WASTELAND

BOOK 01

CITIES IN DUST

WRITTEN BY **ANTONY JOHNSTON**
DRAWN BY **CHRISTOPHER MITTEN**

COVER ART BY **BEN TEMPLESMITH**

LETTERED BY **CHRISTOPHER MITTEN & DOUGLAS E. SHERWOOD**
EDITED BY **JAMES LUCAS JONES**
DESIGNED BY **ANTONY JOHNSTON**
CREATED BY **JOHNSTON & MITTEN**

AN ONI PRESS PUBLICATION

PUBLISHER JOE NOZEMACK
EDITOR IN CHIEF JAMES LUCAS JONES
MANAGING EDITOR RANDAL C. JARRELL
EDITORIAL ASSISTANT DOUGLAS E. SHERWOOD

Oni Press, Inc.
1305 SE Martin Luther King Jr. Blvd, Suite A
Portland, OR 97214
USA
www.onipress.com

www.thebigwet.com

Previously published as issues #1–6 of the Oni Press comic series *Wasteland*.

FIRST EDITION: MARCH 2007
ISBN: 978-193266459-1
1 3 5 7 9 10 8 6 4 2

**ONE HUNDRED YEARS AFTER THE BIG WET.
SOMEWHERE IN AMERICA...**

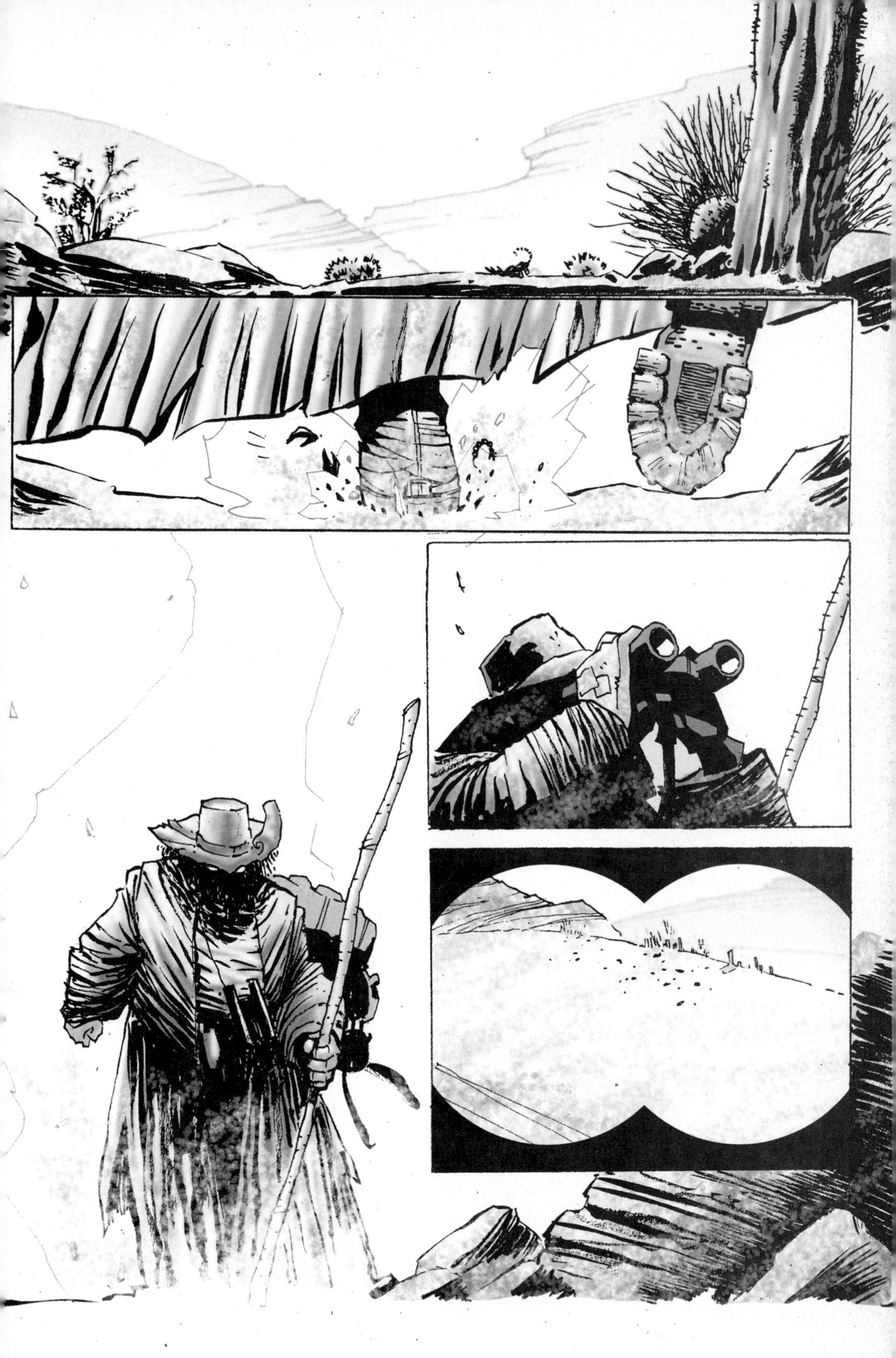

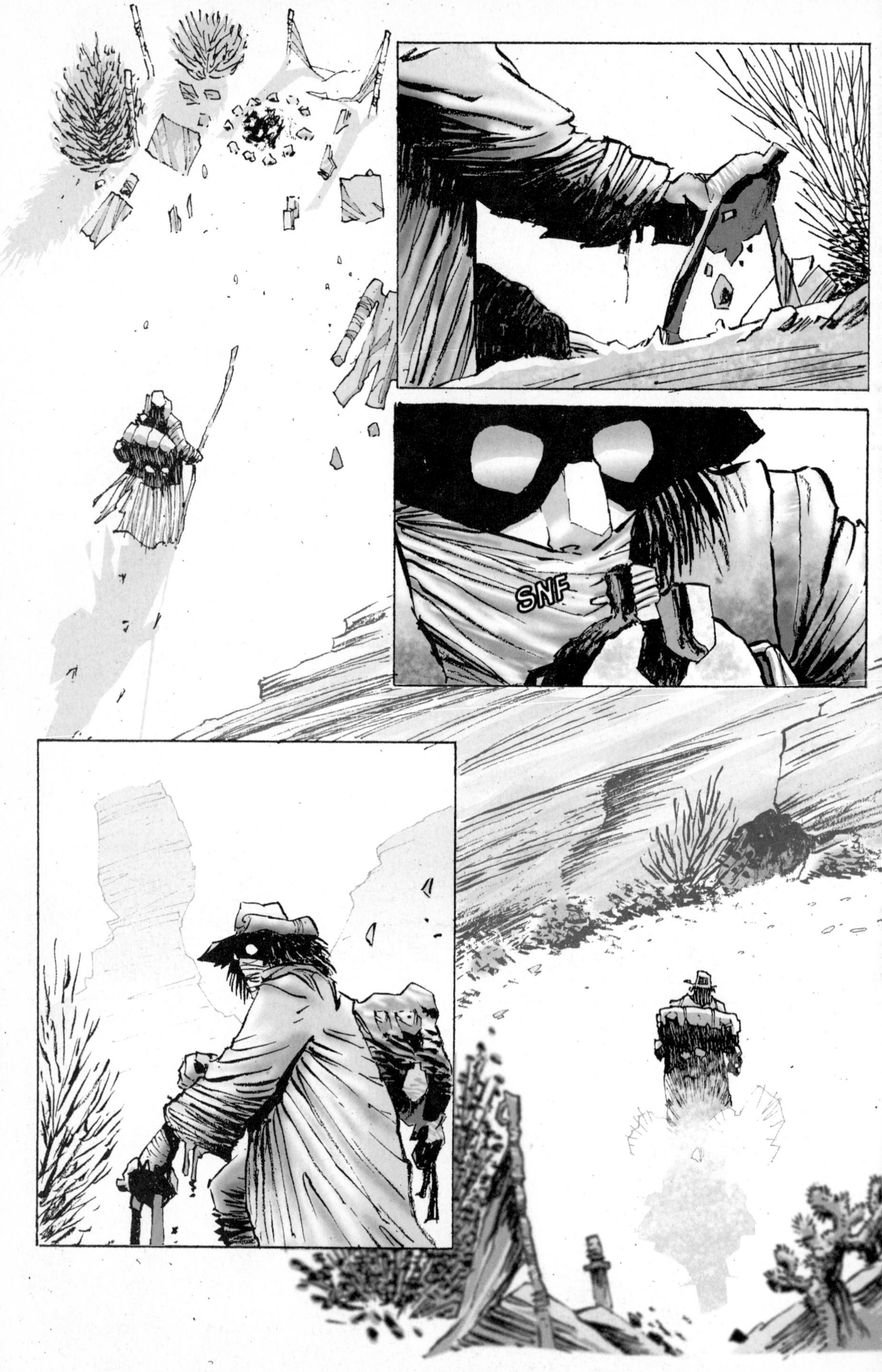
SNF

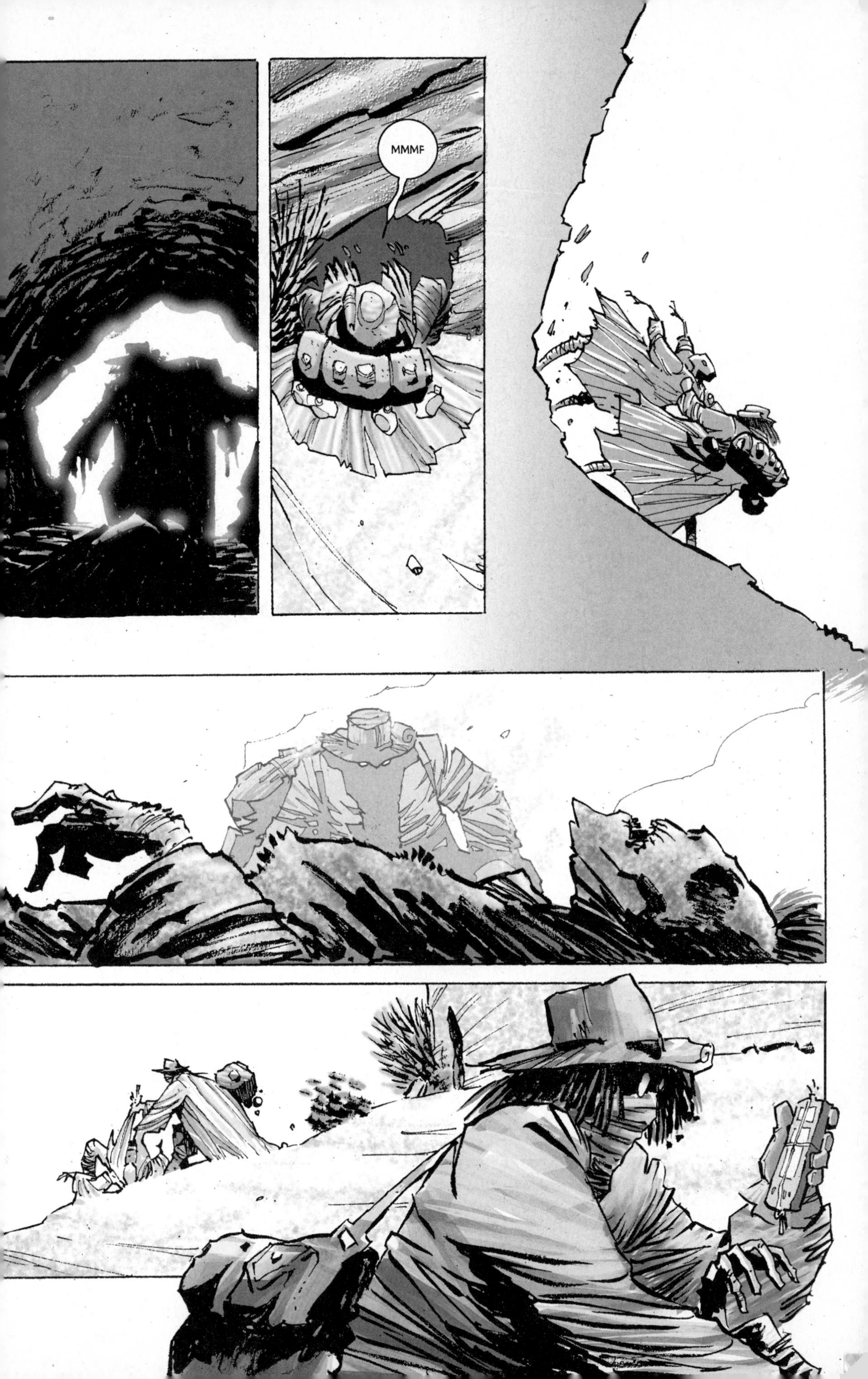
MMMF

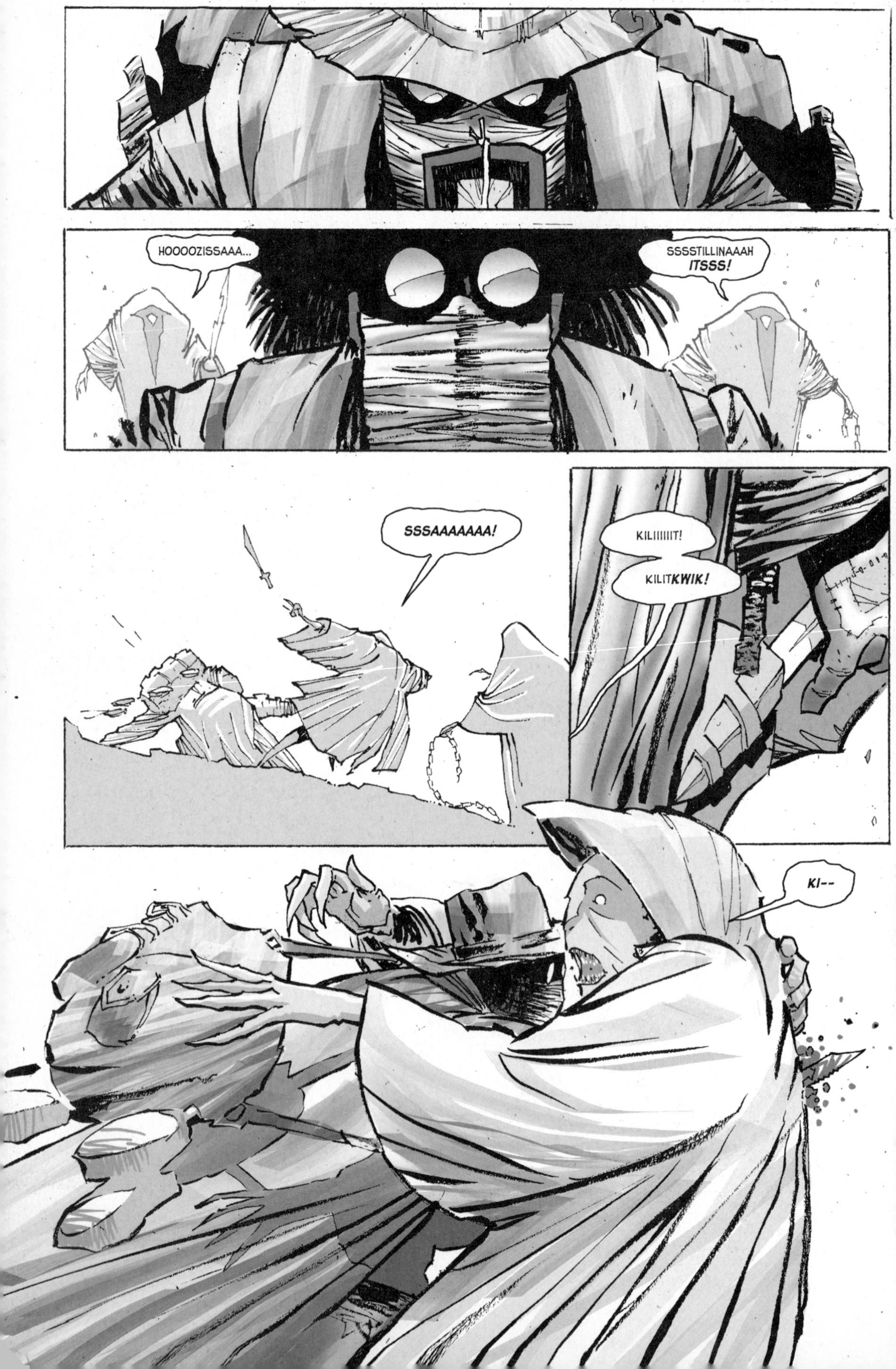
HOOOOZISSAAA...
SSSSTILLINAAAH ITSSS!
SSSAAAAAAAA!
KILIIIIIIT!
KILITKWIK!
KI--

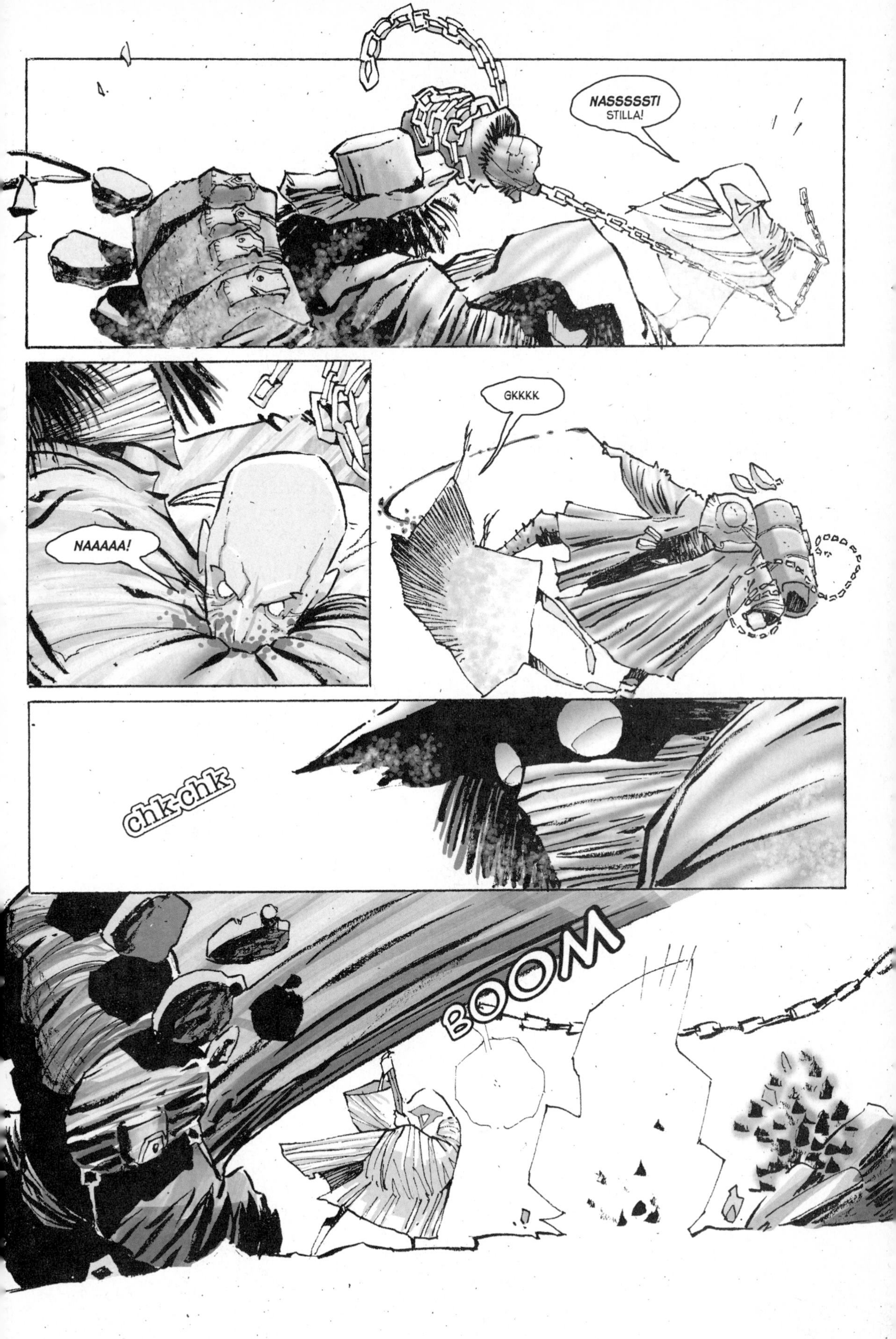
NASSSSSTI STILLA!
NAAAAA!
GKKKK
chk-chk
BOOM

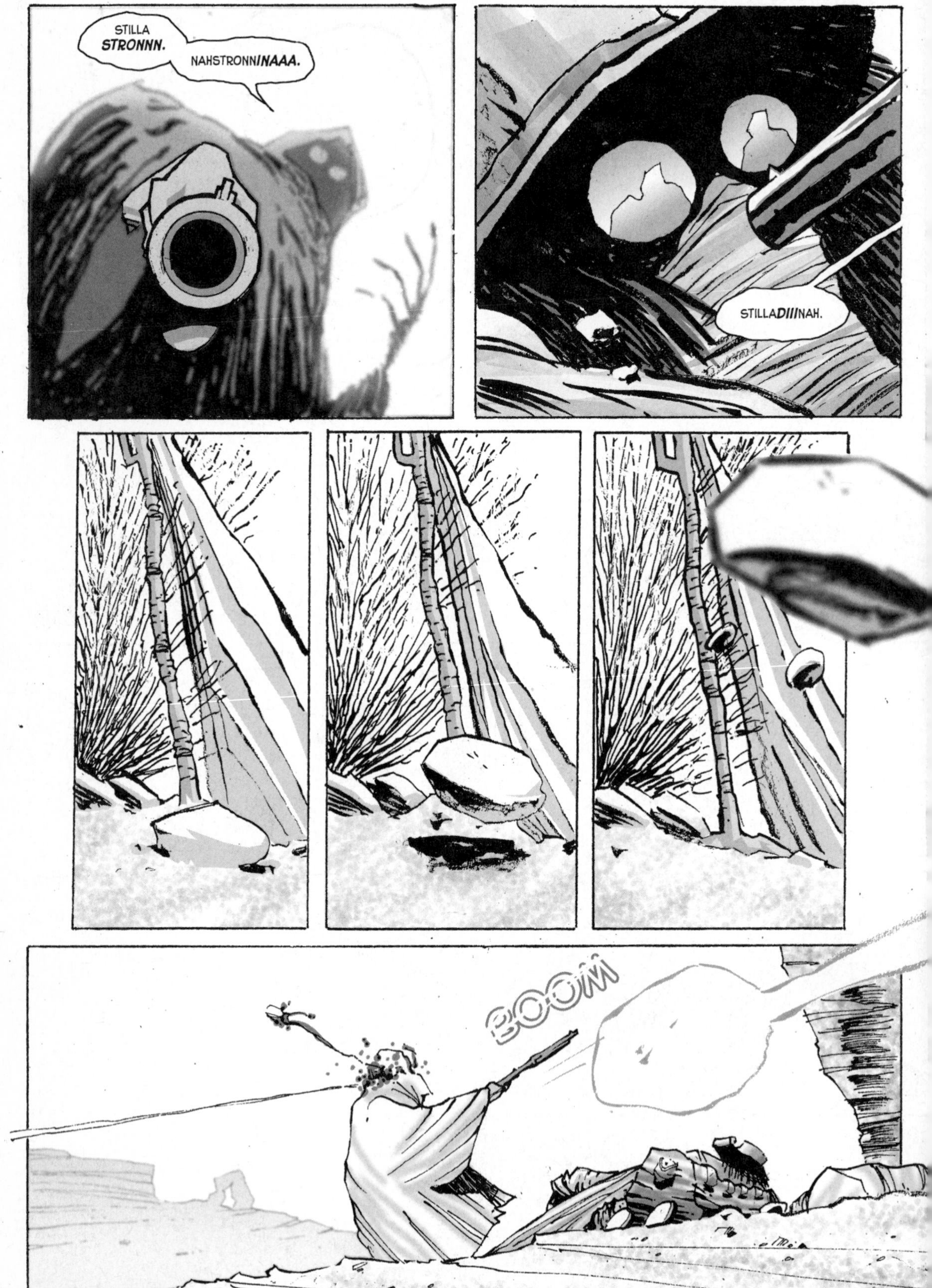
STILLA **STRONNN.**
NAHSTRONN**INAAA.**
STILLA**DIII**NAH.
BOOM

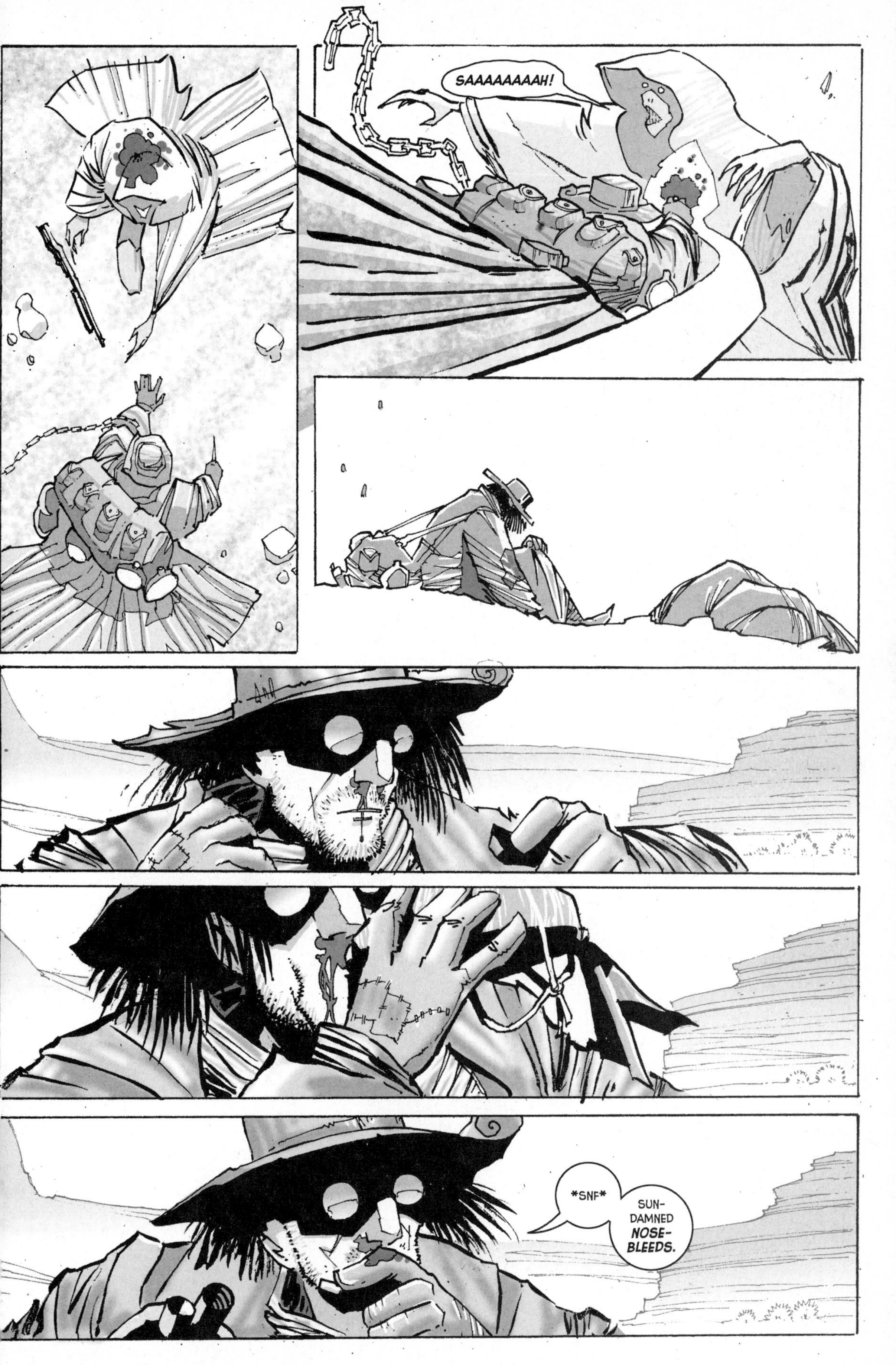
SAAAAAAAAH!
SNF
SUN-DAMNED NOSE-BLEEDS.

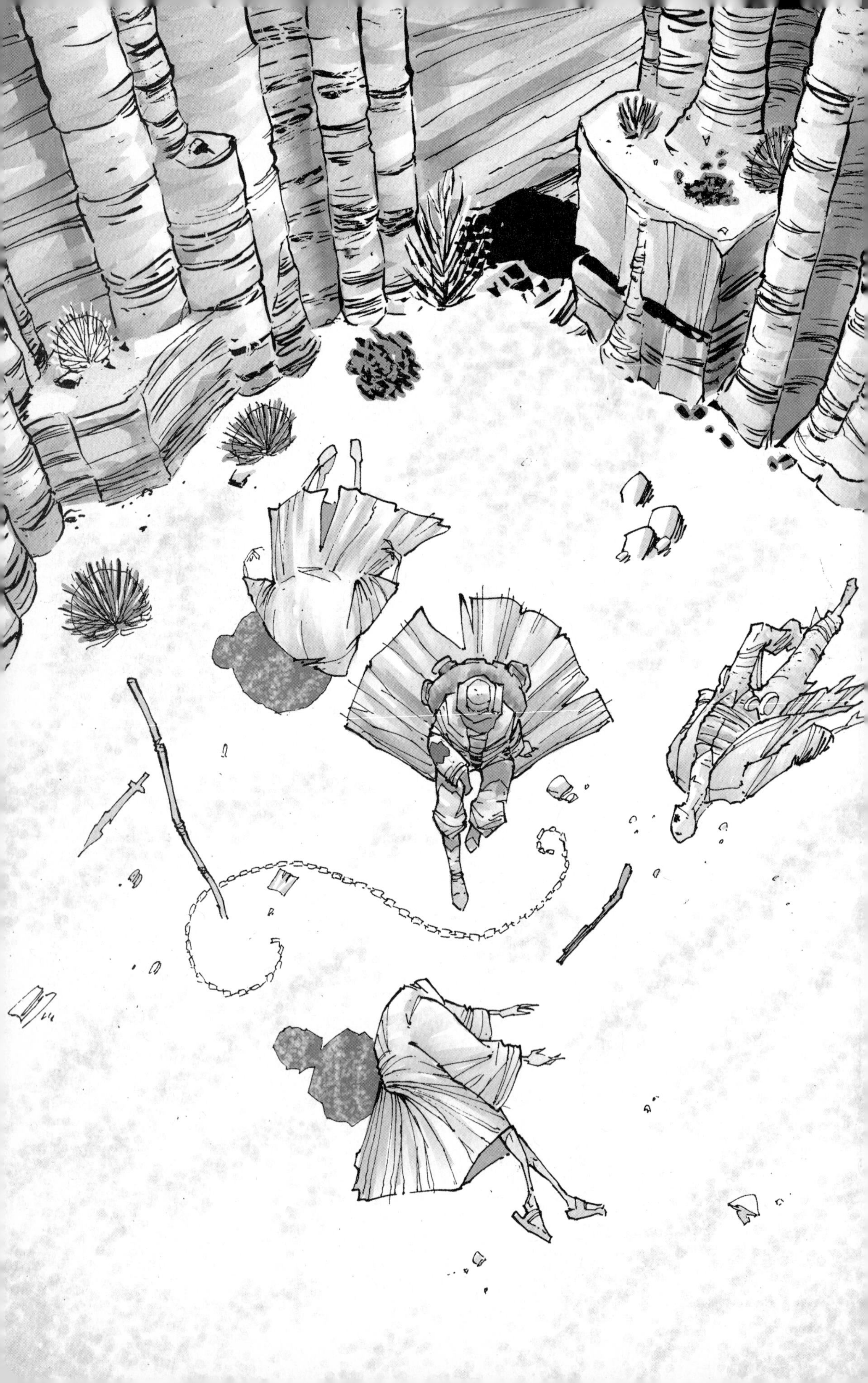

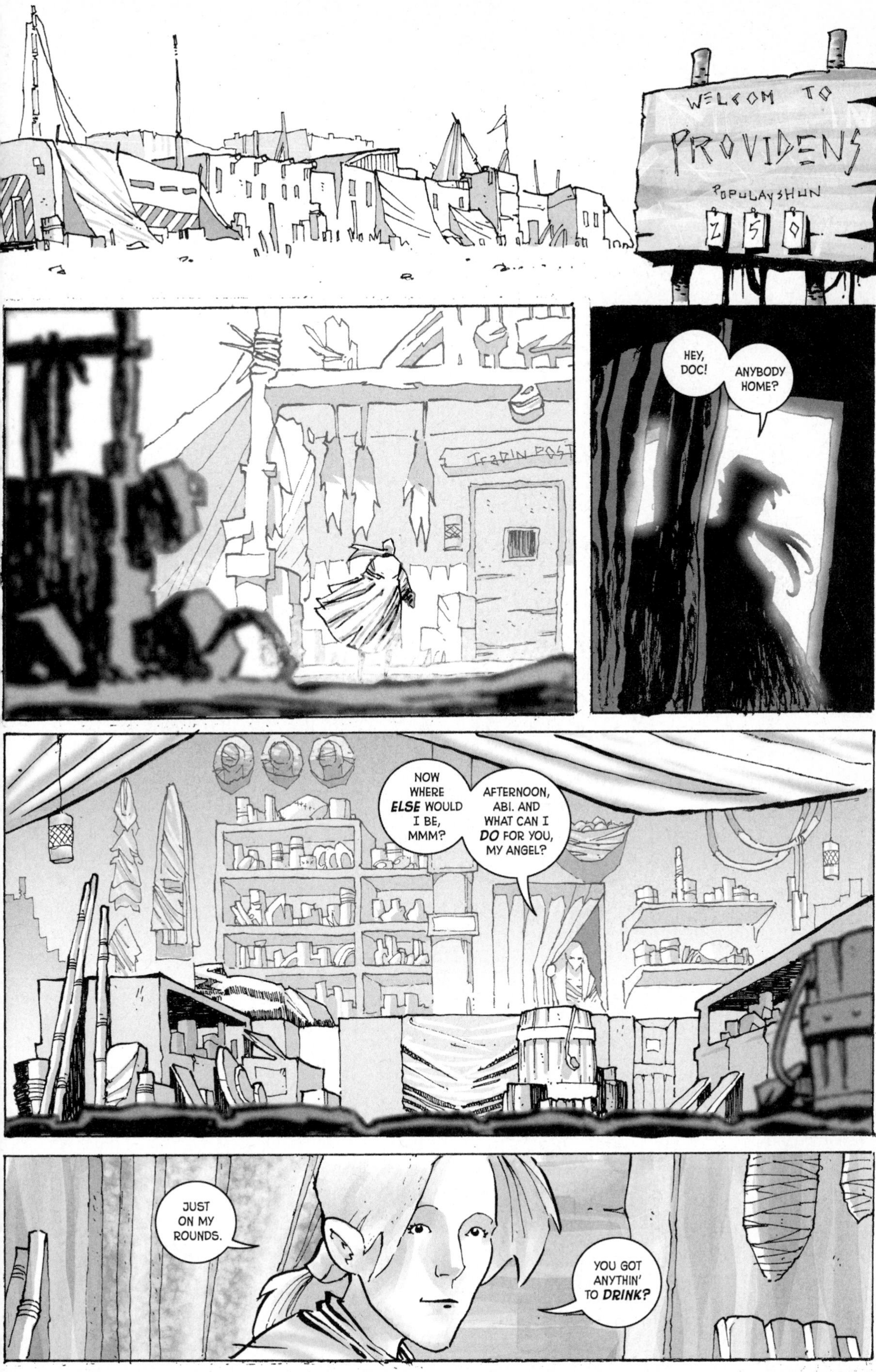
WELCOM TO
PROVIDENS
POPULAYSHUN
2 5 0
TRADIN POST
HEY, DOC!
ANYBODY HOME?
NOW WHERE ELSE WOULD I BE, MMM?
AFTERNOON, ABI. AND WHAT CAN I DO FOR YOU, MY ANGEL?
JUST ON MY ROUNDS.
YOU GOT ANYTHIN' TO DRINK?

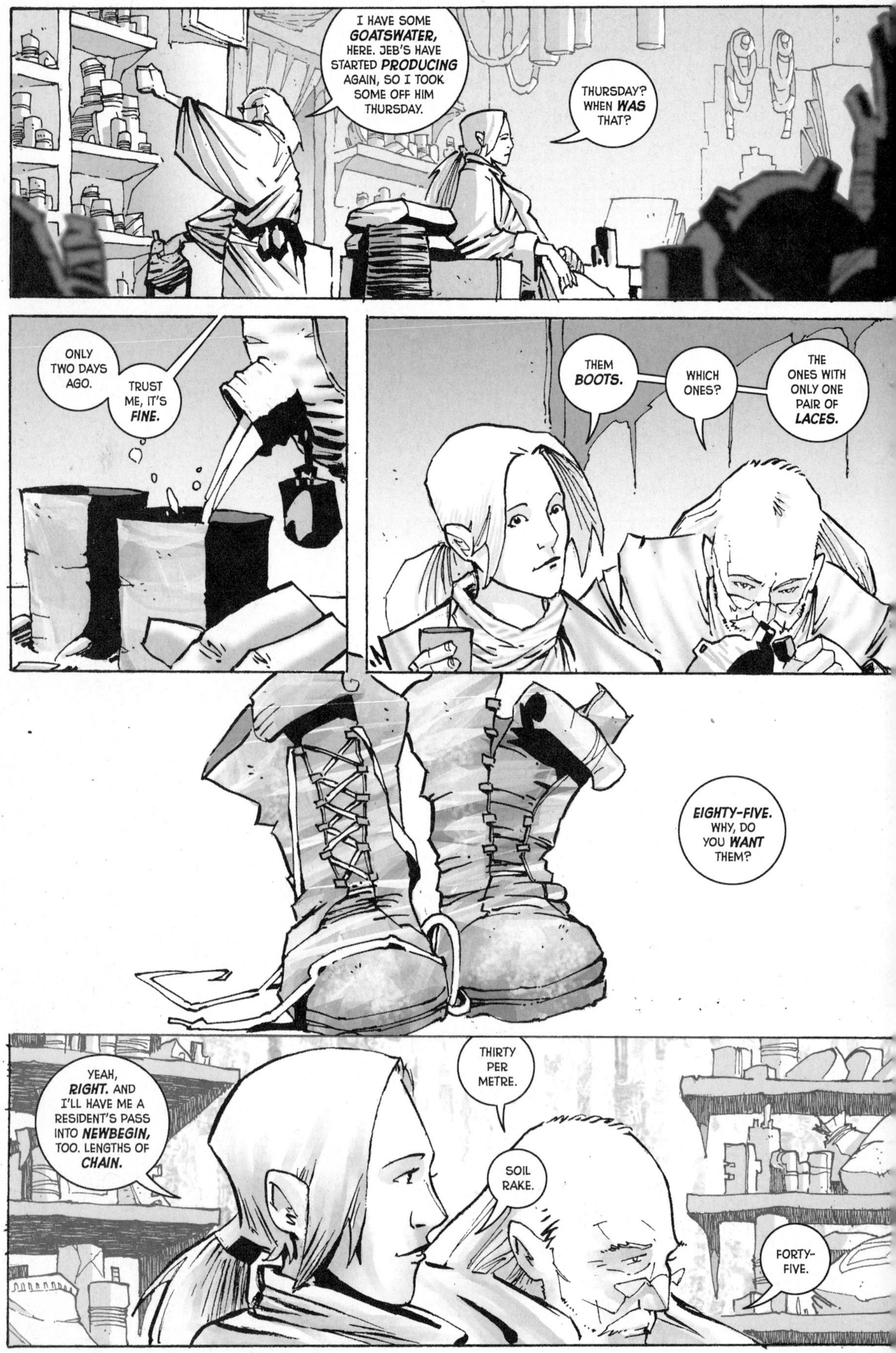
I HAVE SOME GOATSWATER, HERE. JEB'S HAVE STARTED PRODUCING AGAIN, SO I TOOK SOME OFF HIM THURSDAY.
THURSDAY? WHEN WAS THAT?
ONLY TWO DAYS AGO.
TRUST ME, IT'S FINE.
THEM BOOTS.
WHICH ONES?
THE ONES WITH ONLY ONE PAIR OF LACES.
EIGHTY-FIVE. WHY, DO YOU WANT THEM?
YEAH, RIGHT. AND I'LL HAVE ME A RESIDENT'S PASS INTO NEWBEGIN, TOO. LENGTHS OF CHAIN.
THIRTY PER METRE.
SOIL RAKE.
FORTY-FIVE.

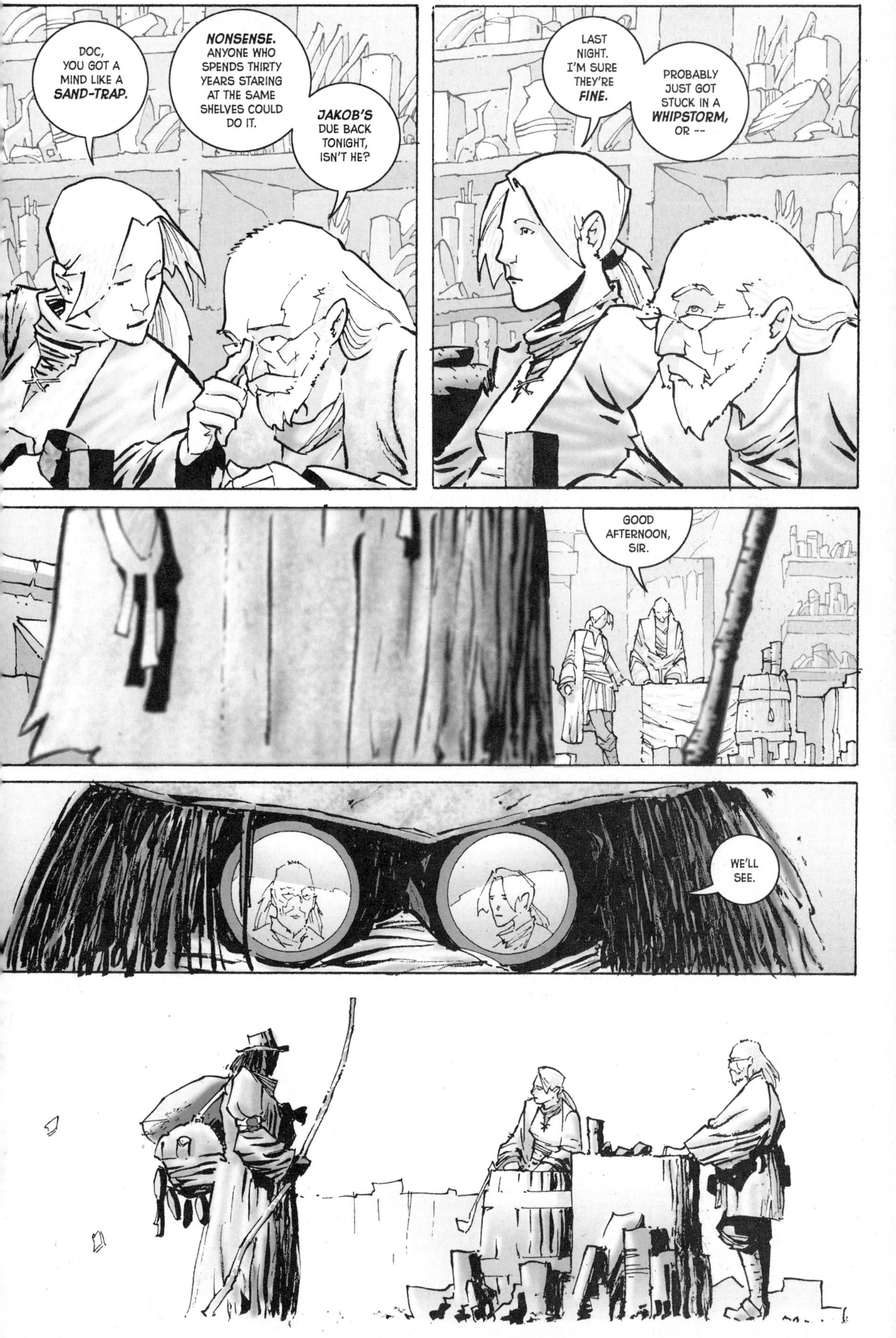
DOC, YOU GOT A MIND LIKE A SAND-TRAP.
NONSENSE. ANYONE WHO SPENDS THIRTY YEARS STARING AT THE SAME SHELVES COULD DO IT.
JAKOB'S DUE BACK TONIGHT, ISN'T HE?
LAST NIGHT. I'M SURE THEY'RE FINE.
PROBABLY JUST GOT STUCK IN A WHIPSTORM, OR --
GOOD AFTERNOON, SIR.
WE'LL SEE.

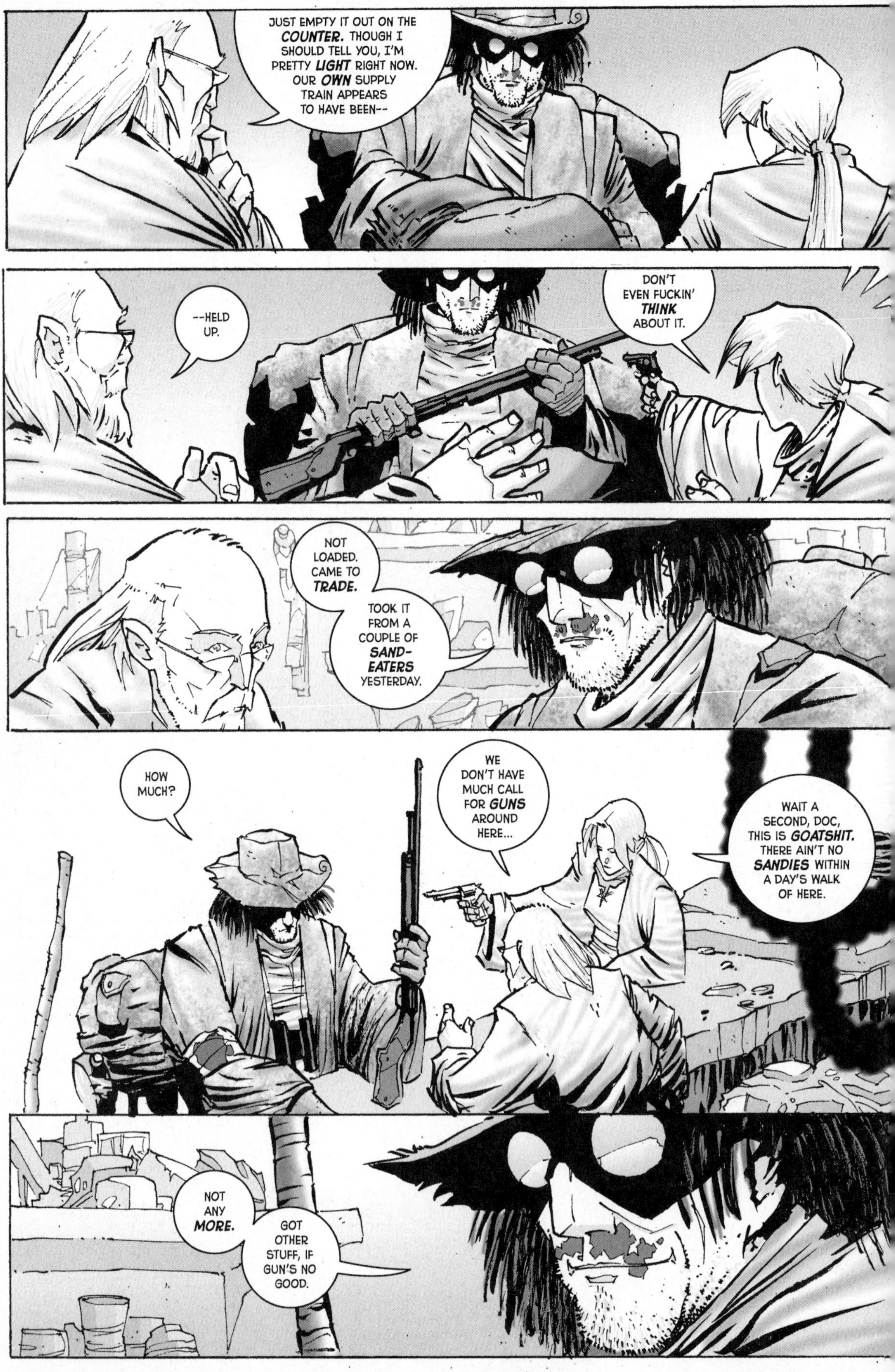
JUST EMPTY IT OUT ON THE COUNTER. THOUGH I SHOULD TELL YOU, I'M PRETTY LIGHT RIGHT NOW. OUR OWN SUPPLY TRAIN APPEARS TO HAVE BEEN--
--HELD UP.
DON'T EVEN FUCKIN' THINK ABOUT IT.
NOT LOADED. CAME TO TRADE.
TOOK IT FROM A COUPLE OF SAND-EATERS YESTERDAY.
HOW MUCH?
WE DON'T HAVE MUCH CALL FOR GUNS AROUND HERE...
WAIT A SECOND, DOC, THIS IS GOATSHIT. THERE AIN'T NO SANDIES WITHIN A DAY'S WALK OF HERE.
NOT ANY MORE.
GOT OTHER STUFF, IF GUN'S NO GOOD.

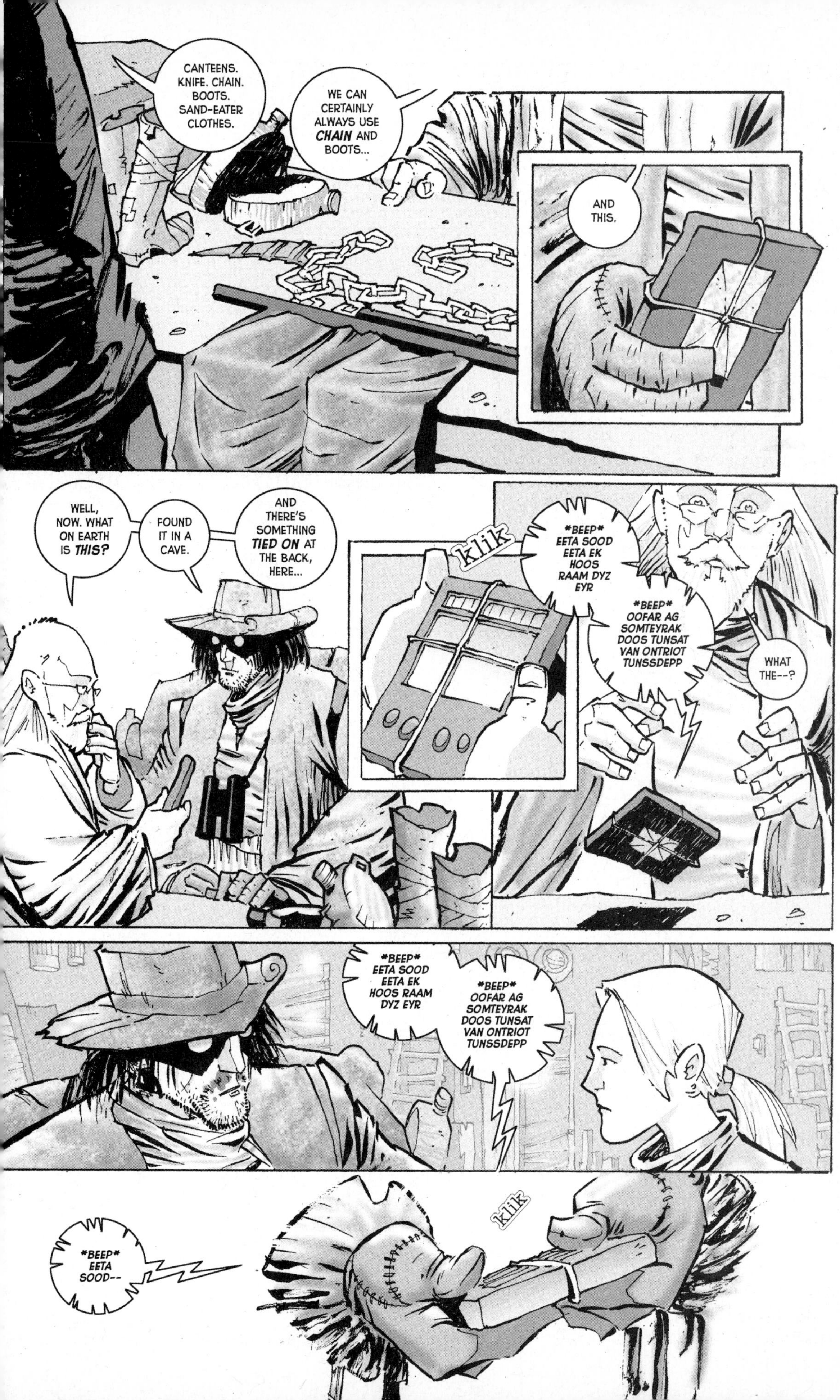
CANTEENS. KNIFE. CHAIN. BOOTS. SAND-EATER CLOTHES.
WE CAN CERTAINLY ALWAYS USE CHAIN AND BOOTS...
AND THIS.
WELL, NOW. WHAT ON EARTH IS THIS?
FOUND IT IN A CAVE.
AND THERE'S SOMETHING TIED ON AT THE BACK, HERE...
klik
BEEP EETA SOOD EETA EK HOOS RAAM DYZ EYR
BEEP OOFAR AG SOMTEYRAK DOOS TUNSAT VAN ONTRIOT TUNSSDEPP
WHAT THE--?
BEEP EETA SOOD EETA EK HOOS RAAM DYZ EYR
BEEP OOFAR AG SOMTEYRAK DOOS TUNSAT VAN ONTRIOT TUNSSDEPP
klik
BEEP EETA SOOD--

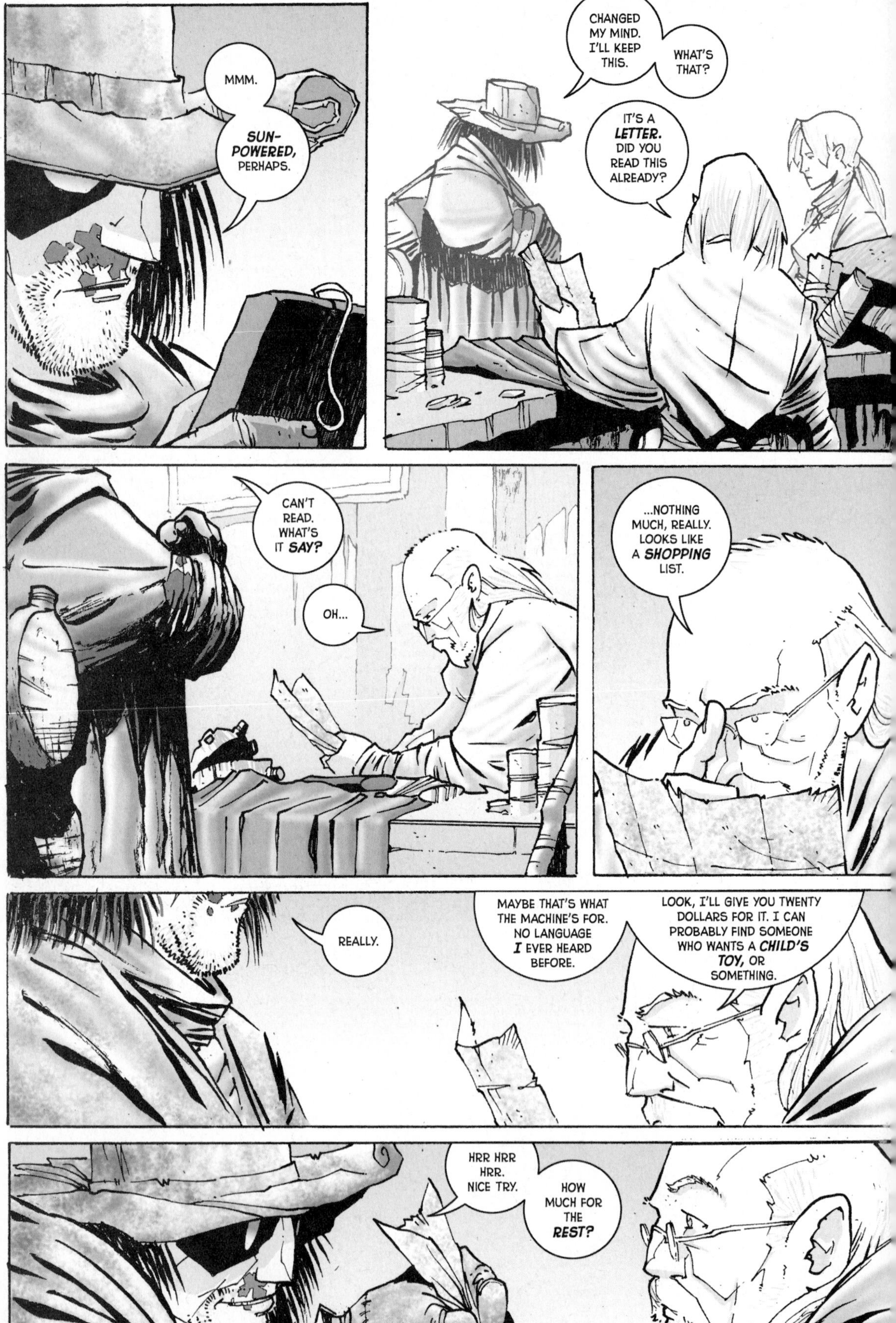
MMM.
SUN-POWERED, PERHAPS.
CHANGED MY MIND. I'LL KEEP THIS.
WHAT'S THAT?
IT'S A LETTER. DID YOU READ THIS ALREADY?
CAN'T READ. WHAT'S IT SAY?
OH...
...NOTHING MUCH, REALLY. LOOKS LIKE A SHOPPING LIST.
REALLY.
MAYBE THAT'S WHAT THE MACHINE'S FOR. NO LANGUAGE I EVER HEARD BEFORE.
LOOK, I'LL GIVE YOU TWENTY DOLLARS FOR IT. I CAN PROBABLY FIND SOMEONE WHO WANTS A CHILD'S TOY, OR SOMETHING.
HRR HRR HRR. NICE TRY.
HOW MUCH FOR THE REST?

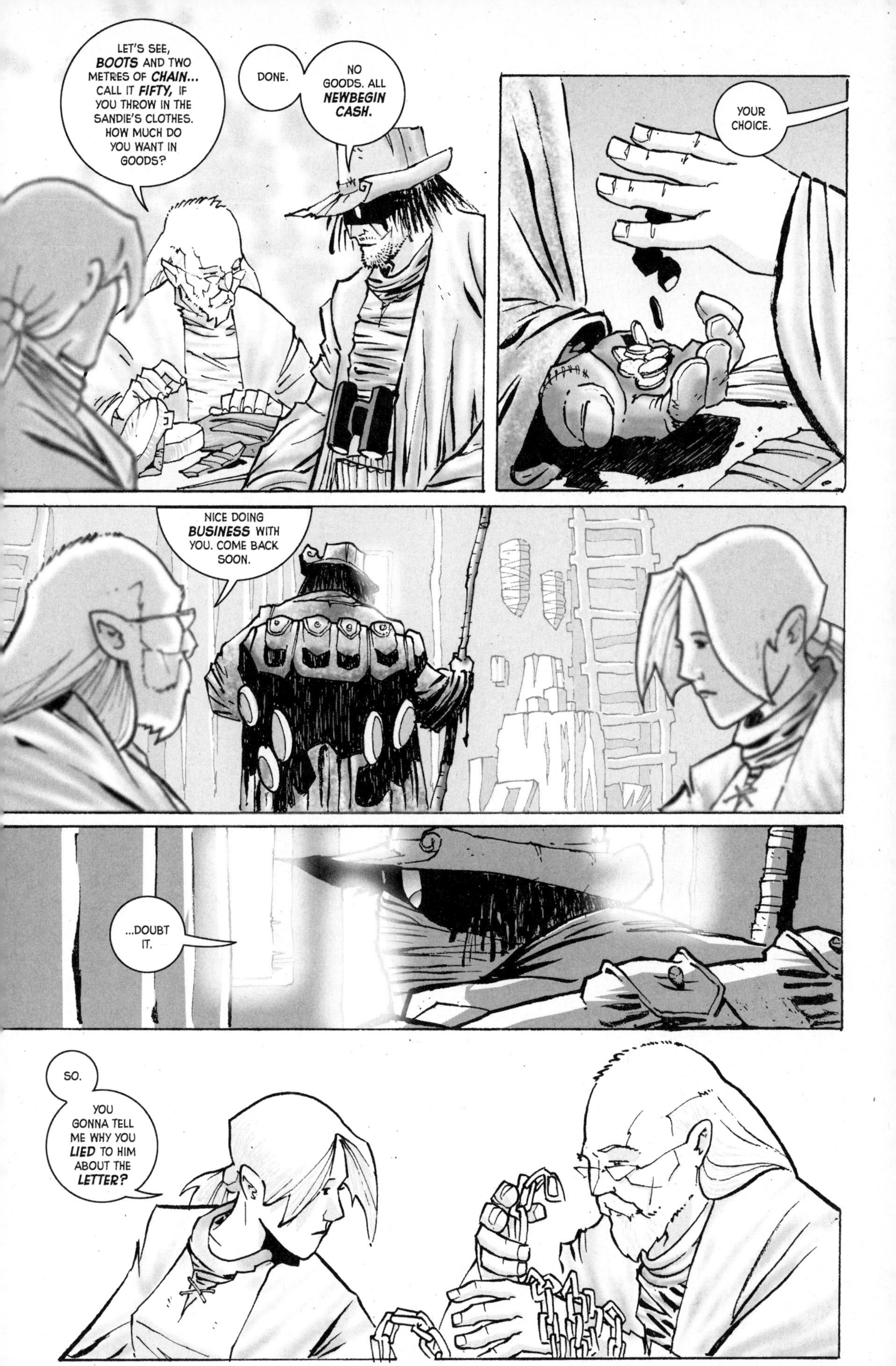
LET'S SEE, BOOTS AND TWO METRES OF CHAIN... CALL IT FIFTY, IF YOU THROW IN THE SANDIE'S CLOTHES. HOW MUCH DO YOU WANT IN GOODS?
DONE.
NO GOODS. ALL NEWBEGIN CASH.
YOUR CHOICE.
NICE DOING BUSINESS WITH YOU. COME BACK SOON.
...DOUBT IT.
SO.
YOU GONNA TELL ME WHY YOU LIED TO HIM ABOUT THE LETTER?

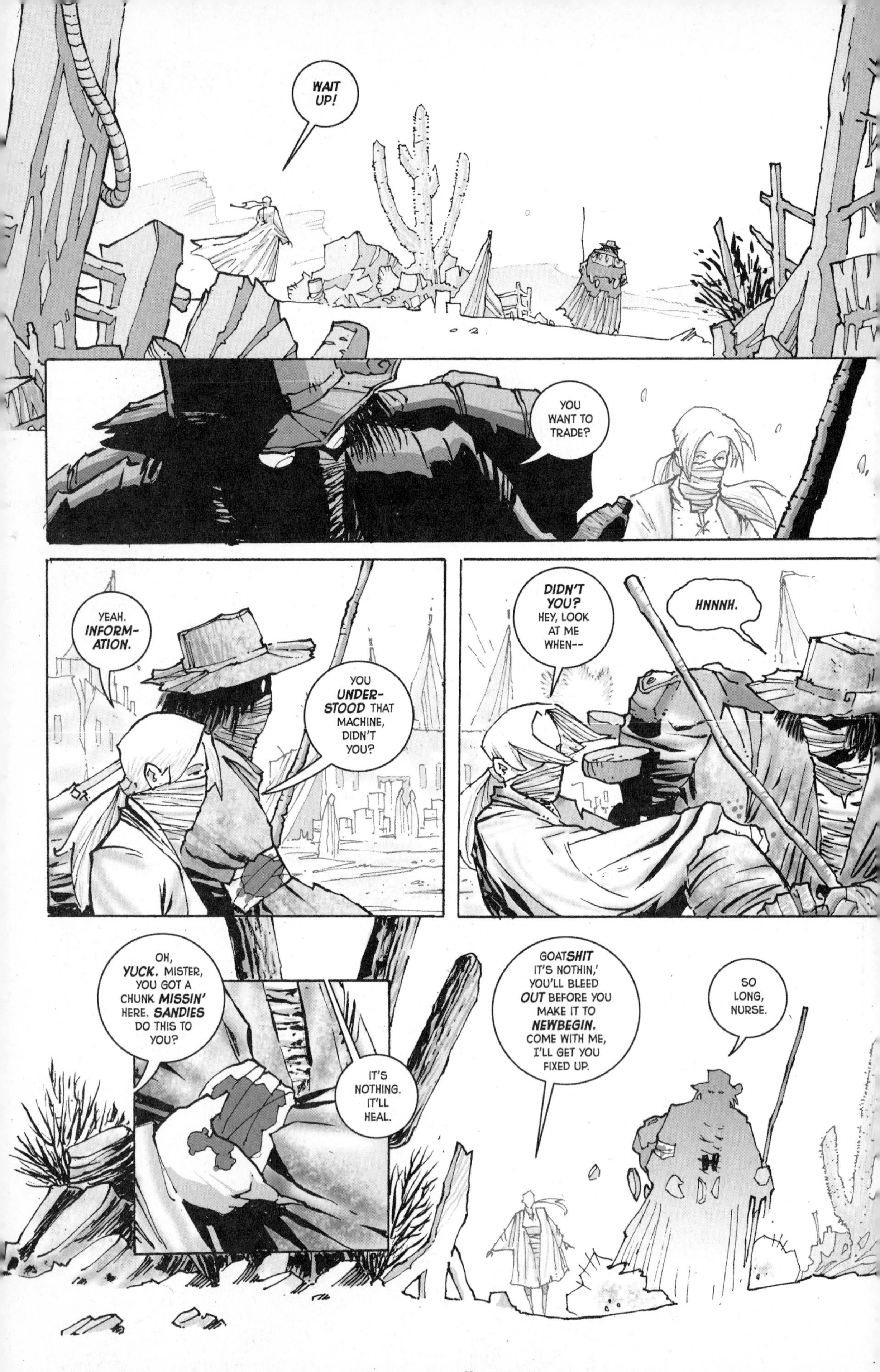
WAIT UP!
YOU WANT TO TRADE?
YEAH. INFORMATION.
YOU UNDERSTOOD THAT MACHINE, DIDN'T YOU?
DIDN'T YOU? HEY, LOOK AT ME WHEN--
HNNNH.
OH, YUCK. MISTER, YOU GOT A CHUNK MISSIN' HERE. SANDIES DO THIS TO YOU?
IT'S NOTHING. IT'LL HEAL.
GOATSHIT IT'S NOTHIN,' YOU'LL BLEED OUT BEFORE YOU MAKE IT TO NEWBEGIN. COME WITH ME, I'LL GET YOU FIXED UP.
SO LONG, NURSE.

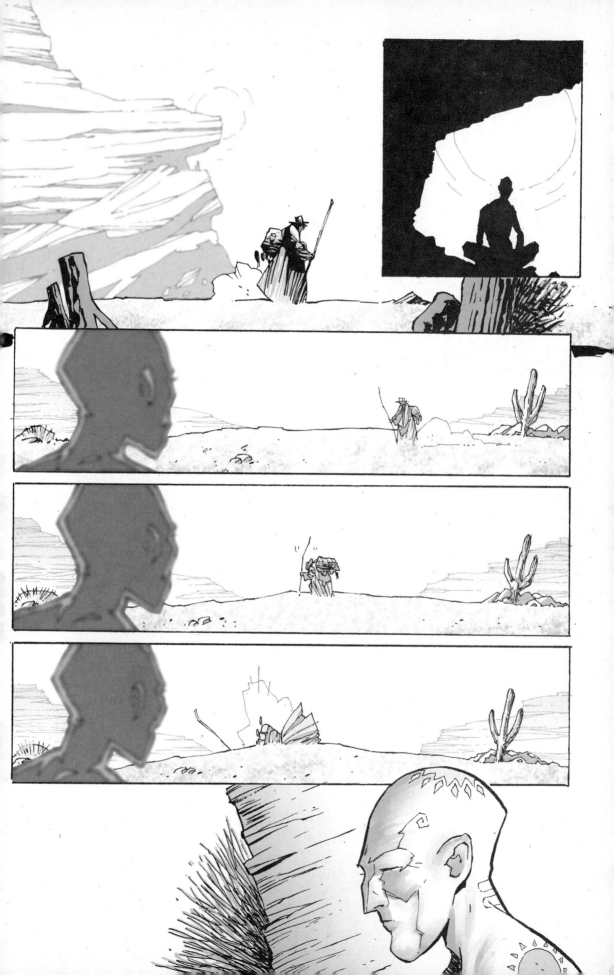

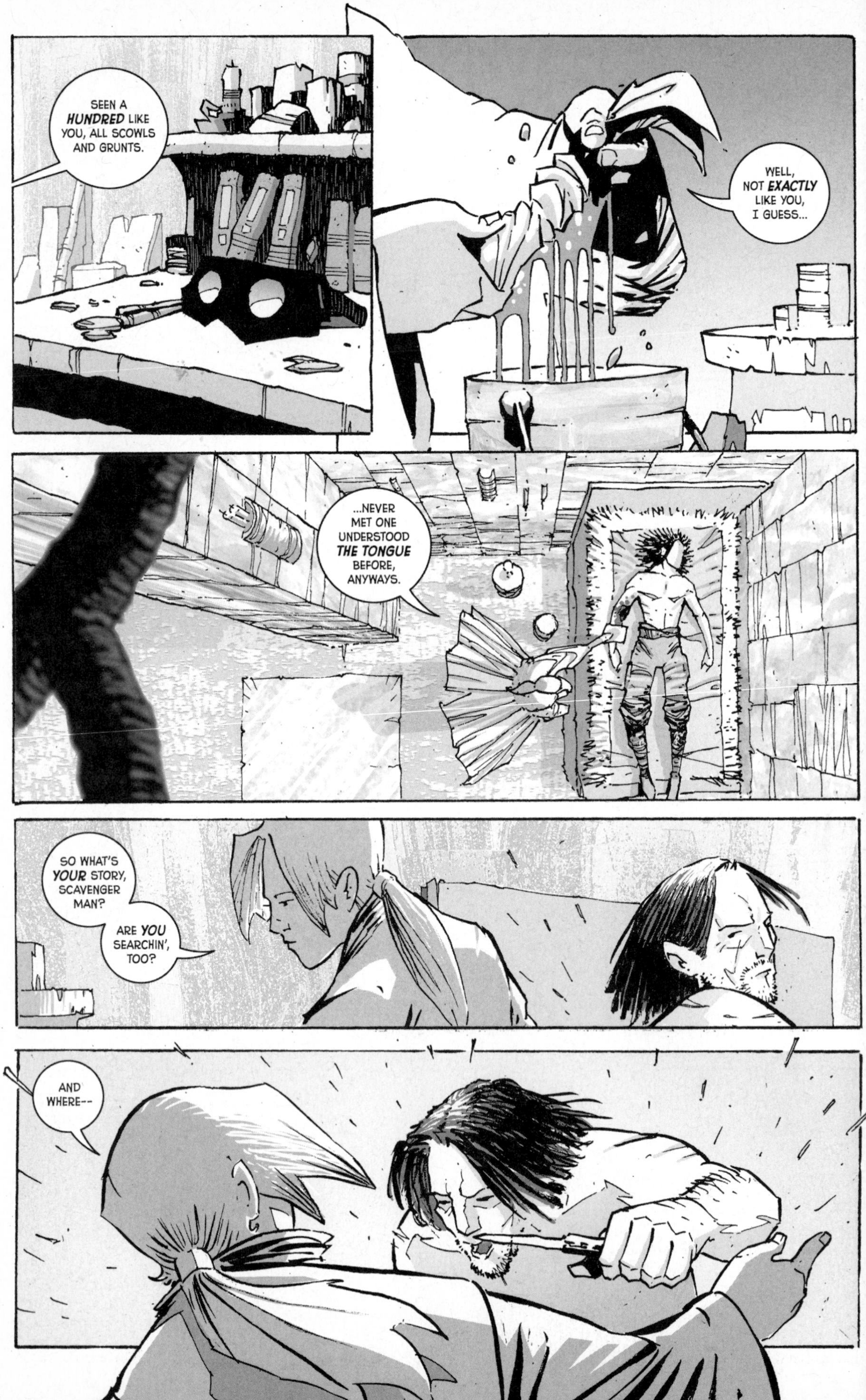
SEEN A HUNDRED LIKE YOU, ALL SCOWLS AND GRUNTS.
WELL, NOT EXACTLY LIKE YOU, I GUESS...
...NEVER MET ONE UNDERSTOOD THE TONGUE BEFORE, ANYWAYS.
SO WHAT'S YOUR STORY, SCAVENGER MAN?
ARE YOU SEARCHIN', TOO?
AND WHERE--

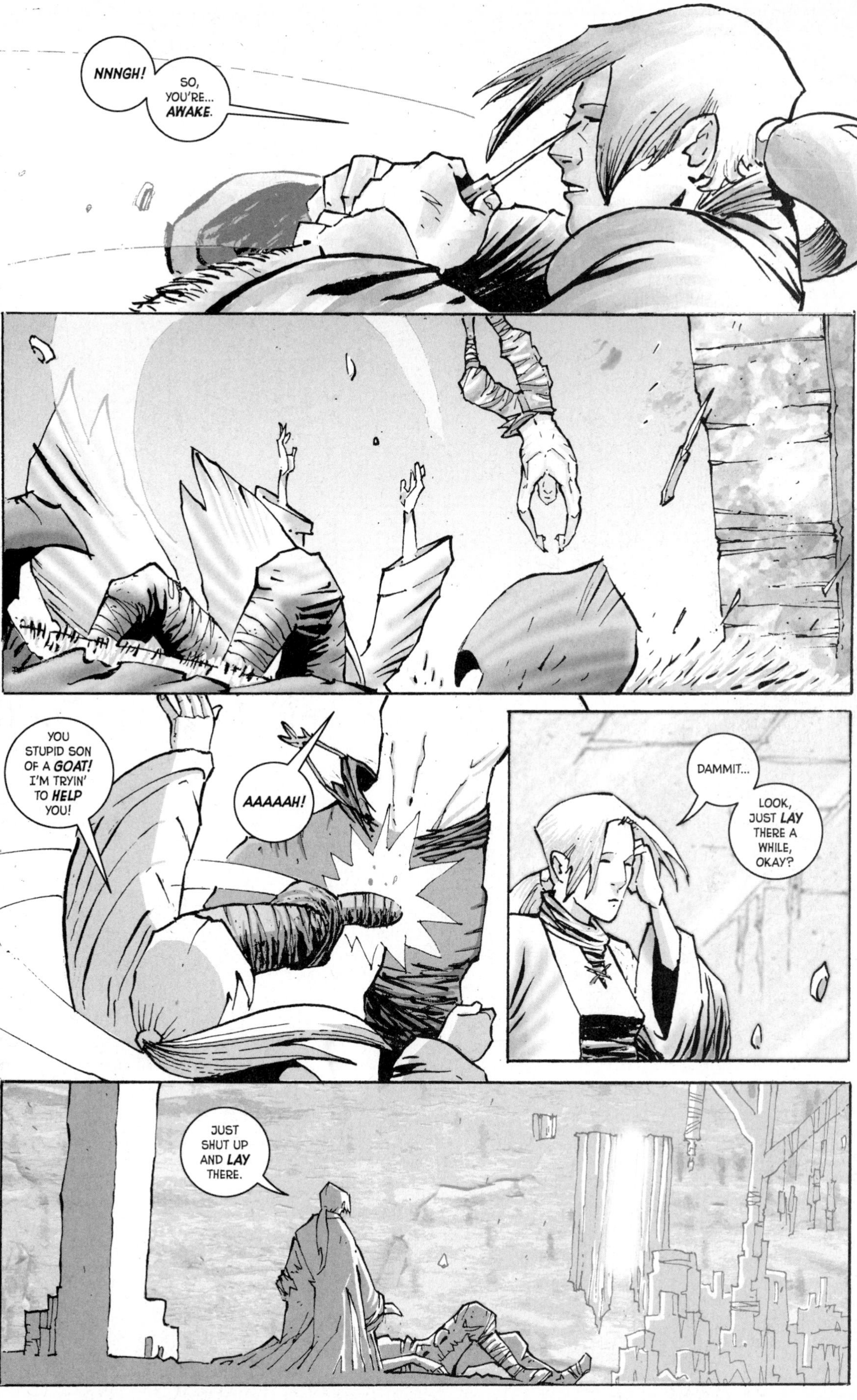
NNNGH!
SO, YOU'RE... AWAKE.
YOU STUPID SON OF A GOAT! I'M TRYIN' TO HELP YOU!
AAAAAH!
DAMMIT...
LOOK, JUST LAY THERE A WHILE, OKAY?
JUST SHUT UP AND LAY THERE.

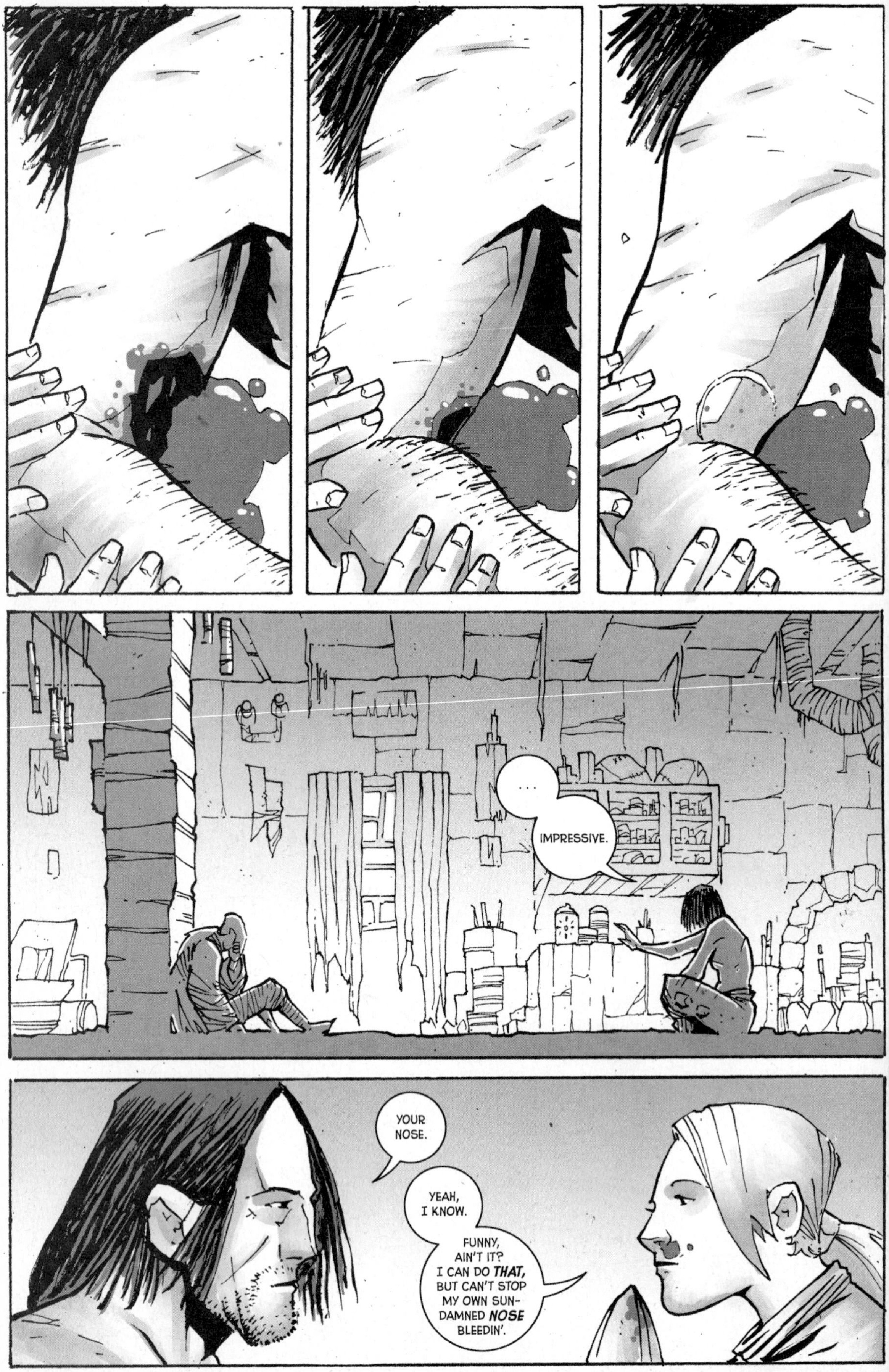
...
IMPRESSIVE.
YOUR NOSE.
YEAH, I KNOW.
FUNNY, AIN'T IT? I CAN DO THAT, BUT CAN'T STOP MY OWN SUN-DAMNED NOSE BLEEDIN'.

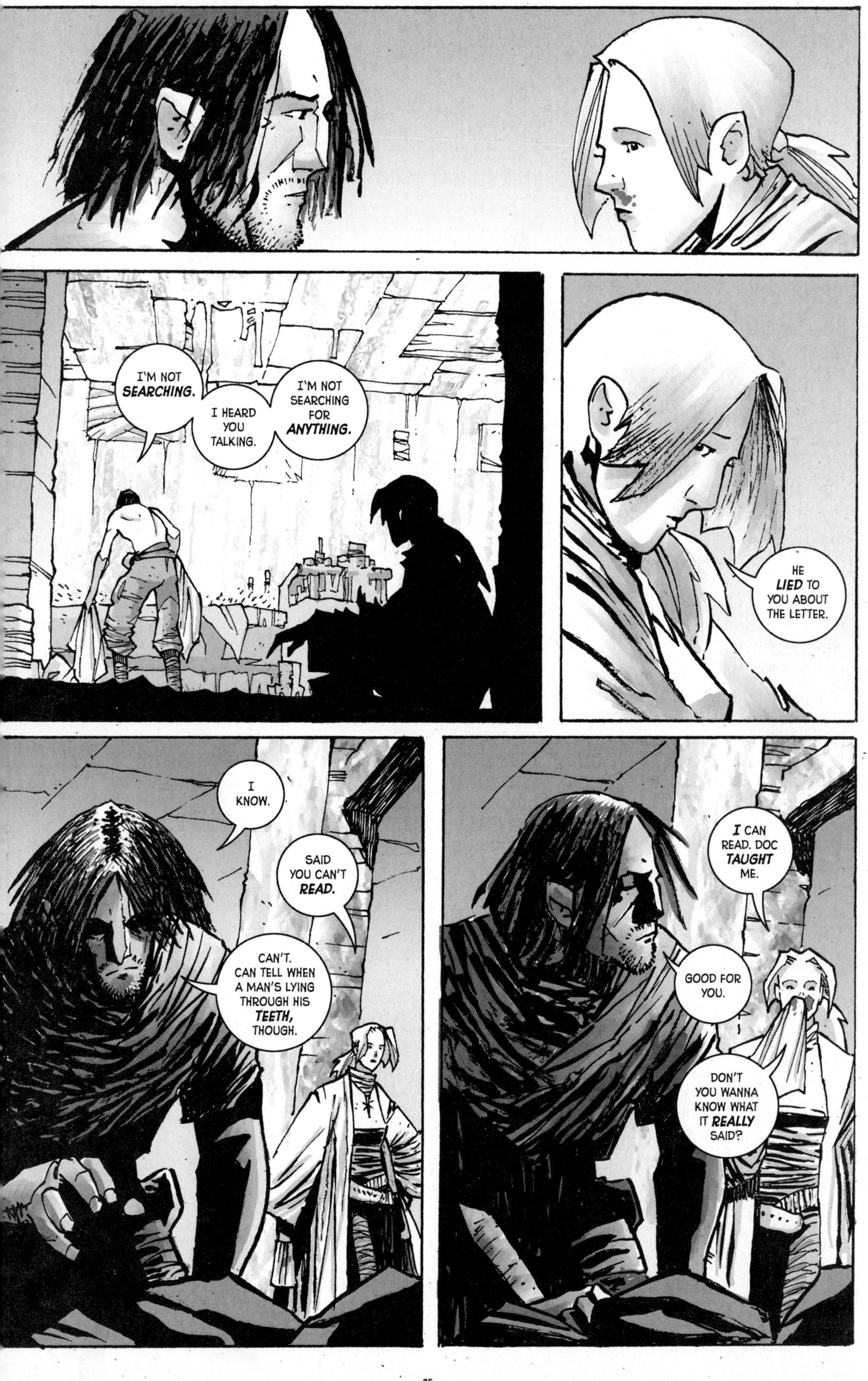
I'M NOT SEARCHING.
I HEARD YOU TALKING.
I'M NOT SEARCHING FOR ANYTHING.
HE LIED TO YOU ABOUT THE LETTER.
I KNOW.
SAID YOU CAN'T READ.
CAN'T. CAN TELL WHEN A MAN'S LYING THROUGH HIS TEETH, THOUGH.
I CAN READ. DOC TAUGHT ME.
GOOD FOR YOU.
DON'T YOU WANNA KNOW WHAT IT REALLY SAID?

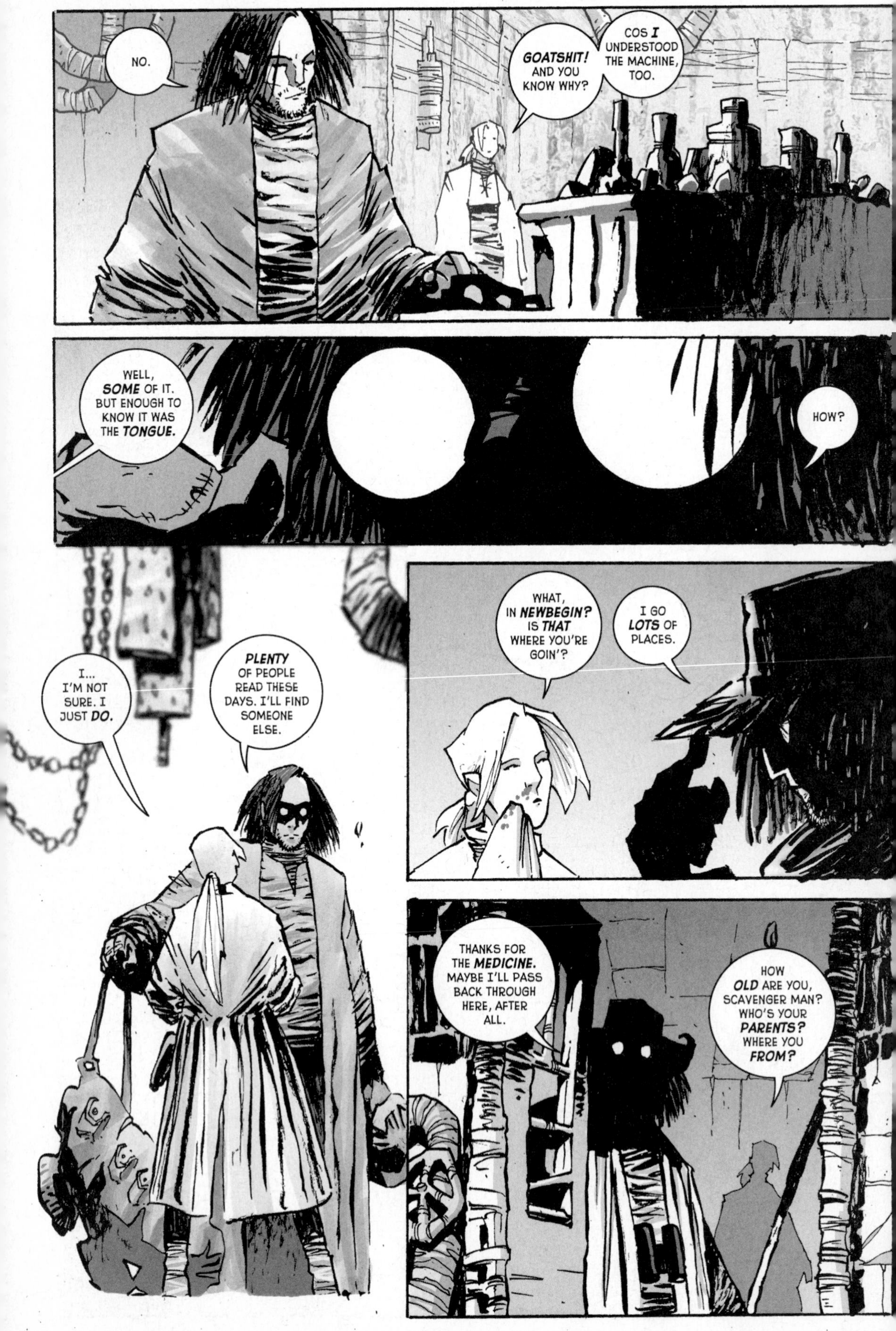
NO.
GOATSHIT! AND YOU KNOW WHY?
COS I UNDERSTOOD THE MACHINE, TOO.
WELL, SOME OF IT. BUT ENOUGH TO KNOW IT WAS THE TONGUE.
HOW?
I... I'M NOT SURE. I JUST DO.
PLENTY OF PEOPLE READ THESE DAYS. I'LL FIND SOMEONE ELSE.
WHAT, IN NEWBEGIN? IS THAT WHERE YOU'RE GOIN'?
I GO LOTS OF PLACES.
THANKS FOR THE MEDICINE. MAYBE I'LL PASS BACK THROUGH HERE, AFTER ALL.
HOW OLD ARE YOU, SCAVENGER MAN? WHO'S YOUR PARENTS? WHERE YOU FROM?

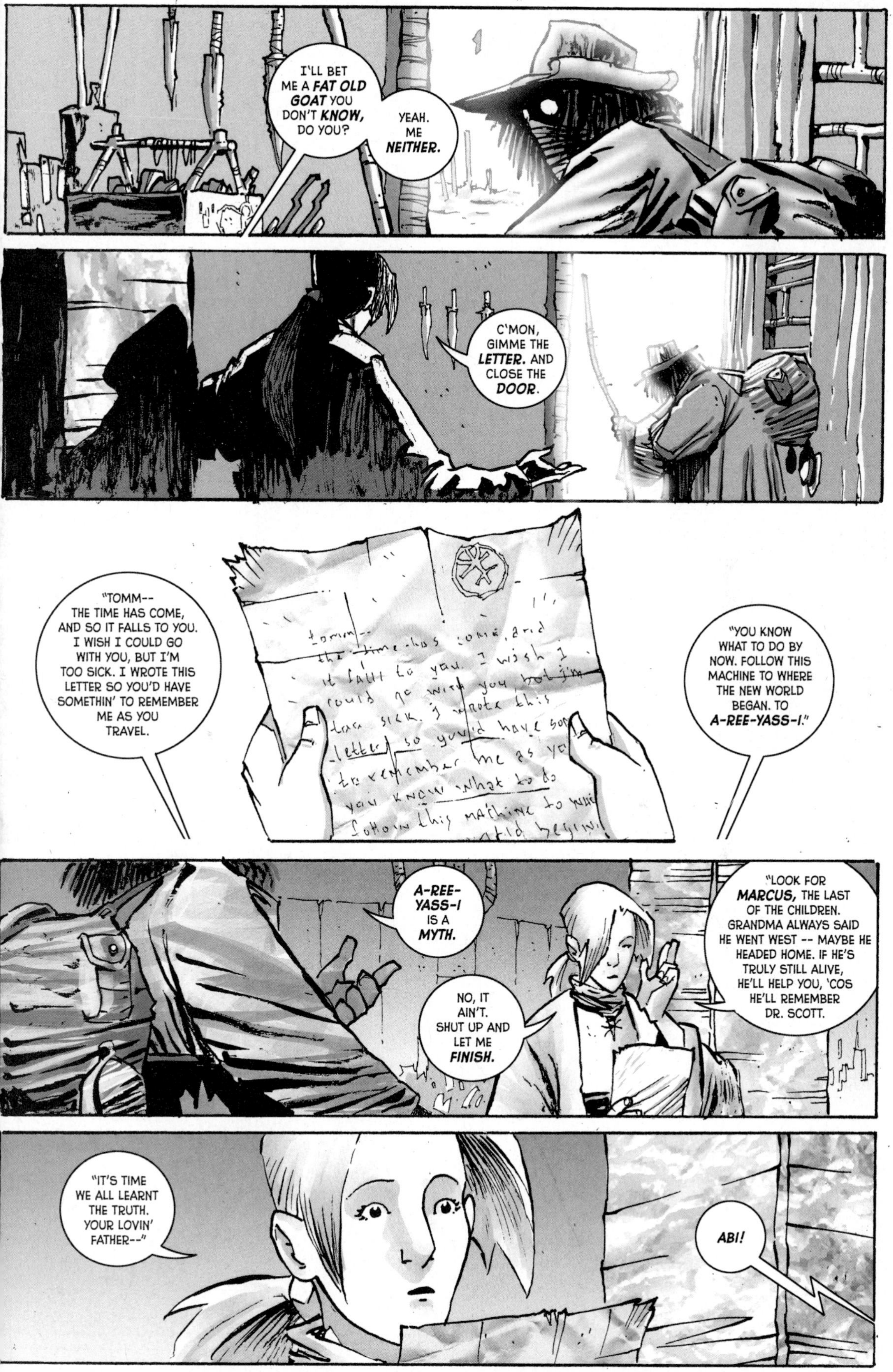

I'LL BET ME A FAT OLD GOAT YOU DON'T KNOW, DO YOU?
YEAH. ME NEITHER.
C'MON, GIMME THE LETTER. AND CLOSE THE DOOR.
"TOMM-- THE TIME HAS COME, AND SO IT FALLS TO YOU. I WISH I COULD GO WITH YOU, BUT I'M TOO SICK. I WROTE THIS LETTER SO YOU'D HAVE SOMETHIN' TO REMEMBER ME AS YOU TRAVEL.
"YOU KNOW WHAT TO DO BY NOW. FOLLOW THIS MACHINE TO WHERE THE NEW WORLD BEGAN. TO A-REE-YASS-I."
A-REE-YASS-I IS A MYTH.
NO, IT AIN'T. SHUT UP AND LET ME FINISH.
"LOOK FOR MARCUS, THE LAST OF THE CHILDREN. GRANDMA ALWAYS SAID HE WENT WEST -- MAYBE HE HEADED HOME. IF HE'S TRULY STILL ALIVE, HE'LL HELP YOU, 'COS HE'LL REMEMBER DR. SCOTT.
"IT'S TIME WE ALL LEARNT THE TRUTH. YOUR LOVIN' FATHER--"
ABI!

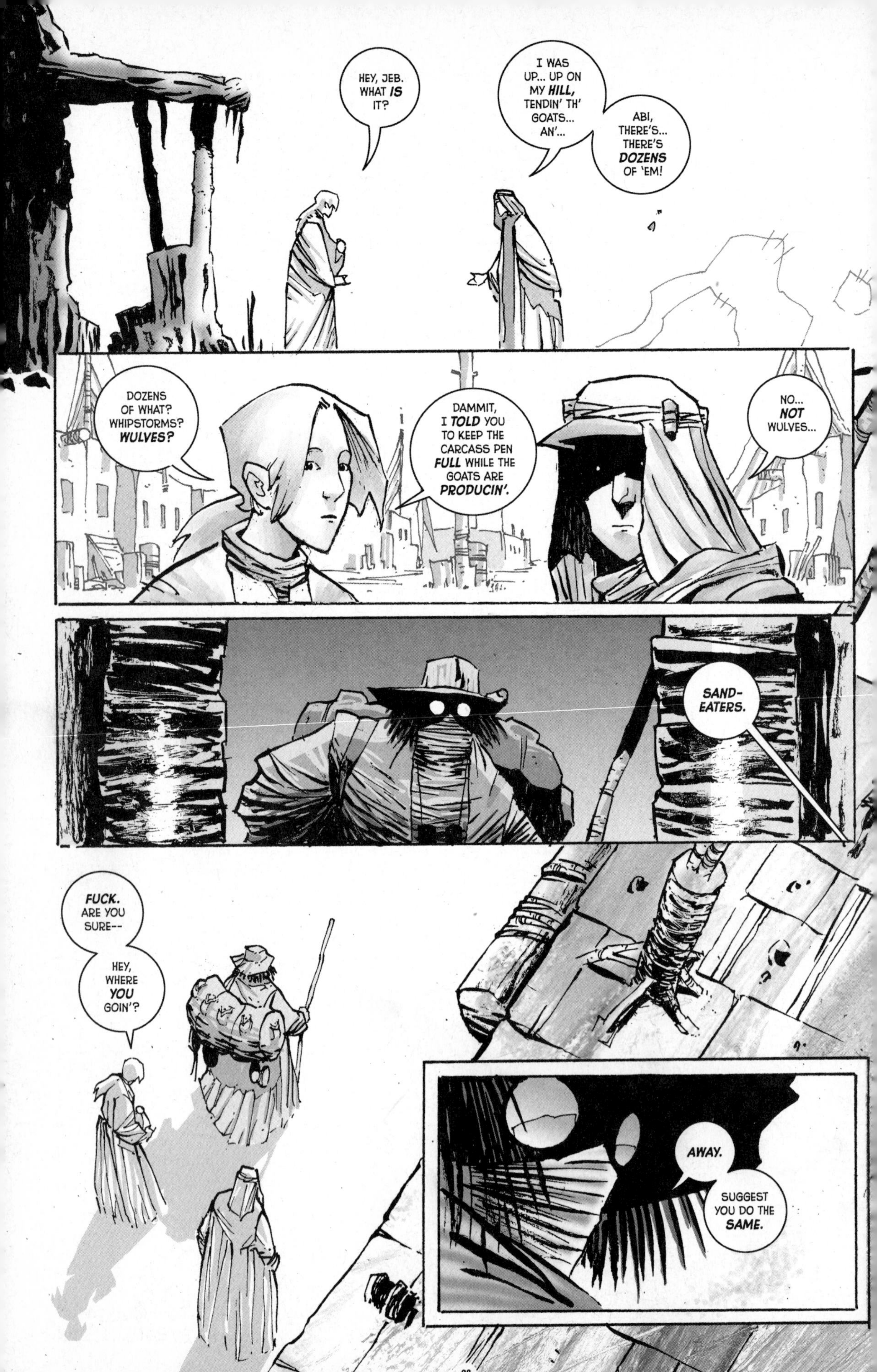
HEY, JEB. WHAT IS IT?
I WAS UP... UP ON MY HILL, TENDIN' TH' GOATS... AN'...
ABI, THERE'S... THERE'S DOZENS OF 'EM!
DOZENS OF WHAT? WHIPSTORMS? WULVES?
DAMMIT, I TOLD YOU TO KEEP THE CARCASS PEN FULL WHILE THE GOATS ARE PRODUCIN'.
NO... NOT WULVES...
SAND-EATERS.
FUCK. ARE YOU SURE--
HEY, WHERE YOU GOIN'?
AWAY.
SUGGEST YOU DO THE SAME.

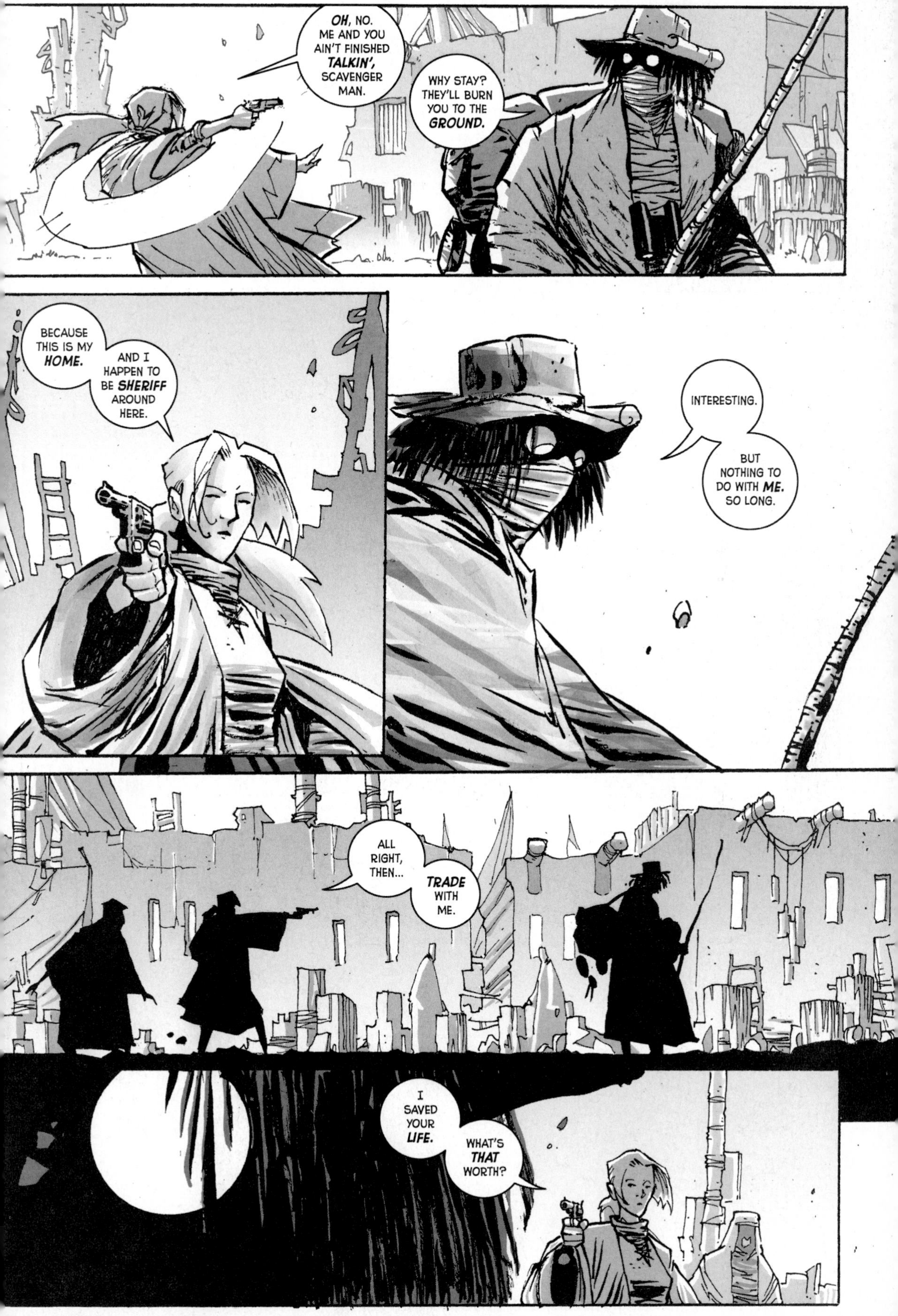
OH, NO. ME AND YOU AIN'T FINISHED TALKIN', SCAVENGER MAN.
WHY STAY? THEY'LL BURN YOU TO THE GROUND.
BECAUSE THIS IS MY HOME.
AND I HAPPEN TO BE SHERIFF AROUND HERE.
INTERESTING.
BUT NOTHING TO DO WITH ME. SO LONG.
ALL RIGHT, THEN...
TRADE WITH ME.
I SAVED YOUR LIFE.
WHAT'S THAT WORTH?

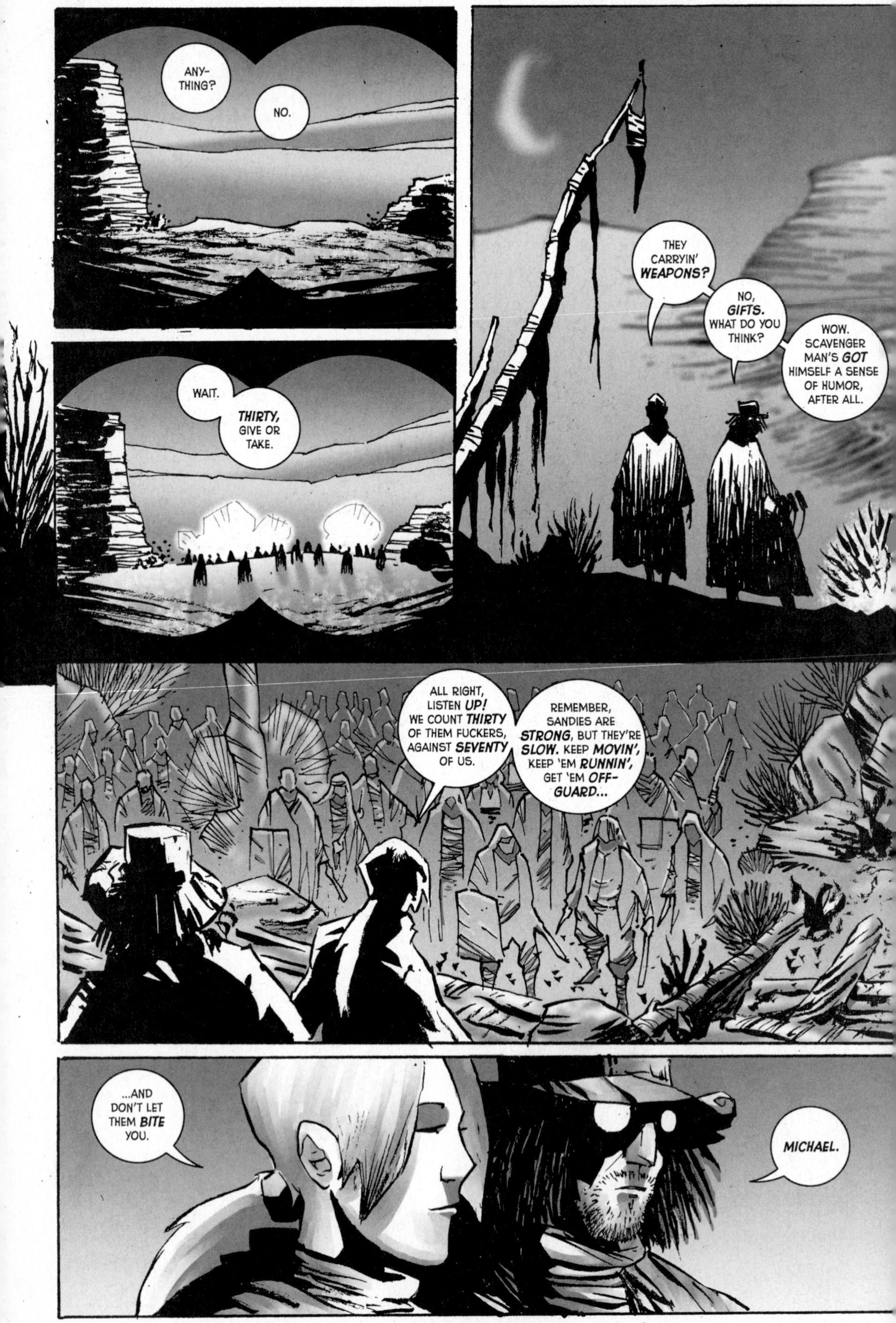
ANY-THING?
NO.
WAIT.
THIRTY, GIVE OR TAKE.
THEY CARRYIN' WEAPONS?
NO, GIFTS. WHAT DO YOU THINK?
WOW. SCAVENGER MAN'S GOT HIMSELF A SENSE OF HUMOR, AFTER ALL.
ALL RIGHT, LISTEN UP! WE COUNT THIRTY OF THEM FUCKERS, AGAINST SEVENTY OF US.
REMEMBER, SANDIES ARE STRONG, BUT THEY'RE SLOW. KEEP MOVIN', KEEP 'EM RUNNIN', GET 'EM OFF-GUARD...
...AND DON'T LET THEM BITE YOU.
MICHAEL.

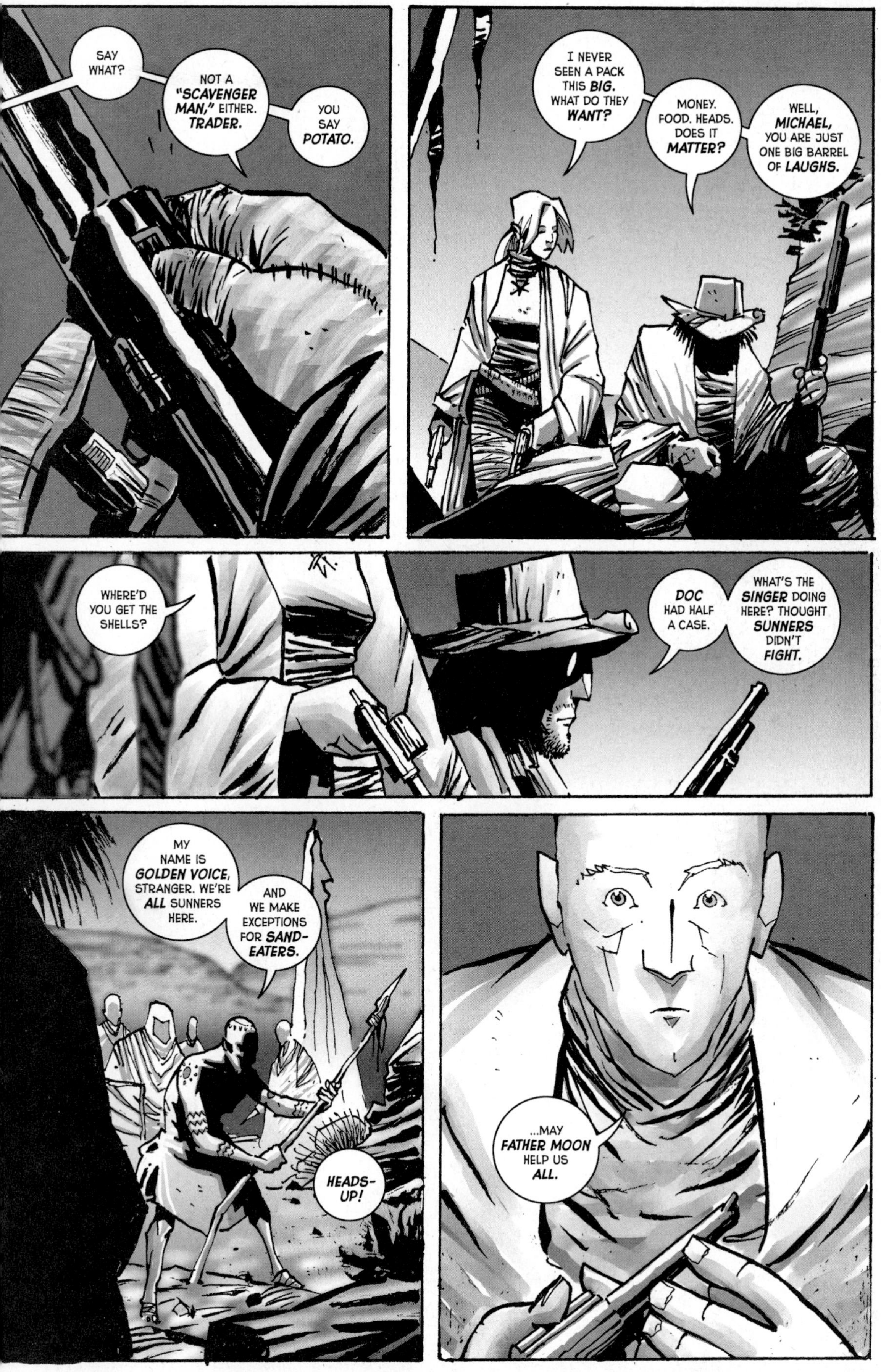
SAY WHAT?
NOT A "SCAVENGER MAN," EITHER. TRADER.
YOU SAY POTATO.
I NEVER SEEN A PACK THIS BIG. WHAT DO THEY WANT?
MONEY. FOOD. HEADS. DOES IT MATTER?
WELL, MICHAEL, YOU ARE JUST ONE BIG BARREL OF LAUGHS.
WHERE'D YOU GET THE SHELLS?
DOC HAD HALF A CASE.
WHAT'S THE SINGER DOING HERE? THOUGHT SUNNERS DIDN'T FIGHT.
MY NAME IS GOLDEN VOICE, STRANGER. WE'RE ALL SUNNERS HERE.
AND WE MAKE EXCEPTIONS FOR SAND-EATERS.
HEADS-UP!
...MAY FATHER MOON HELP US ALL.

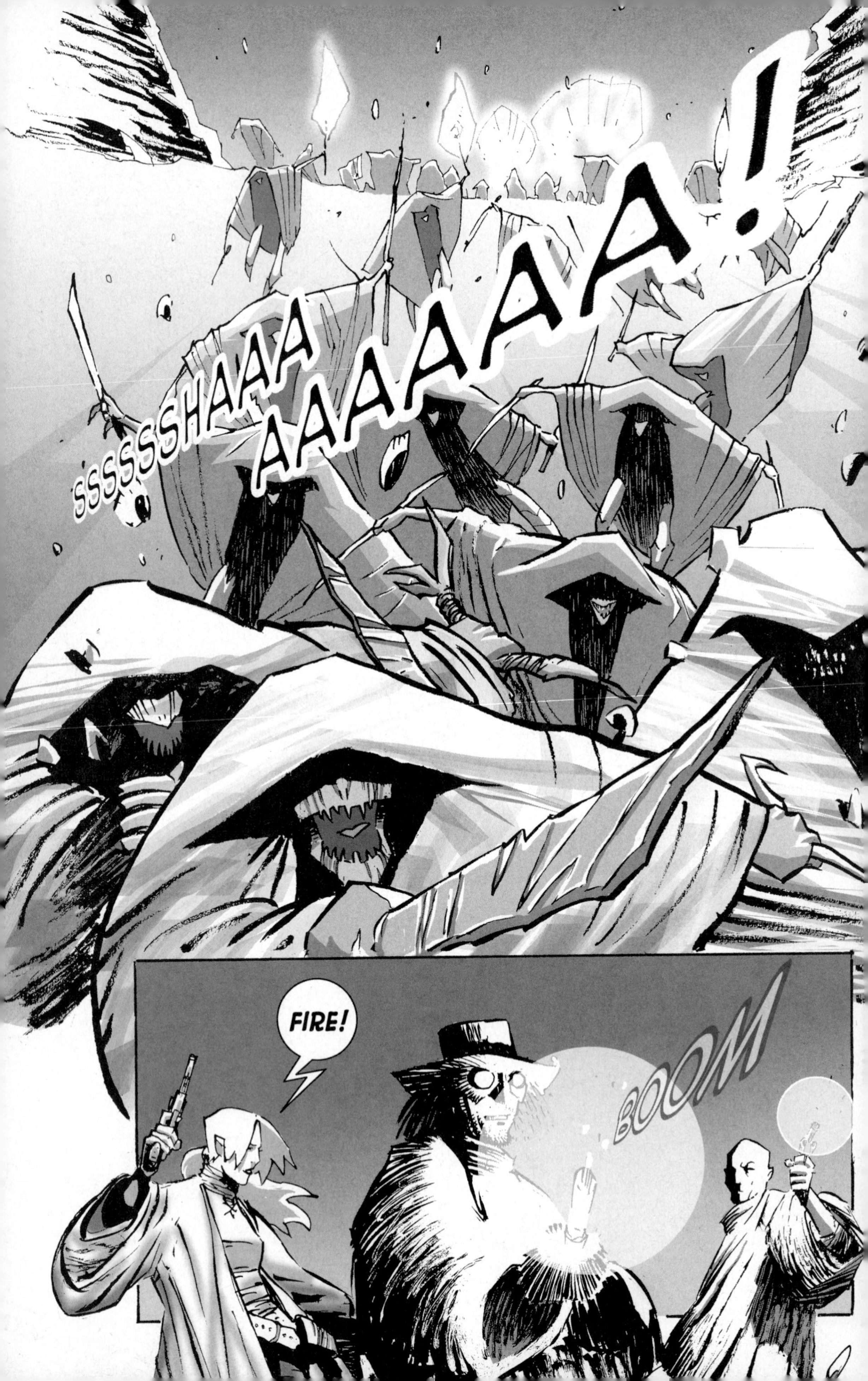
SSSSSSHAAA AAAAAAA!
FIRE!
BOOM

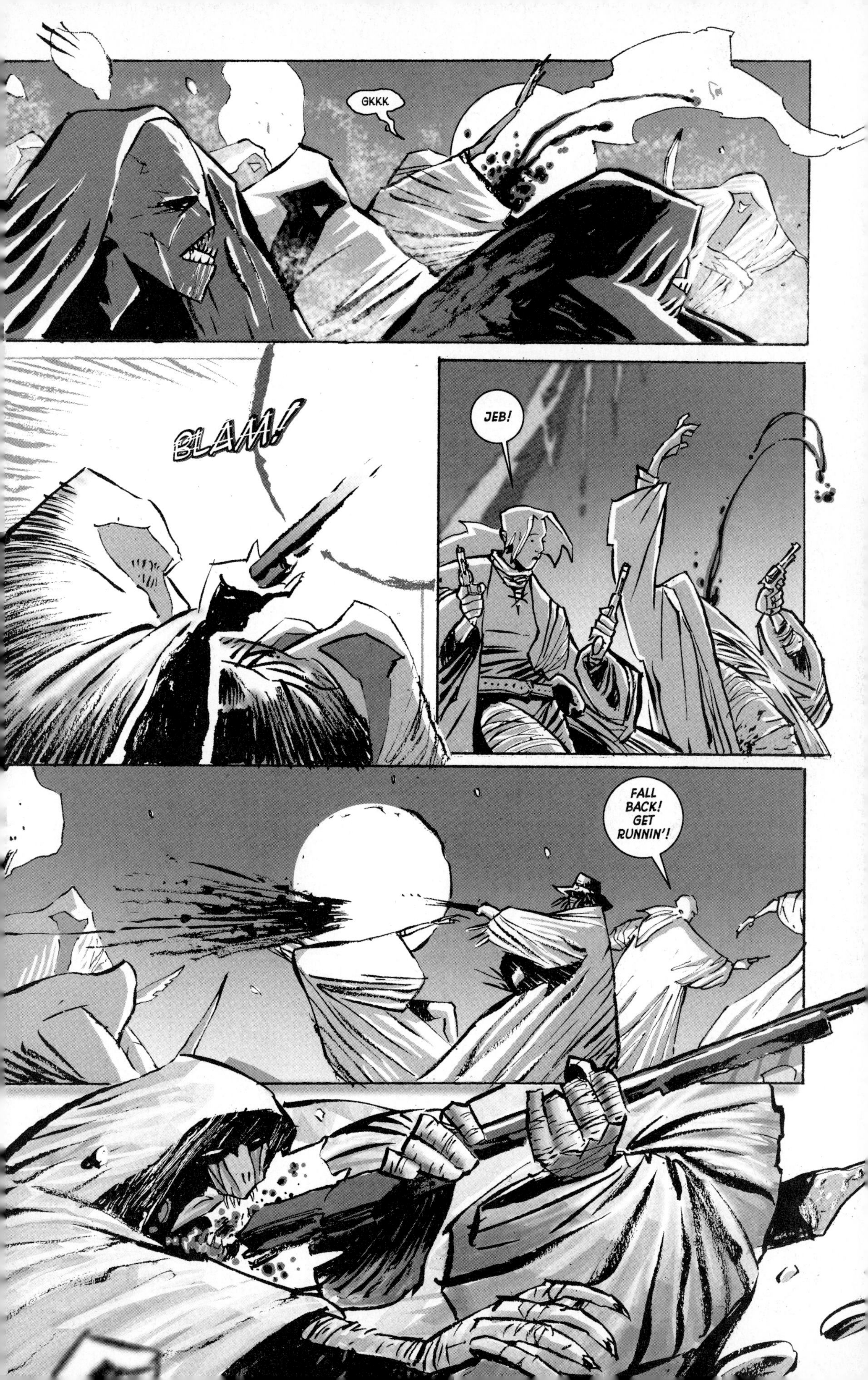
GKKK
BLAM!
JEB!
FALL BACK! GET RUNNIN'!

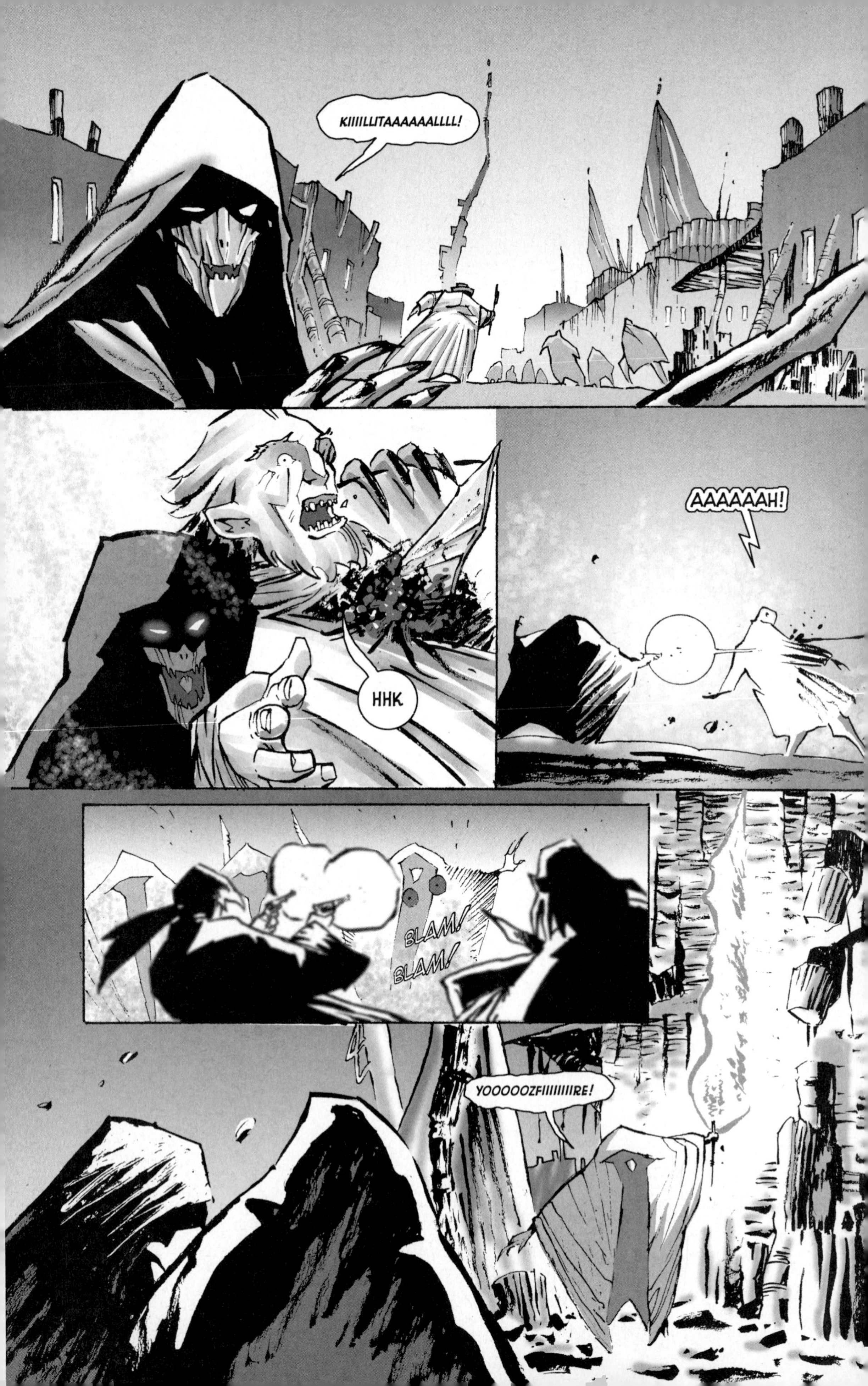
KIIIILLITAAAAAALLLL!
HHK
AAAAAAH!
BLAM!
BLAM!
YOOOOOZFIIIIIIIIRE!

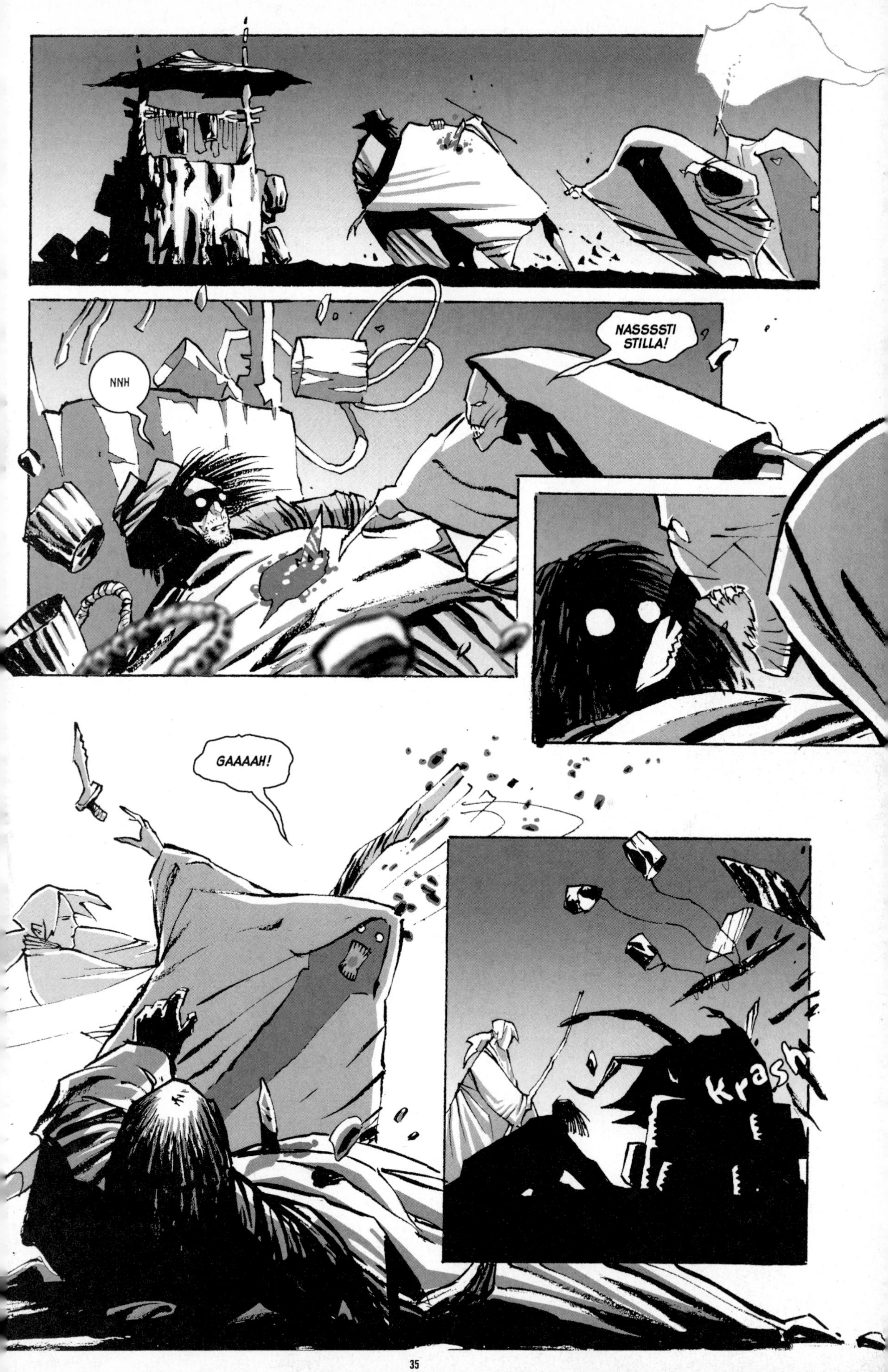
NNH
NASSSSTI STILLA!
GAAAAH!
Krash

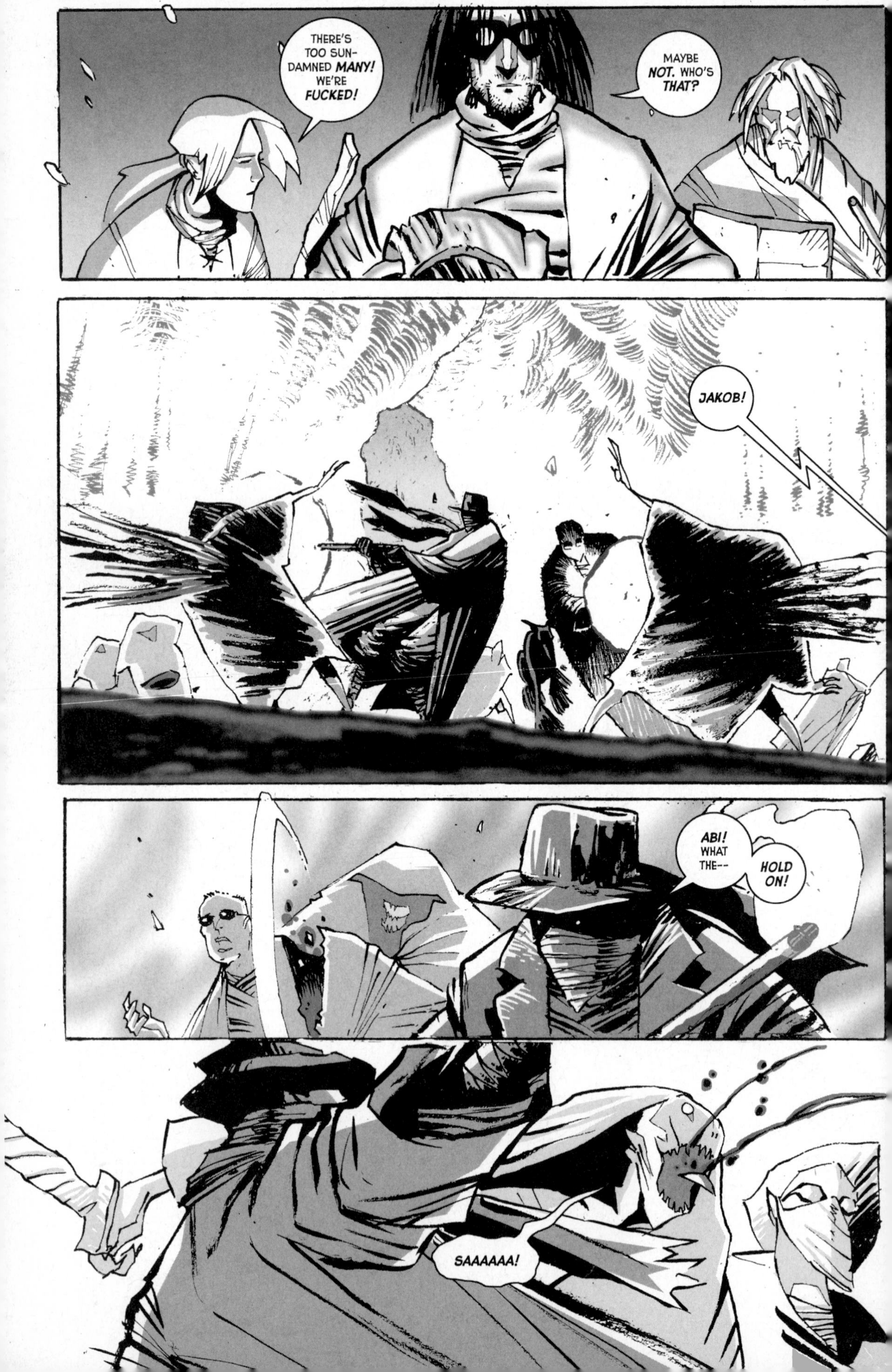
THERE'S TOO SUN-DAMNED MANY! WE'RE FUCKED!
MAYBE NOT. WHO'S THAT?
JAKOB!
ABI! WHAT THE--
HOLD ON!
SAAAAAA!

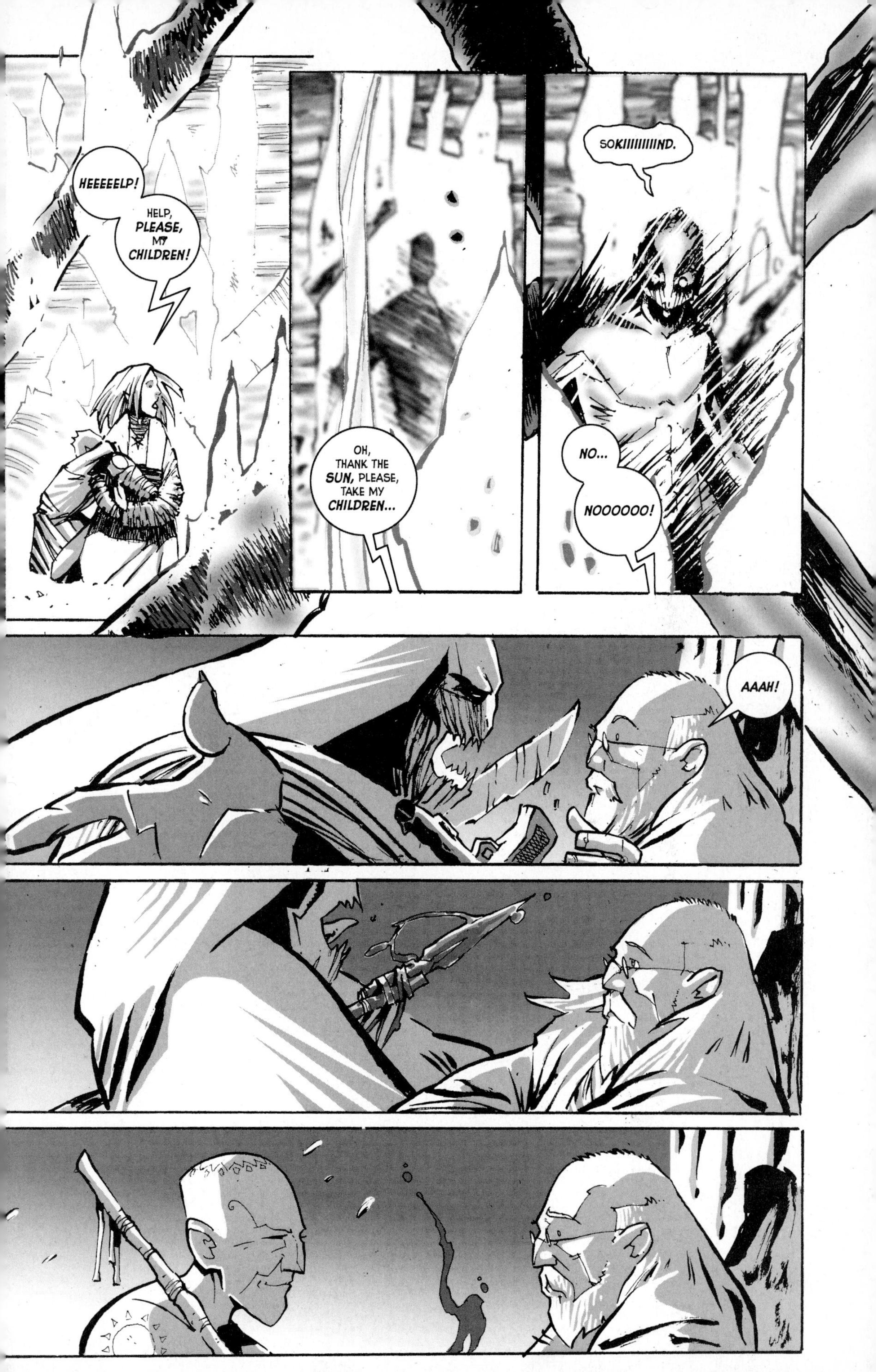
HEEEEELP!
HELP, PLEASE, MY CHILDREN!
OH, THANK THE SUN, PLEASE, TAKE MY CHILDREN...
SOKIIIIIIIIIND.
NO...
NOOOOOO!
AAAH!

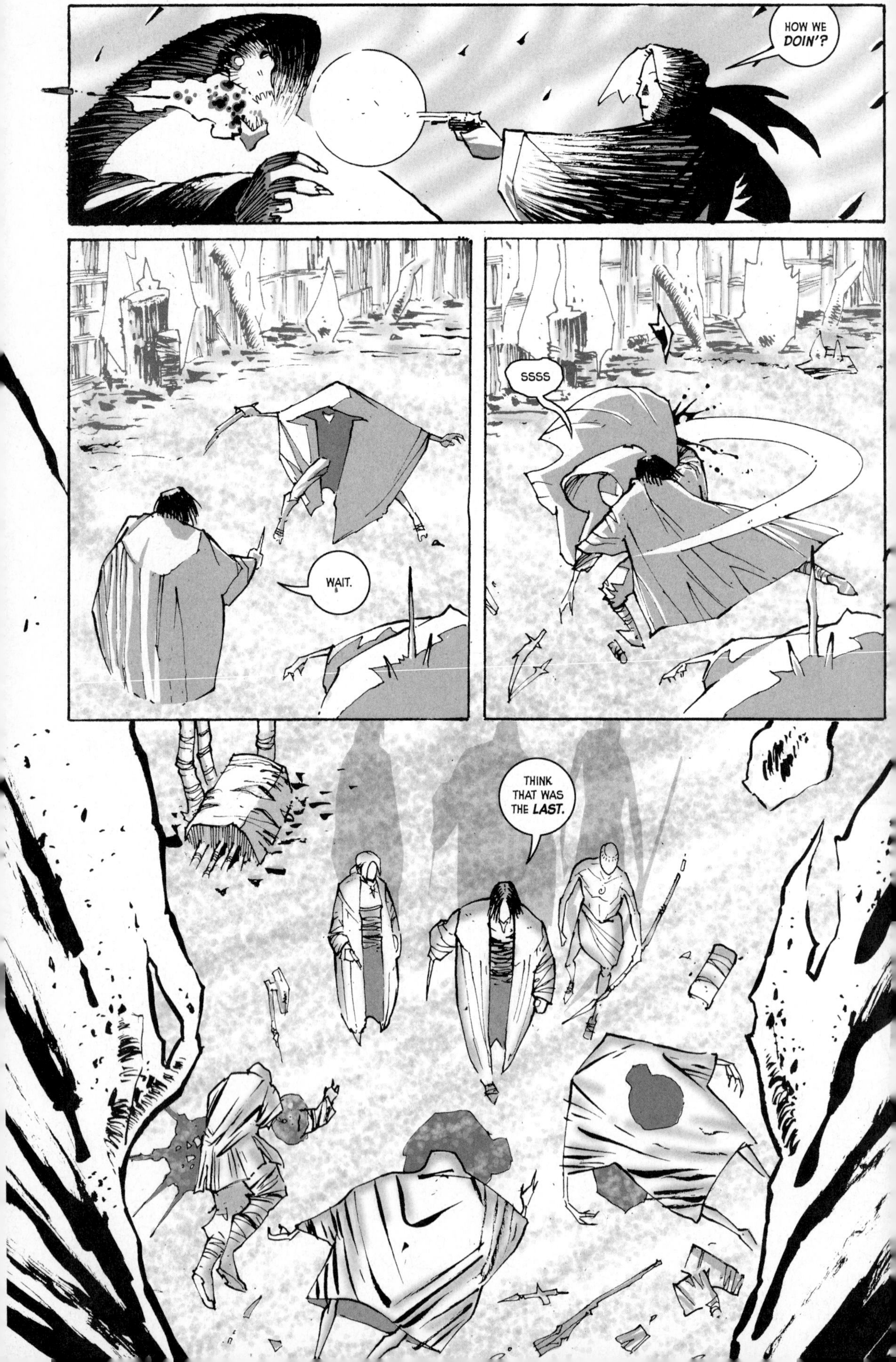
HOW WE DOIN'?
WAIT.
SSSS
THINK THAT WAS THE LAST.

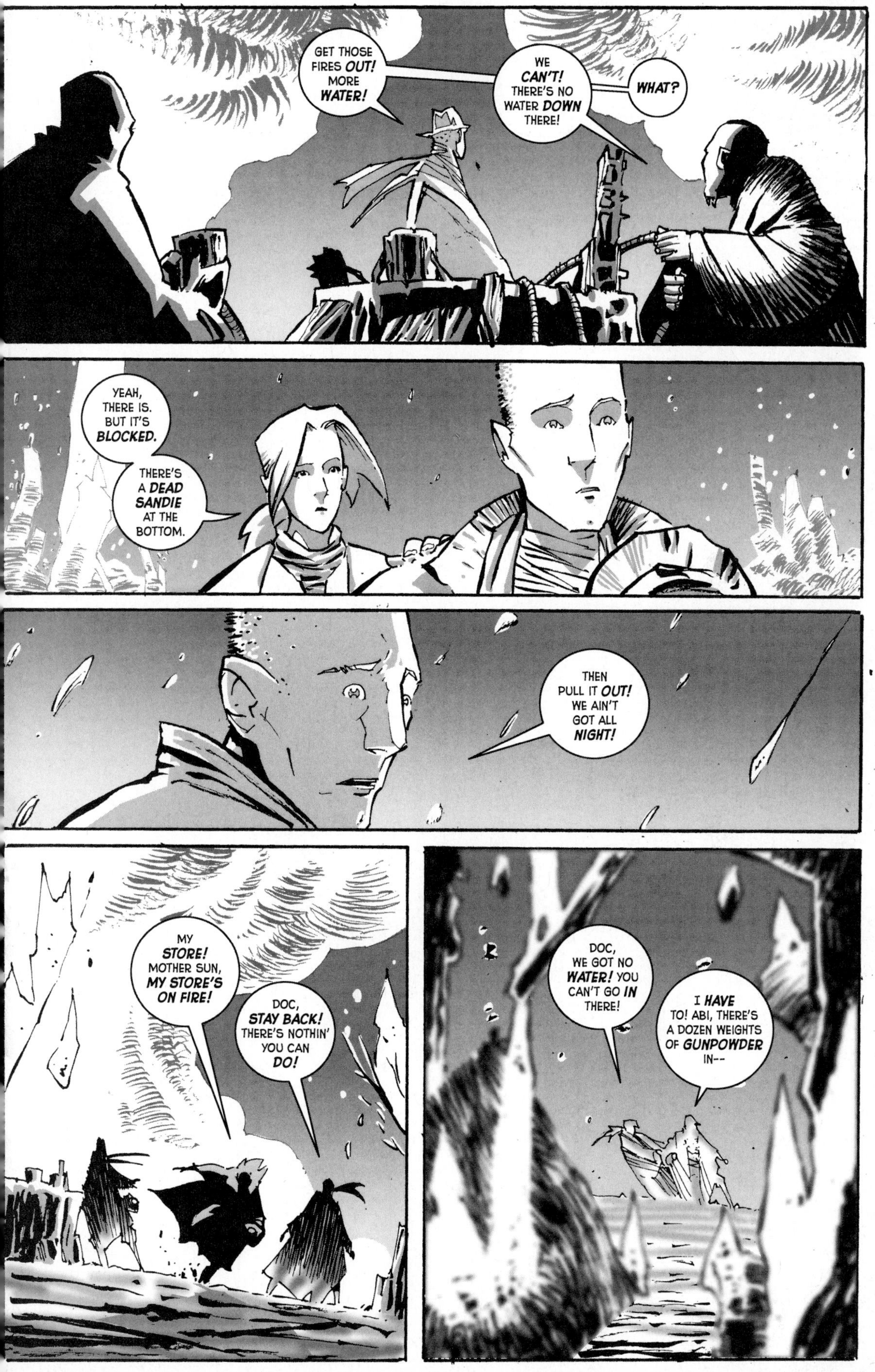
GET THOSE FIRES OUT! MORE WATER!
WE CAN'T! THERE'S NO WATER DOWN THERE!
WHAT?
YEAH, THERE IS. BUT IT'S BLOCKED.
THERE'S A DEAD SANDIE AT THE BOTTOM.
THEN PULL IT OUT! WE AIN'T GOT ALL NIGHT!
MY STORE! MOTHER SUN, MY STORE'S ON FIRE!
DOC, STAY BACK! THERE'S NOTHIN' YOU CAN DO!
DOC, WE GOT NO WATER! YOU CAN'T GO IN THERE!
I HAVE TO! ABI, THERE'S A DOZEN WEIGHTS OF GUNPOWDER IN--

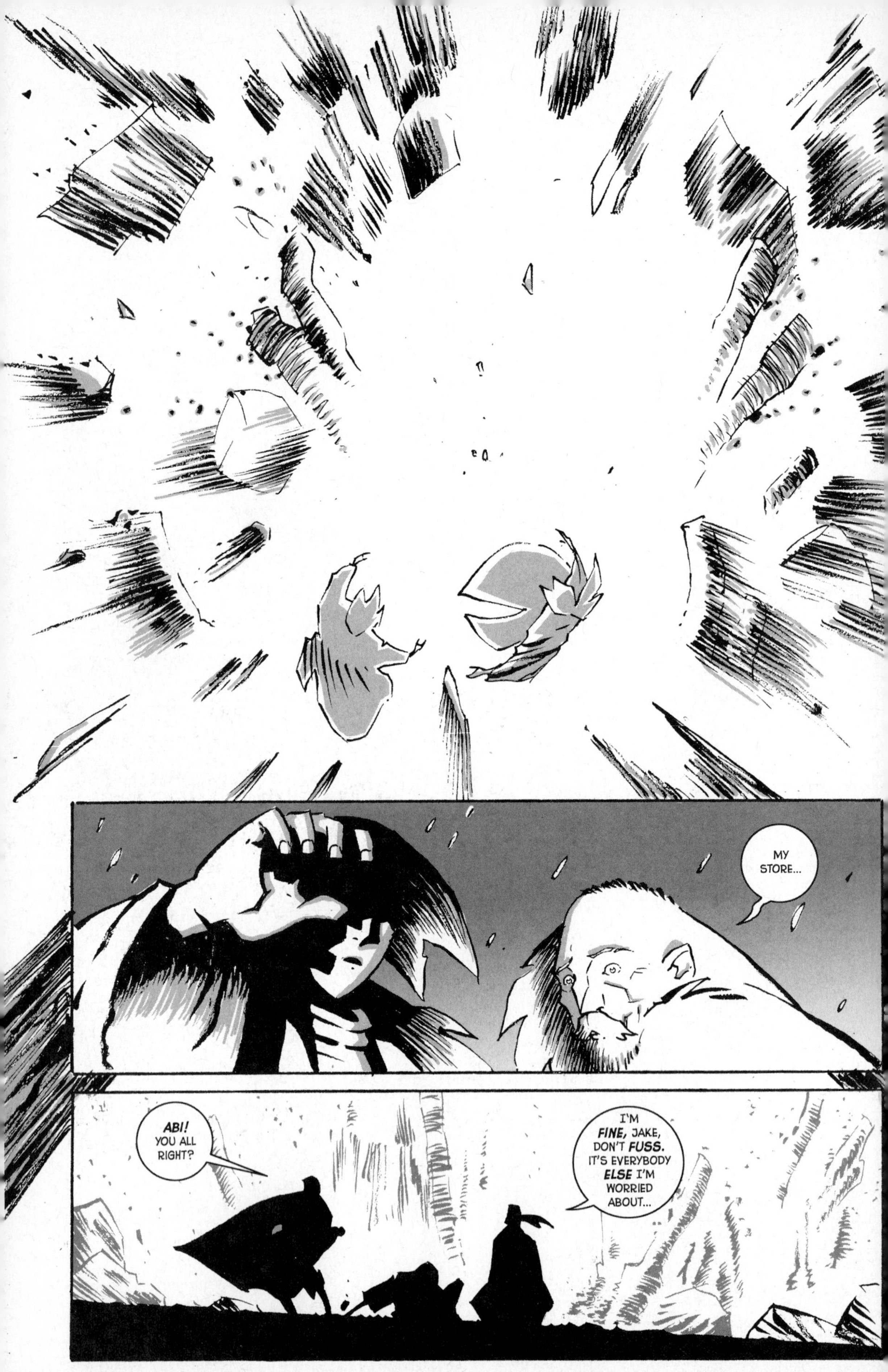
MY STORE...
ABI! YOU ALL RIGHT?
I'M FINE, JAKE, DON'T FUSS. IT'S EVERYBODY ELSE I'M WORRIED ABOUT...

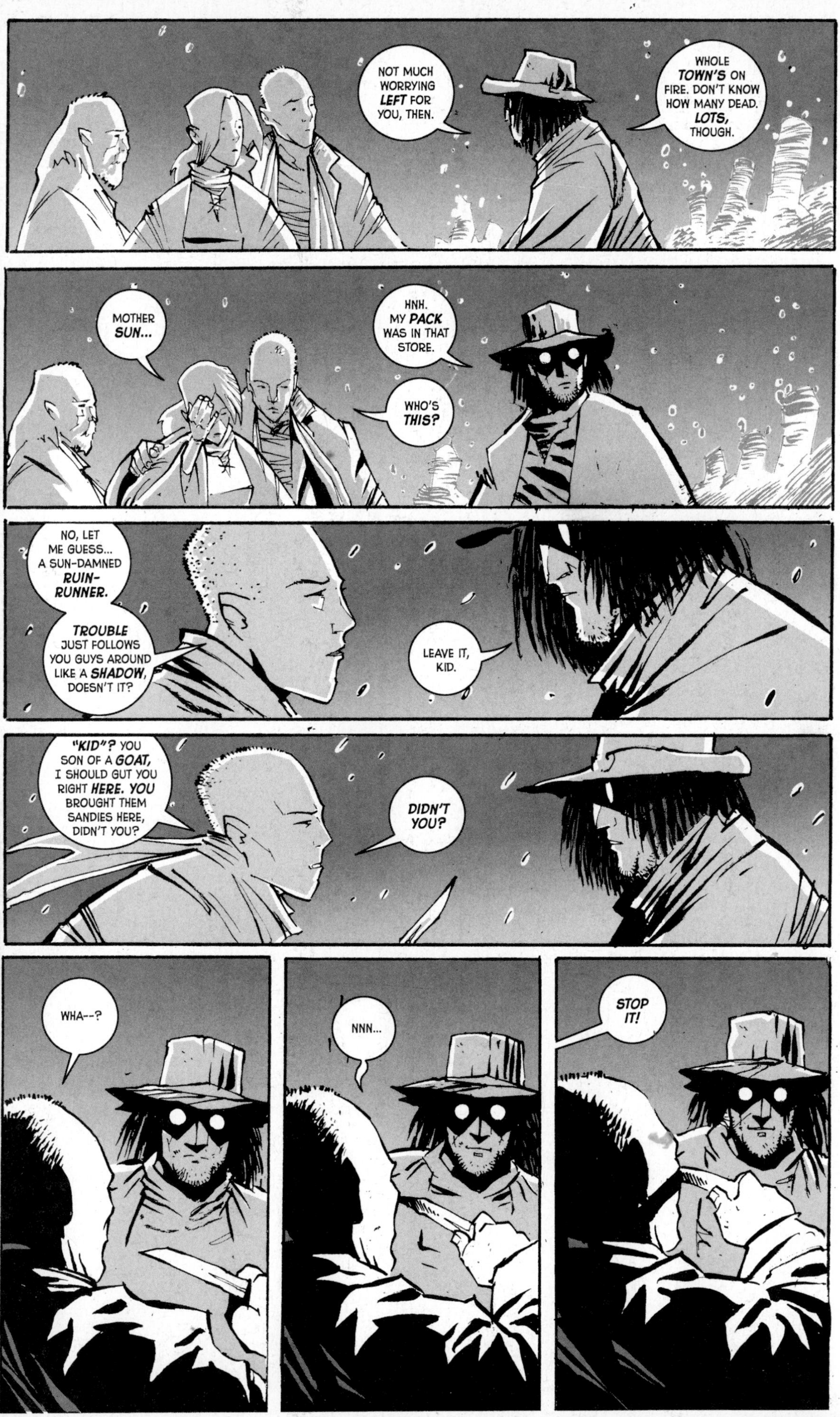
NOT MUCH WORRYING LEFT FOR YOU, THEN.
WHOLE TOWN'S ON FIRE. DON'T KNOW HOW MANY DEAD. LOTS, THOUGH.
MOTHER SUN...
HNH. MY PACK WAS IN THAT STORE.
WHO'S THIS?
NO, LET ME GUESS... A SUN-DAMNED RUIN-RUNNER.
TROUBLE JUST FOLLOWS YOU GUYS AROUND LIKE A SHADOW, DOESN'T IT?
LEAVE IT, KID.
"KID"? YOU SON OF A GOAT, I SHOULD GUT YOU RIGHT HERE. YOU BROUGHT THEM SANDIES HERE, DIDN'T YOU?
DIDN'T YOU?
WHA--?
NNN...
STOP IT!

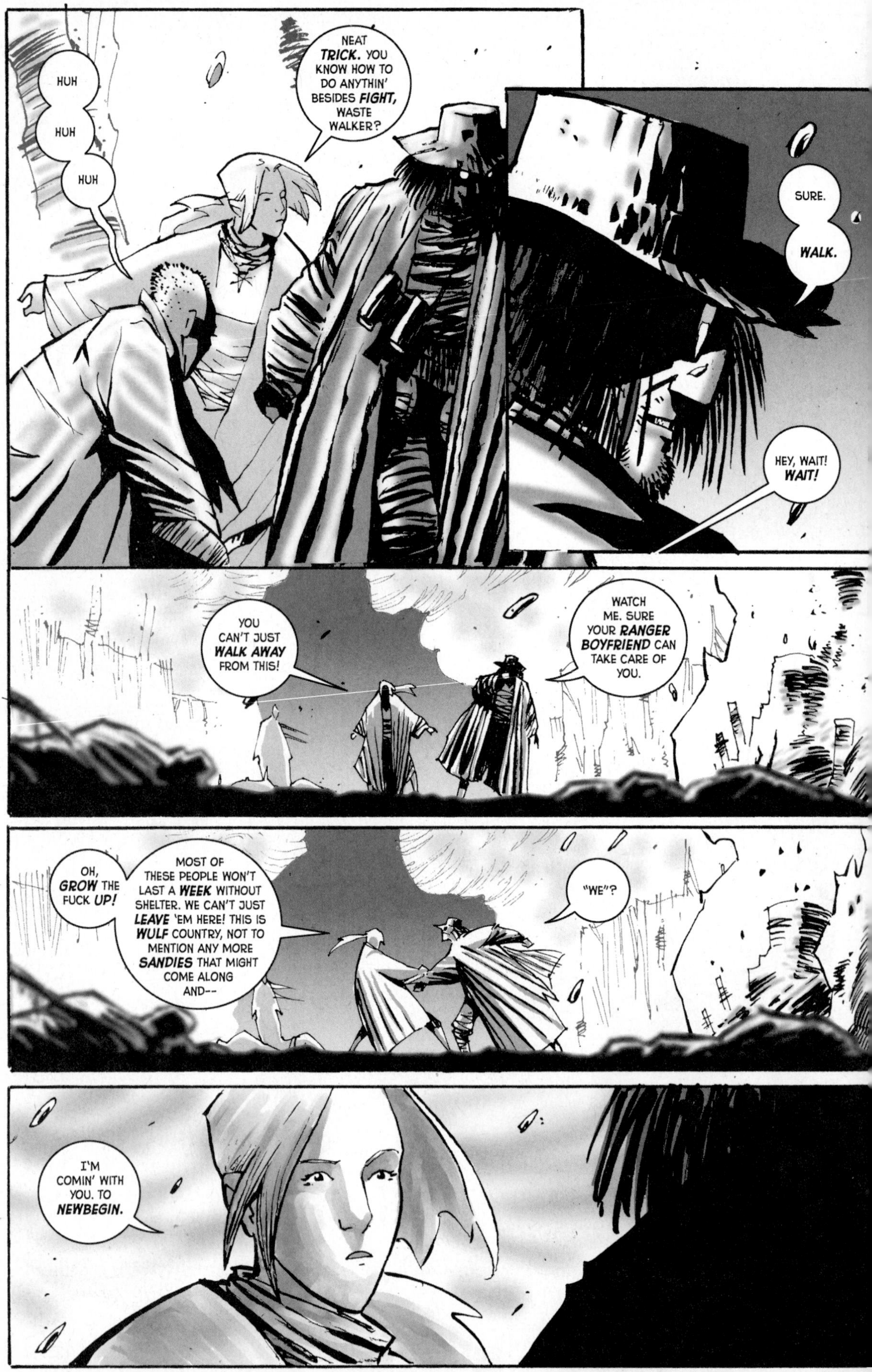
HUH
HUH
HUH
NEAT TRICK. YOU KNOW HOW TO DO ANYTHIN' BESIDES FIGHT, WASTE WALKER?
SURE.
WALK.
HEY, WAIT! WAIT!
YOU CAN'T JUST WALK AWAY FROM THIS!
WATCH ME. SURE YOUR RANGER BOYFRIEND CAN TAKE CARE OF YOU.
OH, GROW THE FUCK UP!
MOST OF THESE PEOPLE WON'T LAST A WEEK WITHOUT SHELTER. WE CAN'T JUST LEAVE 'EM HERE! THIS IS WULF COUNTRY, NOT TO MENTION ANY MORE SANDIES THAT MIGHT COME ALONG AND--
"WE"?
I'M COMIN' WITH YOU. TO NEWBEGIN.

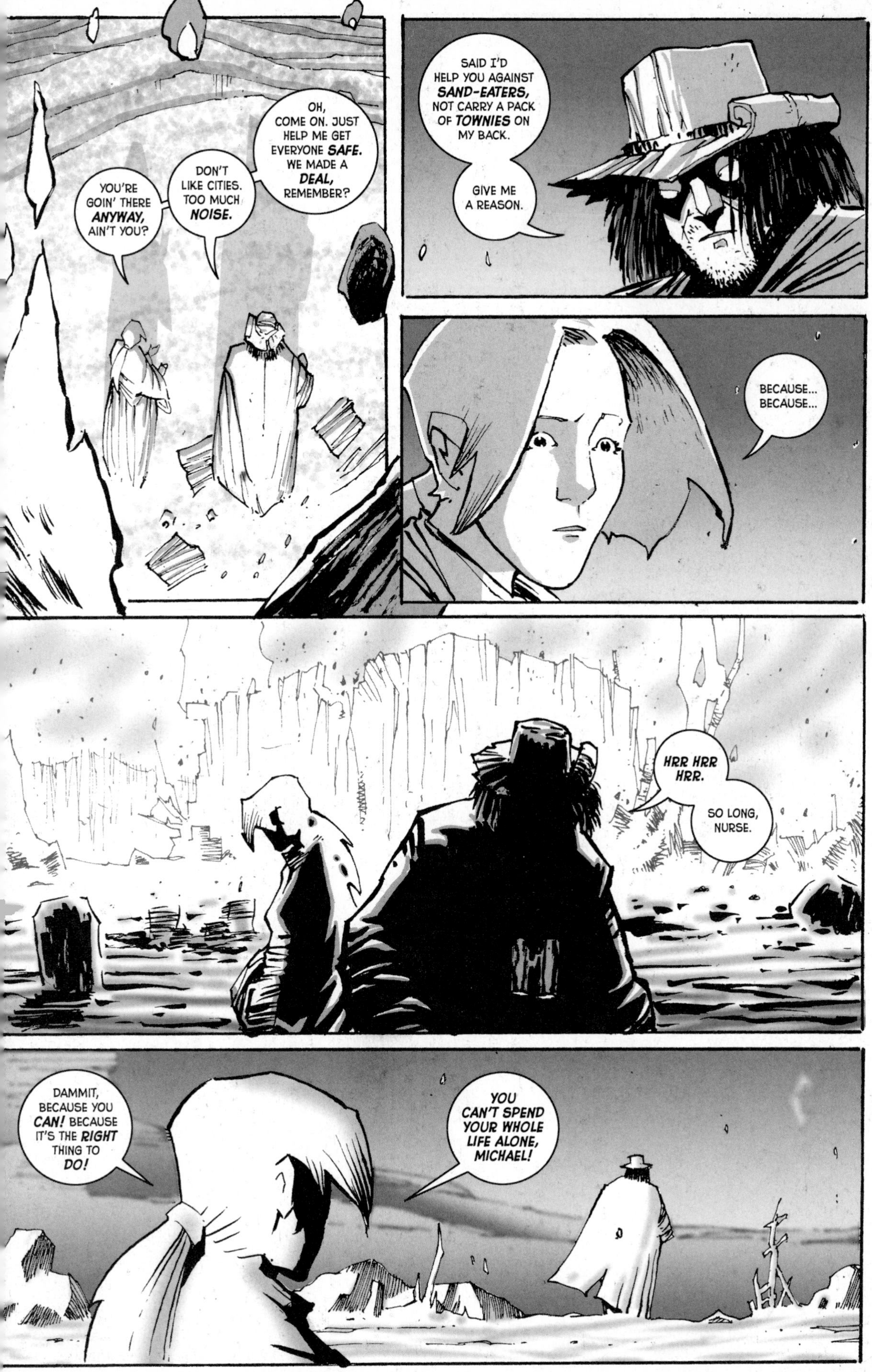
YOU'RE GOIN' THERE ANYWAY, AIN'T YOU?
DON'T LIKE CITIES. TOO MUCH NOISE.
OH, COME ON. JUST HELP ME GET EVERYONE SAFE. WE MADE A DEAL, REMEMBER?
SAID I'D HELP YOU AGAINST SAND-EATERS, NOT CARRY A PACK OF TOWNIES ON MY BACK.
GIVE ME A REASON.
BECAUSE... BECAUSE...
HRR HRR HRR.
SO LONG, NURSE.
DAMMIT, BECAUSE YOU CAN! BECAUSE IT'S THE RIGHT THING TO DO!
YOU CAN'T SPEND YOUR WHOLE LIFE ALONE, MICHAEL!

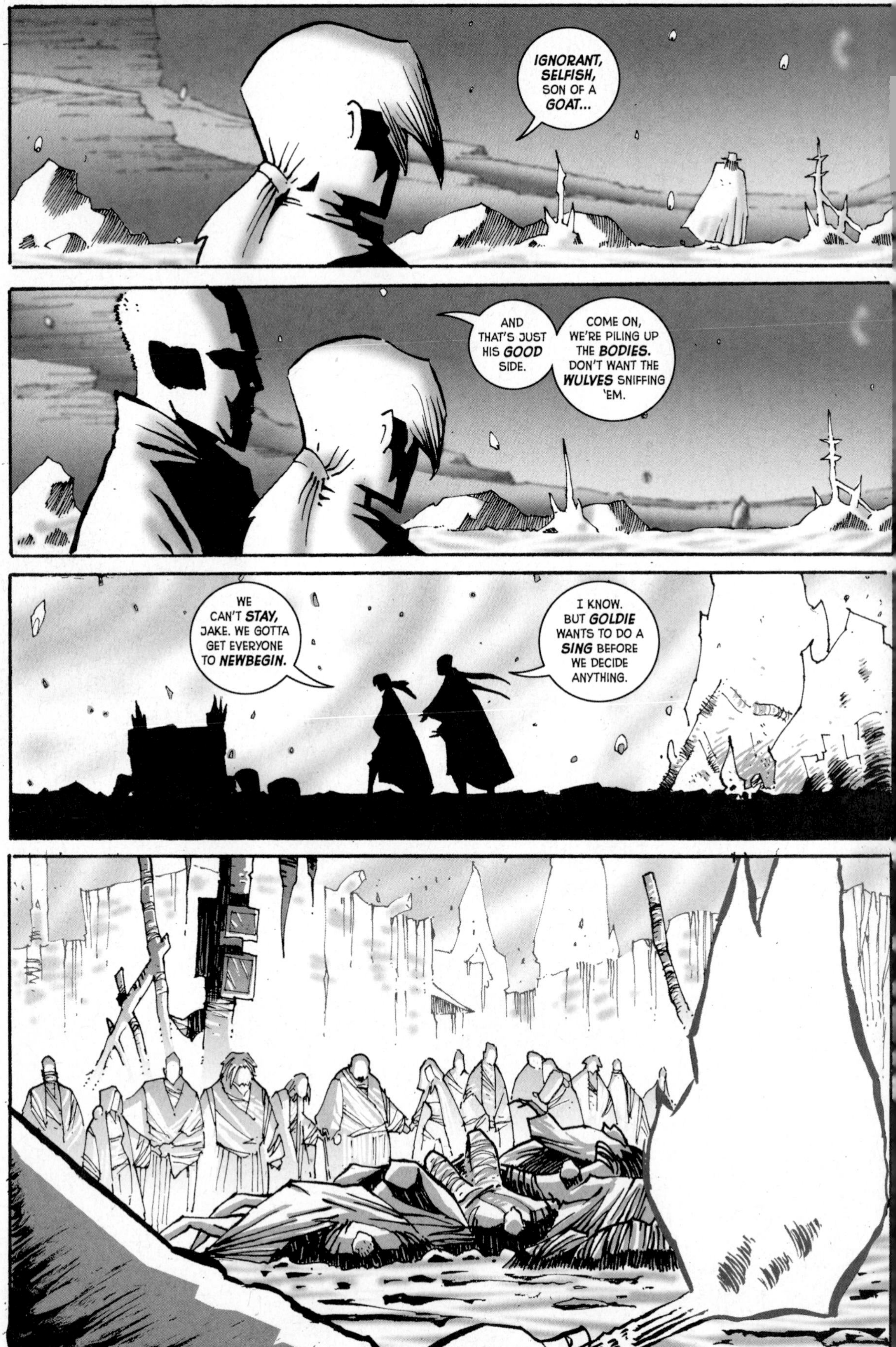
IGNORANT, SELFISH, SON OF A GOAT...
AND THAT'S JUST HIS GOOD SIDE.
COME ON, WE'RE PILING UP THE BODIES. DON'T WANT THE WULVES SNIFFING 'EM.
WE CAN'T STAY, JAKE. WE GOTTA GET EVERYONE TO NEWBEGIN.
I KNOW. BUT GOLDIE WANTS TO DO A SING BEFORE WE DECIDE ANYTHING.

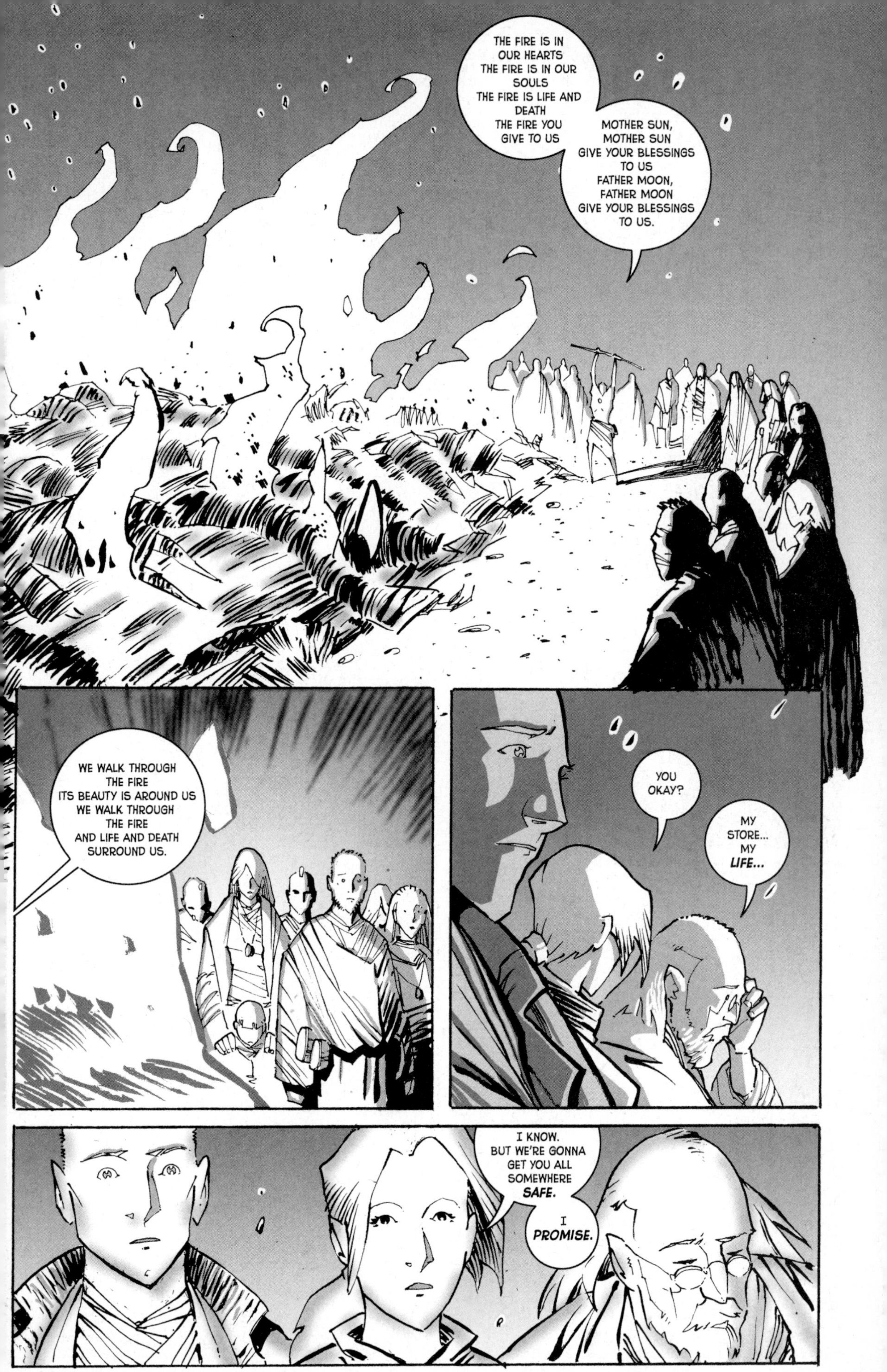
THE FIRE IS IN OUR HEARTS THE FIRE IS IN OUR SOULS THE FIRE IS LIFE AND DEATH THE FIRE YOU GIVE TO US
MOTHER SUN, MOTHER SUN GIVE YOUR BLESSINGS TO US FATHER MOON, FATHER MOON GIVE YOUR BLESSINGS TO US.
WE WALK THROUGH THE FIRE ITS BEAUTY IS AROUND US WE WALK THROUGH THE FIRE AND LIFE AND DEATH SURROUND US.
YOU OKAY?
MY STORE... MY LIFE...
I KNOW. BUT WE'RE GONNA GET YOU ALL SOMEWHERE SAFE.
I PROMISE.

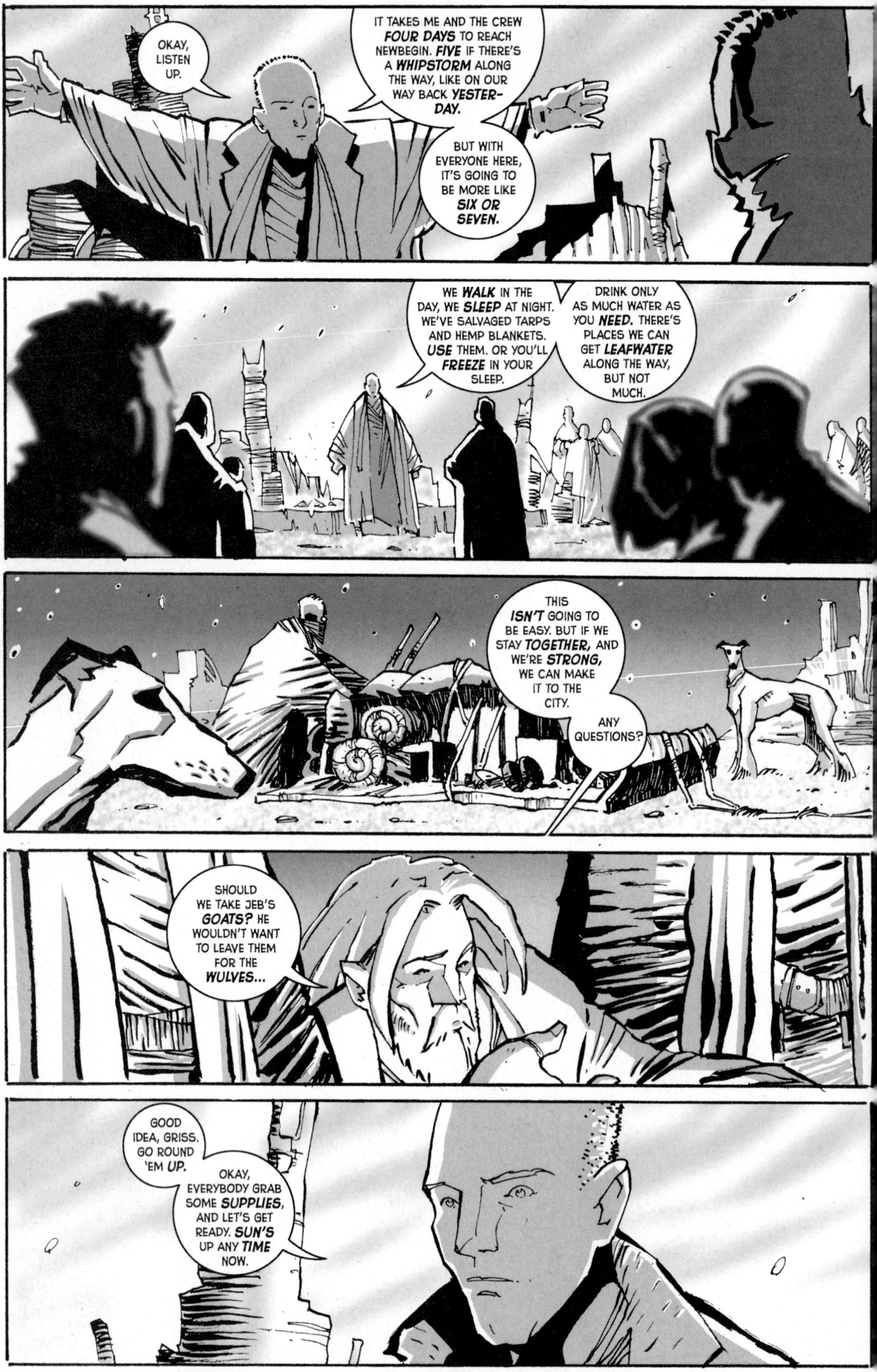
OKAY, LISTEN UP.
IT TAKES ME AND THE CREW FOUR DAYS TO REACH NEWBEGIN. FIVE IF THERE'S A WHIPSTORM ALONG THE WAY, LIKE ON OUR WAY BACK YESTER-DAY.
BUT WITH EVERYONE HERE, IT'S GOING TO BE MORE LIKE SIX OR SEVEN.
WE WALK IN THE DAY, WE SLEEP AT NIGHT. WE'VE SALVAGED TARPS AND HEMP BLANKETS. USE THEM. OR YOU'LL FREEZE IN YOUR SLEEP.
DRINK ONLY AS MUCH WATER AS YOU NEED. THERE'S PLACES WE CAN GET LEAFWATER ALONG THE WAY, BUT NOT MUCH.
THIS ISN'T GOING TO BE EASY. BUT IF WE STAY TOGETHER, AND WE'RE STRONG, WE CAN MAKE IT TO THE CITY.
ANY QUESTIONS?
SHOULD WE TAKE JEB'S GOATS? HE WOULDN'T WANT TO LEAVE THEM FOR THE WULVES...
GOOD IDEA, GRISS. GO ROUND 'EM UP.
OKAY, EVERYBODY GRAB SOME SUPPLIES, AND LET'S GET READY. SUN'S UP ANY TIME NOW.

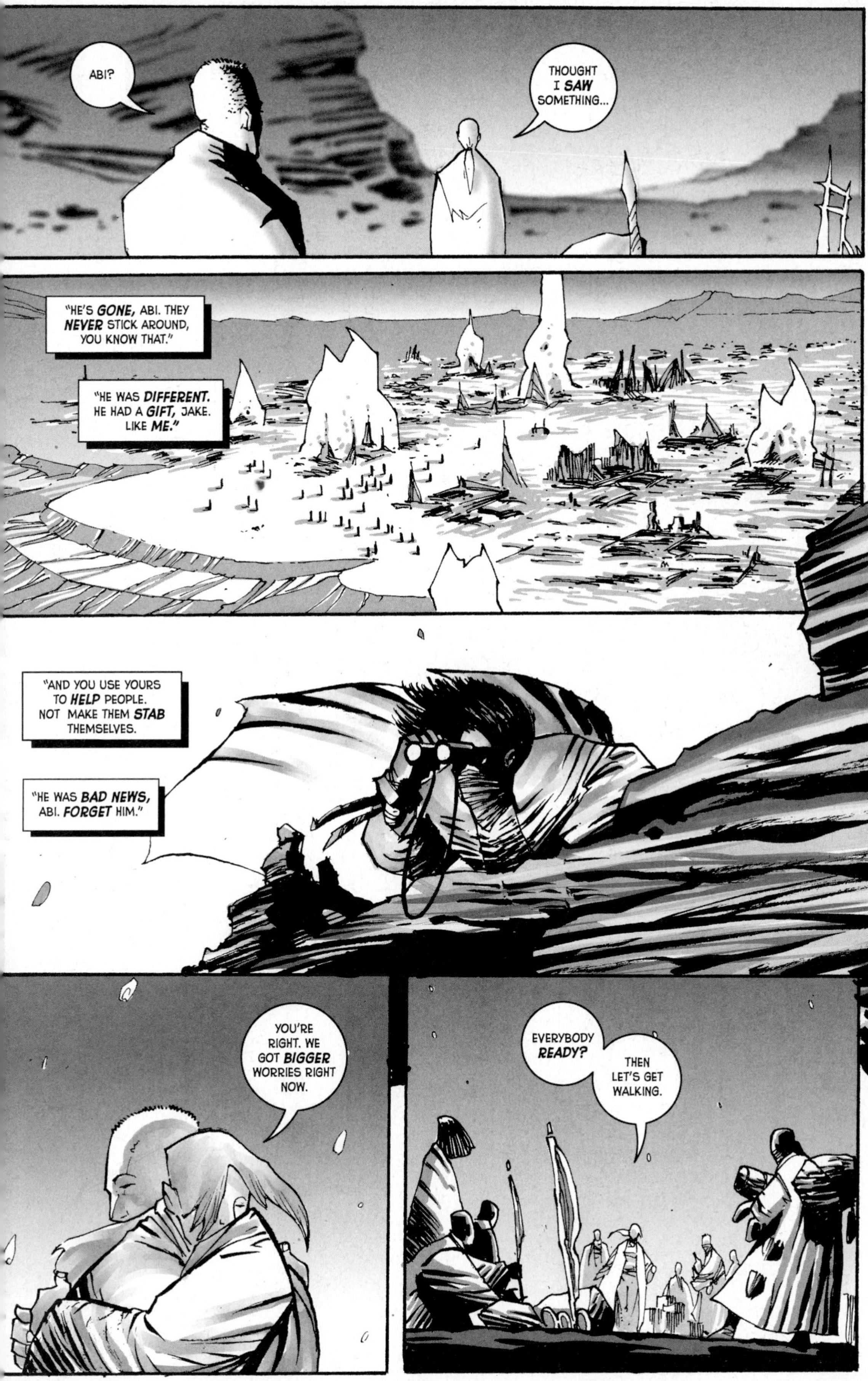
ABI?
THOUGHT I SAW SOMETHING...
"HE'S GONE, ABI. THEY NEVER STICK AROUND, YOU KNOW THAT."
"HE WAS DIFFERENT. HE HAD A GIFT, JAKE. LIKE ME."
"AND YOU USE YOURS TO HELP PEOPLE. NOT MAKE THEM STAB THEMSELVES.
"HE WAS BAD NEWS, ABI. FORGET HIM."
YOU'RE RIGHT. WE GOT BIGGER WORRIES RIGHT NOW.
EVERYBODY READY?
THEN LET'S GET WALKING.

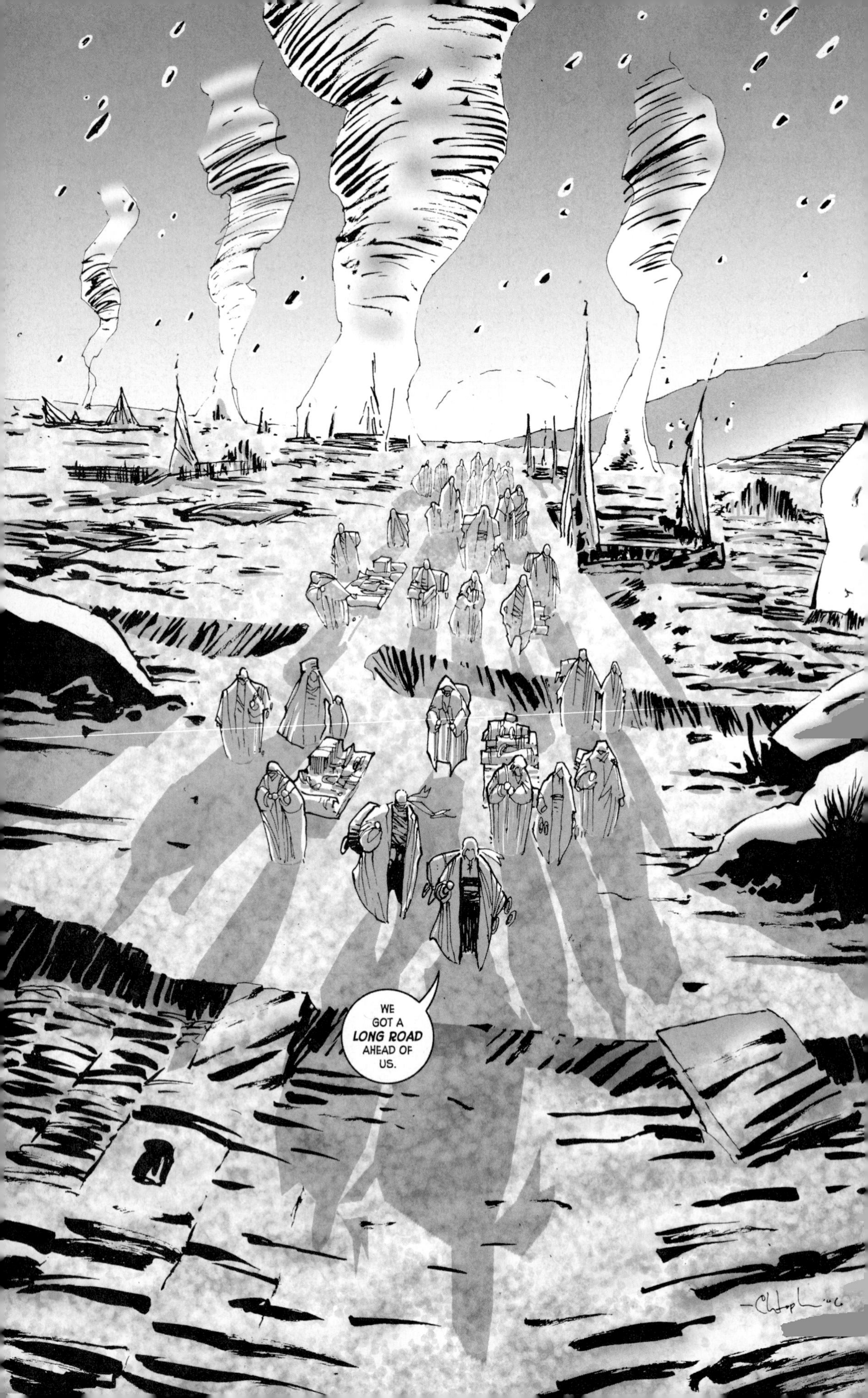
WE GOT A LONG ROAD AHEAD OF US.

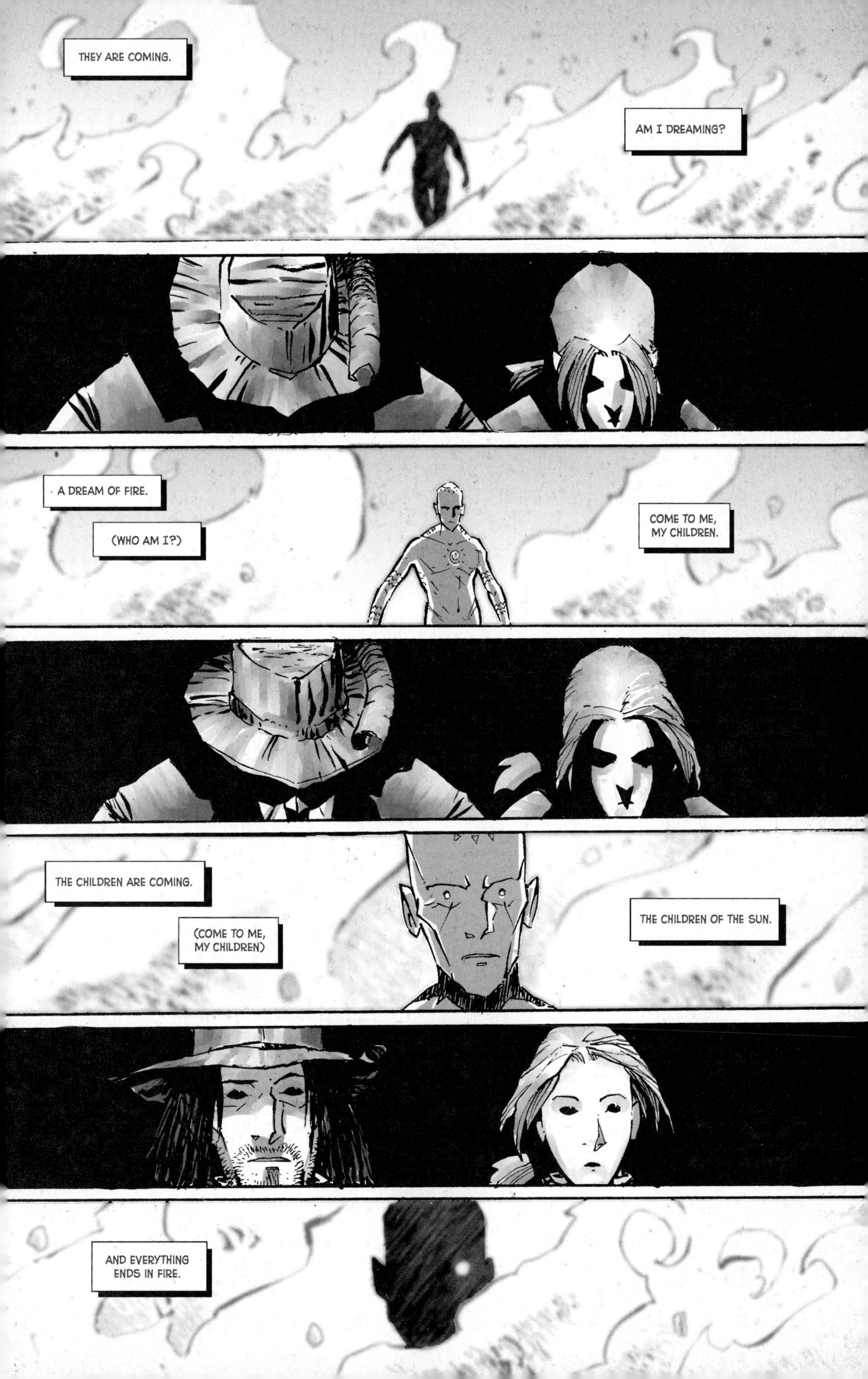
THEY ARE COMING.
AM I DREAMING?
A DREAM OF FIRE.
(WHO AM I?)
COME TO ME, MY CHILDREN.
THE CHILDREN ARE COMING.
(COME TO ME, MY CHILDREN)
THE CHILDREN OF THE SUN.
AND EVERYTHING ENDS IN FIRE.

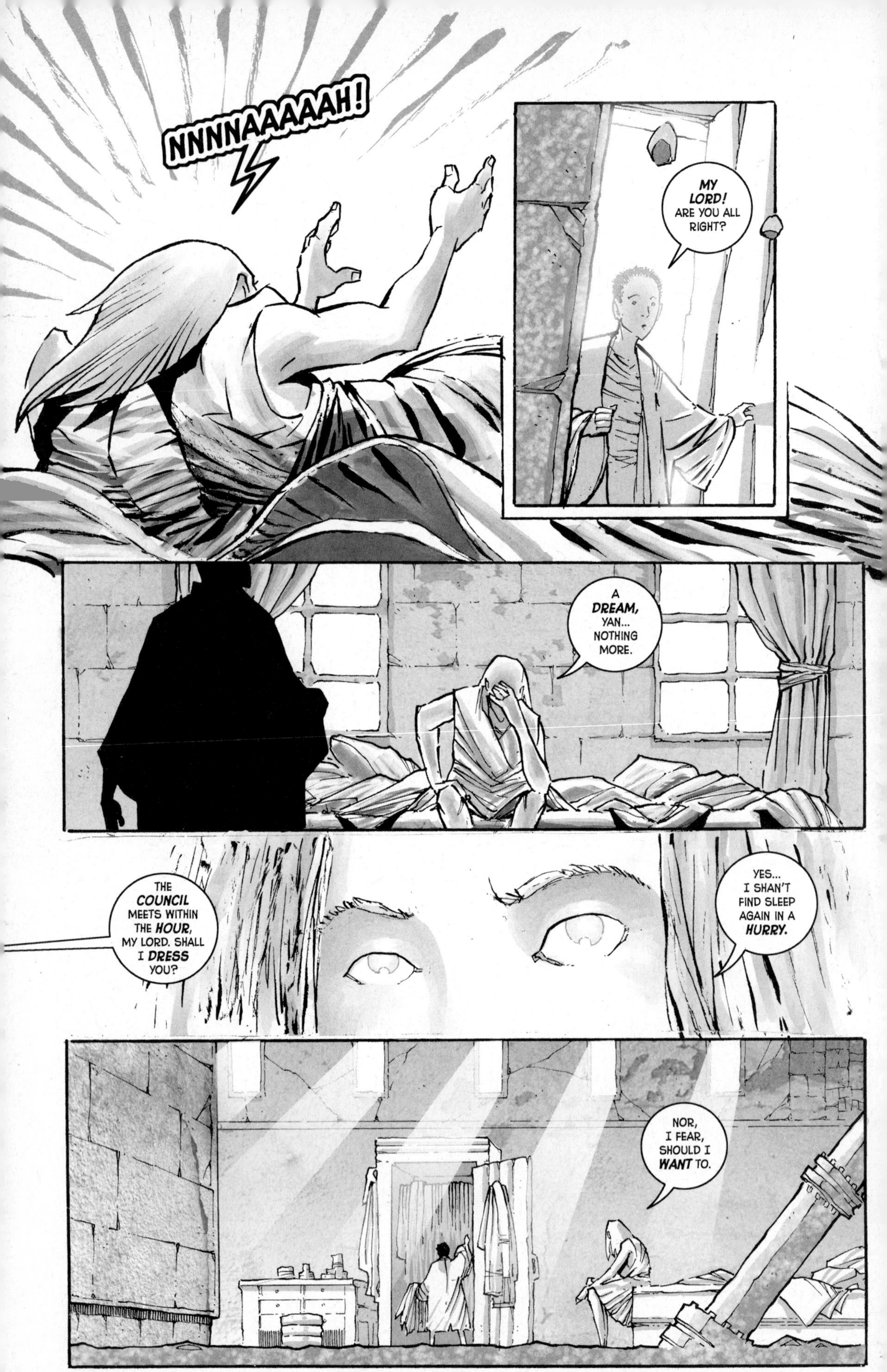
NNNNAAAAAH!
MY LORD! ARE YOU ALL RIGHT?
A DREAM, YAN... NOTHING MORE.
THE COUNCIL MEETS WITHIN THE HOUR, MY LORD. SHALL I DRESS YOU?
YES... I SHAN'T FIND SLEEP AGAIN IN A HURRY.
NOR, I FEAR, SHOULD I WANT TO.

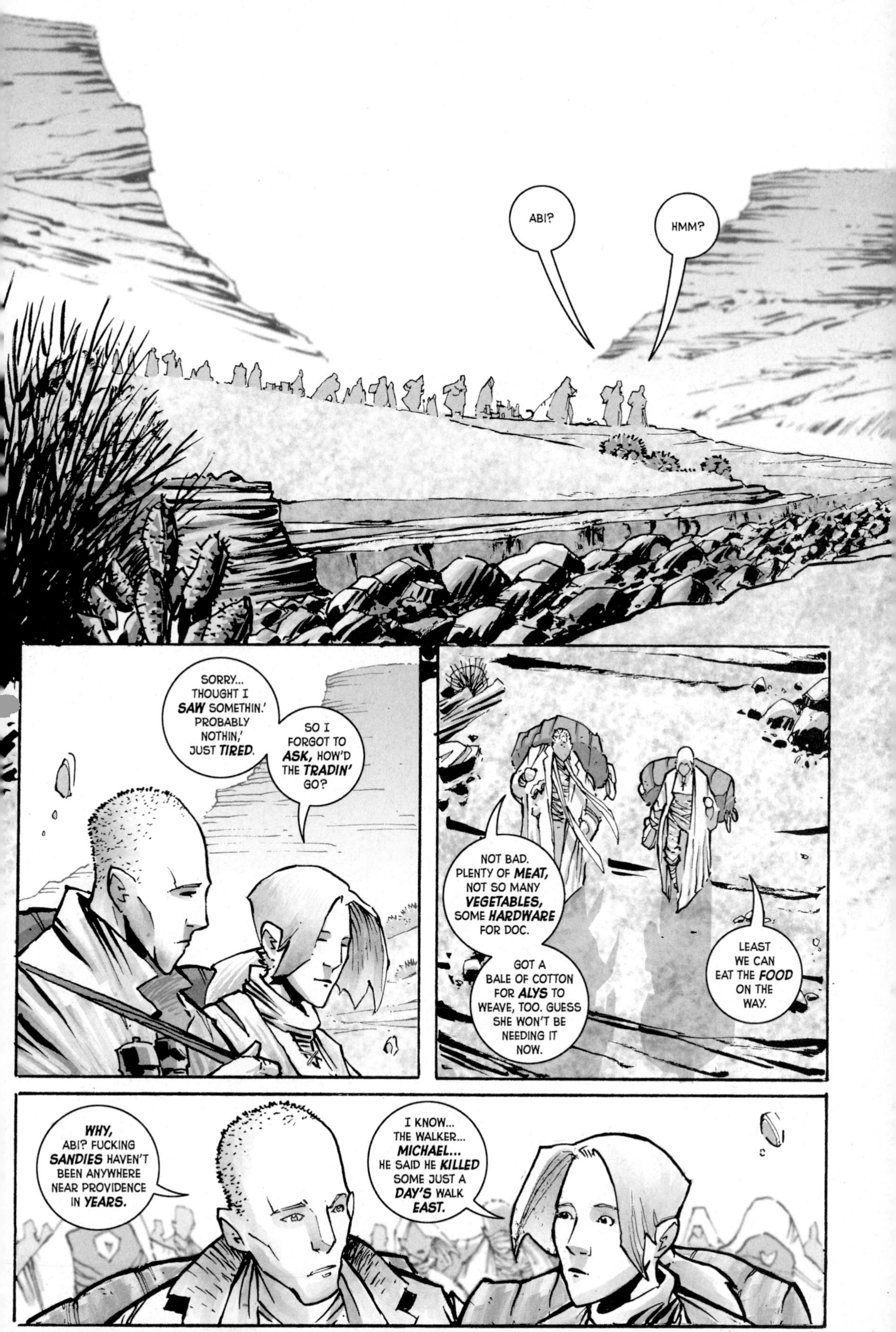
ABI?
HMM?
SORRY... THOUGHT I SAW SOMETHIN.' PROBABLY NOTHIN,' JUST TIRED.
SO I FORGOT TO ASK, HOW'D THE TRADIN' GO?
NOT BAD. PLENTY OF MEAT, NOT SO MANY VEGETABLES, SOME HARDWARE FOR DOC.
GOT A BALE OF COTTON FOR ALYS TO WEAVE, TOO. GUESS SHE WON'T BE NEEDING IT NOW.
LEAST WE CAN EAT THE FOOD ON THE WAY.
WHY, ABI? FUCKING SANDIES HAVEN'T BEEN ANYWHERE NEAR PROVIDENCE IN YEARS.
I KNOW... THE WALKER... MICHAEL... HE SAID HE KILLED SOME JUST A DAY'S WALK EAST.

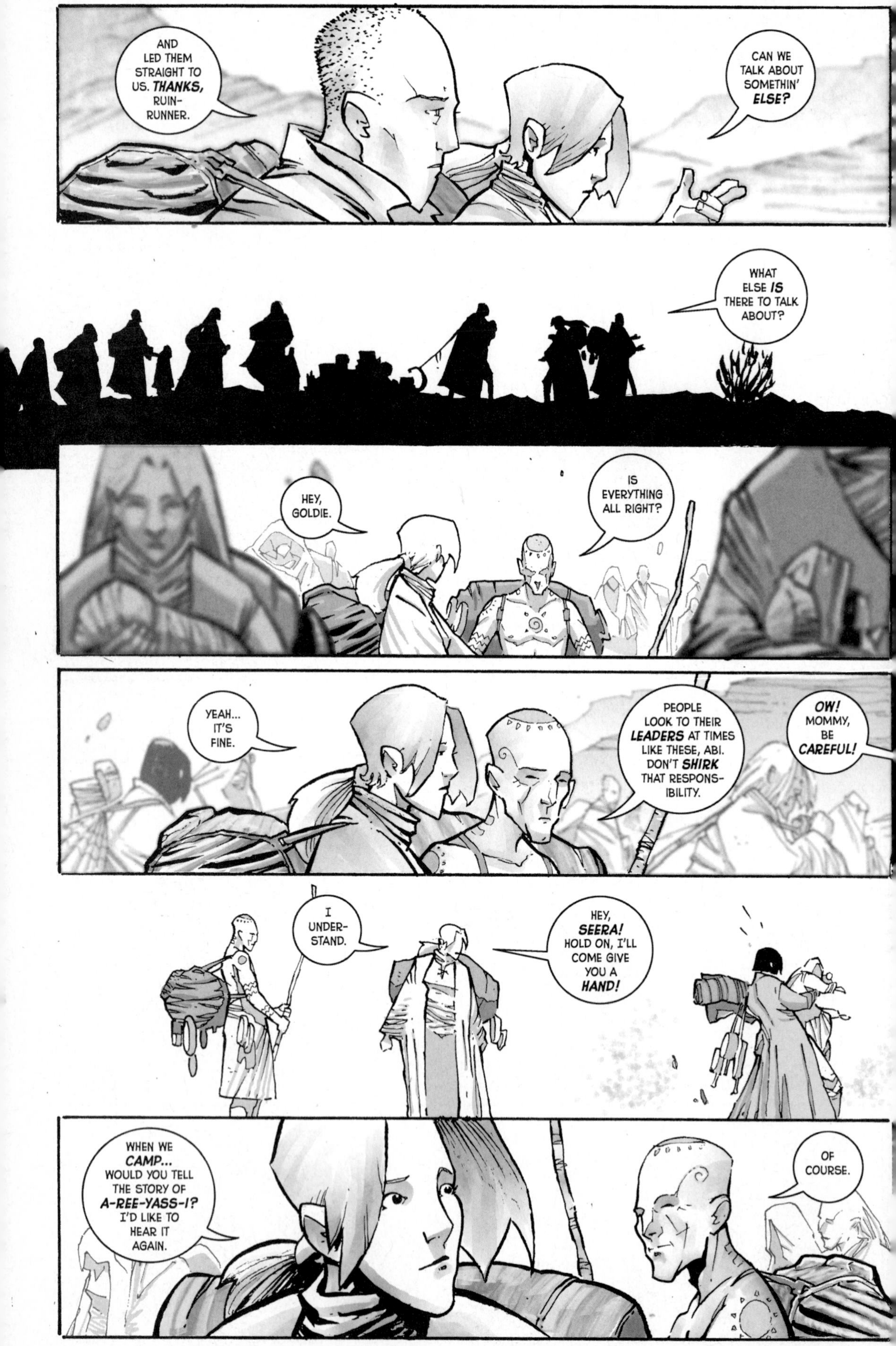
AND LED THEM STRAIGHT TO US. THANKS, RUIN-RUNNER.
CAN WE TALK ABOUT SOMETHIN' ELSE?
WHAT ELSE IS THERE TO TALK ABOUT?
HEY, GOLDIE.
IS EVERYTHING ALL RIGHT?
YEAH... IT'S FINE.
PEOPLE LOOK TO THEIR LEADERS AT TIMES LIKE THESE, ABI. DON'T SHIRK THAT RESPONS-IBILITY.
OW! MOMMY, BE CAREFUL!
I UNDER-STAND.
HEY, SEERA! HOLD ON, I'LL COME GIVE YOU A HAND!
WHEN WE CAMP... WOULD YOU TELL THE STORY OF A-REE-YASS-I? I'D LIKE TO HEAR IT AGAIN.
OF COURSE.

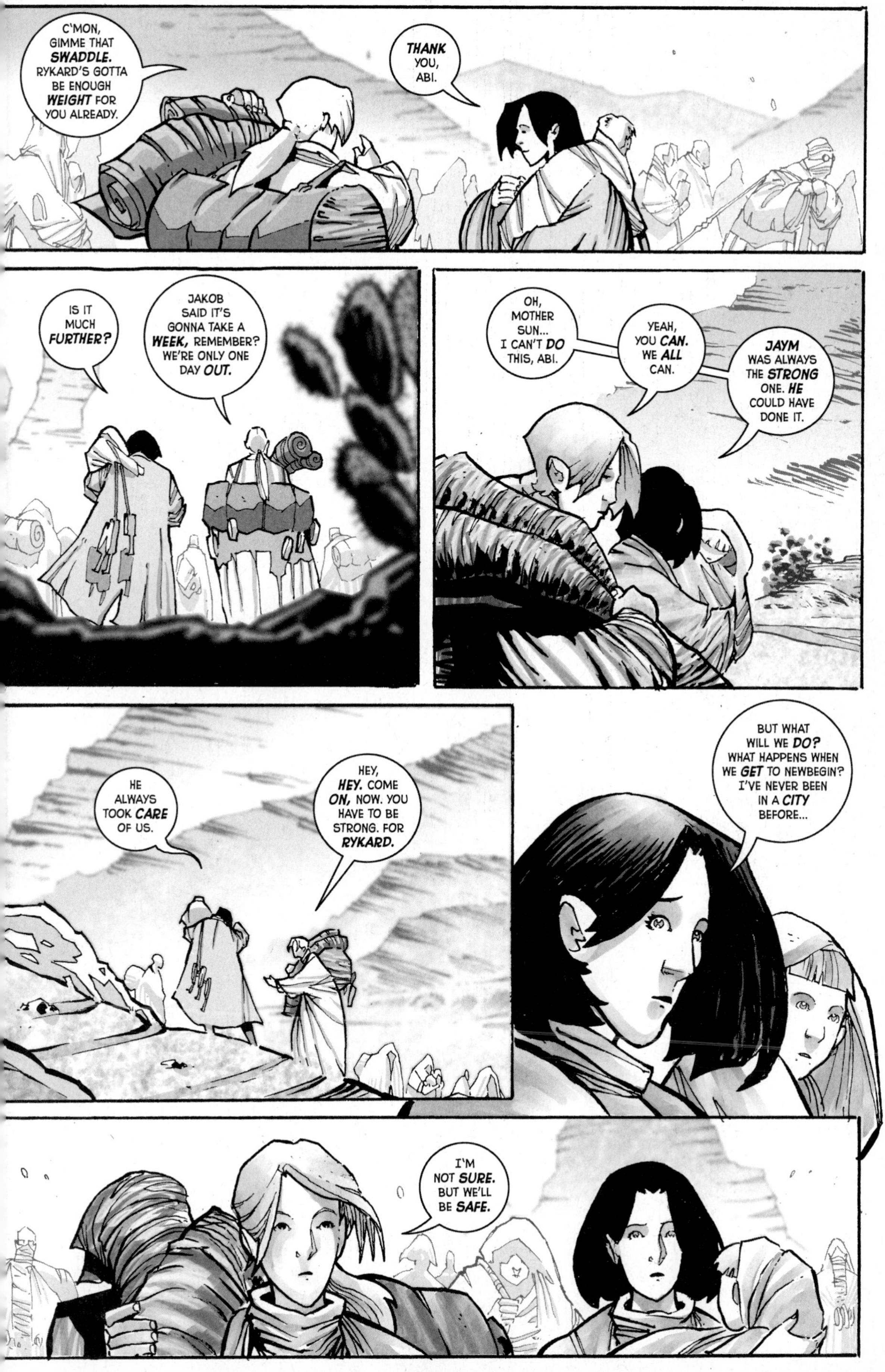
C'MON, GIMME THAT SWADDLE. RYKARD'S GOTTA BE ENOUGH WEIGHT FOR YOU ALREADY.
THANK YOU, ABI.
IS IT MUCH FURTHER?
JAKOB SAID IT'S GONNA TAKE A WEEK, REMEMBER? WE'RE ONLY ONE DAY OUT.
OH, MOTHER SUN... I CAN'T DO THIS, ABI.
YEAH, YOU CAN. WE ALL CAN.
JAYM WAS ALWAYS THE STRONG ONE. HE COULD HAVE DONE IT.
HE ALWAYS TOOK CARE OF US.
HEY, HEY. COME ON, NOW. YOU HAVE TO BE STRONG. FOR RYKARD.
BUT WHAT WILL WE DO? WHAT HAPPENS WHEN WE GET TO NEWBEGIN? I'VE NEVER BEEN IN A CITY BEFORE...
I'M NOT SURE. BUT WE'LL BE SAFE.

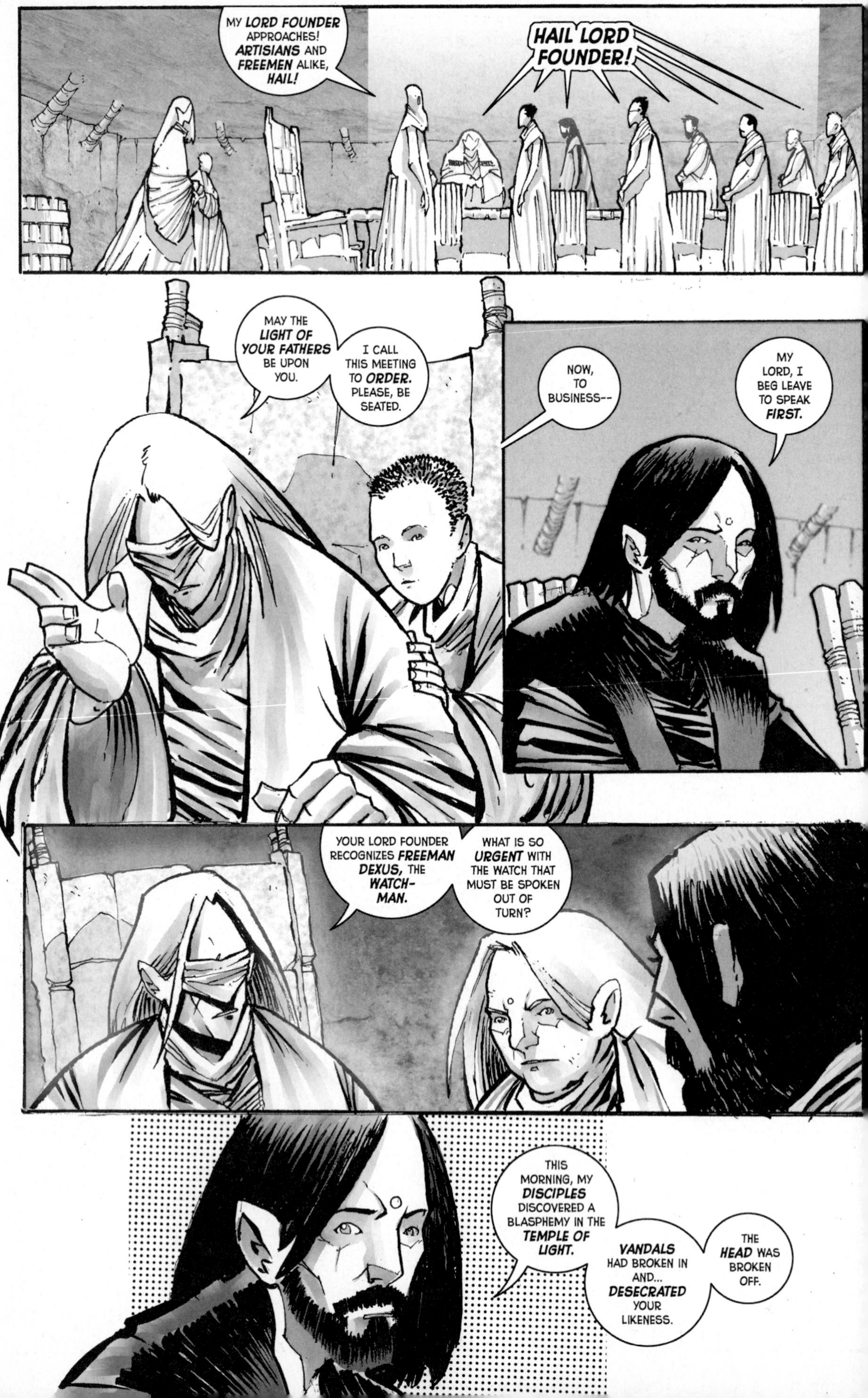
MY LORD FOUNDER APPROACHES! ARTISIANS AND FREEMEN ALIKE, HAIL!
HAIL LORD FOUNDER!
MAY THE LIGHT OF YOUR FATHERS BE UPON YOU.
I CALL THIS MEETING TO ORDER. PLEASE, BE SEATED.
NOW, TO BUSINESS--
MY LORD, I BEG LEAVE TO SPEAK FIRST.
YOUR LORD FOUNDER RECOGNIZES FREEMAN DEXUS, THE WATCH-MAN.
WHAT IS SO URGENT WITH THE WATCH THAT MUST BE SPOKEN OUT OF TURN?
THIS MORNING, MY DISCIPLES DISCOVERED A BLASPHEMY IN THE TEMPLE OF LIGHT.
VANDALS HAD BROKEN IN AND... DESECRATED YOUR LIKENESS.
THE HEAD WAS BROKEN OFF.

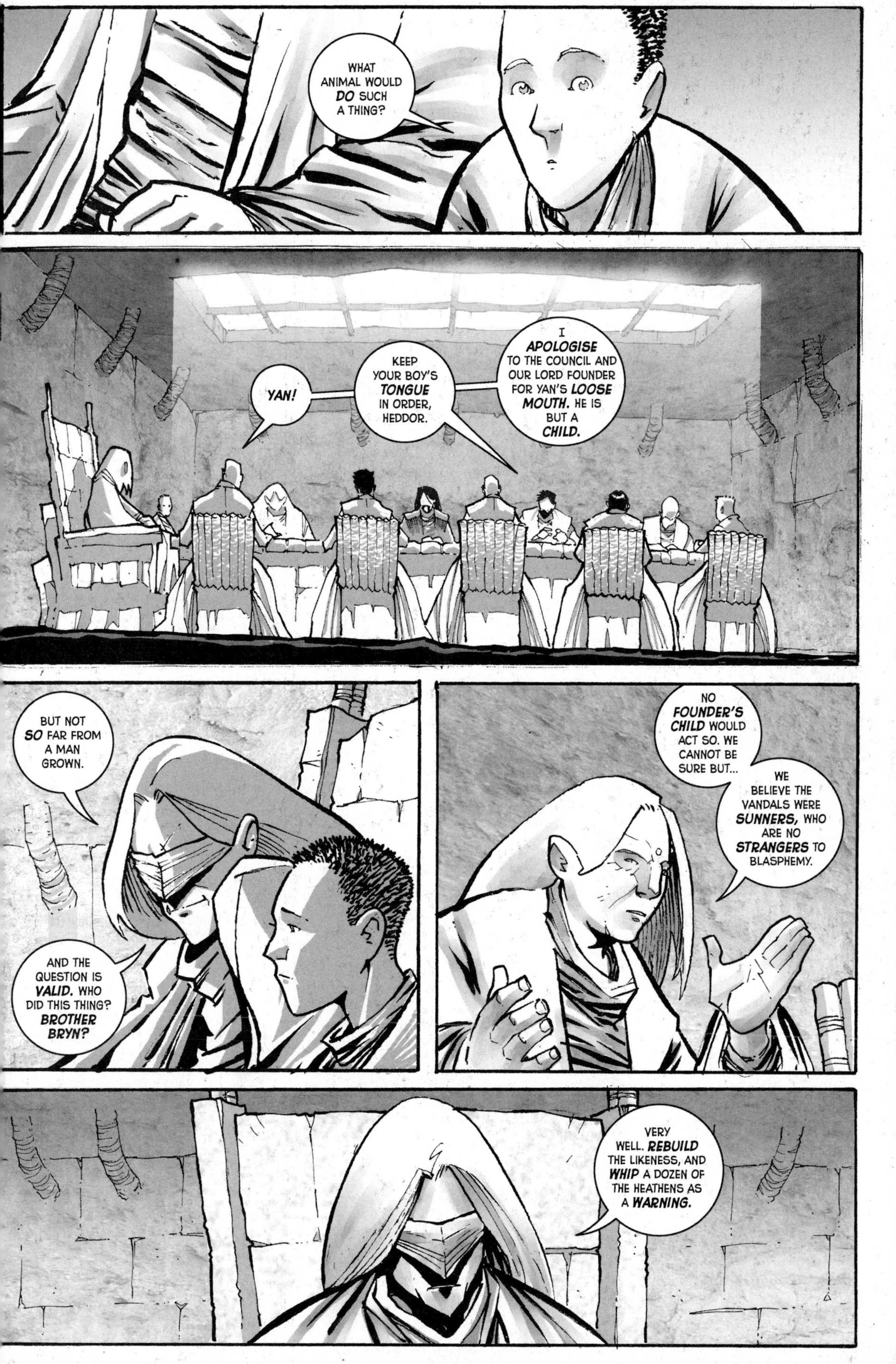
WHAT ANIMAL WOULD DO SUCH A THING?
YAN!
KEEP YOUR BOY'S TONGUE IN ORDER, HEDDOR.
I APOLOGISE TO THE COUNCIL AND OUR LORD FOUNDER FOR YAN'S LOOSE MOUTH. HE IS BUT A CHILD.
BUT NOT SO FAR FROM A MAN GROWN.
AND THE QUESTION IS VALID. WHO DID THIS THING? BROTHER BRYN?
NO FOUNDER'S CHILD WOULD ACT SO. WE CANNOT BE SURE BUT...
WE BELIEVE THE VANDALS WERE SUNNERS, WHO ARE NO STRANGERS TO BLASPHEMY.
VERY WELL. REBUILD THE LIKENESS, AND WHIP A DOZEN OF THE HEATHENS AS A WARNING.

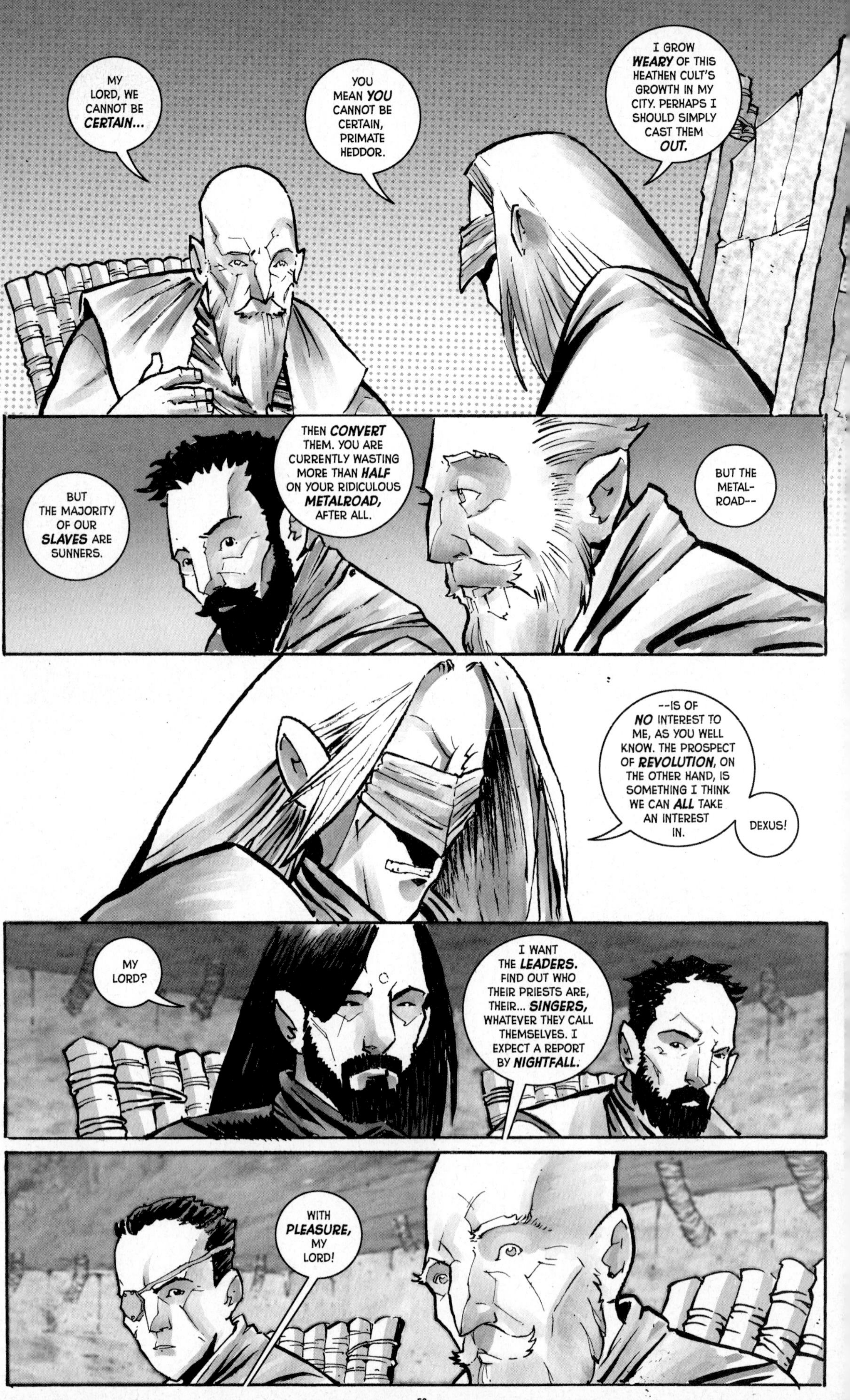
MY LORD, WE CANNOT BE CERTAIN...
YOU MEAN YOU CANNOT BE CERTAIN, PRIMATE HEDDOR.
I GROW WEARY OF THIS HEATHEN CULT'S GROWTH IN MY CITY. PERHAPS I SHOULD SIMPLY CAST THEM OUT.
BUT THE MAJORITY OF OUR SLAVES ARE SUNNERS.
THEN CONVERT THEM. YOU ARE CURRENTLY WASTING MORE THAN HALF ON YOUR RIDICULOUS METALROAD, AFTER ALL.
BUT THE METAL-ROAD--
--IS OF NO INTEREST TO ME, AS YOU WELL KNOW. THE PROSPECT OF REVOLUTION, ON THE OTHER HAND, IS SOMETHING I THINK WE CAN ALL TAKE AN INTEREST IN.
DEXUS!
MY LORD?
I WANT THE LEADERS. FIND OUT WHO THEIR PRIESTS ARE, THEIR... SINGERS, WHATEVER THEY CALL THEMSELVES. I EXPECT A REPORT BY NIGHTFALL.
WITH PLEASURE, MY LORD!

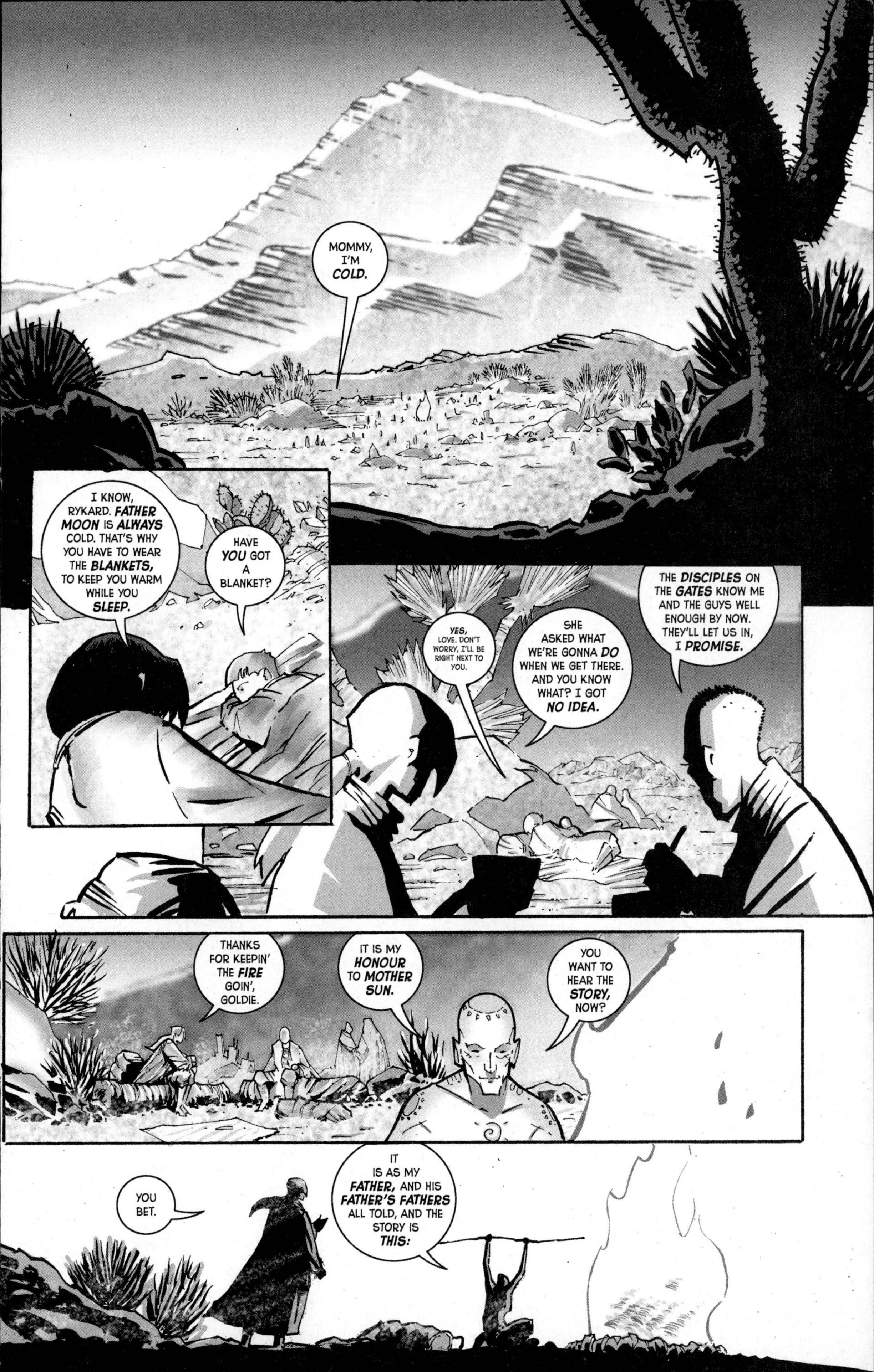
MOMMY, I'M COLD.
I KNOW, RYKARD. FATHER MOON IS ALWAYS COLD. THAT'S WHY YOU HAVE TO WEAR THE BLANKETS, TO KEEP YOU WARM WHILE YOU SLEEP.
HAVE YOU GOT A BLANKET?
YES, LOVE. DON'T WORRY, I'LL BE RIGHT NEXT TO YOU.
SHE ASKED WHAT WE'RE GONNA DO WHEN WE GET THERE. AND YOU KNOW WHAT? I GOT NO IDEA.
THE DISCIPLES ON THE GATES KNOW ME AND THE GUYS WELL ENOUGH BY NOW. THEY'LL LET US IN, I PROMISE.
THANKS FOR KEEPIN' THE FIRE GOIN', GOLDIE.
IT IS MY HONOUR TO MOTHER SUN.
YOU WANT TO HEAR THE STORY, NOW?
YOU BET.
IT IS AS MY FATHER, AND HIS FATHER'S FATHERS ALL TOLD, AND THE STORY IS THIS:

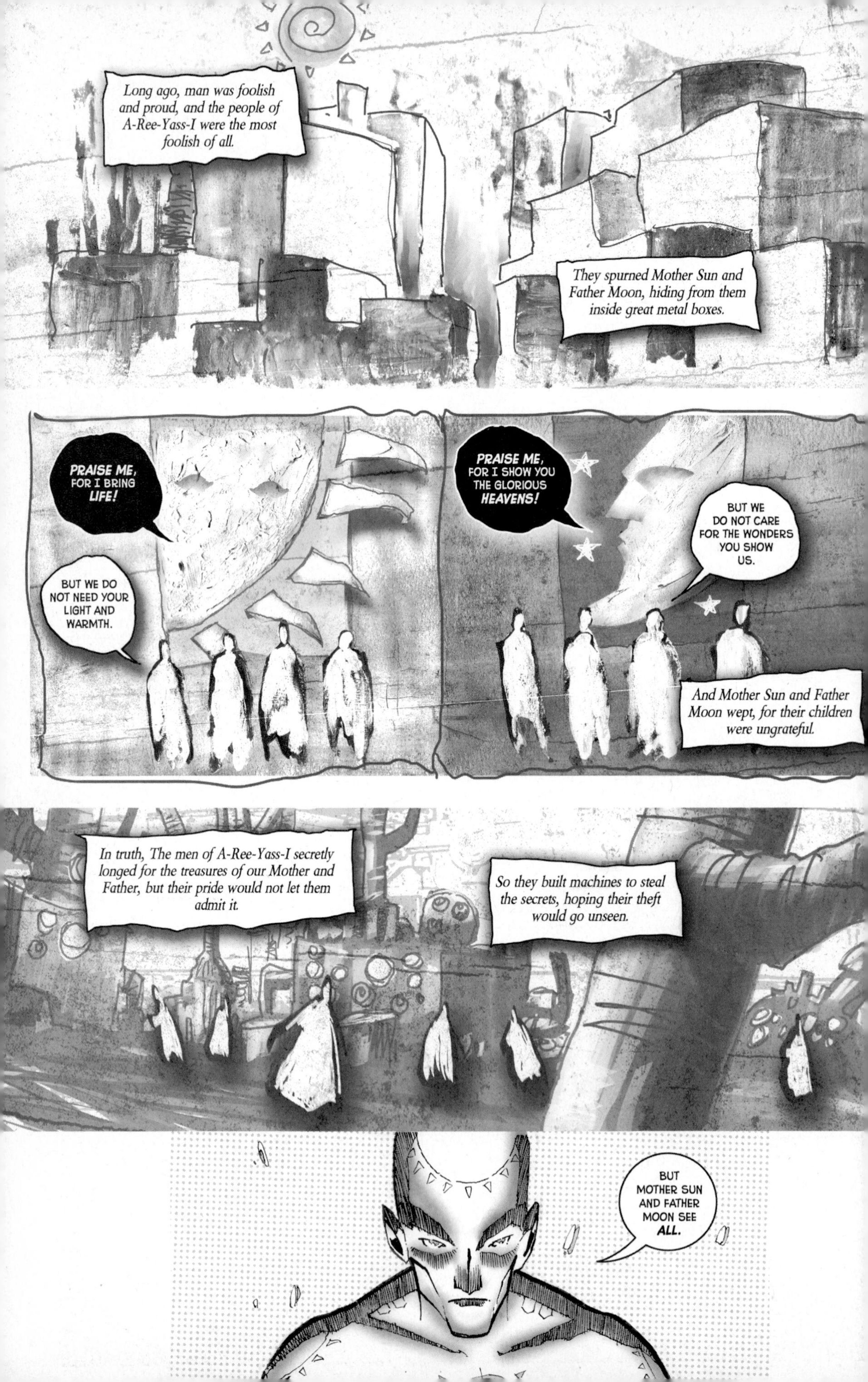
Long ago, man was foolish and proud, and the people of A-Ree-Yass-I were the most foolish of all.
They spurned Mother Sun and Father Moon, hiding from them inside great metal boxes.
PRAISE ME, FOR I BRING LIFE!
BUT WE DO NOT NEED YOUR LIGHT AND WARMTH.
PRAISE ME, FOR I SHOW YOU THE GLORIOUS HEAVENS!
BUT WE DO NOT CARE FOR THE WONDERS YOU SHOW US.
And Mother Sun and Father Moon wept, for their children were ungrateful.
In truth, The men of A-Ree-Yass-I secretly longed for the treasures of our Mother and Father, but their pride would not let them admit it.
So they built machines to steal the secrets, hoping their theft would go unseen.
BUT MOTHER SUN AND FATHER MOON SEE ALL.

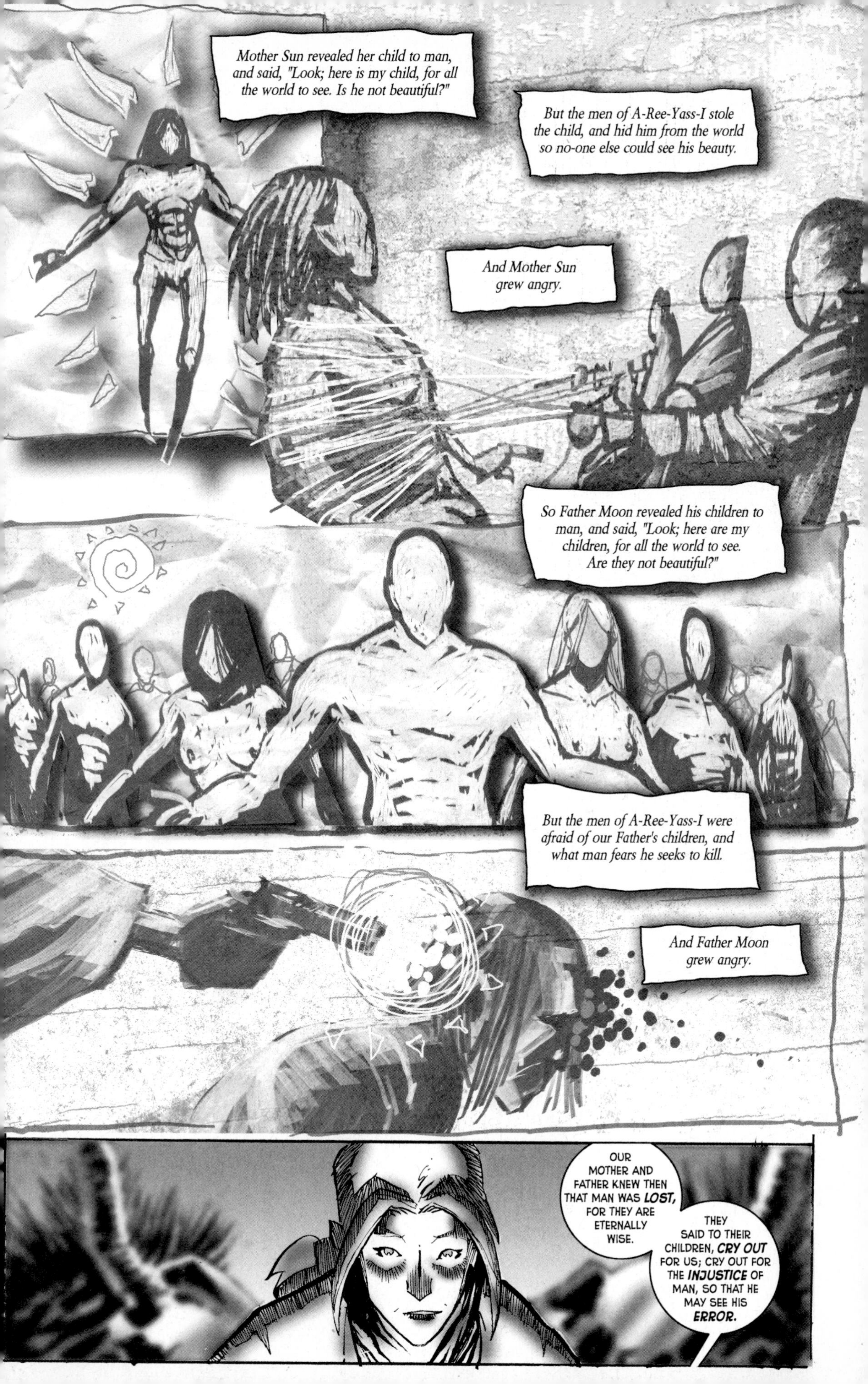

Mother Sun revealed her child to man, and said, "Look; here is my child, for all the world to see. Is he not beautiful?"
But the men of A-Ree-Yass-I stole the child, and hid him from the world so no-one else could see his beauty.
And Mother Sun grew angry.
So Father Moon revealed his children to man, and said, "Look; here are my children, for all the world to see. Are they not beautiful?"
But the men of A-Ree-Yass-I were afraid of our Father's children, and what man fears he seeks to kill.
And Father Moon grew angry.
OUR MOTHER AND FATHER KNEW THEN THAT MAN WAS LOST, FOR THEY ARE ETERNALLY WISE.
THEY SAID TO THEIR CHILDREN, CRY OUT FOR US; CRY OUT FOR THE INJUSTICE OF MAN, SO THAT HE MAY SEE HIS ERROR.

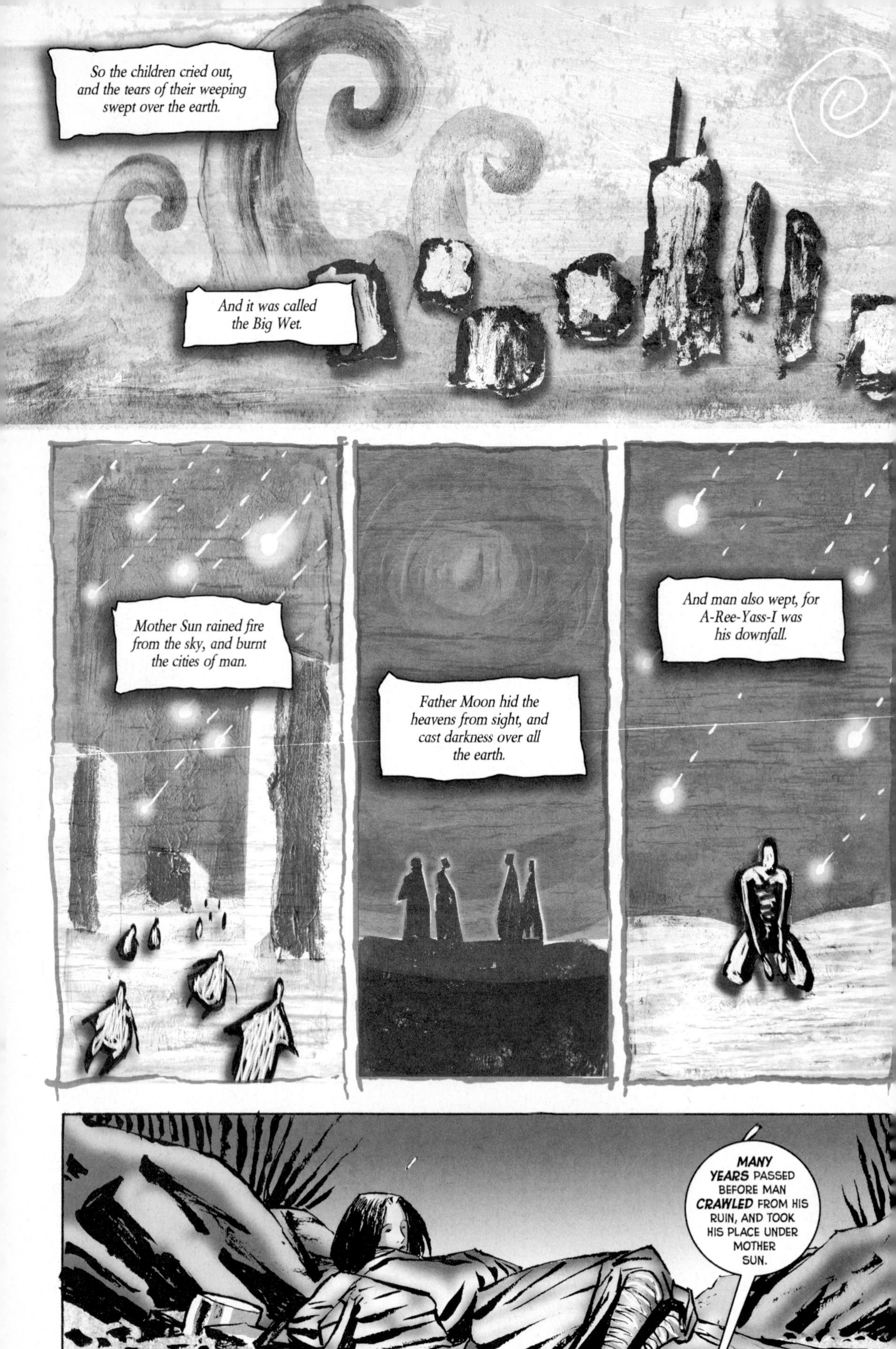
So the children cried out, and the tears of their weeping swept over the earth.
And it was called the Big Wet.
Mother Sun rained fire from the sky, and burnt the cities of man.
Father Moon hid the heavens from sight, and cast darkness over all the earth.
And man also wept, for A-Ree-Yass-I was his downfall.
MANY YEARS PASSED BEFORE MAN CRAWLED FROM HIS RUIN, AND TOOK HIS PLACE UNDER MOTHER SUN.

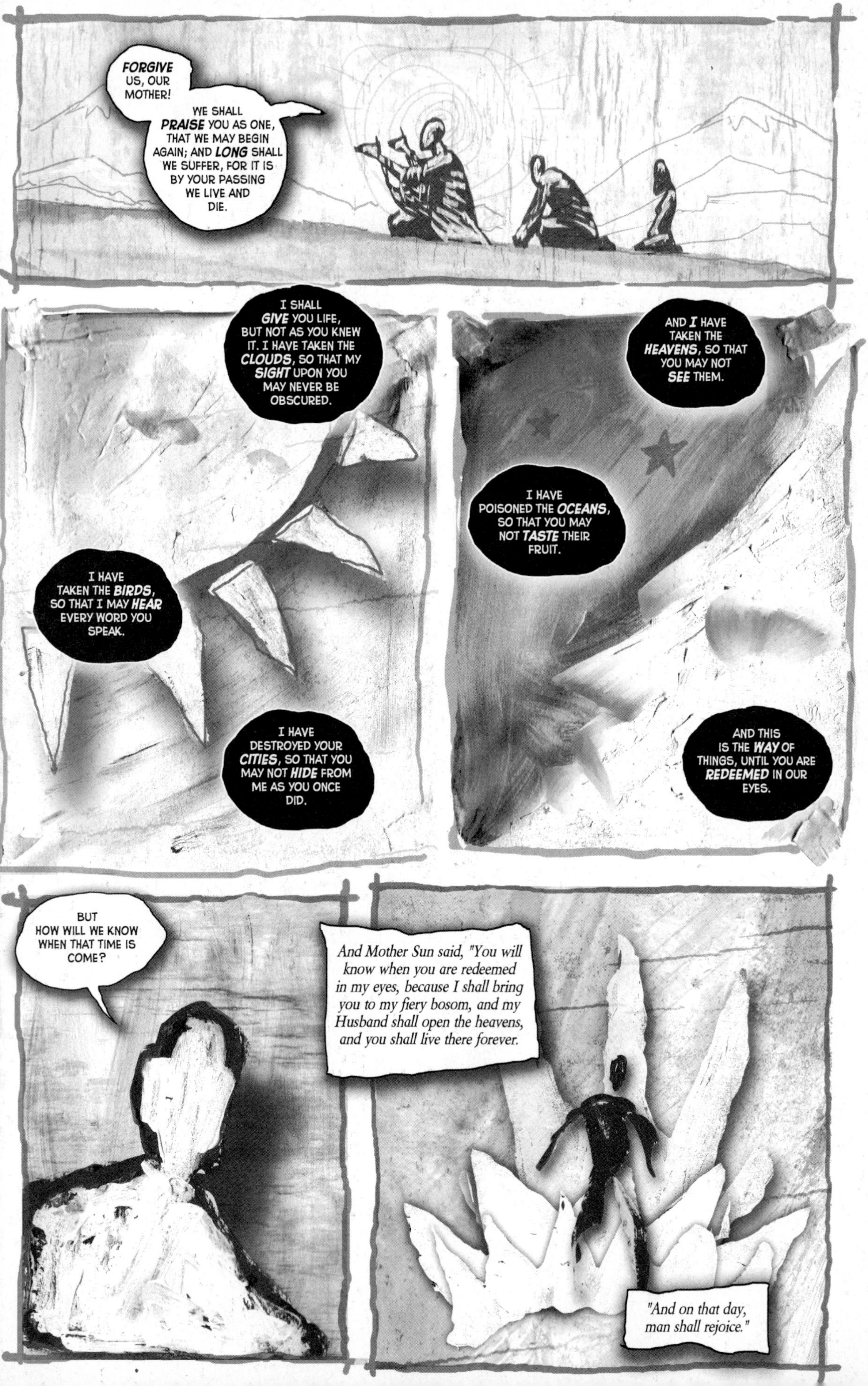
FORGIVE US, OUR MOTHER!
WE SHALL PRAISE YOU AS ONE, THAT WE MAY BEGIN AGAIN; AND LONG SHALL WE SUFFER, FOR IT IS BY YOUR PASSING WE LIVE AND DIE.
I SHALL GIVE YOU LIFE, BUT NOT AS YOU KNEW IT. I HAVE TAKEN THE CLOUDS, SO THAT MY SIGHT UPON YOU MAY NEVER BE OBSCURED.
I HAVE TAKEN THE BIRDS, SO THAT I MAY HEAR EVERY WORD YOU SPEAK.
I HAVE DESTROYED YOUR CITIES, SO THAT YOU MAY NOT HIDE FROM ME AS YOU ONCE DID.
AND I HAVE TAKEN THE HEAVENS, SO THAT YOU MAY NOT SEE THEM.
I HAVE POISONED THE OCEANS, SO THAT YOU MAY NOT TASTE THEIR FRUIT.
AND THIS IS THE WAY OF THINGS, UNTIL YOU ARE REDEEMED IN OUR EYES.
BUT HOW WILL WE KNOW WHEN THAT TIME IS COME?
And Mother Sun said, "You will know when you are redeemed in my eyes, because I shall bring you to my fiery bosom, and my Husband shall open the heavens, and you shall live there forever.
"And on that day, man shall rejoice."

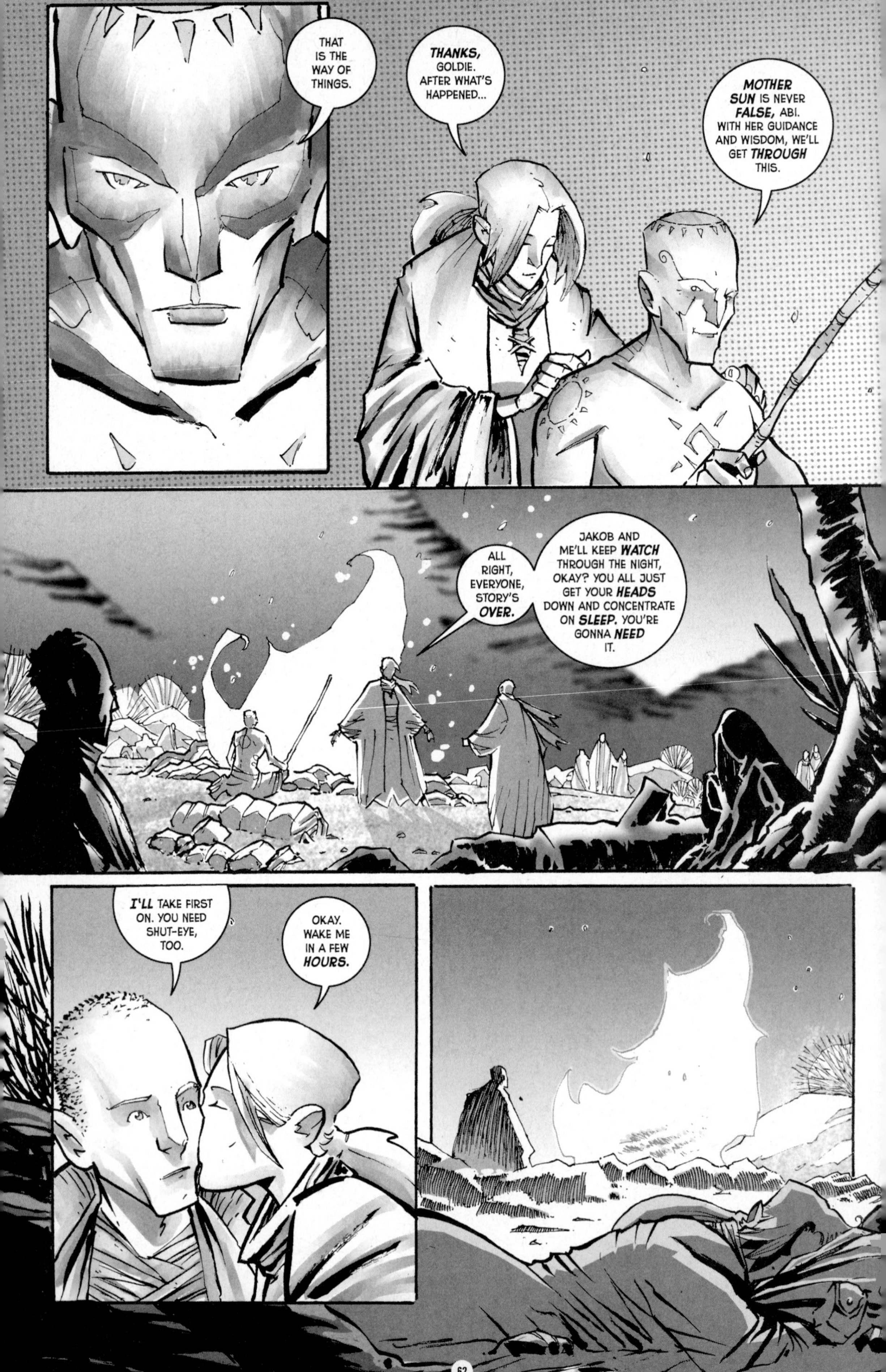
THAT IS THE WAY OF THINGS.
THANKS, GOLDIE. AFTER WHAT'S HAPPENED...
MOTHER SUN IS NEVER FALSE, ABI. WITH HER GUIDANCE AND WISDOM, WE'LL GET THROUGH THIS.
ALL RIGHT, EVERYONE, STORY'S OVER.
JAKOB AND ME'LL KEEP WATCH THROUGH THE NIGHT, OKAY? YOU ALL JUST GET YOUR HEADS DOWN AND CONCENTRATE ON SLEEP. YOU'RE GONNA NEED IT.
I'LL TAKE FIRST ON. YOU NEED SHUT-EYE, TOO.
OKAY. WAKE ME IN A FEW HOURS.

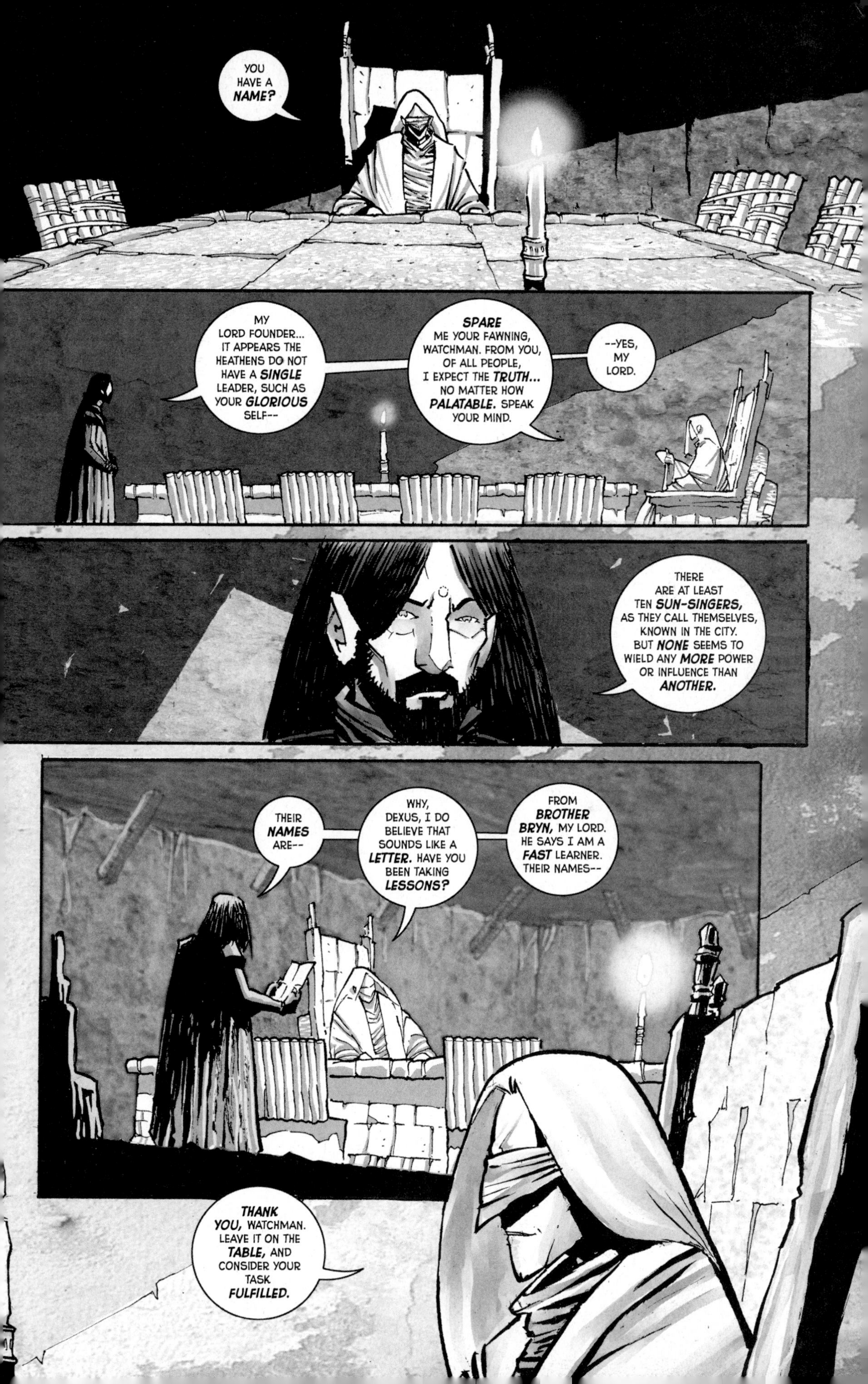
YOU HAVE A NAME?
MY LORD FOUNDER... IT APPEARS THE HEATHENS DO NOT HAVE A SINGLE LEADER, SUCH AS YOUR GLORIOUS SELF--
SPARE ME YOUR FAWNING, WATCHMAN. FROM YOU, OF ALL PEOPLE, I EXPECT THE TRUTH... NO MATTER HOW PALATABLE. SPEAK YOUR MIND.
--YES, MY LORD.
THERE ARE AT LEAST TEN SUN-SINGERS, AS THEY CALL THEMSELVES, KNOWN IN THE CITY. BUT NONE SEEMS TO WIELD ANY MORE POWER OR INFLUENCE THAN ANOTHER.
THEIR NAMES ARE--
WHY, DEXUS, I DO BELIEVE THAT SOUNDS LIKE A LETTER. HAVE YOU BEEN TAKING LESSONS?
FROM BROTHER BRYN, MY LORD. HE SAYS I AM A FAST LEARNER. THEIR NAMES--
THANK YOU, WATCHMAN. LEAVE IT ON THE TABLE, AND CONSIDER YOUR TASK FULFILLED.

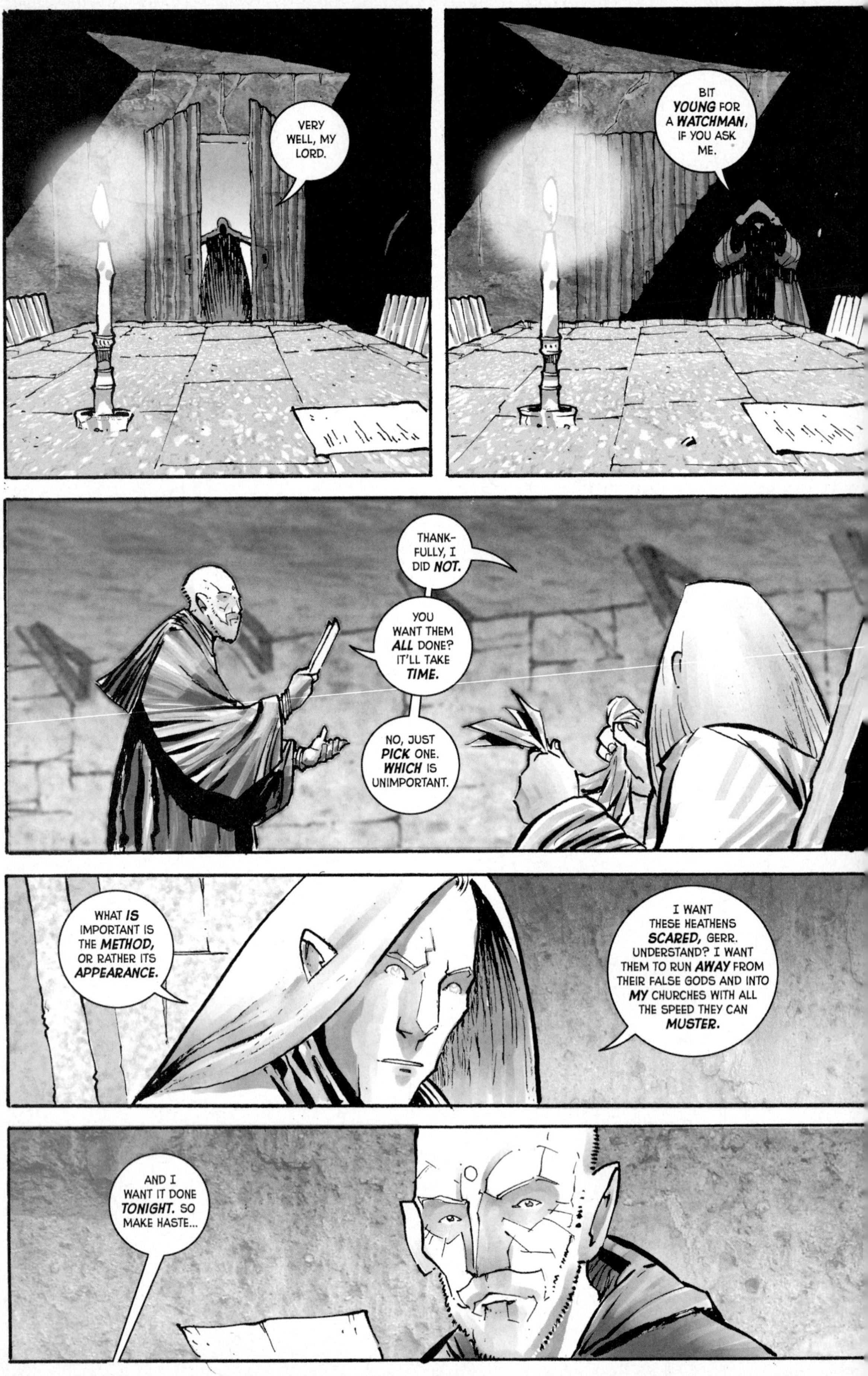
VERY WELL, MY LORD.
BIT YOUNG FOR A WATCHMAN, IF YOU ASK ME.
THANK-FULLY, I DID NOT.
YOU WANT THEM ALL DONE? IT'LL TAKE TIME.
NO, JUST PICK ONE. WHICH IS UNIMPORTANT.
WHAT IS IMPORTANT IS THE METHOD, OR RATHER ITS APPEARANCE.
I WANT THESE HEATHENS SCARED, GERR. UNDERSTAND? I WANT THEM TO RUN AWAY FROM THEIR FALSE GODS AND INTO MY CHURCHES WITH ALL THE SPEED THEY CAN MUSTER.
AND I WANT IT DONE TONIGHT. SO MAKE HASTE...

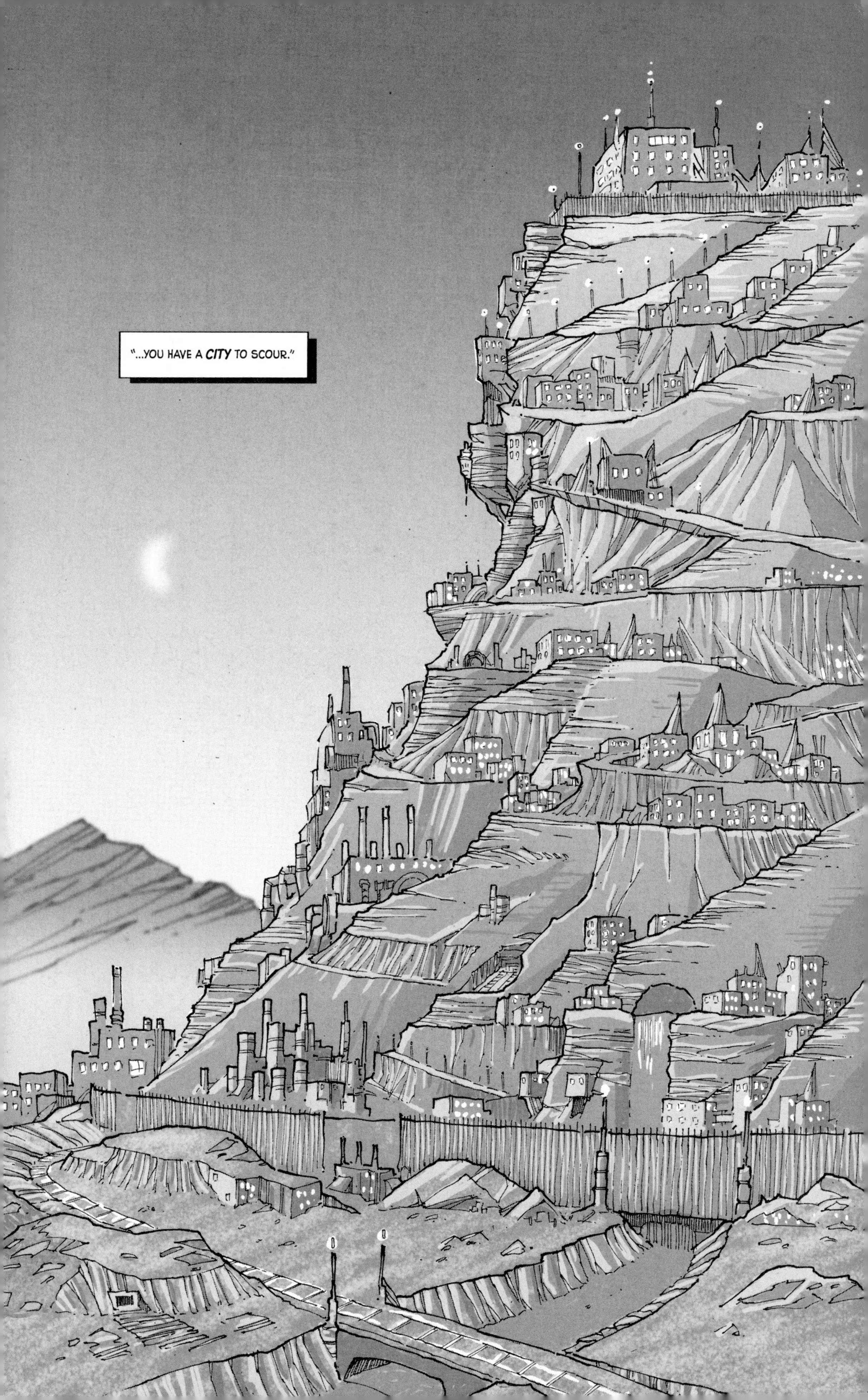
"...YOU HAVE A CITY TO SCOUR."

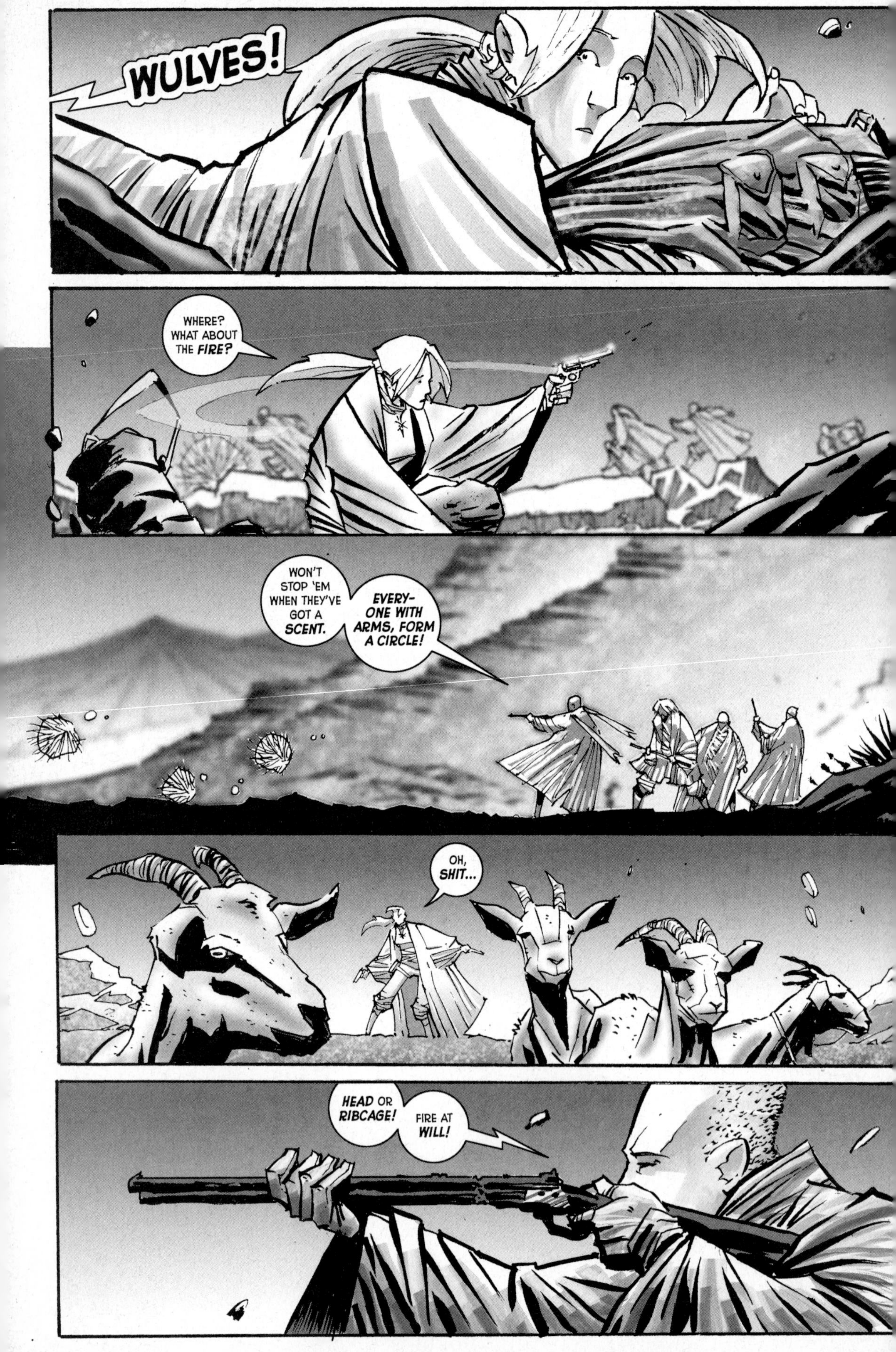
WULVES!
WHERE? WHAT ABOUT THE FIRE?
WON'T STOP 'EM WHEN THEY'VE GOT A SCENT.
EVERY-ONE WITH ARMS, FORM A CIRCLE!
OH, SHIT...
HEAD OR RIBCAGE!
FIRE AT WILL!

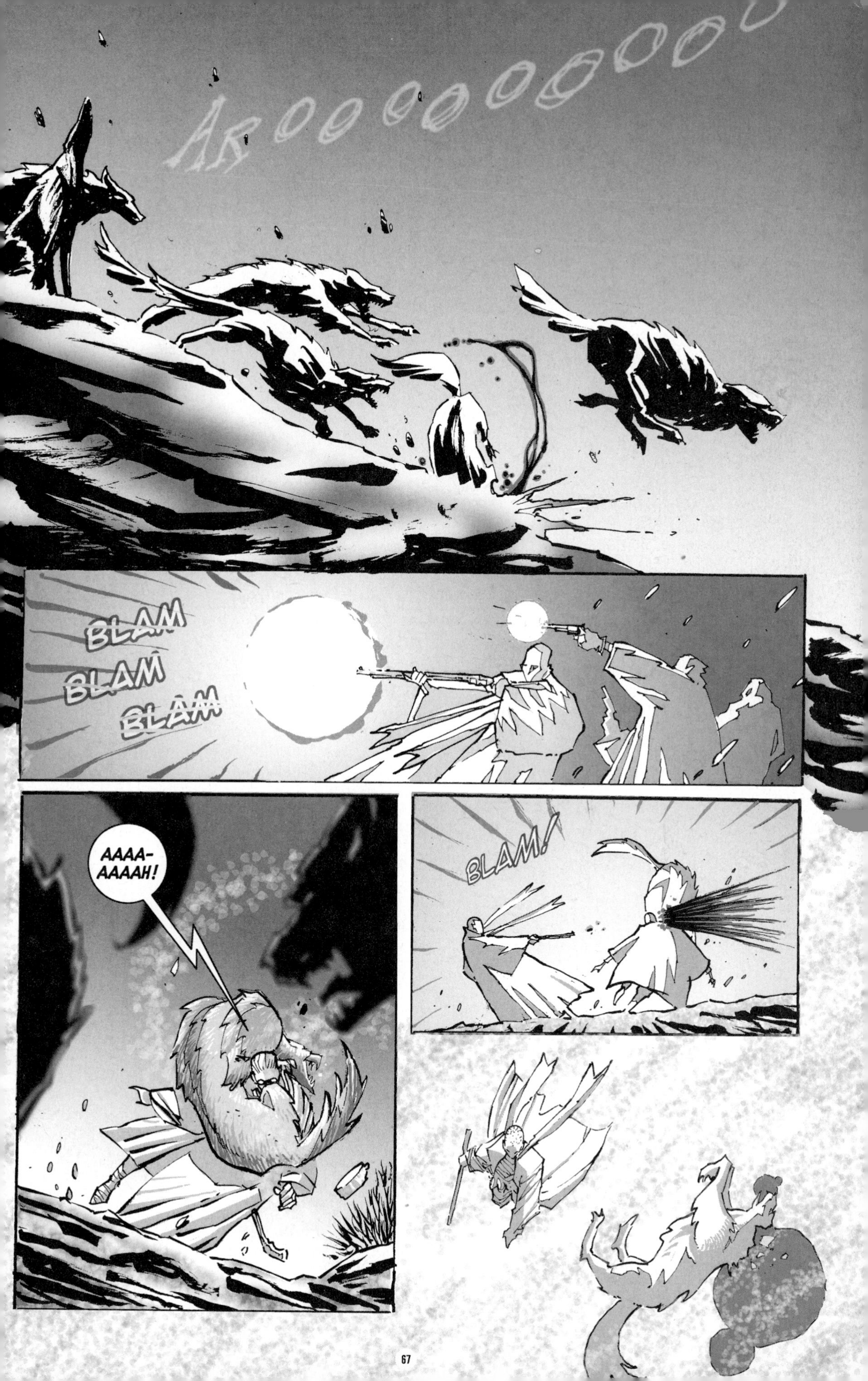
AROOOOOOOOOO
BLAM
BLAM
BLAM
AAAA-
AAAAH!
BLAM!

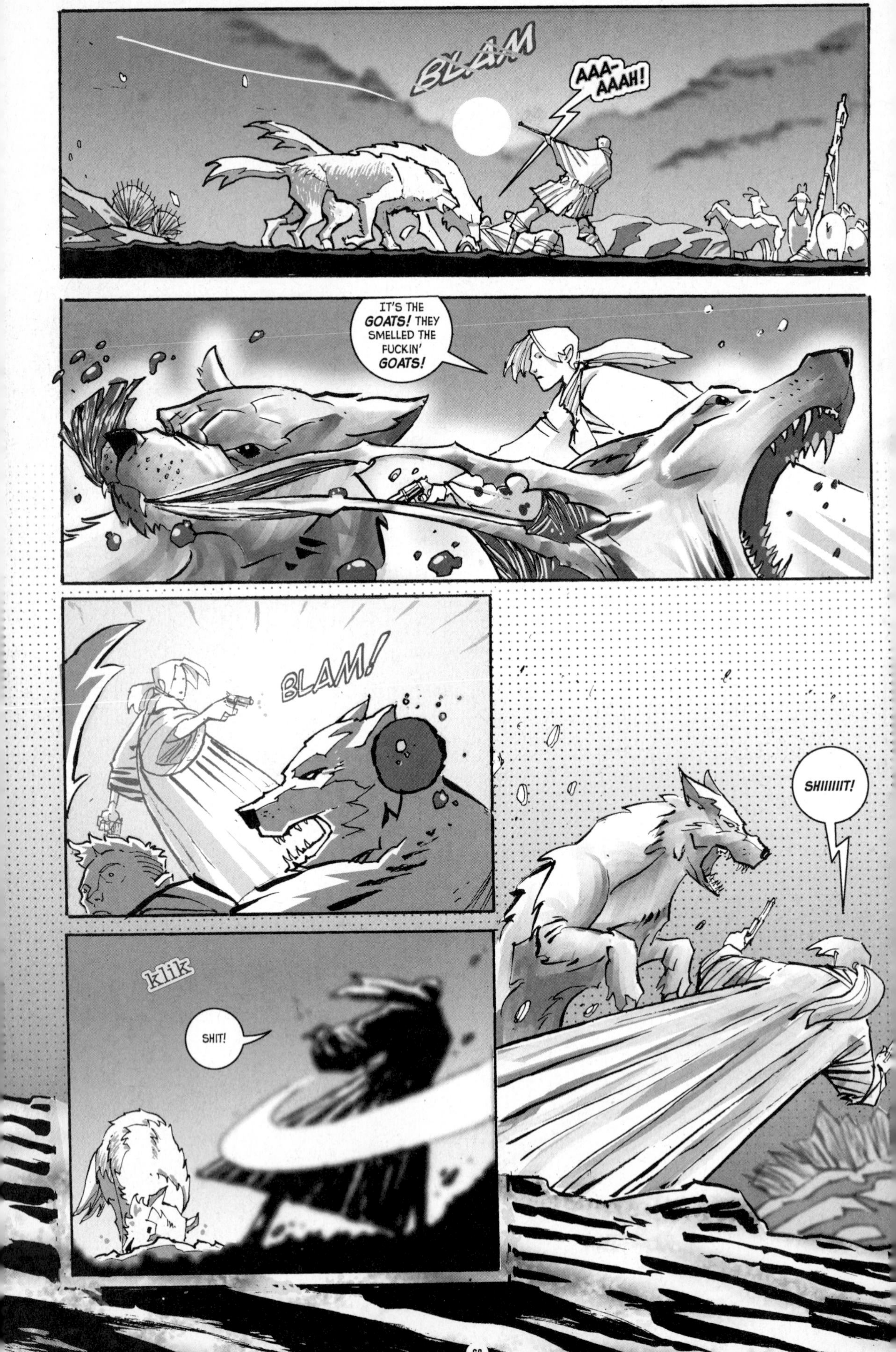
BLAM
AAA-AAAH!
IT'S THE GOATS! THEY SMELLED THE FUCKIN' GOATS!
BLAM!
SHIIIIIIT!
klik
SHIT!

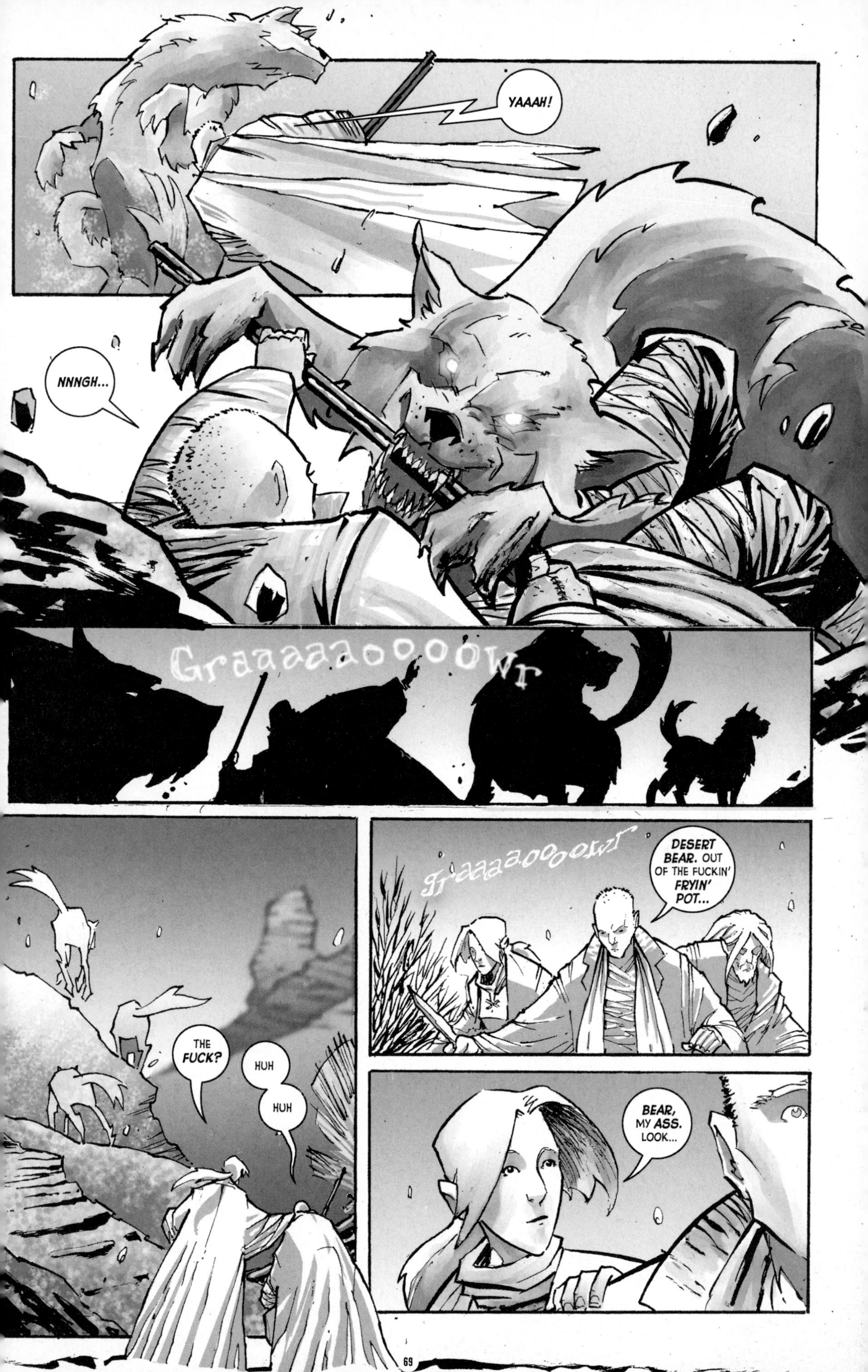

YAAAH!
NNNGH...
Graaaaaoooowr
THE FUCK?
HUH
HUH
Graaaaaoooowr
DESERT BEAR. OUT OF THE FUCKIN' FRYIN' POT...
BEAR, MY ASS. LOOK...

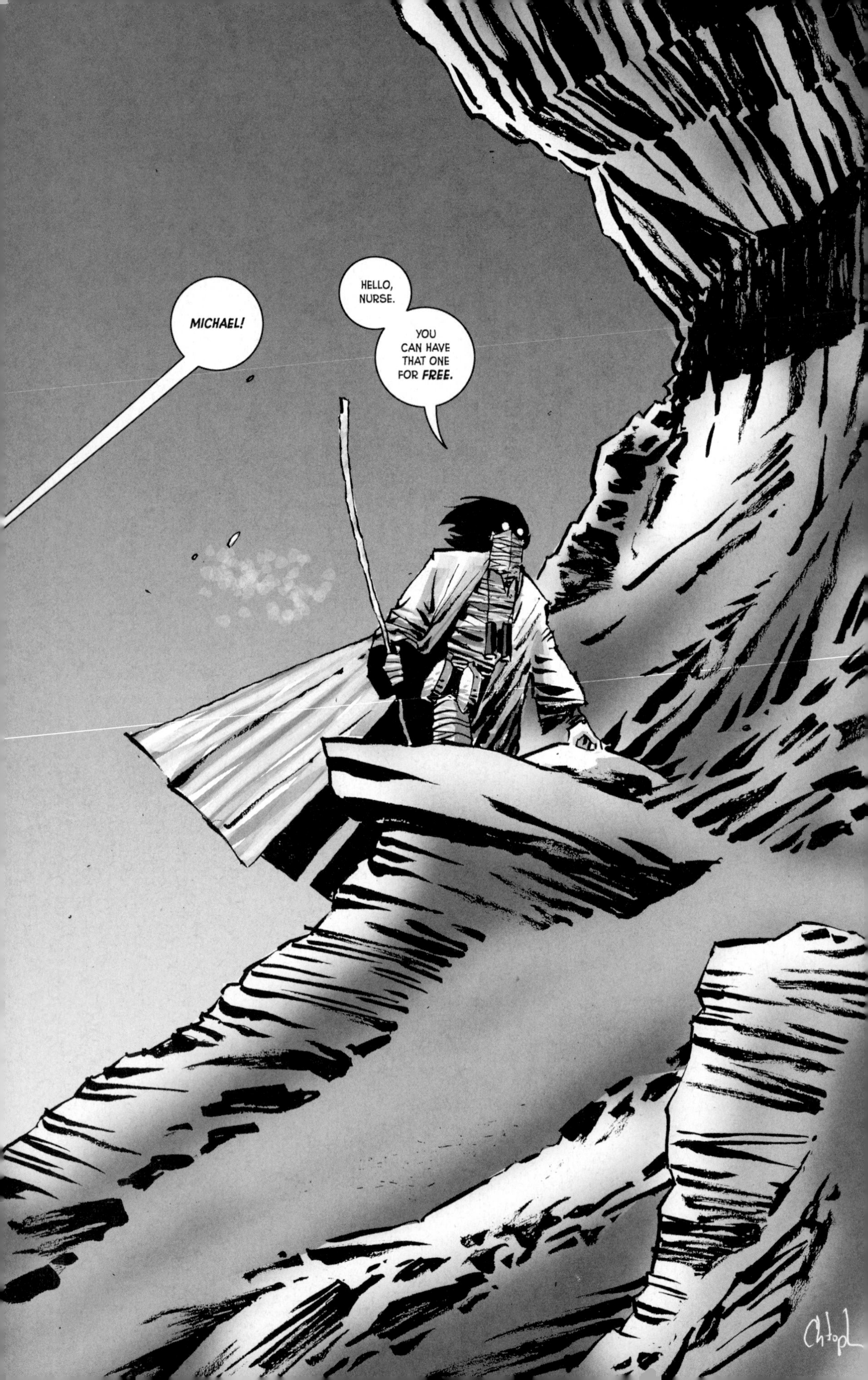
MICHAEL!
HELLO, NURSE.
YOU CAN HAVE THAT ONE FOR FREE.

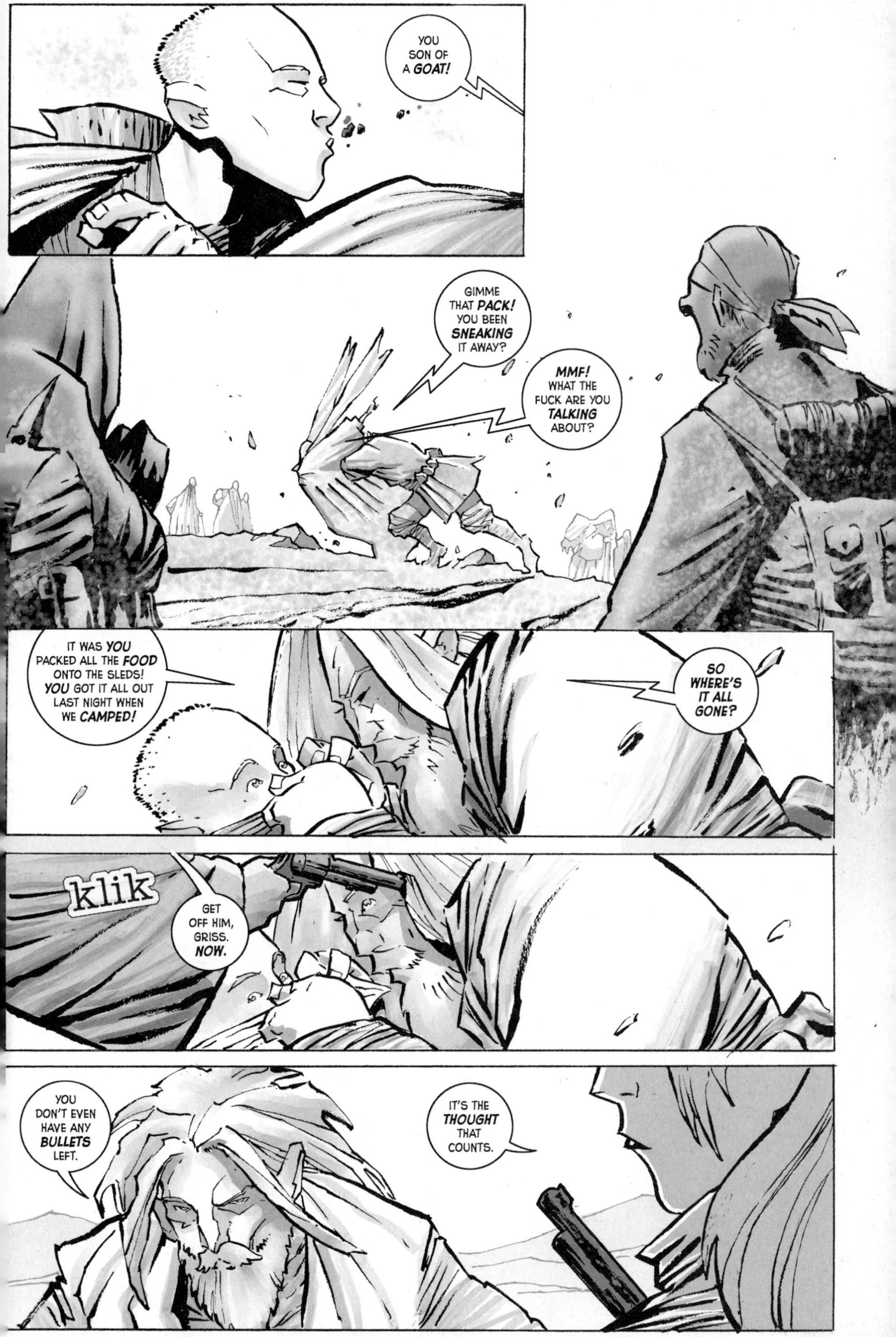

YOU SON OF A GOAT!
GIMME THAT PACK! YOU BEEN SNEAKING IT AWAY?
MMF! WHAT THE FUCK ARE YOU TALKING ABOUT?
IT WAS YOU PACKED ALL THE FOOD ONTO THE SLEDS! YOU GOT IT ALL OUT LAST NIGHT WHEN WE CAMPED!
SO WHERE'S IT ALL GONE?
klik
GET OFF HIM, GRISS. NOW.
YOU DON'T EVEN HAVE ANY BULLETS LEFT.
IT'S THE THOUGHT THAT COUNTS.

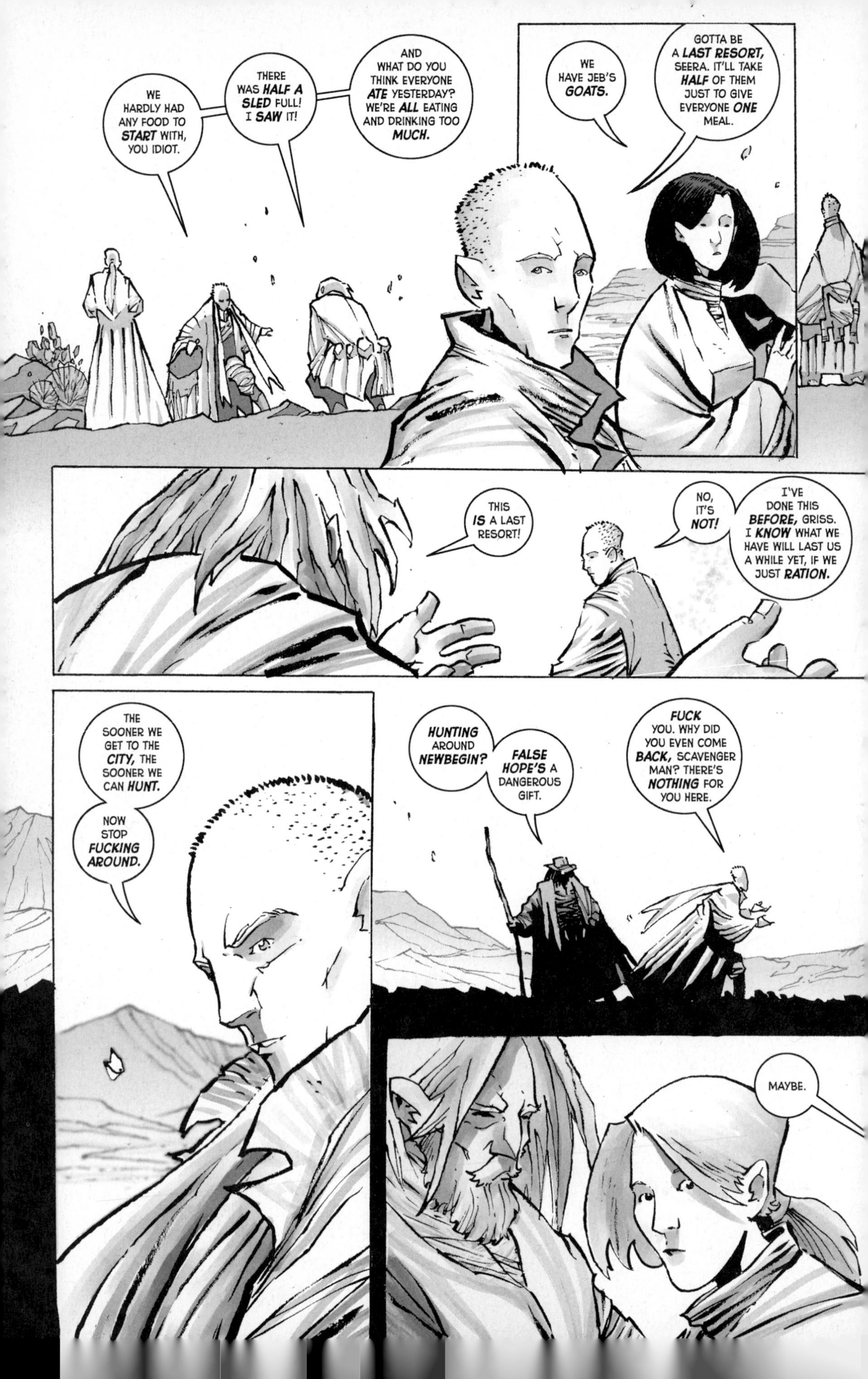

WE HARDLY HAD ANY FOOD TO START WITH, YOU IDIOT.
THERE WAS HALF A SLED FULL! I SAW IT!
AND WHAT DO YOU THINK EVERYONE ATE YESTERDAY? WE'RE ALL EATING AND DRINKING TOO MUCH.
WE HAVE JEB'S GOATS.
GOTTA BE A LAST RESORT, SEERA. IT'LL TAKE HALF OF THEM JUST TO GIVE EVERYONE ONE MEAL.
THIS IS A LAST RESORT!
NO, IT'S NOT!
I'VE DONE THIS BEFORE, GRISS. I KNOW WHAT WE HAVE WILL LAST US A WHILE YET, IF WE JUST RATION.
THE SOONER WE GET TO THE CITY, THE SOONER WE CAN HUNT.
NOW STOP FUCKING AROUND.
HUNTING AROUND NEWBEGIN?
FALSE HOPE'S A DANGEROUS GIFT.
FUCK YOU. WHY DID YOU EVEN COME BACK, SCAVENGER MAN? THERE'S NOTHING FOR YOU HERE.
MAYBE.

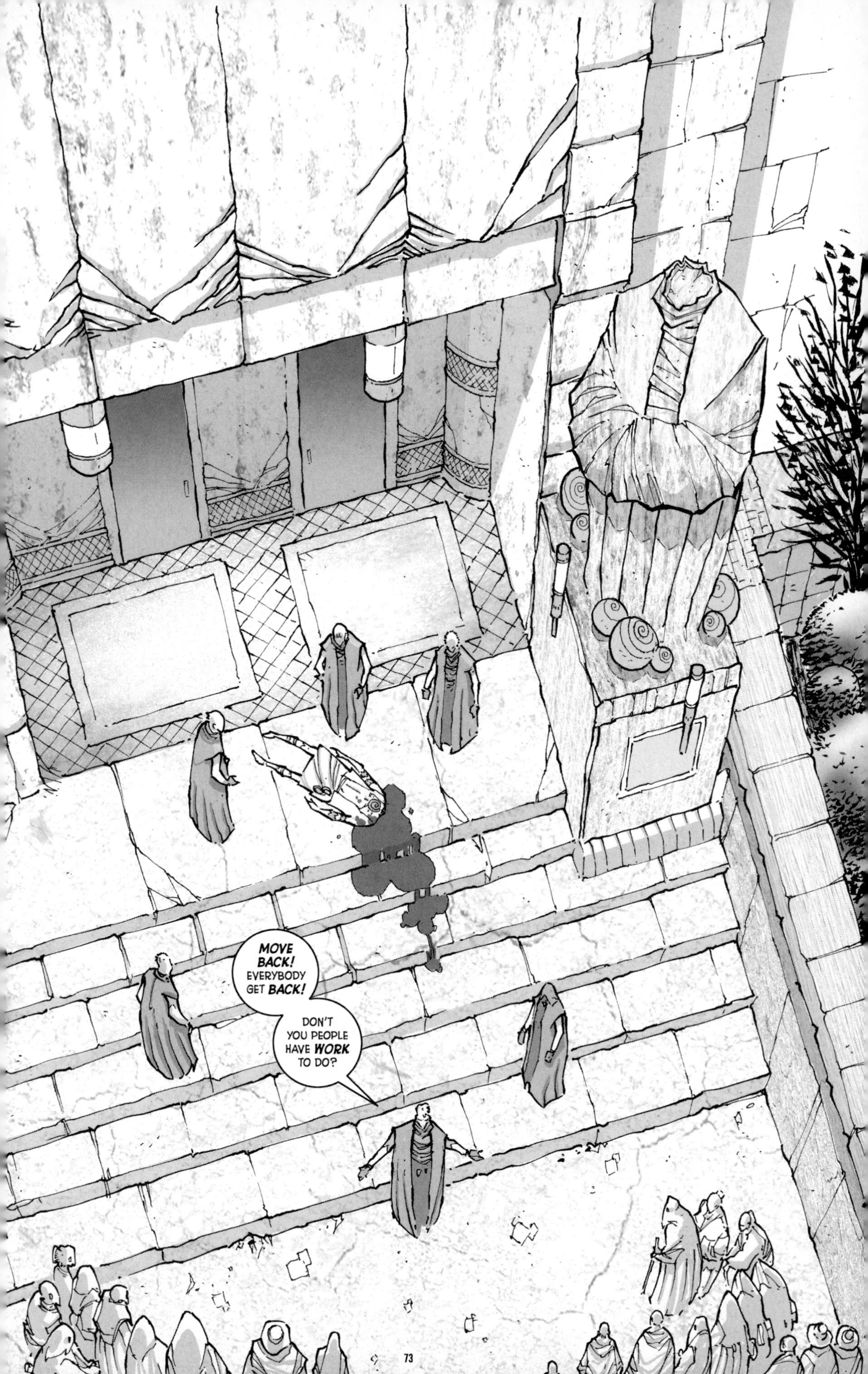
MOVE BACK! EVERYBODY GET BACK!
DON'T YOU PEOPLE HAVE WORK TO DO?

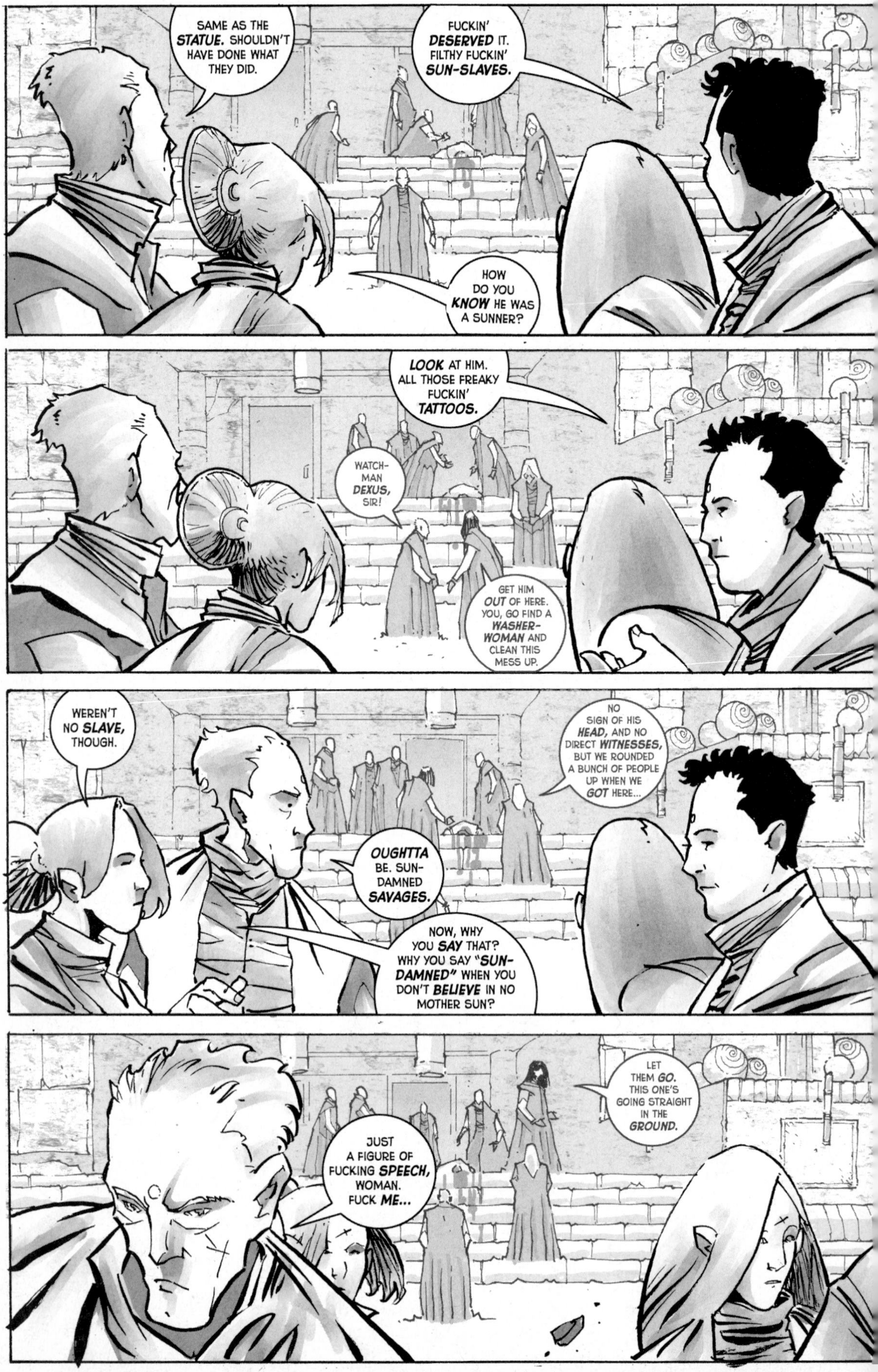
SAME AS THE STATUE. SHOULDN'T HAVE DONE WHAT THEY DID.
FUCKIN' DESERVED IT. FILTHY FUCKIN' SUN-SLAVES.
HOW DO YOU KNOW HE WAS A SUNNER?
LOOK AT HIM. ALL THOSE FREAKY FUCKIN' TATTOOS.
WATCH-MAN DEXUS, SIR!
GET HIM OUT OF HERE. YOU, GO FIND A WASHER-WOMAN AND CLEAN THIS MESS UP.
WEREN'T NO SLAVE, THOUGH.
NO SIGN OF HIS HEAD, AND NO DIRECT WITNESSES, BUT WE ROUNDED A BUNCH OF PEOPLE UP WHEN WE GOT HERE...
OUGHTTA BE. SUN-DAMNED SAVAGES.
NOW, WHY YOU SAY THAT? WHY YOU SAY "SUN-DAMNED" WHEN YOU DON'T BELIEVE IN NO MOTHER SUN?
LET THEM GO. THIS ONE'S GOING STRAIGHT IN THE GROUND.
JUST A FIGURE OF FUCKING SPEECH, WOMAN. FUCK ME...

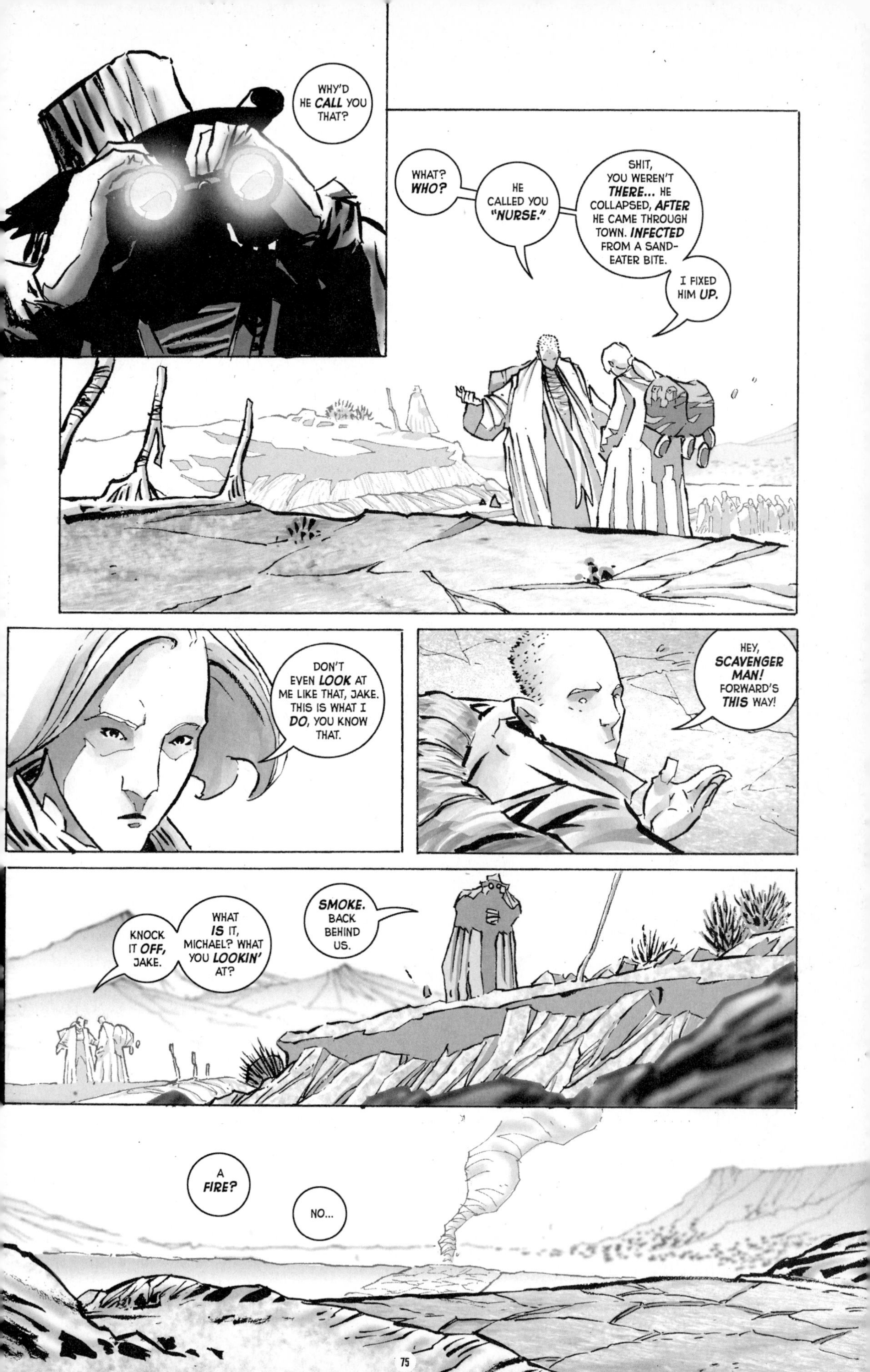
WHY'D HE **CALL** YOU THAT?
WHAT? **WHO?**
HE CALLED YOU **"NURSE."**
SHIT, YOU WEREN'T **THERE...** HE COLLAPSED, **AFTER** HE CAME THROUGH TOWN. **INFECTED** FROM A SAND-EATER BITE.
I FIXED HIM **UP.**
DON'T EVEN **LOOK** AT ME LIKE THAT, JAKE. THIS IS WHAT I **DO**, YOU KNOW THAT.
HEY, **SCAVENGER MAN!** FORWARD'S **THIS** WAY!
KNOCK IT **OFF,** JAKE.
WHAT **IS** IT, MICHAEL? WHAT YOU **LOOKIN'** AT?
SMOKE. BACK BEHIND US.
A **FIRE?**
NO...

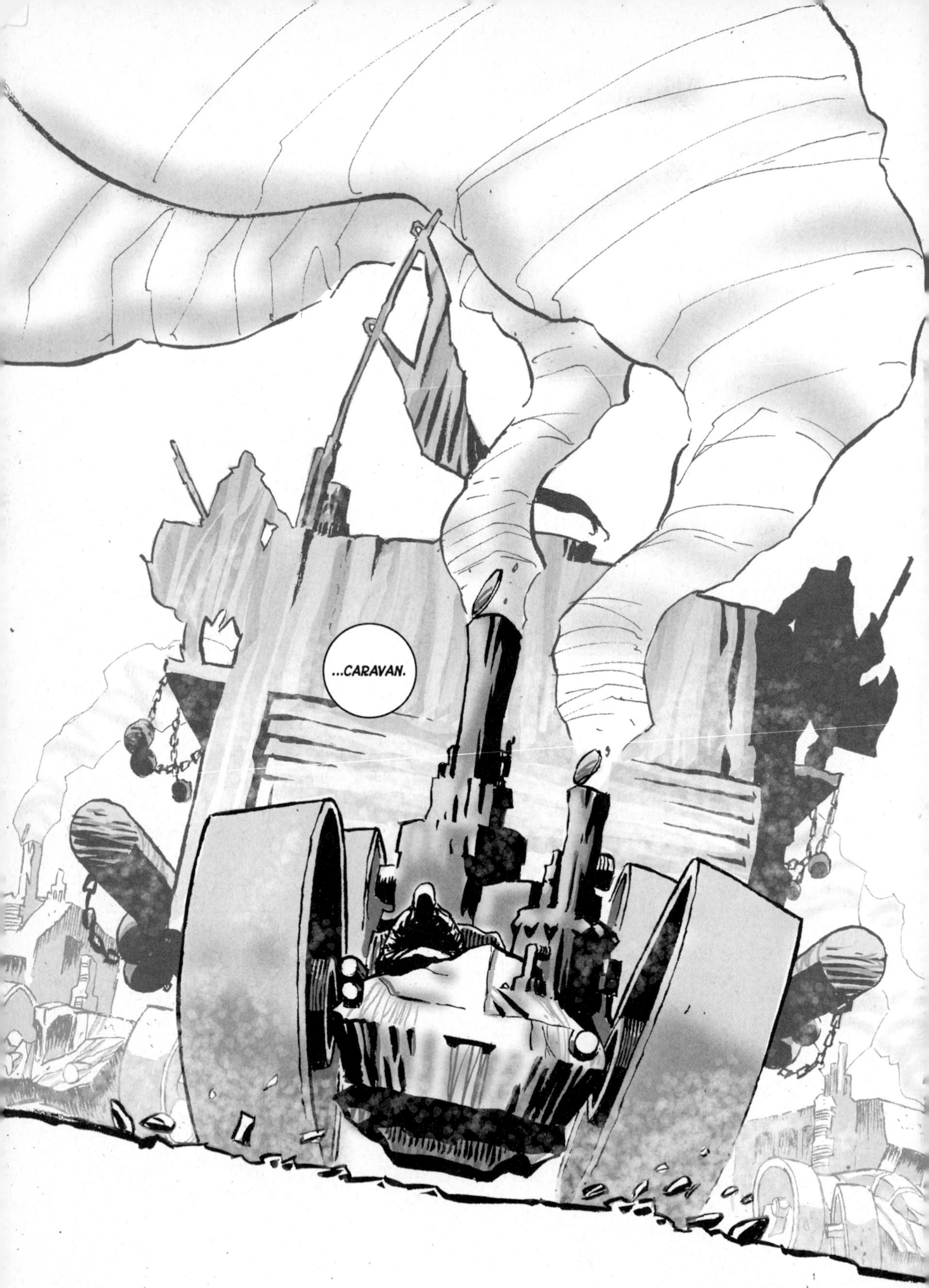
...CARAVAN.

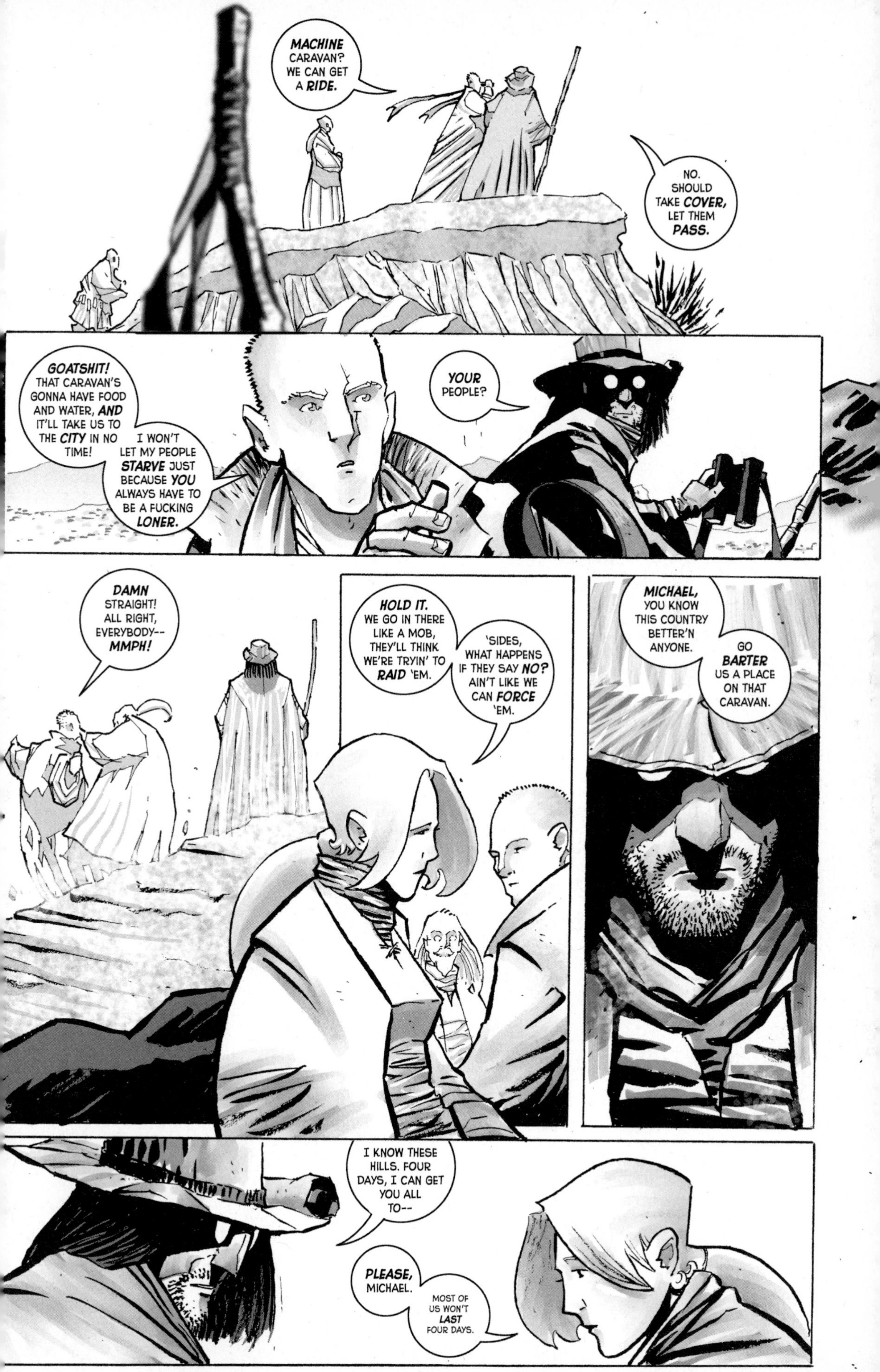
MACHINE CARAVAN? WE CAN GET A RIDE.
NO. SHOULD TAKE COVER, LET THEM PASS.
GOATSHIT! THAT CARAVAN'S GONNA HAVE FOOD AND WATER, AND IT'LL TAKE US TO THE CITY IN NO TIME!
I WON'T LET MY PEOPLE STARVE JUST BECAUSE YOU ALWAYS HAVE TO BE A FUCKING LONER.
YOUR PEOPLE?
DAMN STRAIGHT! ALL RIGHT, EVERYBODY-- MMPH!
HOLD IT. WE GO IN THERE LIKE A MOB, THEY'LL THINK WE'RE TRYIN' TO RAID 'EM.
'SIDES, WHAT HAPPENS IF THEY SAY NO? AIN'T LIKE WE CAN FORCE 'EM.
MICHAEL, YOU KNOW THIS COUNTRY BETTER'N ANYONE.
GO BARTER US A PLACE ON THAT CARAVAN.
I KNOW THESE HILLS. FOUR DAYS, I CAN GET YOU ALL TO--
PLEASE, MICHAEL.
MOST OF US WON'T LAST FOUR DAYS.

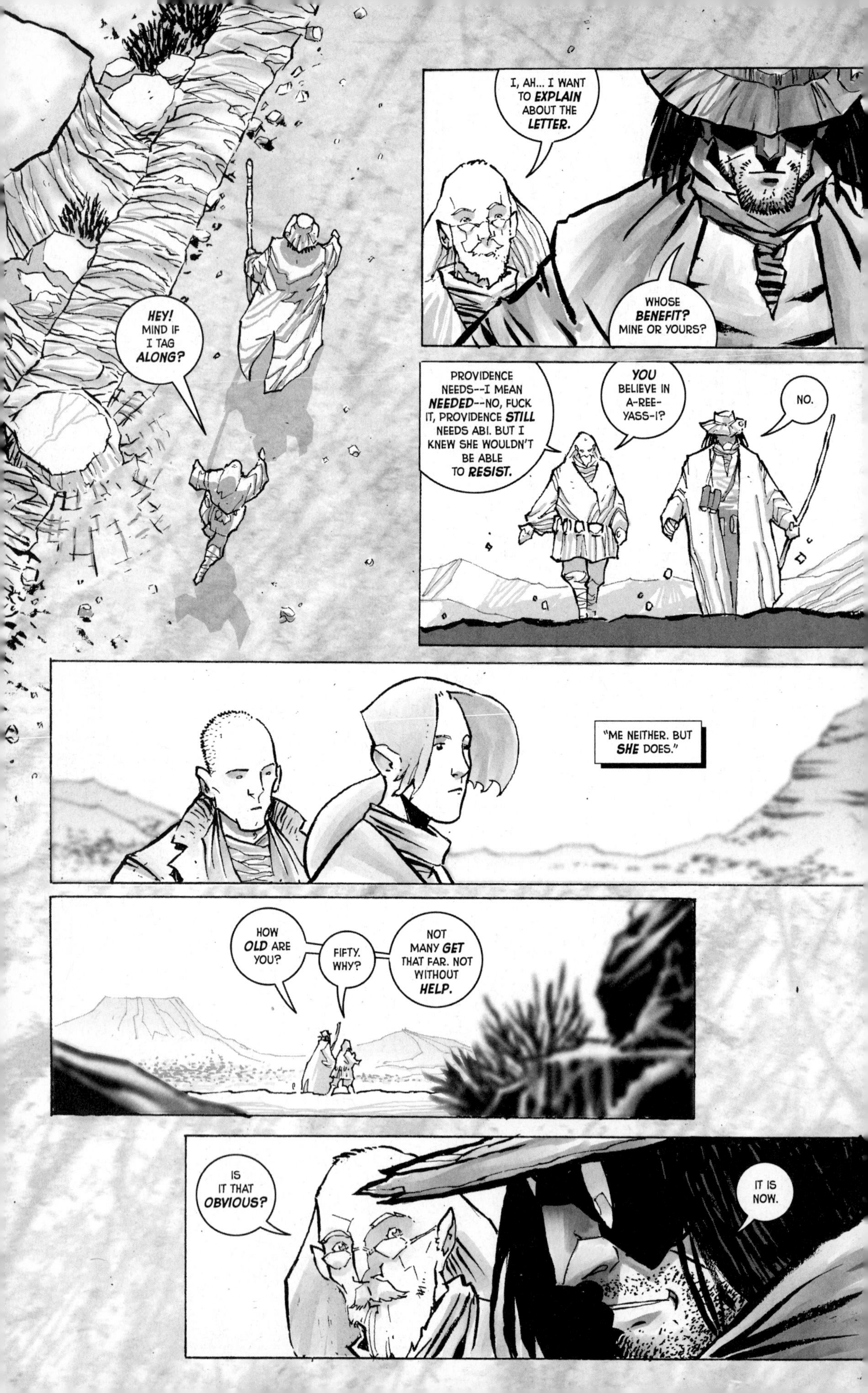
HEY! MIND IF I TAG ALONG?
I, AH... I WANT TO EXPLAIN ABOUT THE LETTER.
WHOSE BENEFIT? MINE OR YOURS?
PROVIDENCE NEEDS--I MEAN NEEDED--NO, FUCK IT, PROVIDENCE STILL NEEDS ABI. BUT I KNEW SHE WOULDN'T BE ABLE TO RESIST.
YOU BELIEVE IN A-REE-YASS-I?
NO.
"ME NEITHER. BUT SHE DOES."
HOW OLD ARE YOU?
FIFTY. WHY?
NOT MANY GET THAT FAR. NOT WITHOUT HELP.
IS IT THAT OBVIOUS?
IT IS NOW.

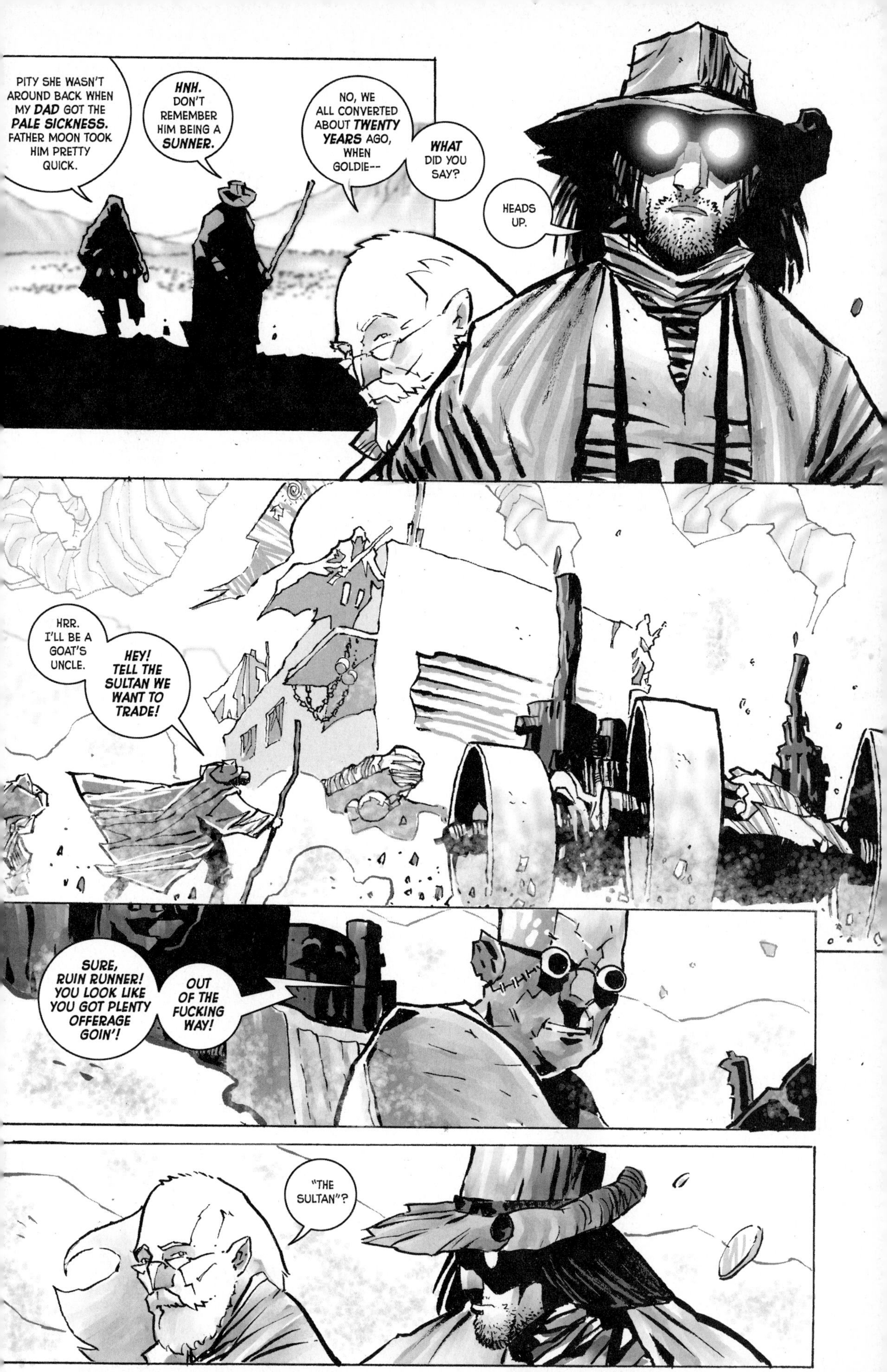
PITY SHE WASN'T AROUND BACK WHEN MY DAD GOT THE PALE SICKNESS. FATHER MOON TOOK HIM PRETTY QUICK.
HNH. DON'T REMEMBER HIM BEING A SUNNER.
NO, WE ALL CONVERTED ABOUT TWENTY YEARS AGO, WHEN GOLDIE--
WHAT DID YOU SAY?
HEADS UP.
HRR. I'LL BE A GOAT'S UNCLE.
HEY! TELL THE SULTAN WE WANT TO TRADE!
SURE, RUIN RUNNER! YOU LOOK LIKE YOU GOT PLENTY OFFERAGE GOIN'!
OUT OF THE FUCKING WAY!
"THE SULTAN"?

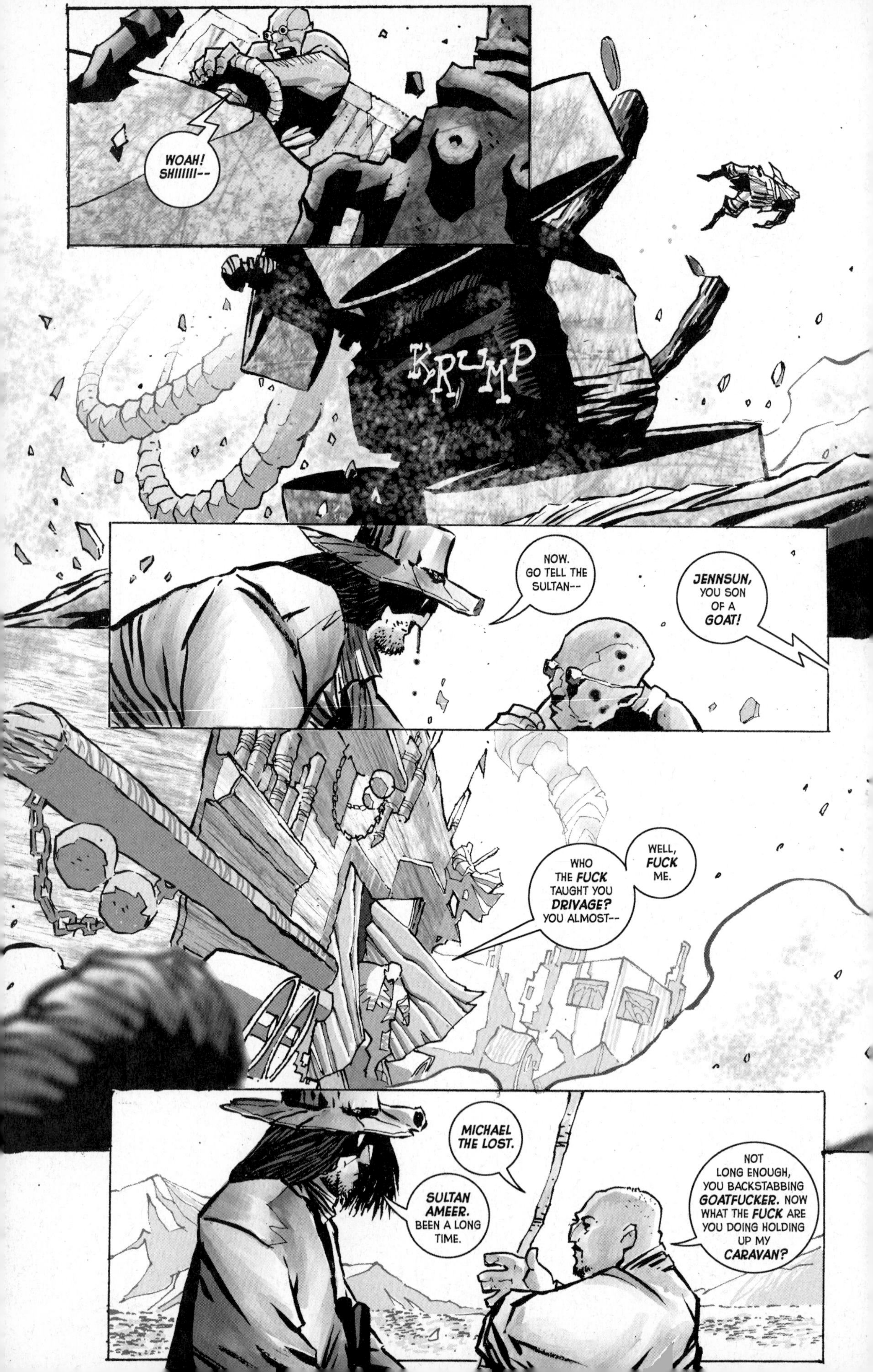
WOAH! SHIIIIII--
KRUMP
NOW. GO TELL THE SULTAN--
JENNSUN, YOU SON OF A GOAT!
WELL, FUCK ME.
WHO THE FUCK TAUGHT YOU DRIVAGE? YOU ALMOST--
MICHAEL THE LOST.
SULTAN AMEER. BEEN A LONG TIME.
NOT LONG ENOUGH, YOU BACKSTABBING GOATFUCKER. NOW WHAT THE FUCK ARE YOU DOING HOLDING UP MY CARAVAN?

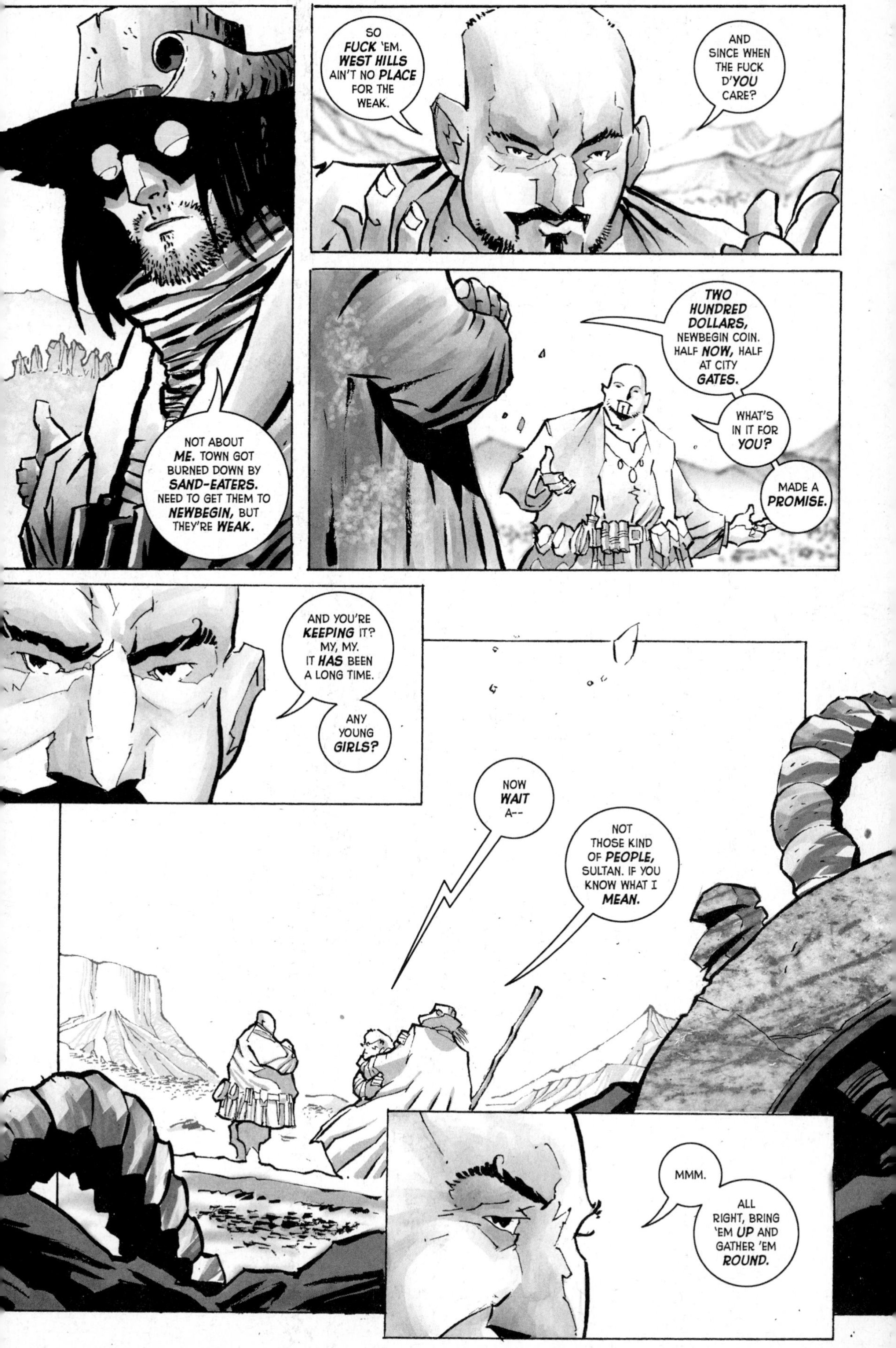
SO FUCK 'EM. WEST HILLS AIN'T NO PLACE FOR THE WEAK.
AND SINCE WHEN THE FUCK D'YOU CARE?
NOT ABOUT ME. TOWN GOT BURNED DOWN BY SAND-EATERS. NEED TO GET THEM TO NEWBEGIN, BUT THEY'RE WEAK.
TWO HUNDRED DOLLARS, NEWBEGIN COIN. HALF NOW, HALF AT CITY GATES.
WHAT'S IN IT FOR YOU?
MADE A PROMISE.
AND YOU'RE KEEPING IT? MY, MY. IT HAS BEEN A LONG TIME.
ANY YOUNG GIRLS?
NOW WAIT A--
NOT THOSE KIND OF PEOPLE, SULTAN. IF YOU KNOW WHAT I MEAN.
MMM.
ALL RIGHT, BRING 'EM UP AND GATHER 'EM ROUND.

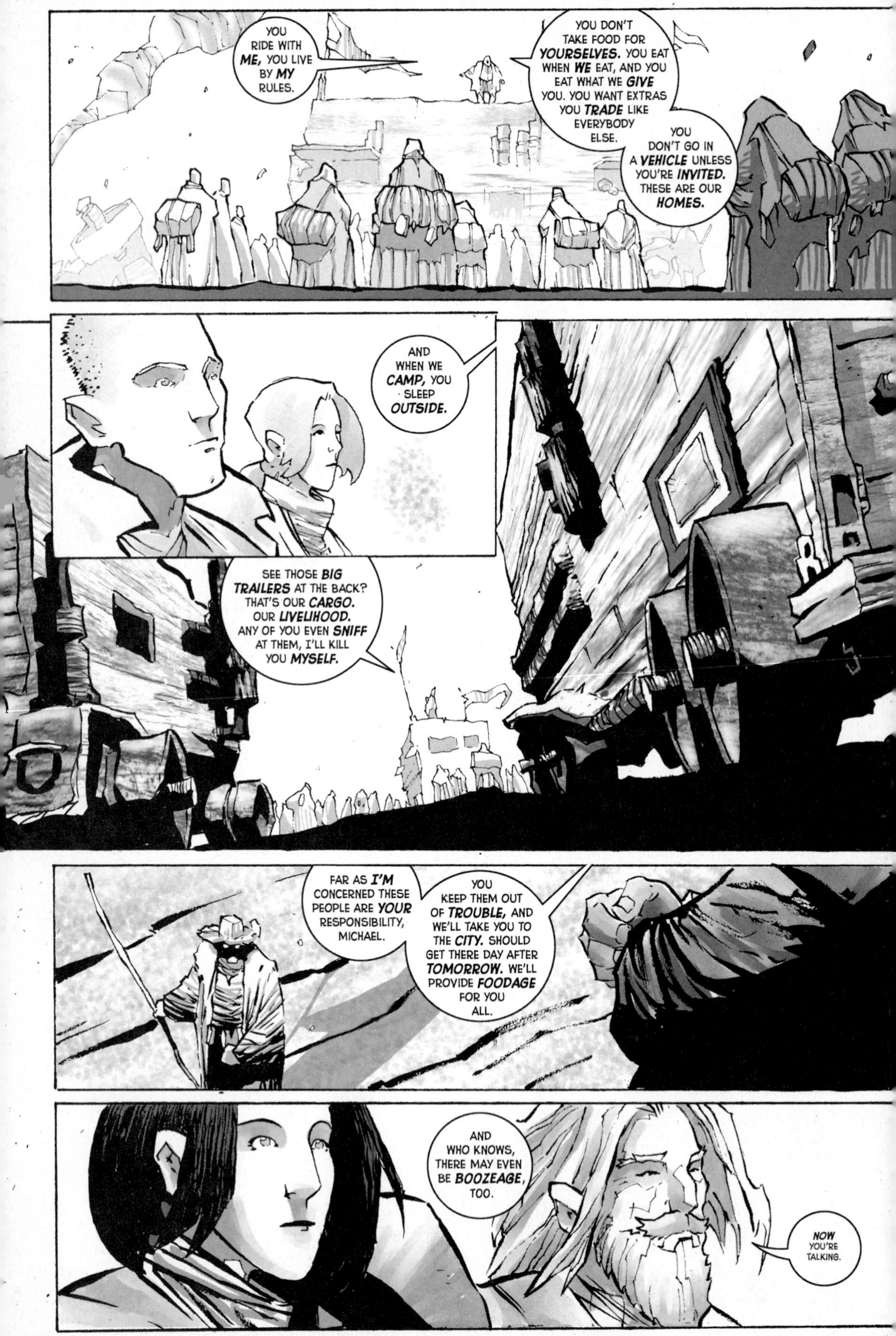
YOU RIDE WITH ME, YOU LIVE BY MY RULES.
YOU DON'T TAKE FOOD FOR YOURSELVES. YOU EAT WHEN WE EAT, AND YOU EAT WHAT WE GIVE YOU. YOU WANT EXTRAS YOU TRADE LIKE EVERYBODY ELSE.
YOU DON'T GO IN A VEHICLE UNLESS YOU'RE INVITED. THESE ARE OUR HOMES.
AND WHEN WE CAMP, YOU SLEEP OUTSIDE.
SEE THOSE BIG TRAILERS AT THE BACK? THAT'S OUR CARGO. OUR LIVELIHOOD. ANY OF YOU EVEN SNIFF AT THEM, I'LL KILL YOU MYSELF.
FAR AS I'M CONCERNED THESE PEOPLE ARE YOUR RESPONSIBILITY, MICHAEL.
YOU KEEP THEM OUT OF TROUBLE, AND WE'LL TAKE YOU TO THE CITY. SHOULD GET THERE DAY AFTER TOMORROW. WE'LL PROVIDE FOODAGE FOR YOU ALL.
AND WHO KNOWS, THERE MAY EVEN BE BOOZEAGE, TOO.
NOW YOU'RE TALKING.

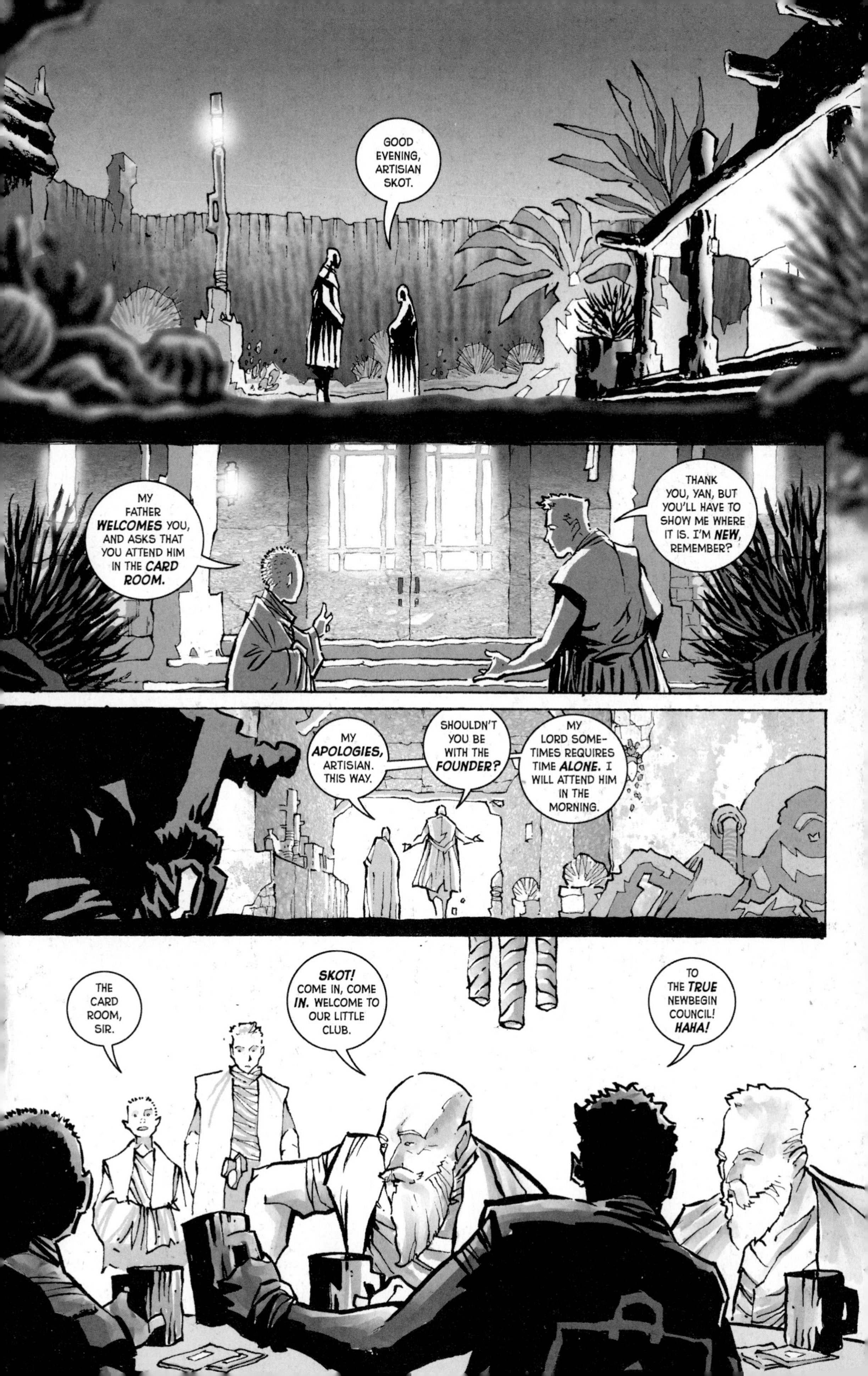
GOOD EVENING, ARTISIAN SKOT.
MY FATHER WELCOMES YOU, AND ASKS THAT YOU ATTEND HIM IN THE CARD ROOM.
THANK YOU, YAN, BUT YOU'LL HAVE TO SHOW ME WHERE IT IS. I'M NEW, REMEMBER?
MY APOLOGIES, ARTISIAN. THIS WAY.
SHOULDN'T YOU BE WITH THE FOUNDER?
MY LORD SOME-TIMES REQUIRES TIME ALONE. I WILL ATTEND HIM IN THE MORNING.
THE CARD ROOM, SIR.
SKOT! COME IN, COME IN. WELCOME TO OUR LITTLE CLUB.
TO THE TRUE NEWBEGIN COUNCIL! HAHA!

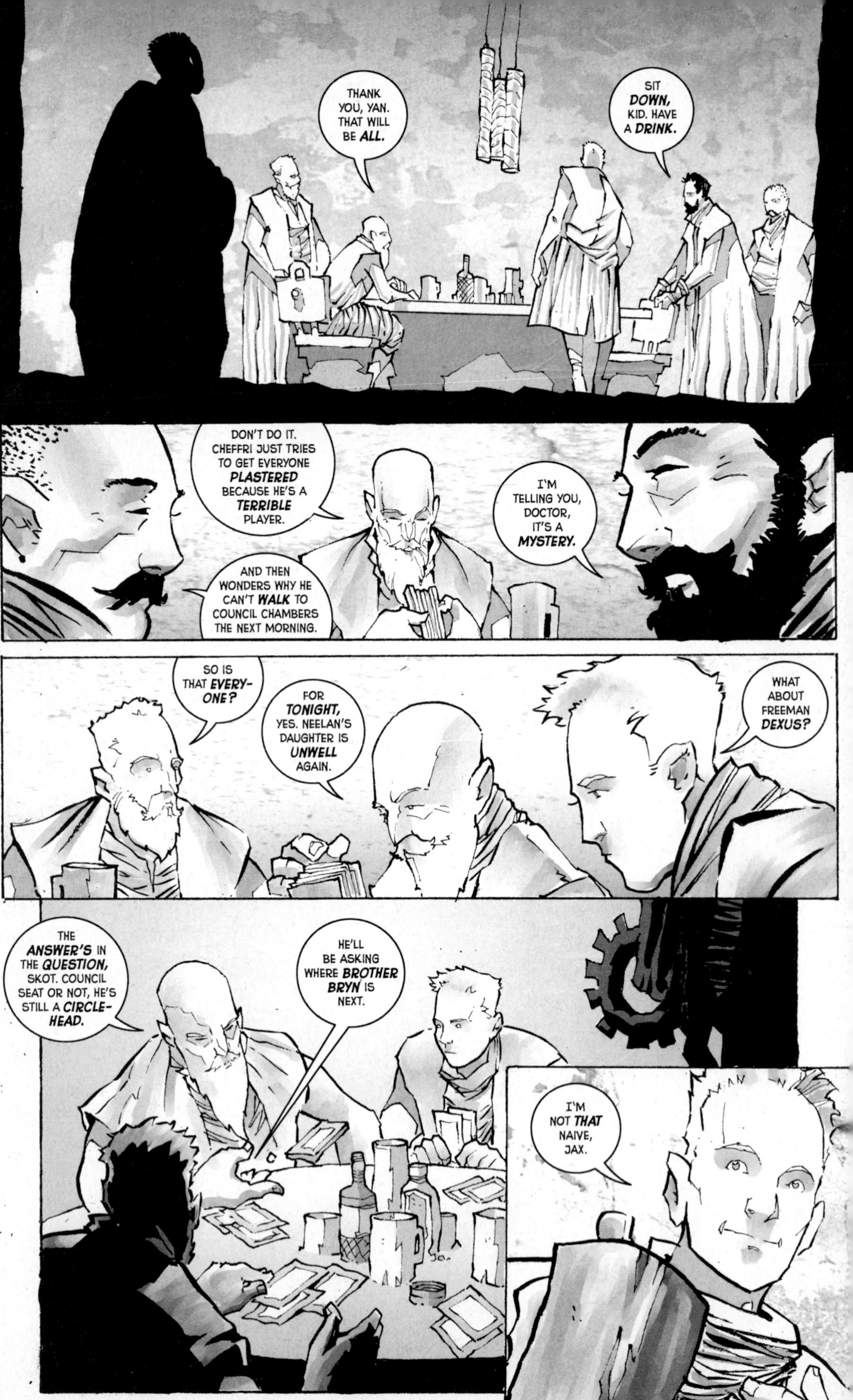
THANK YOU, YAN. THAT WILL BE ALL.
SIT DOWN, KID. HAVE A DRINK.
DON'T DO IT. CHEFFRI JUST TRIES TO GET EVERYONE PLASTERED BECAUSE HE'S A TERRIBLE PLAYER.
I'M TELLING YOU, DOCTOR, IT'S A MYSTERY.
AND THEN WONDERS WHY HE CAN'T WALK TO COUNCIL CHAMBERS THE NEXT MORNING.
SO IS THAT EVERY-ONE?
FOR TONIGHT, YES. NEELAN'S DAUGHTER IS UNWELL AGAIN.
WHAT ABOUT FREEMAN DEXUS?
THE ANSWER'S IN THE QUESTION, SKOT. COUNCIL SEAT OR NOT, HE'S STILL A CIRCLE-HEAD.
HE'LL BE ASKING WHERE BROTHER BRYN IS NEXT.
I'M NOT THAT NAIVE, JAX.

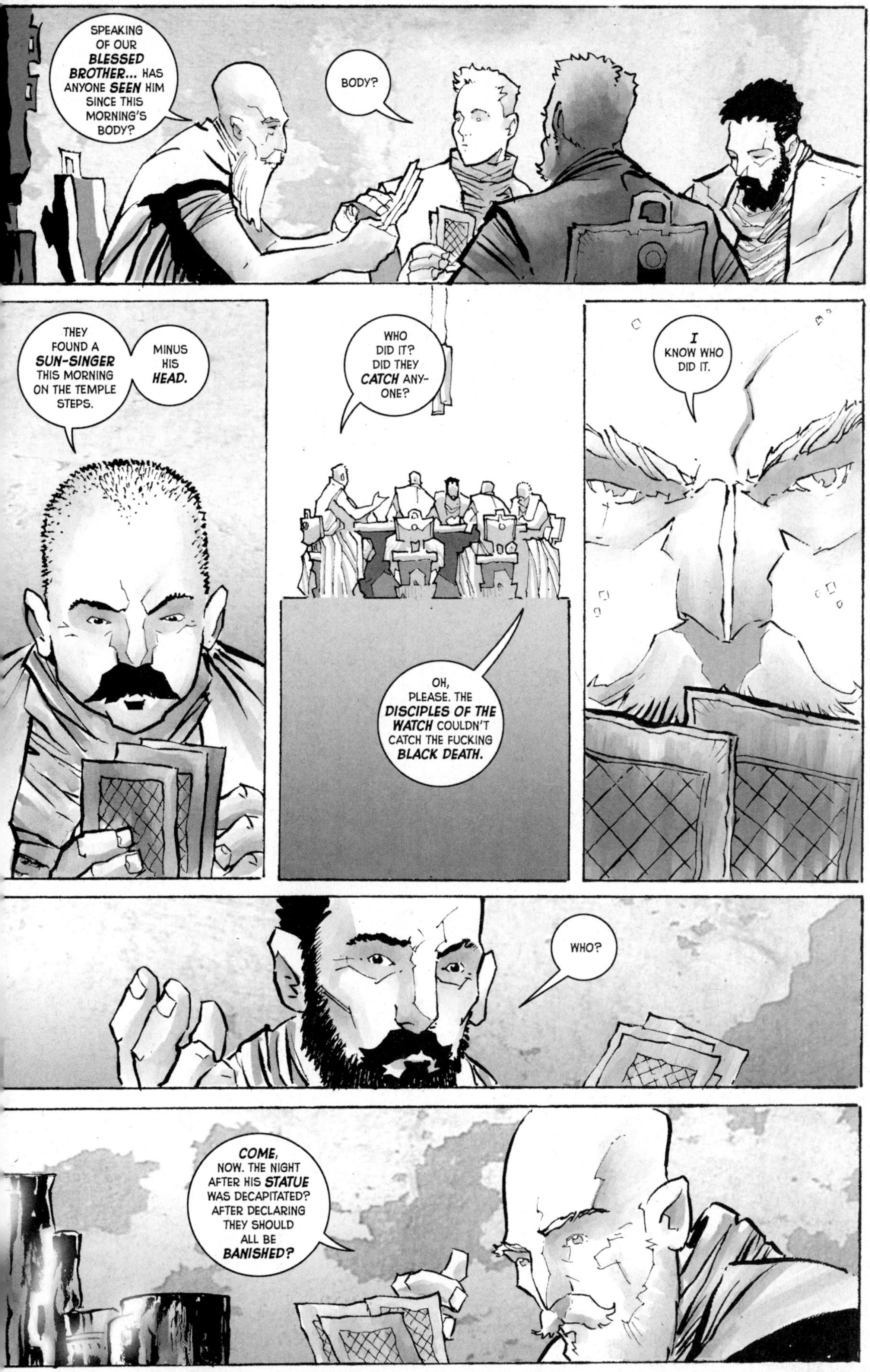
SPEAKING OF OUR BLESSED BROTHER... HAS ANYONE SEEN HIM SINCE THIS MORNING'S BODY?
BODY?
THEY FOUND A SUN-SINGER THIS MORNING ON THE TEMPLE STEPS.
MINUS HIS HEAD.
WHO DID IT? DID THEY CATCH ANY-ONE?
OH, PLEASE. THE DISCIPLES OF THE WATCH COULDN'T CATCH THE FUCKING BLACK DEATH.
I KNOW WHO DID IT.
WHO?
COME, NOW. THE NIGHT AFTER HIS STATUE WAS DECAPITATED? AFTER DECLARING THEY SHOULD ALL BE BANISHED?

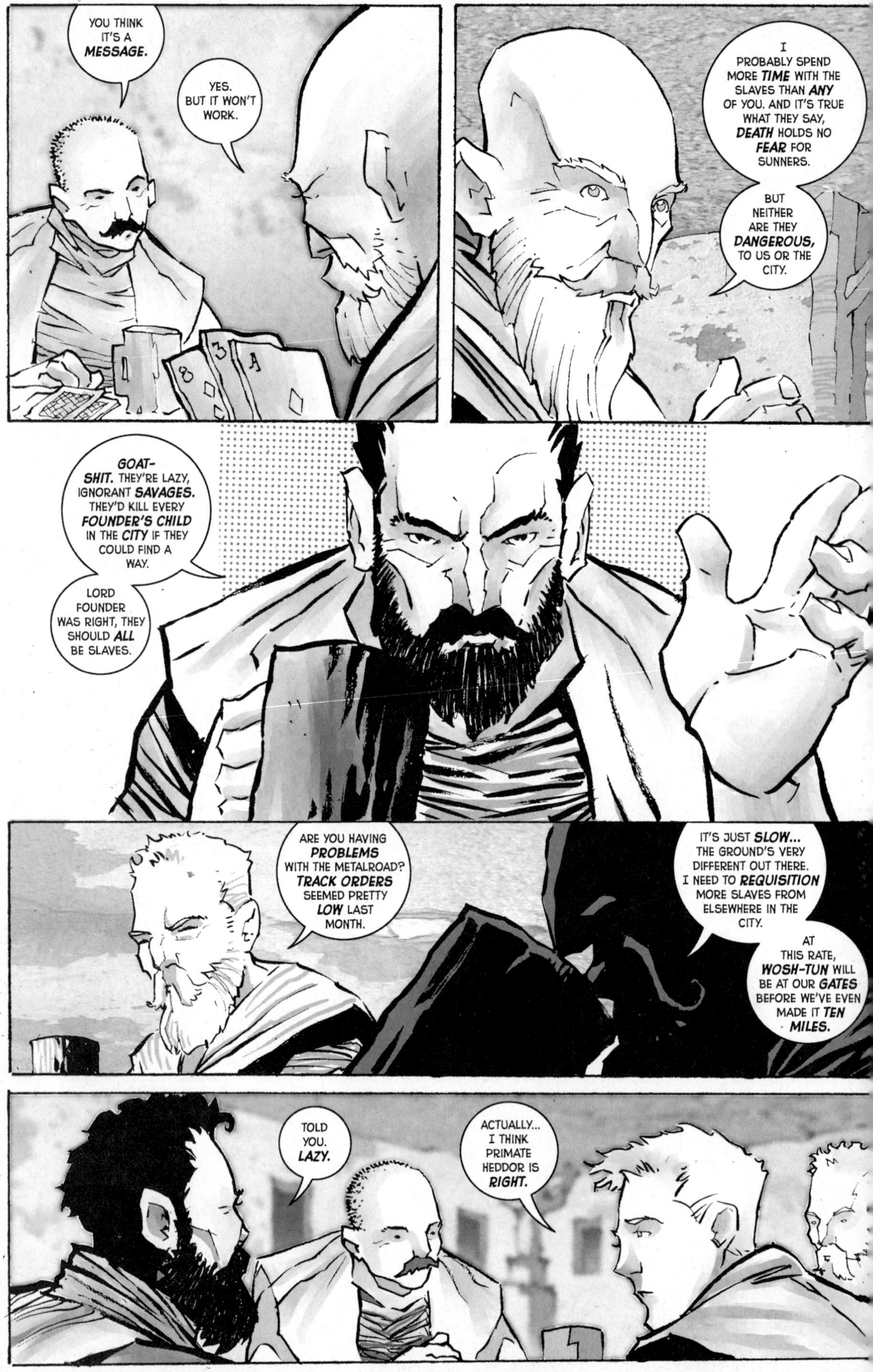

YOU THINK IT'S A MESSAGE.
YES. BUT IT WON'T WORK.
I PROBABLY SPEND MORE TIME WITH THE SLAVES THAN ANY OF YOU. AND IT'S TRUE WHAT THEY SAY, DEATH HOLDS NO FEAR FOR SUNNERS.
BUT NEITHER ARE THEY DANGEROUS, TO US OR THE CITY.
GOAT-SHIT. THEY'RE LAZY, IGNORANT SAVAGES. THEY'D KILL EVERY FOUNDER'S CHILD IN THE CITY IF THEY COULD FIND A WAY.
LORD FOUNDER WAS RIGHT, THEY SHOULD ALL BE SLAVES.
ARE YOU HAVING PROBLEMS WITH THE METALROAD? TRACK ORDERS SEEMED PRETTY LOW LAST MONTH.
IT'S JUST SLOW... THE GROUND'S VERY DIFFERENT OUT THERE. I NEED TO REQUISITION MORE SLAVES FROM ELSEWHERE IN THE CITY.
AT THIS RATE, WOSH-TUN WILL BE AT OUR GATES BEFORE WE'VE EVEN MADE IT TEN MILES.
TOLD YOU. LAZY.
ACTUALLY... I THINK PRIMATE HEDDOR IS RIGHT.

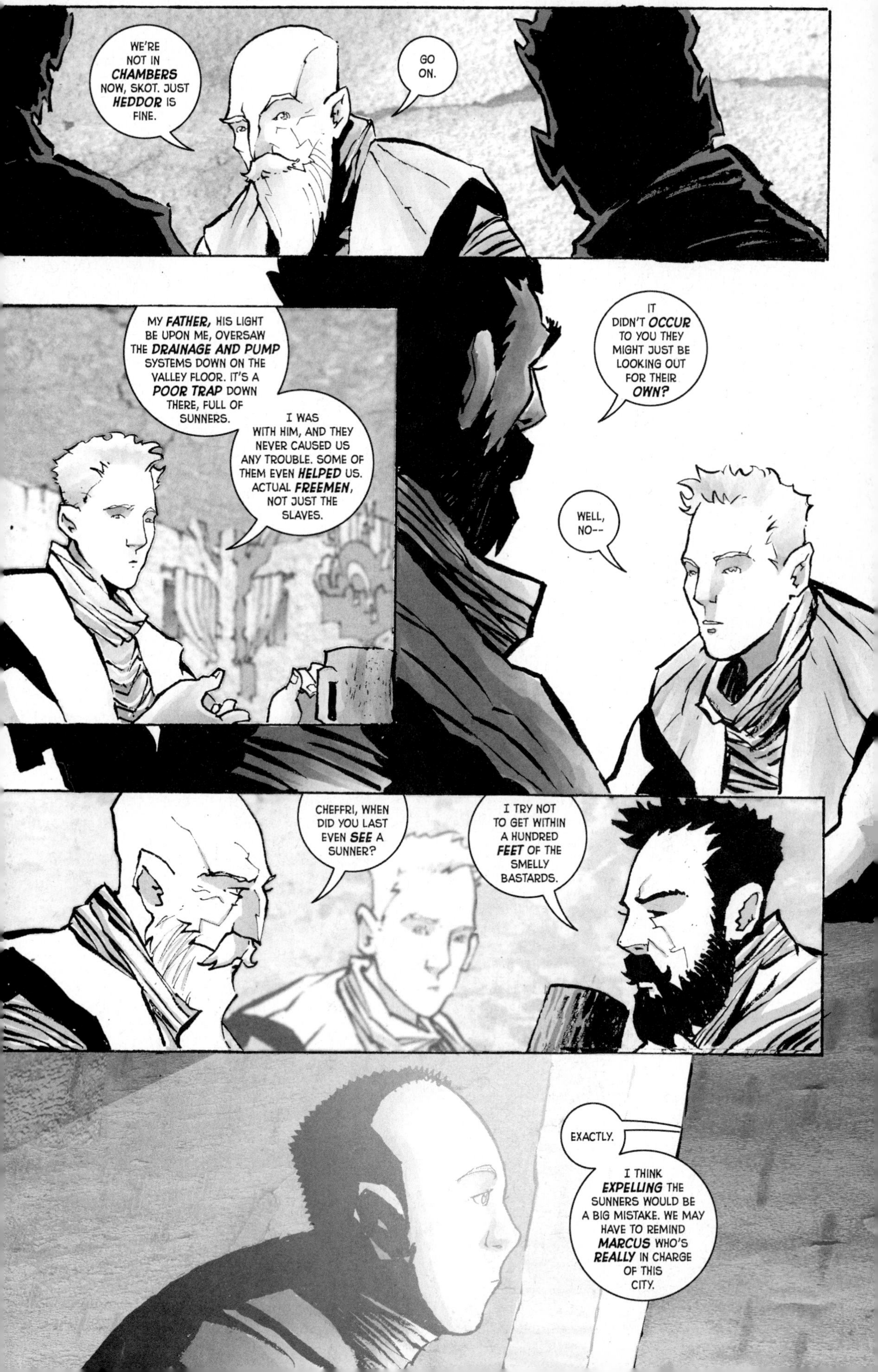
WE'RE NOT IN CHAMBERS NOW, SKOT. JUST HEDDOR IS FINE.
GO ON.
MY FATHER, HIS LIGHT BE UPON ME, OVERSAW THE DRAINAGE AND PUMP SYSTEMS DOWN ON THE VALLEY FLOOR. IT'S A POOR TRAP DOWN THERE, FULL OF SUNNERS.
I WAS WITH HIM, AND THEY NEVER CAUSED US ANY TROUBLE. SOME OF THEM EVEN HELPED US. ACTUAL FREEMEN, NOT JUST THE SLAVES.
IT DIDN'T OCCUR TO YOU THEY MIGHT JUST BE LOOKING OUT FOR THEIR OWN?
WELL, NO--
CHEFFRI, WHEN DID YOU LAST EVEN SEE A SUNNER?
I TRY NOT TO GET WITHIN A HUNDRED FEET OF THE SMELLY BASTARDS.
EXACTLY.
I THINK EXPELLING THE SUNNERS WOULD BE A BIG MISTAKE. WE MAY HAVE TO REMIND MARCUS WHO'S REALLY IN CHARGE OF THIS CITY.

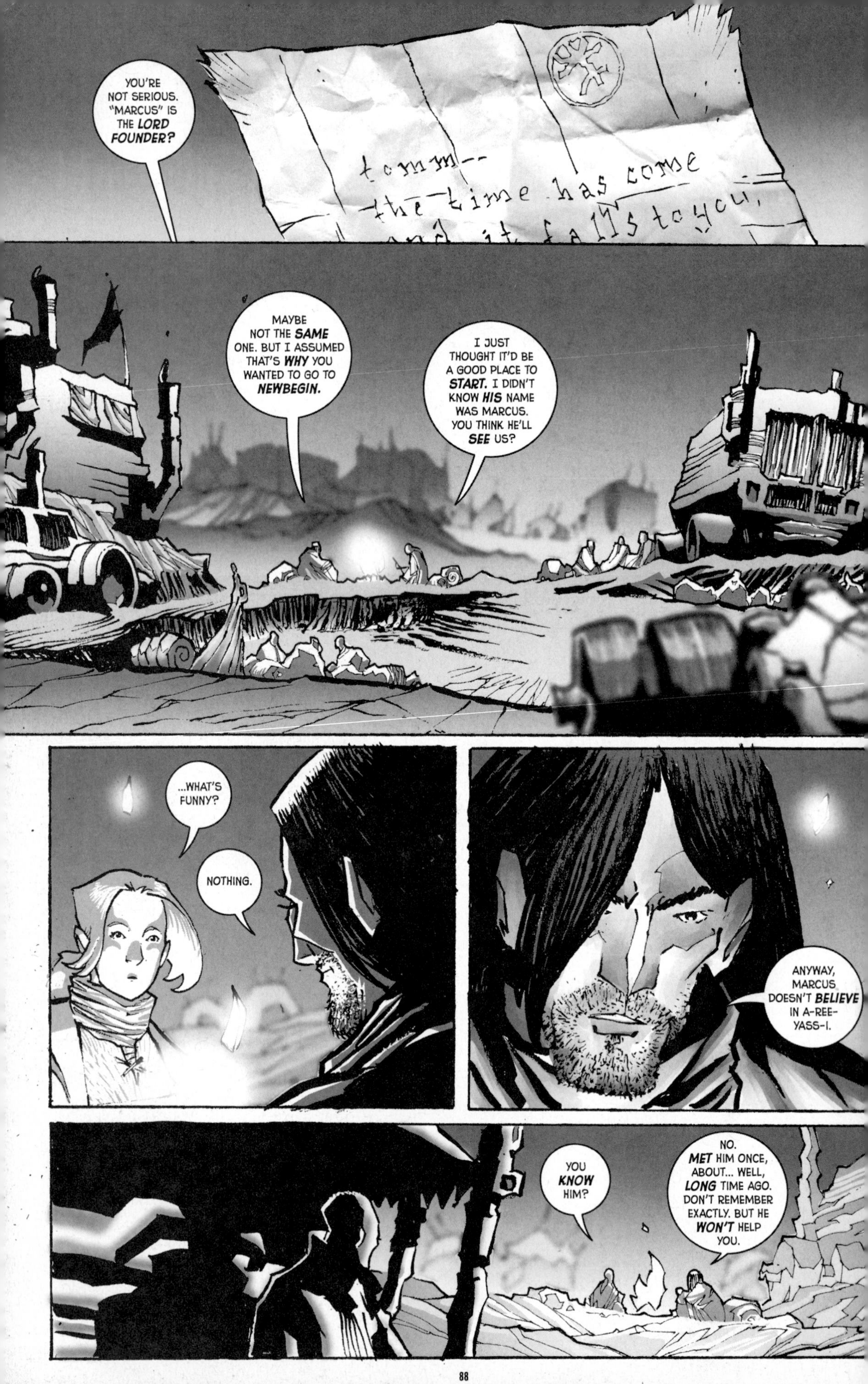
YOU'RE NOT SERIOUS. "MARCUS" IS THE LORD FOUNDER?
tomm-- the time has come and it falls to you.
MAYBE NOT THE SAME ONE. BUT I ASSUMED THAT'S WHY YOU WANTED TO GO TO NEWBEGIN.
I JUST THOUGHT IT'D BE A GOOD PLACE TO START. I DIDN'T KNOW HIS NAME WAS MARCUS. YOU THINK HE'LL SEE US?
...WHAT'S FUNNY?
NOTHING.
ANYWAY, MARCUS DOESN'T BELIEVE IN A-REE-YASS-I.
YOU KNOW HIM?
NO. MET HIM ONCE, ABOUT... WELL, LONG TIME AGO. DON'T REMEMBER EXACTLY. BUT HE WON'T HELP YOU.

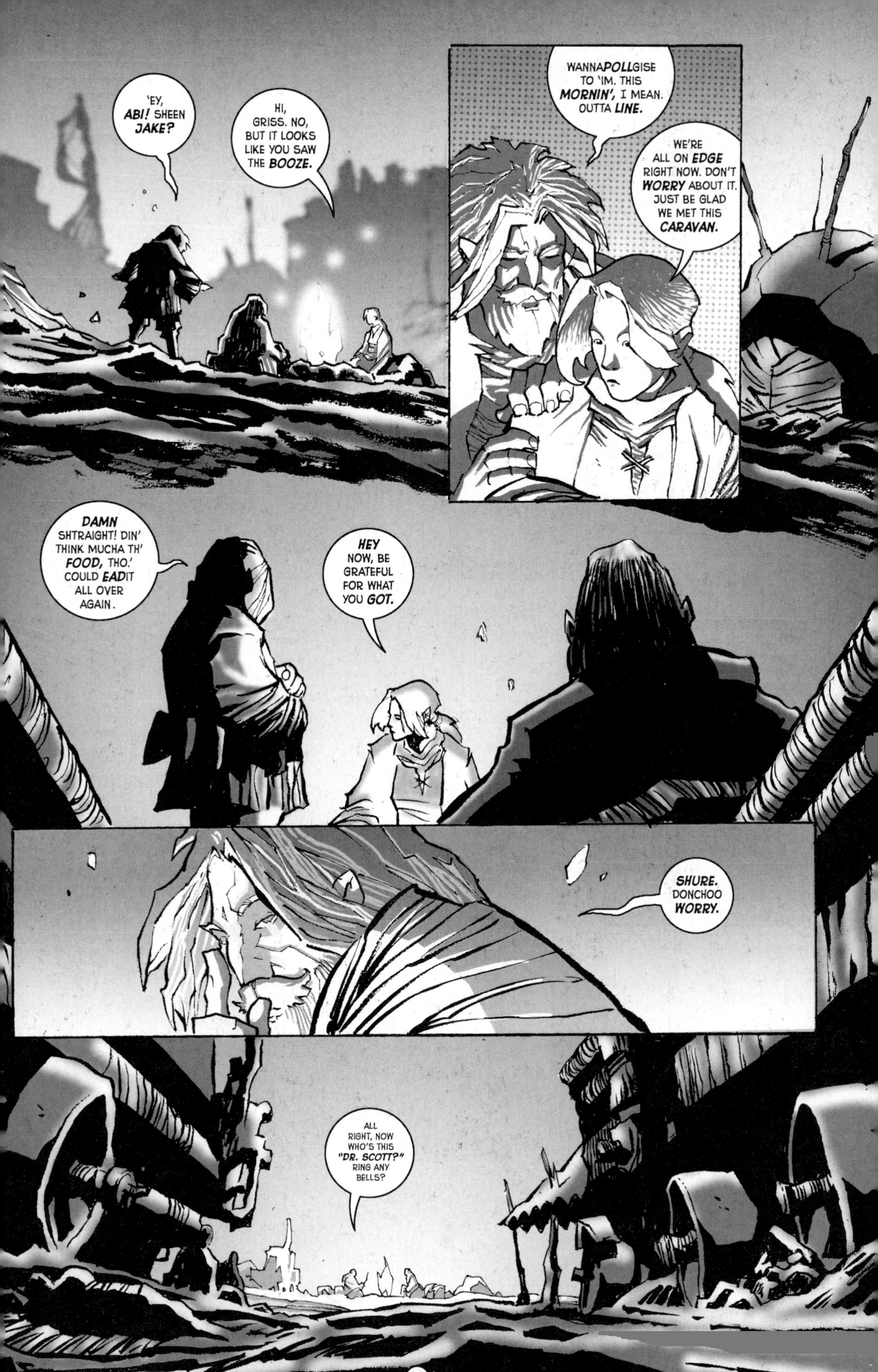
'EY, ABI! SHEEN JAKE?
HI, GRISS. NO, BUT IT LOOKS LIKE YOU SAW THE BOOZE.
WANNAPOLLGISE TO 'IM. THIS MORNIN', I MEAN. OUTTA LINE.
WE'RE ALL ON EDGE RIGHT NOW. DON'T WORRY ABOUT IT. JUST BE GLAD WE MET THIS CARAVAN.
DAMN SHTRAIGHT! DIN' THINK MUCHA TH' FOOD, THO.' COULD EADIT ALL OVER AGAIN.
HEY NOW, BE GRATEFUL FOR WHAT YOU GOT.
SHURE. DONCHOO WORRY.
ALL RIGHT, NOW WHO'S THIS "DR. SCOTT?" RING ANY BELLS?

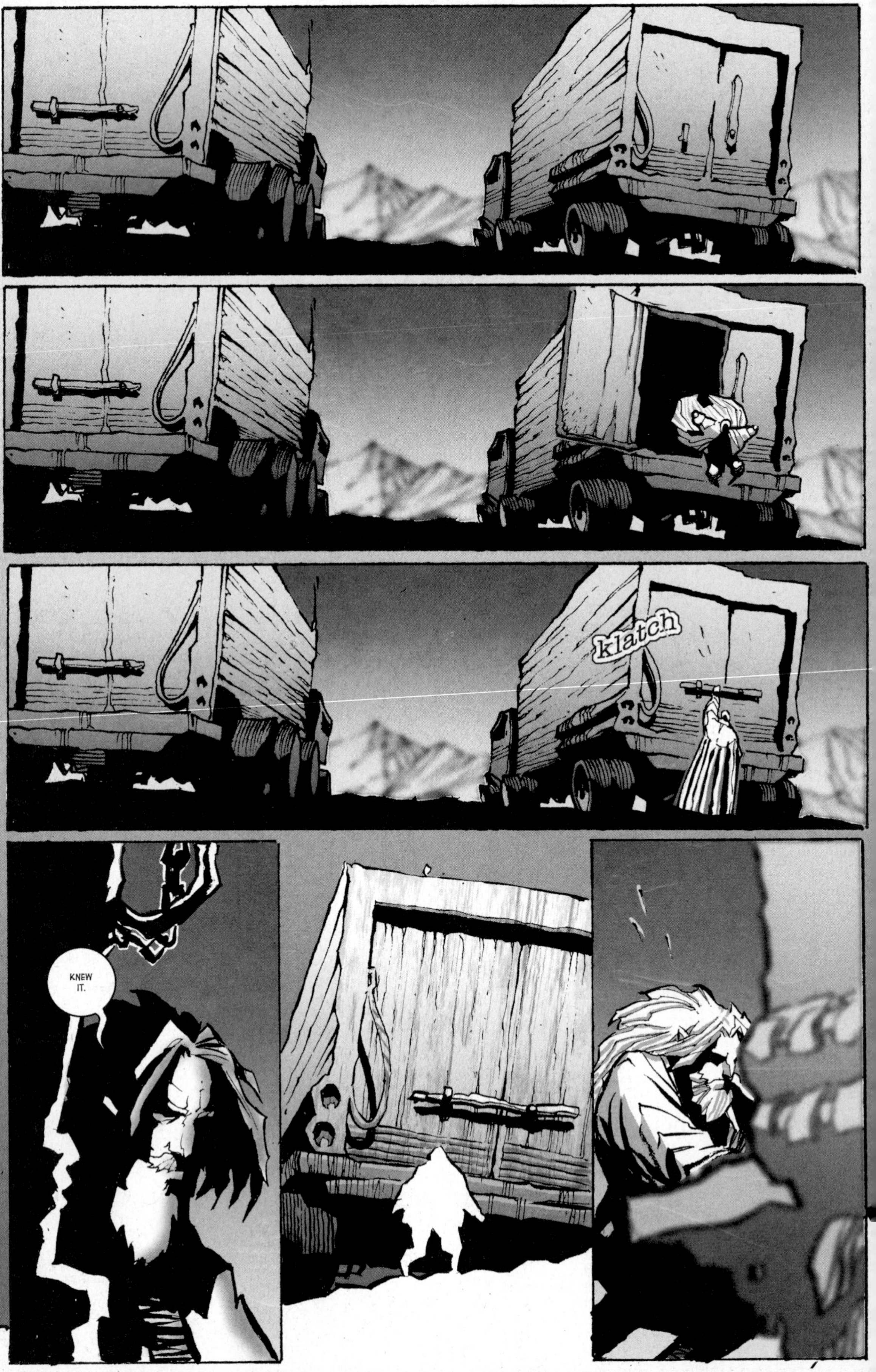
klatch
KNEW IT.

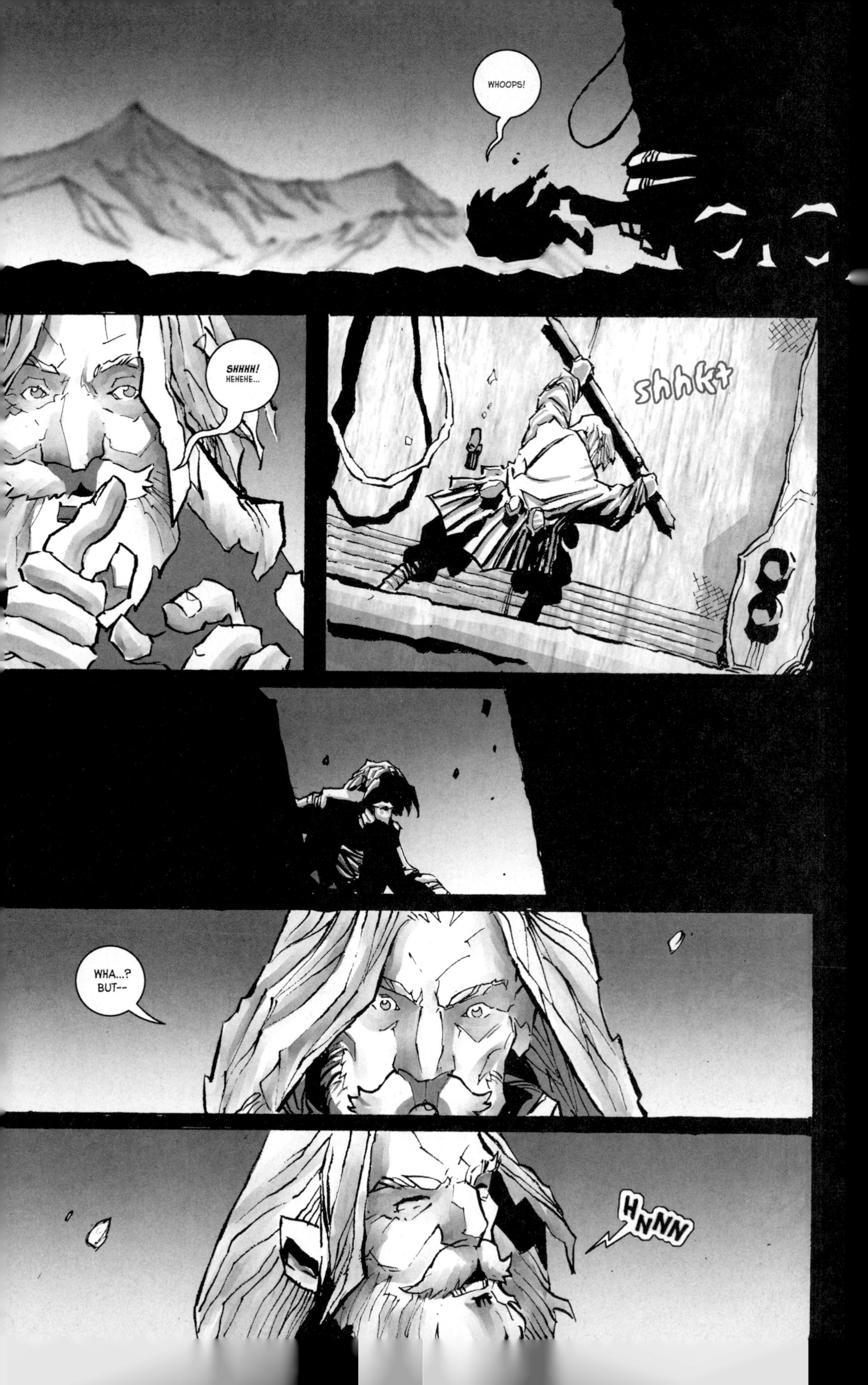
WHOOPS!
SHHHH! HEHEHE...
shhkt
WHA...? BUT--
HNNN

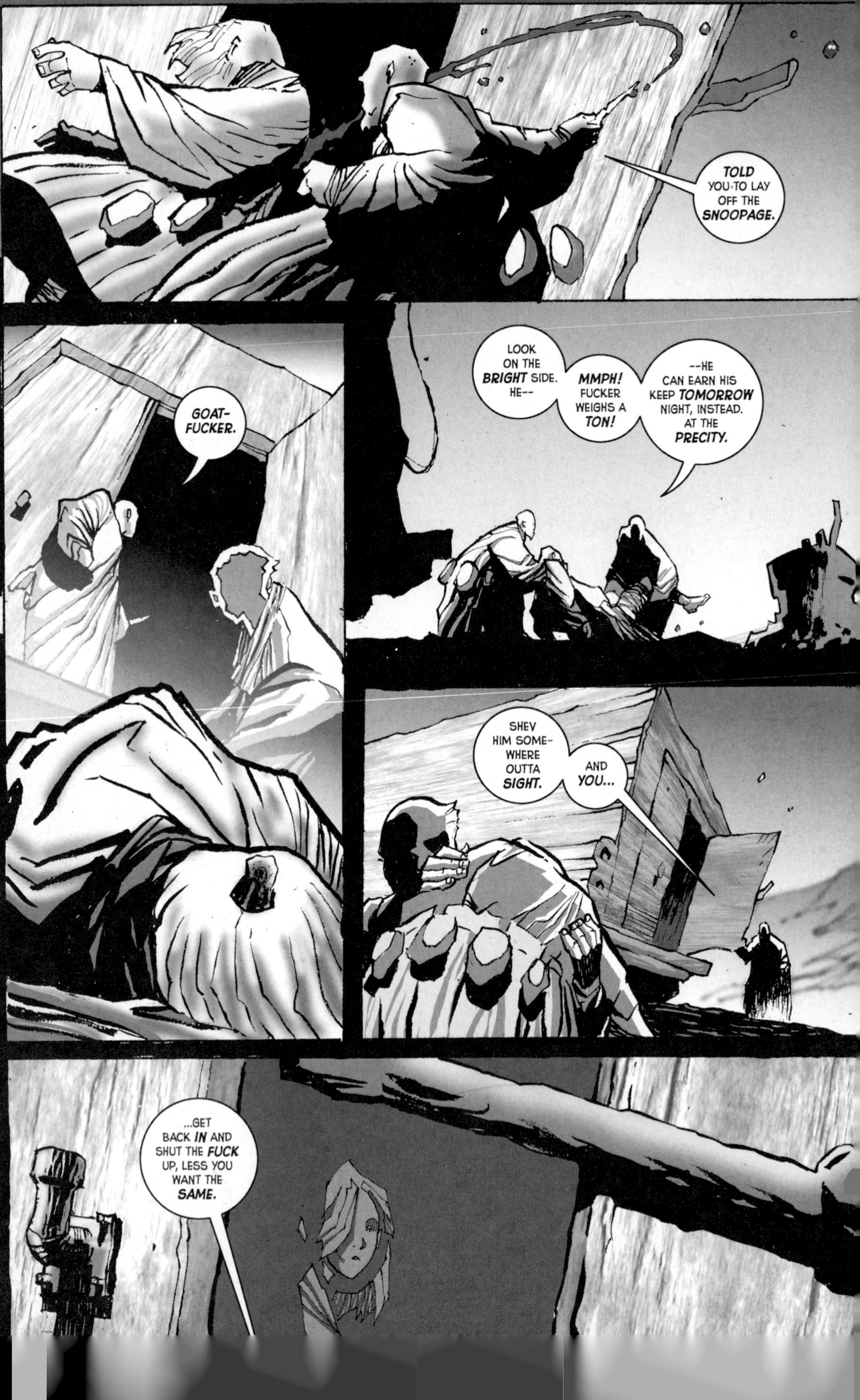
TOLD YOU TO LAY OFF THE SNOOPAGE.
GOAT-FUCKER.
LOOK ON THE BRIGHT SIDE. HE--
MMPH! FUCKER WEIGHS A TON!
--HE CAN EARN HIS KEEP TOMORROW NIGHT, INSTEAD. AT THE PRECITY.
SHEV HIM SOME-WHERE OUTTA SIGHT.
AND YOU...
...GET BACK IN AND SHUT THE FUCK UP, LESS YOU WANT THE SAME.

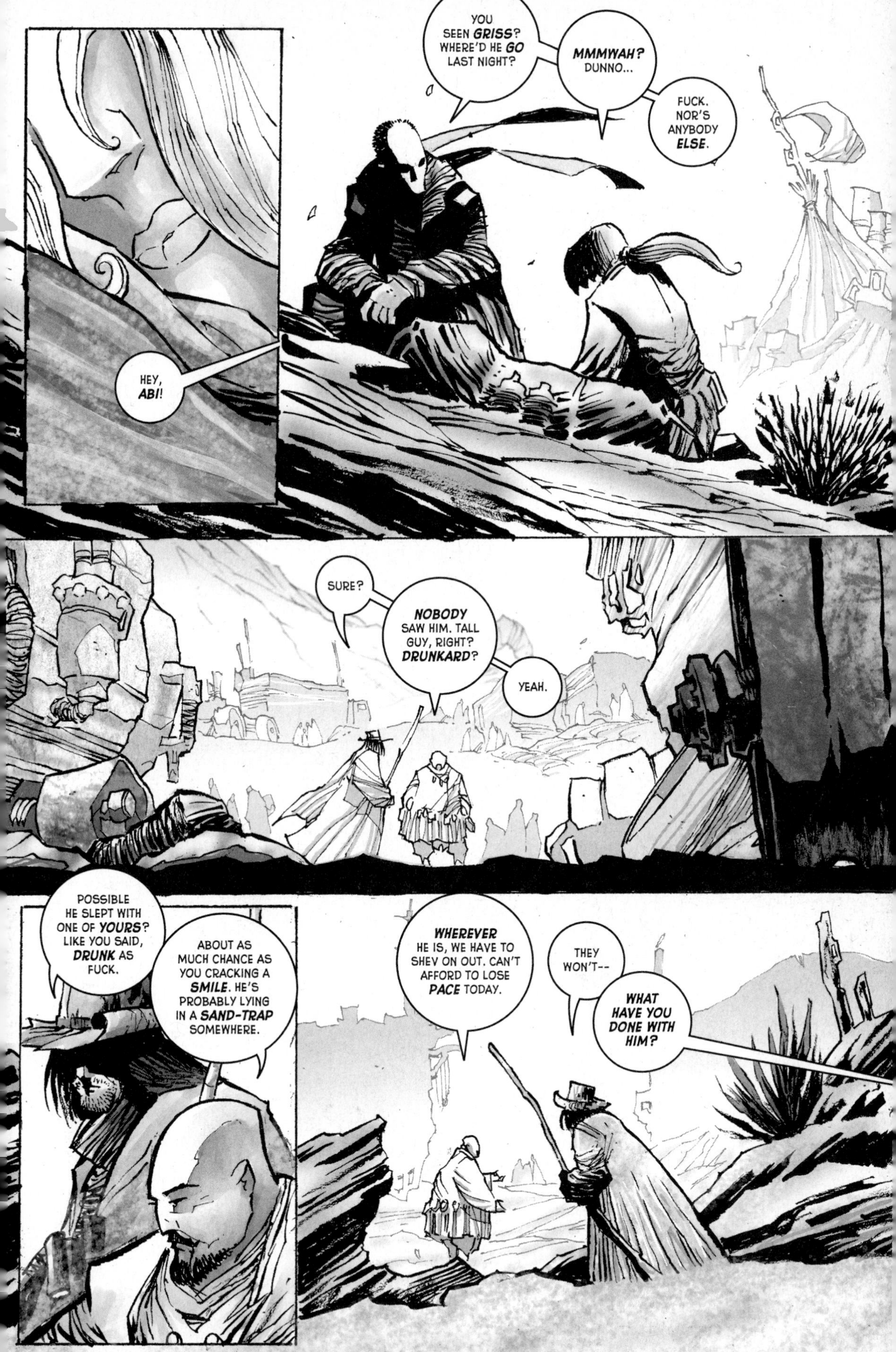
YOU SEEN GRISS? WHERE'D HE GO LAST NIGHT?
MMMWAH? DUNNO...
FUCK. NOR'S ANYBODY ELSE.
HEY, ABI!
SURE?
NOBODY SAW HIM. TALL GUY, RIGHT? DRUNKARD?
YEAH.
POSSIBLE HE SLEPT WITH ONE OF YOURS? LIKE YOU SAID, DRUNK AS FUCK.
ABOUT AS MUCH CHANCE AS YOU CRACKING A SMILE. HE'S PROBABLY LYING IN A SAND-TRAP SOMEWHERE.
WHEREVER HE IS, WE HAVE TO SHEY ON OUT. CAN'T AFFORD TO LOSE PACE TODAY.
THEY WON'T--
WHAT HAVE YOU DONE WITH HIM?

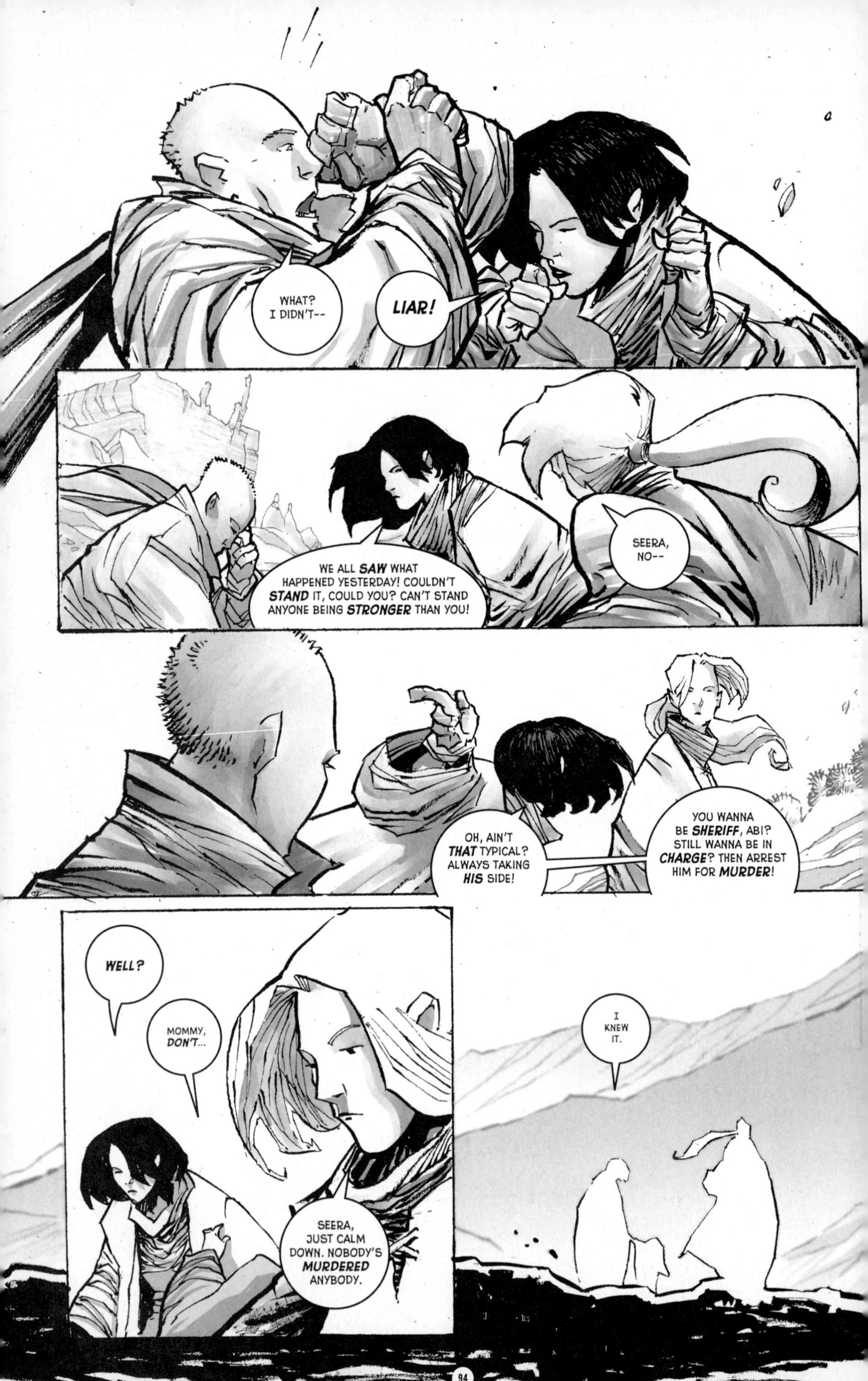
WHAT? I DIDN'T--
LIAR!
WE ALL SAW WHAT HAPPENED YESTERDAY! COULDN'T STAND IT, COULD YOU? CAN'T STAND ANYONE BEING STRONGER THAN YOU!
SEERA, NO--
YOU WANNA BE SHERIFF, ABI? STILL WANNA BE IN CHARGE? THEN ARREST HIM FOR MURDER!
OH, AIN'T THAT TYPICAL? ALWAYS TAKING HIS SIDE!
WELL?
MOMMY, DON'T...
SEERA, JUST CALM DOWN. NOBODY'S MURDERED ANYBODY.
I KNEW IT.

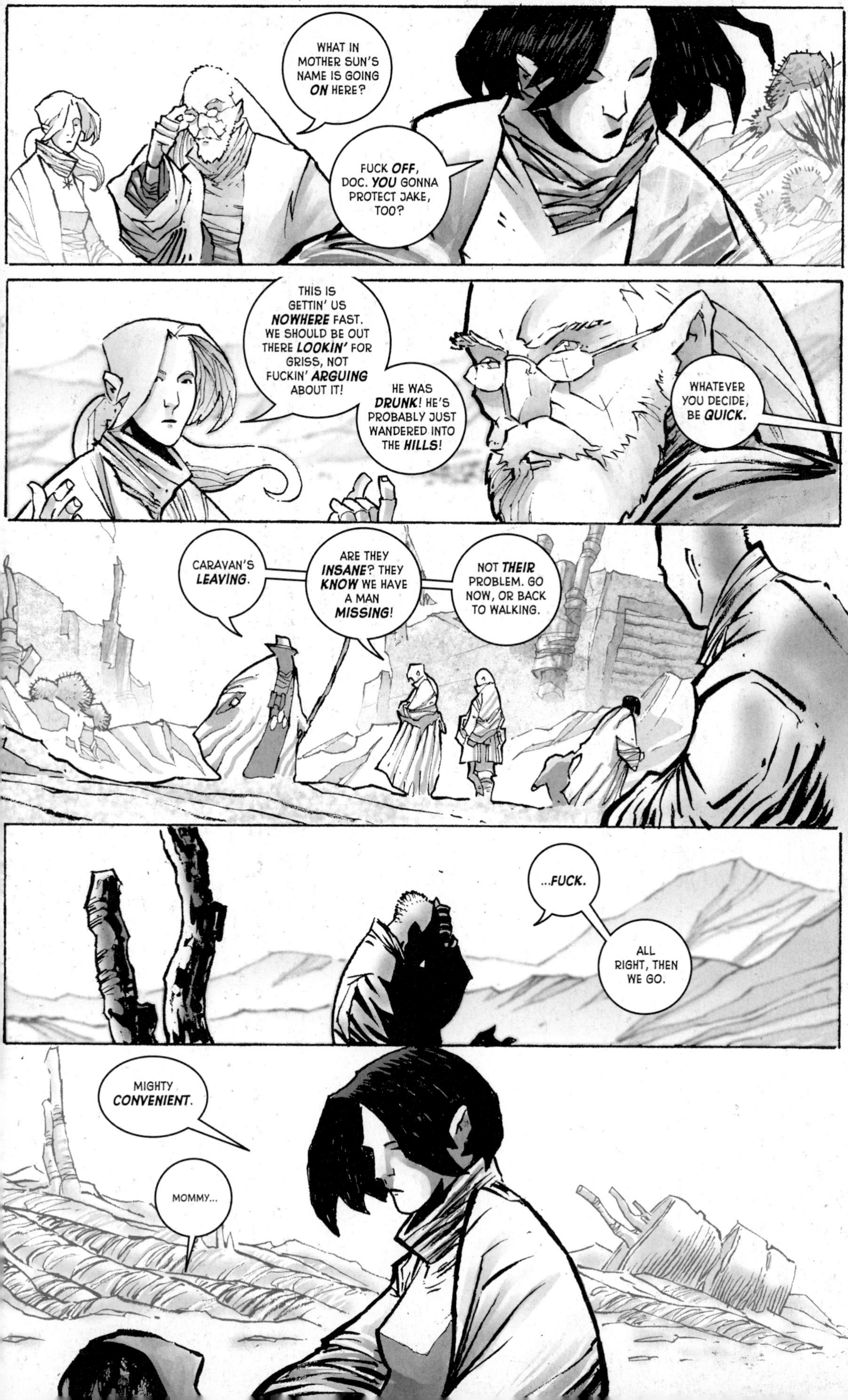
WHAT IN MOTHER SUN'S NAME IS GOING ON HERE?
FUCK OFF, DOC. YOU GONNA PROTECT JAKE, TOO?
THIS IS GETTIN' US NOWHERE FAST. WE SHOULD BE OUT THERE LOOKIN' FOR GRISS, NOT FUCKIN' ARGUING ABOUT IT!
HE WAS DRUNK! HE'S PROBABLY JUST WANDERED INTO THE HILLS!
WHATEVER YOU DECIDE, BE QUICK.
CARAVAN'S LEAVING.
ARE THEY INSANE? THEY KNOW WE HAVE A MAN MISSING!
NOT THEIR PROBLEM. GO NOW, OR BACK TO WALKING.
...FUCK.
ALL RIGHT, THEN WE GO.
MIGHTY CONVENIENT.
MOMMY...

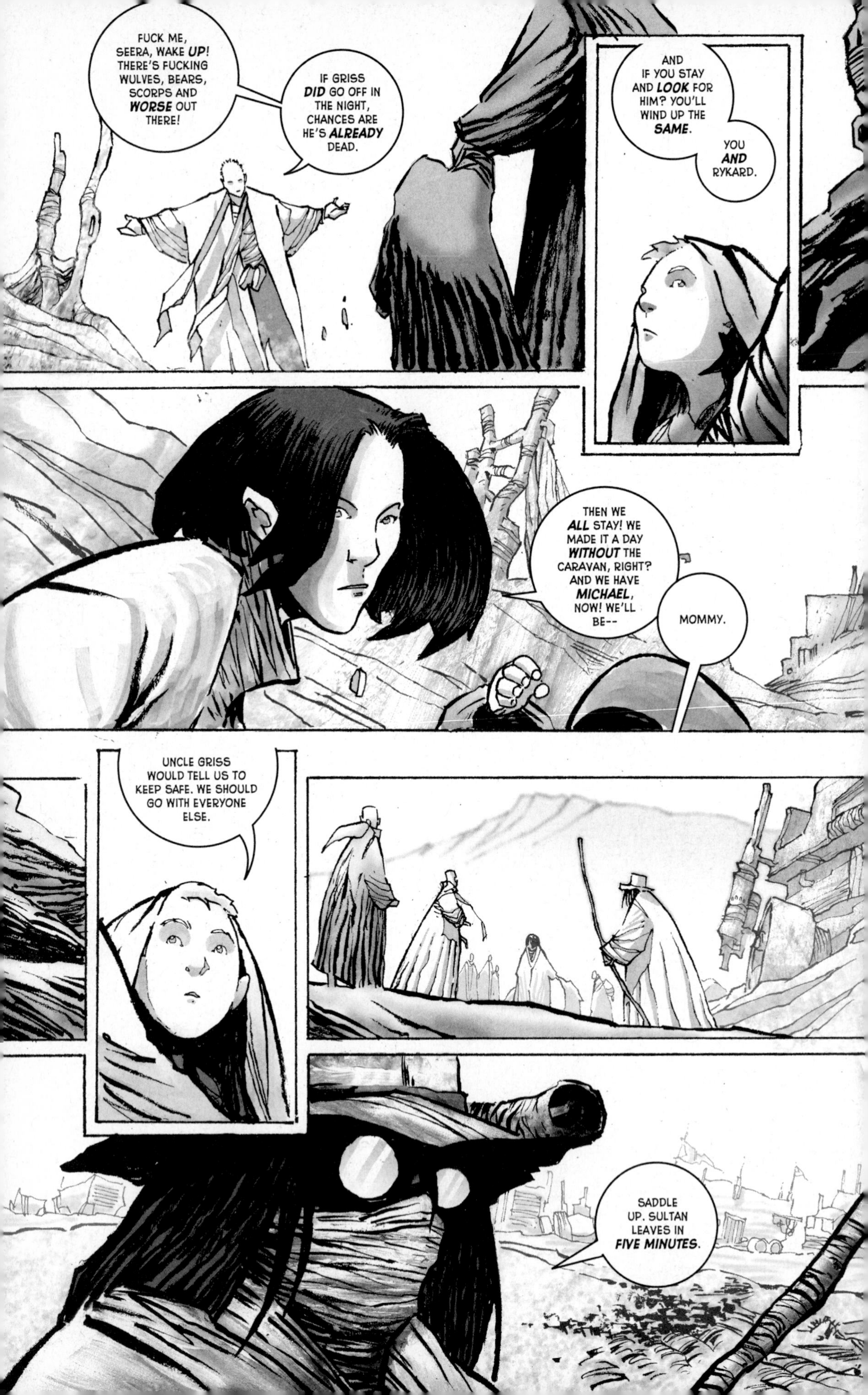
FUCK ME, SEERA, WAKE UP! THERE'S FUCKING WULVES, BEARS, SCORPS AND WORSE OUT THERE!
IF GRISS DID GO OFF IN THE NIGHT, CHANCES ARE HE'S ALREADY DEAD.
AND IF YOU STAY AND LOOK FOR HIM? YOU'LL WIND UP THE SAME.
YOU AND RYKARD.
THEN WE ALL STAY! WE MADE IT A DAY WITHOUT THE CARAVAN, RIGHT? AND WE HAVE MICHAEL, NOW! WE'LL BE--
MOMMY.
UNCLE GRISS WOULD TELL US TO KEEP SAFE. WE SHOULD GO WITH EVERYONE ELSE.
SADDLE UP. SULTAN LEAVES IN FIVE MINUTES.

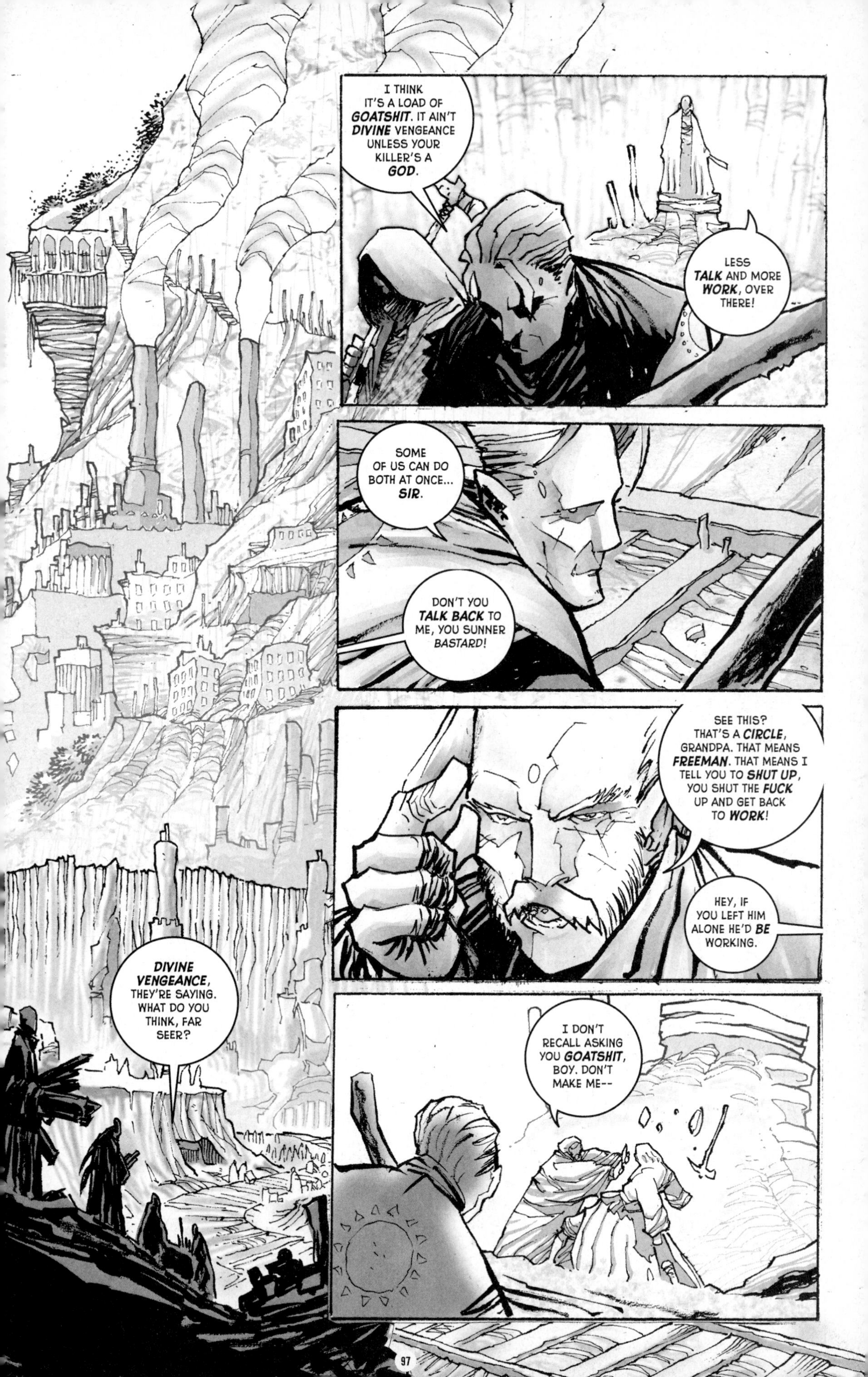
DIVINE VENGEANCE, THEY'RE SAYING. WHAT DO YOU THINK, FAR SEER?
I THINK IT'S A LOAD OF GOATSHIT. IT AIN'T DIVINE VENGEANCE UNLESS YOUR KILLER'S A GOD.
LESS TALK AND MORE WORK, OVER THERE!
SOME OF US CAN DO BOTH AT ONCE... SIR.
DON'T YOU TALK BACK TO ME, YOU SUNNER BASTARD!
SEE THIS? THAT'S A CIRCLE, GRANDPA. THAT MEANS FREEMAN. THAT MEANS I TELL YOU TO SHUT UP, YOU SHUT THE FUCK UP AND GET BACK TO WORK!
HEY, IF YOU LEFT HIM ALONE HE'D BE WORKING.
I DON'T RECALL ASKING YOU GOATSHIT, BOY. DON'T MAKE ME--

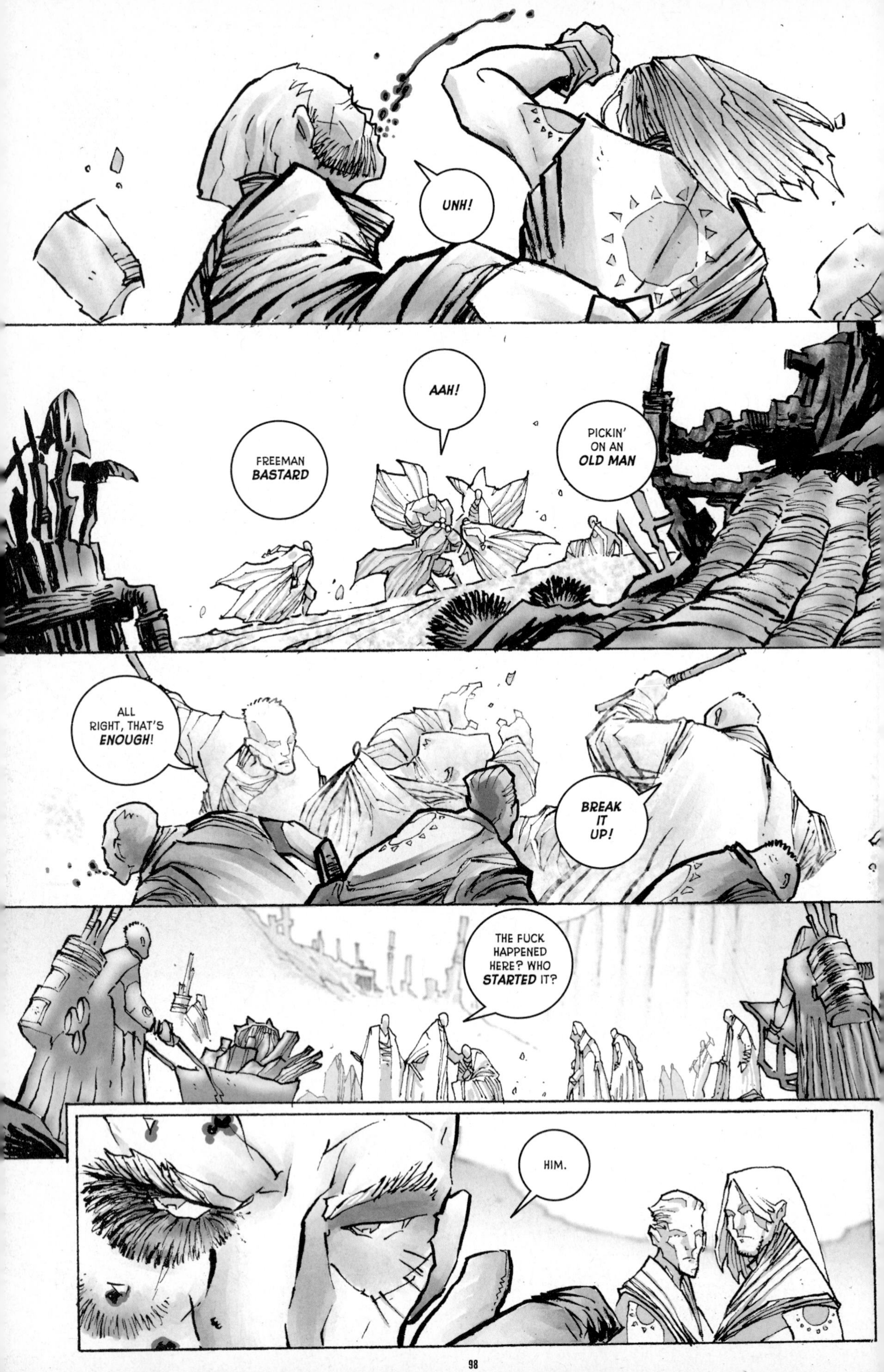
UNH!
FREEMAN BASTARD
AAH!
PICKIN' ON AN OLD MAN
ALL RIGHT, THAT'S ENOUGH!
BREAK IT UP!
THE FUCK HAPPENED HERE? WHO STARTED IT?
HIM.

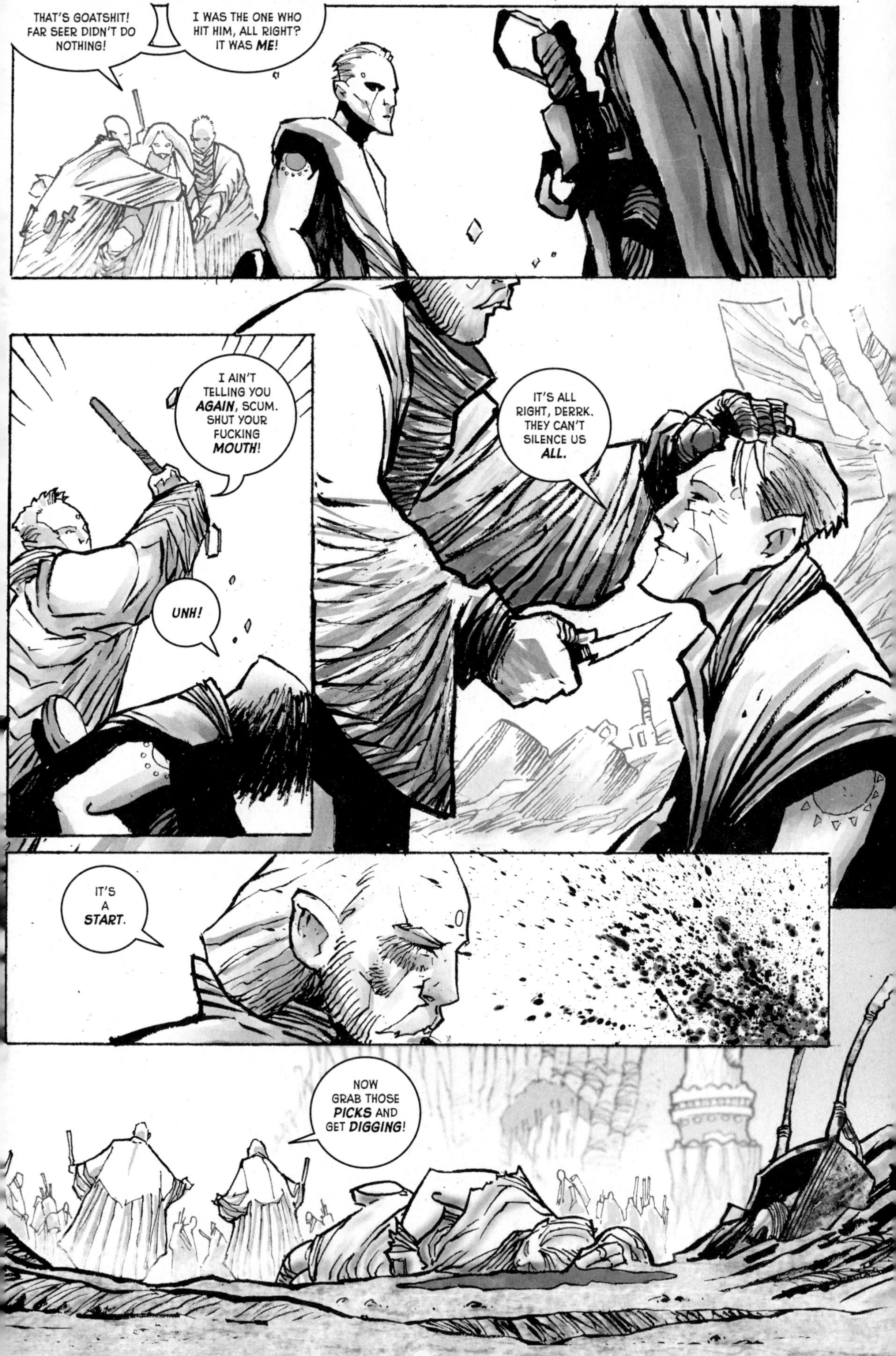
THAT'S GOATSHIT! FAR SEER DIDN'T DO NOTHING!
I WAS THE ONE WHO HIT HIM, ALL RIGHT? IT WAS ME!
I AIN'T TELLING YOU AGAIN, SCUM. SHUT YOUR FUCKING MOUTH!
UNH!
IT'S ALL RIGHT, DERRK. THEY CAN'T SILENCE US ALL.
IT'S A START.
NOW GRAB THOSE PICKS AND GET DIGGING!

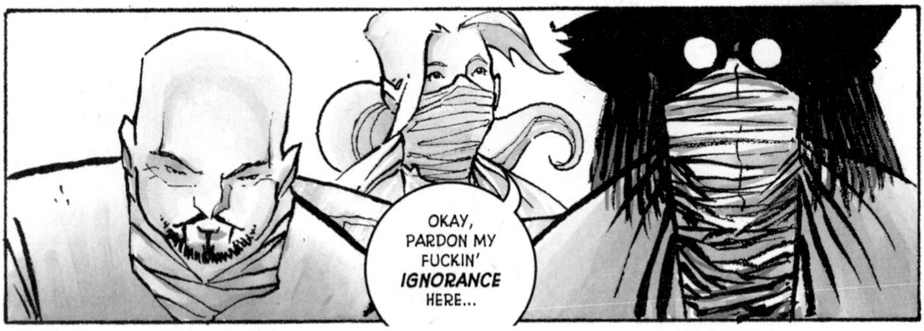
OKAY, PARDON MY FUCKIN' IGNORANCE HERE...
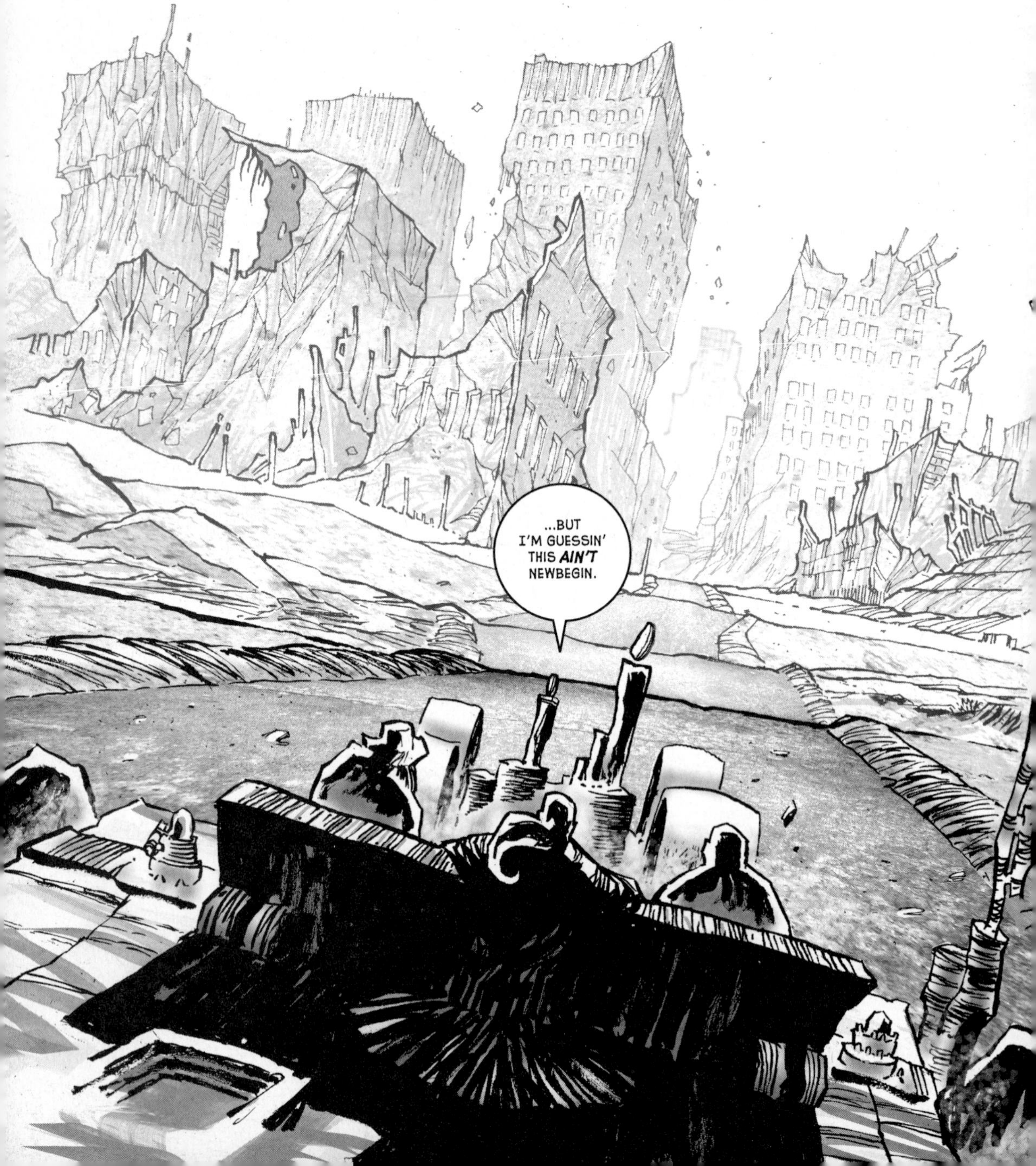
...BUT I'M GUESSIN' THIS AIN'T NEWBEGIN.

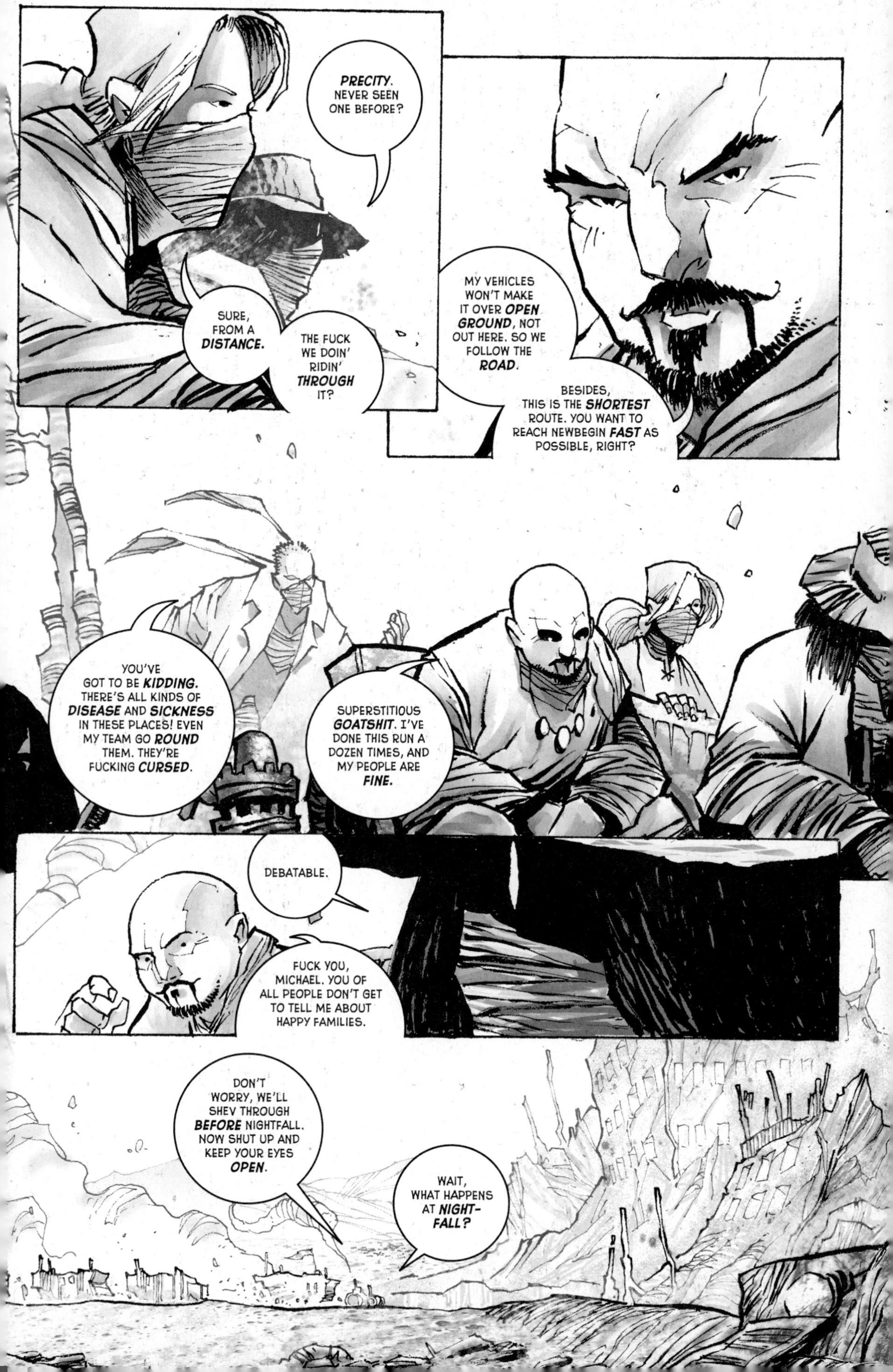
PRECITY. NEVER SEEN ONE BEFORE?
SURE, FROM A DISTANCE.
THE FUCK WE DOIN' RIDIN' THROUGH IT?
MY VEHICLES WON'T MAKE IT OVER OPEN GROUND, NOT OUT HERE. SO WE FOLLOW THE ROAD.
BESIDES, THIS IS THE SHORTEST ROUTE. YOU WANT TO REACH NEWBEGIN FAST AS POSSIBLE, RIGHT?
YOU'VE GOT TO BE KIDDING. THERE'S ALL KINDS OF DISEASE AND SICKNESS IN THESE PLACES! EVEN MY TEAM GO ROUND THEM. THEY'RE FUCKING CURSED.
SUPERSTITIOUS GOATSHIT. I'VE DONE THIS RUN A DOZEN TIMES, AND MY PEOPLE ARE FINE.
DEBATABLE.
FUCK YOU, MICHAEL. YOU OF ALL PEOPLE DON'T GET TO TELL ME ABOUT HAPPY FAMILIES.
DON'T WORRY, WE'LL SHEV THROUGH BEFORE NIGHTFALL. NOW SHUT UP AND KEEP YOUR EYES OPEN.
WAIT, WHAT HAPPENS AT NIGHT-FALL?

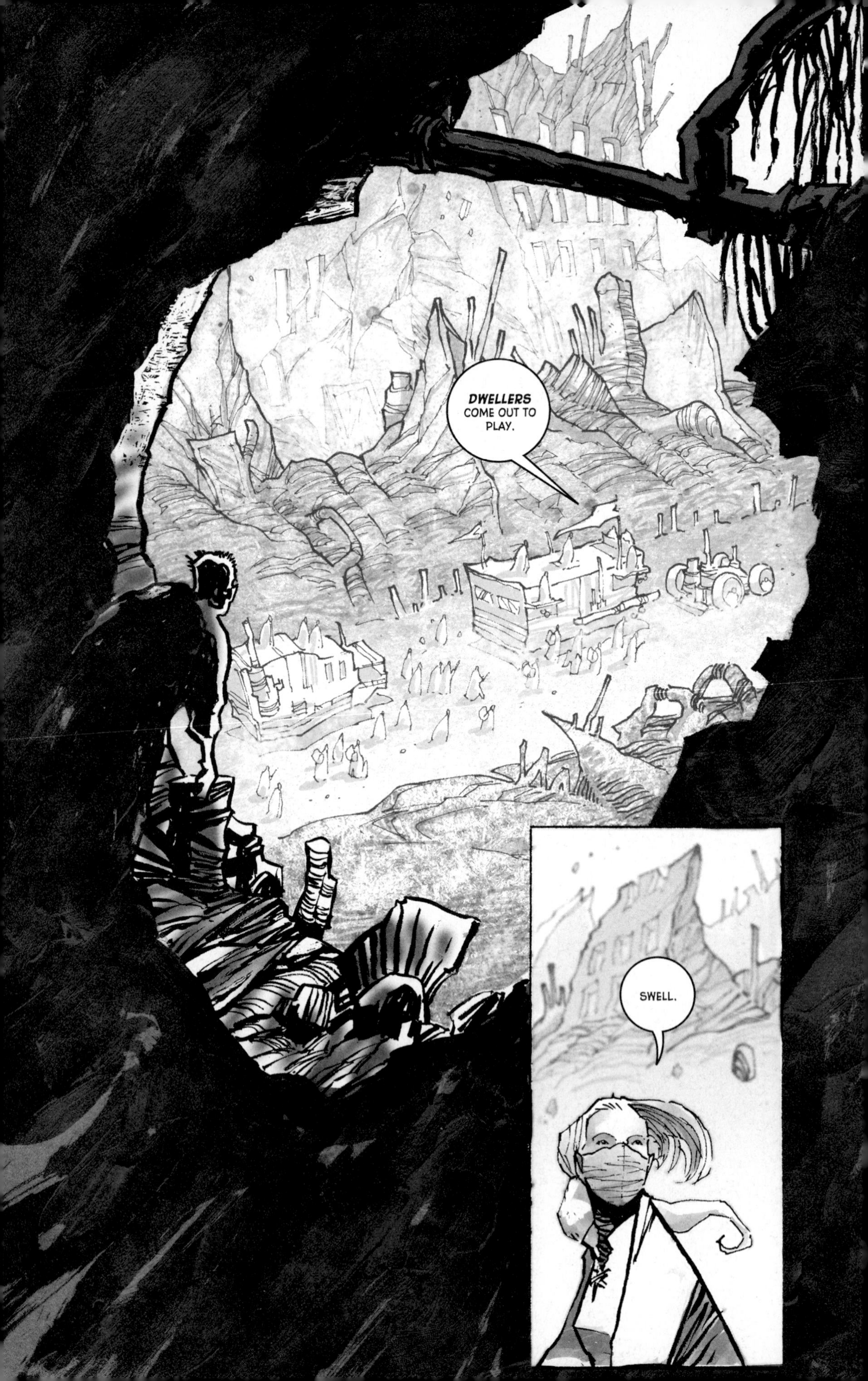
DWELLERS COME OUT TO PLAY.
SWELL.

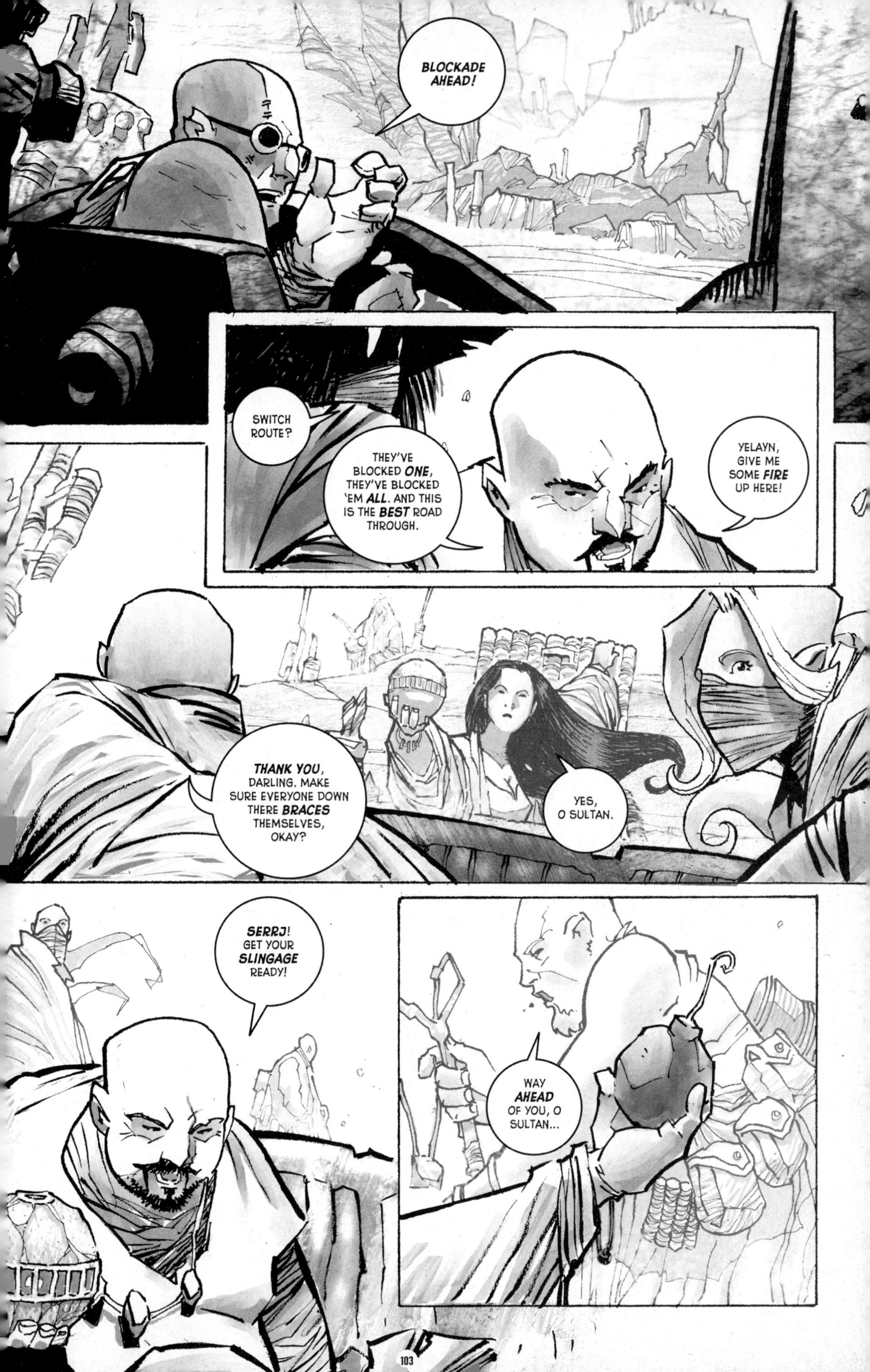

BLOCKADE AHEAD!
SWITCH ROUTE?
THEY'VE BLOCKED ONE, THEY'VE BLOCKED 'EM ALL. AND THIS IS THE BEST ROAD THROUGH.
YELAYN, GIVE ME SOME FIRE UP HERE!
THANK YOU, DARLING. MAKE SURE EVERYONE DOWN THERE BRACES THEMSELVES, OKAY?
YES, O SULTAN.
SERRJ! GET YOUR SLINGAGE READY!
WAY AHEAD OF YOU, O SULTAN...

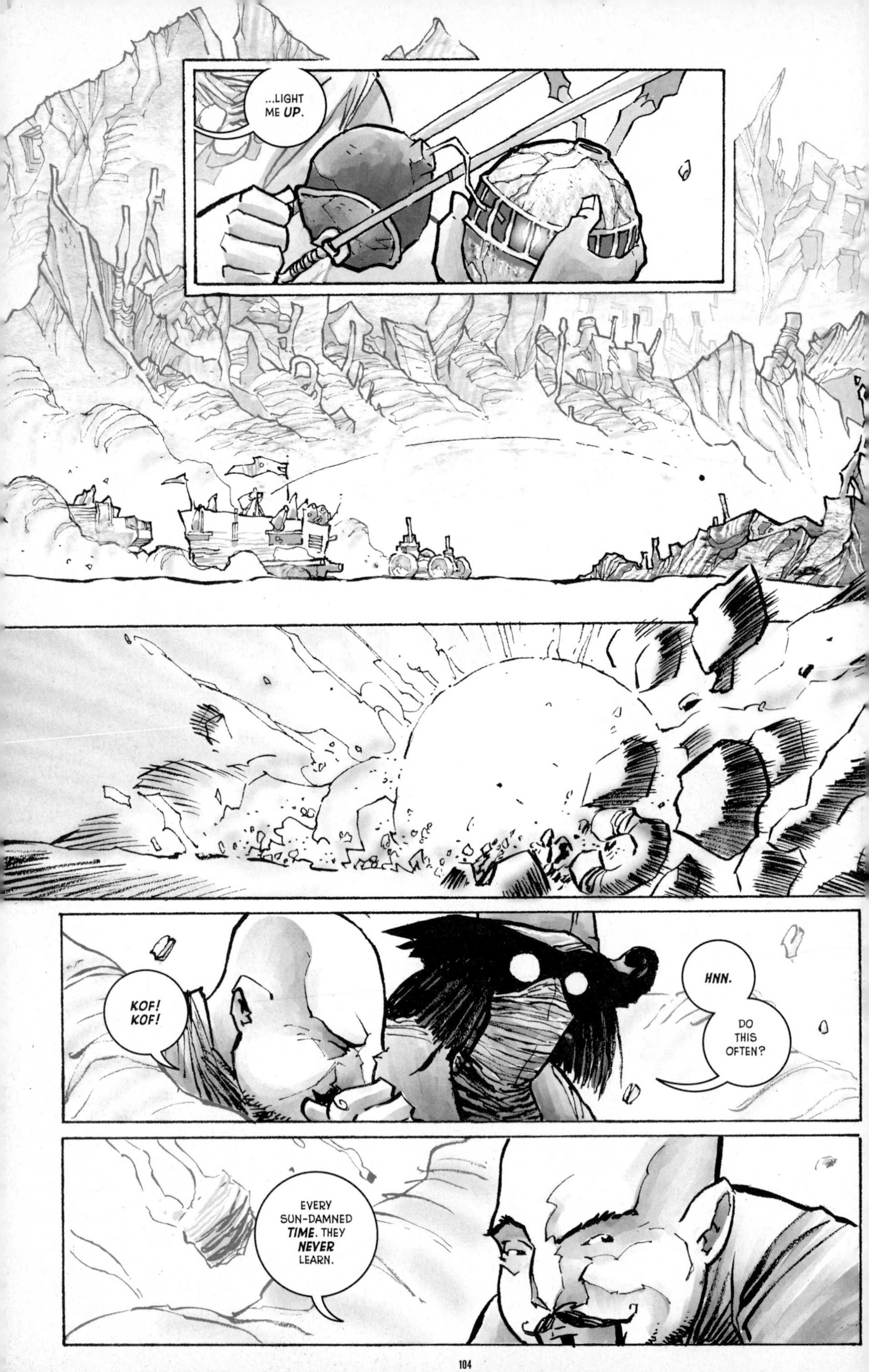
...LIGHT ME UP.
KOF! KOF!
HNN.
DO THIS OFTEN?
EVERY SUN-DAMNED TIME. THEY NEVER LEARN.

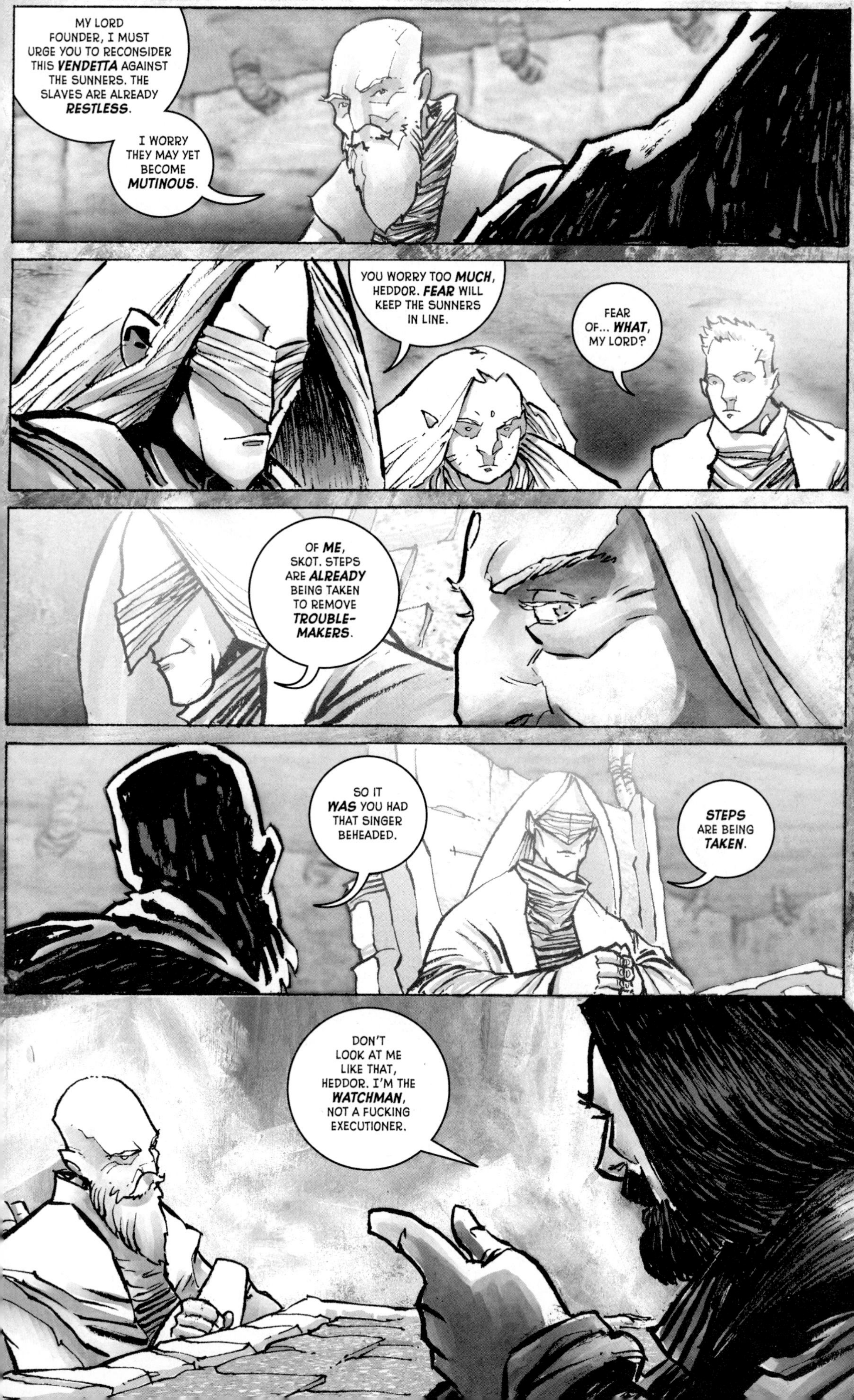
MY LORD FOUNDER, I MUST URGE YOU TO RECONSIDER THIS VENDETTA AGAINST THE SUNNERS. THE SLAVES ARE ALREADY RESTLESS.
I WORRY THEY MAY YET BECOME MUTINOUS.
YOU WORRY TOO MUCH, HEDDOR. FEAR WILL KEEP THE SUNNERS IN LINE.
FEAR OF... WHAT, MY LORD?
OF ME, SKOT. STEPS ARE ALREADY BEING TAKEN TO REMOVE TROUBLE-MAKERS.
SO IT WAS YOU HAD THAT SINGER BEHEADED.
STEPS ARE BEING TAKEN.
DON'T LOOK AT ME LIKE THAT, HEDDOR. I'M THE WATCHMAN, NOT A FUCKING EXECUTIONER.

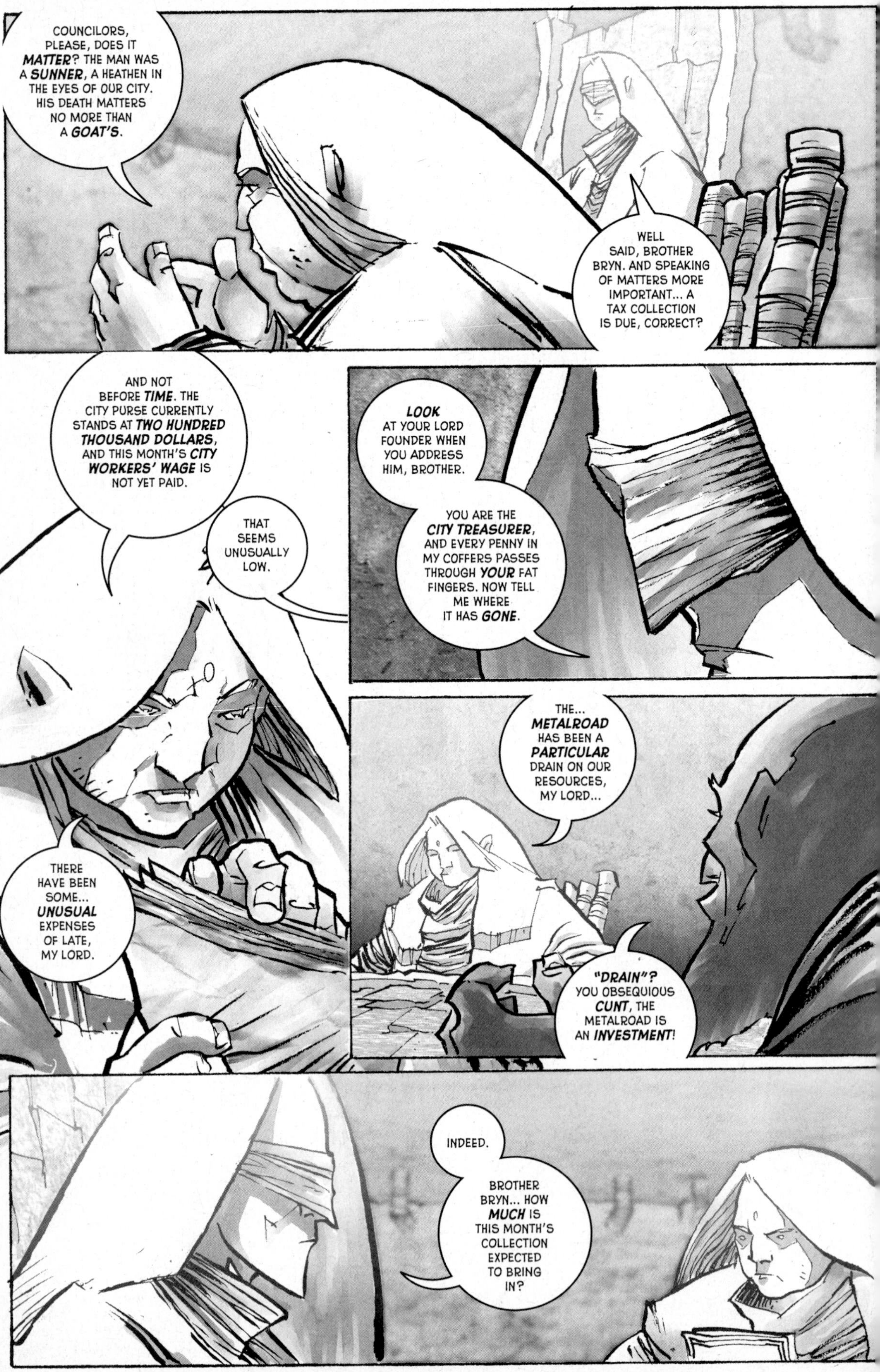
COUNCILORS, PLEASE, DOES IT MATTER? THE MAN WAS A SUNNER, A HEATHEN IN THE EYES OF OUR CITY. HIS DEATH MATTERS NO MORE THAN A GOAT'S.
WELL SAID, BROTHER BRYN. AND SPEAKING OF MATTERS MORE IMPORTANT... A TAX COLLECTION IS DUE, CORRECT?
AND NOT BEFORE TIME. THE CITY PURSE CURRENTLY STANDS AT TWO HUNDRED THOUSAND DOLLARS, AND THIS MONTH'S CITY WORKERS' WAGE IS NOT YET PAID.
THAT SEEMS UNUSUALLY LOW.
LOOK AT YOUR LORD FOUNDER WHEN YOU ADDRESS HIM, BROTHER.
YOU ARE THE CITY TREASURER, AND EVERY PENNY IN MY COFFERS PASSES THROUGH YOUR FAT FINGERS. NOW TELL ME WHERE IT HAS GONE.
THERE HAVE BEEN SOME... UNUSUAL EXPENSES OF LATE, MY LORD.
THE... METALROAD HAS BEEN A PARTICULAR DRAIN ON OUR RESOURCES, MY LORD...
"DRAIN"? YOU OBSEQUIOUS CUNT, THE METALROAD IS AN INVESTMENT!
INDEED.
BROTHER BRYN... HOW MUCH IS THIS MONTH'S COLLECTION EXPECTED TO BRING IN?

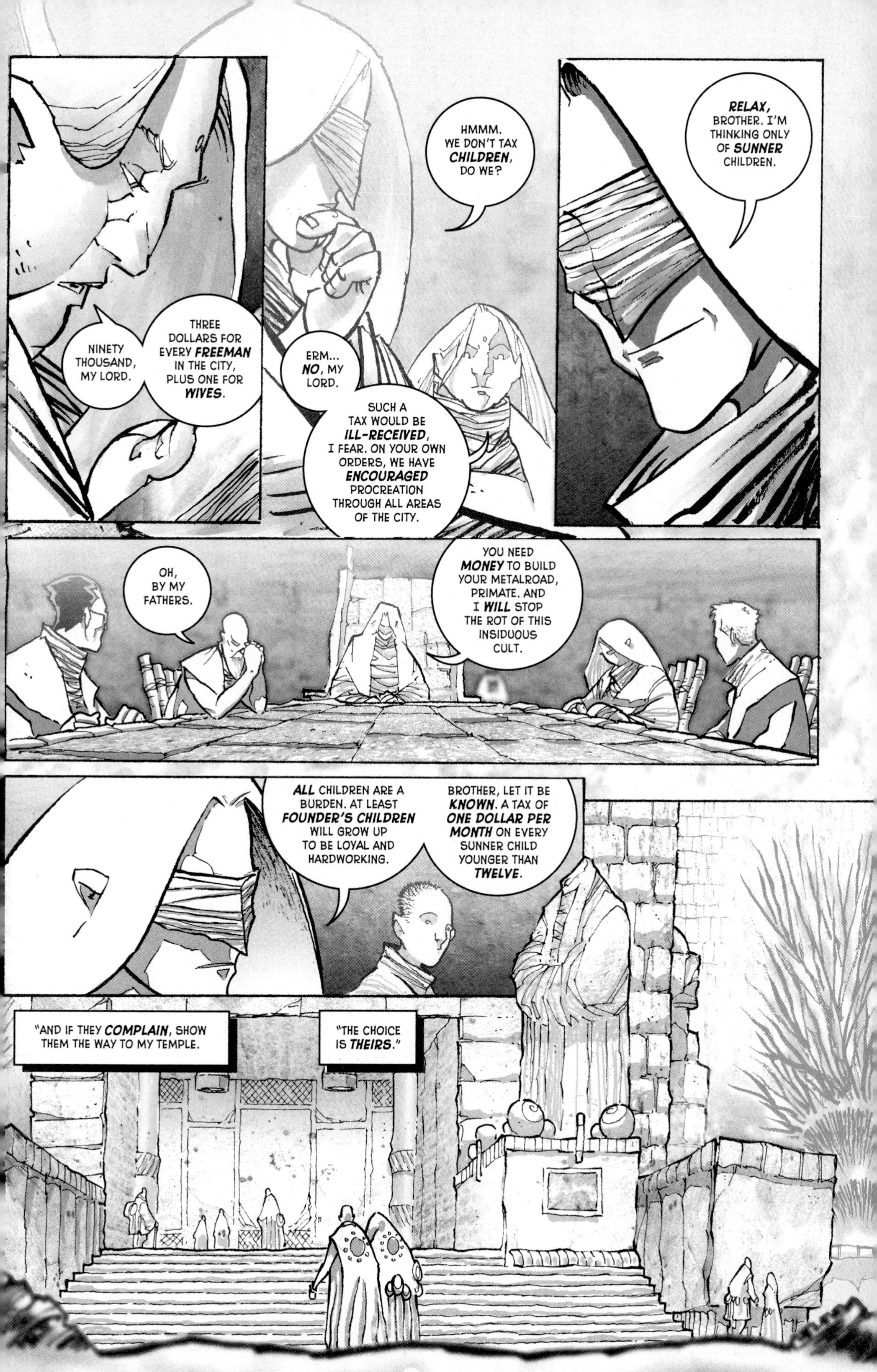
NINETY THOUSAND, MY LORD.
THREE DOLLARS FOR EVERY FREEMAN IN THE CITY, PLUS ONE FOR WIVES.
HMMM. WE DON'T TAX CHILDREN, DO WE?
ERM... NO, MY LORD.
SUCH A TAX WOULD BE ILL-RECEIVED, I FEAR. ON YOUR OWN ORDERS, WE HAVE ENCOURAGED PROCREATION THROUGH ALL AREAS OF THE CITY.
RELAX, BROTHER. I'M THINKING ONLY OF SUNNER CHILDREN.
OH, BY MY FATHERS.
YOU NEED MONEY TO BUILD YOUR METALROAD, PRIMATE. AND I WILL STOP THE ROT OF THIS INSIDUOUS CULT.
ALL CHILDREN ARE A BURDEN. AT LEAST FOUNDER'S CHILDREN WILL GROW UP TO BE LOYAL AND HARDWORKING.
BROTHER, LET IT BE KNOWN. A TAX OF ONE DOLLAR PER MONTH ON EVERY SUNNER CHILD YOUNGER THAN TWELVE.
"AND IF THEY COMPLAIN, SHOW THEM THE WAY TO MY TEMPLE.
"THE CHOICE IS THEIRS."

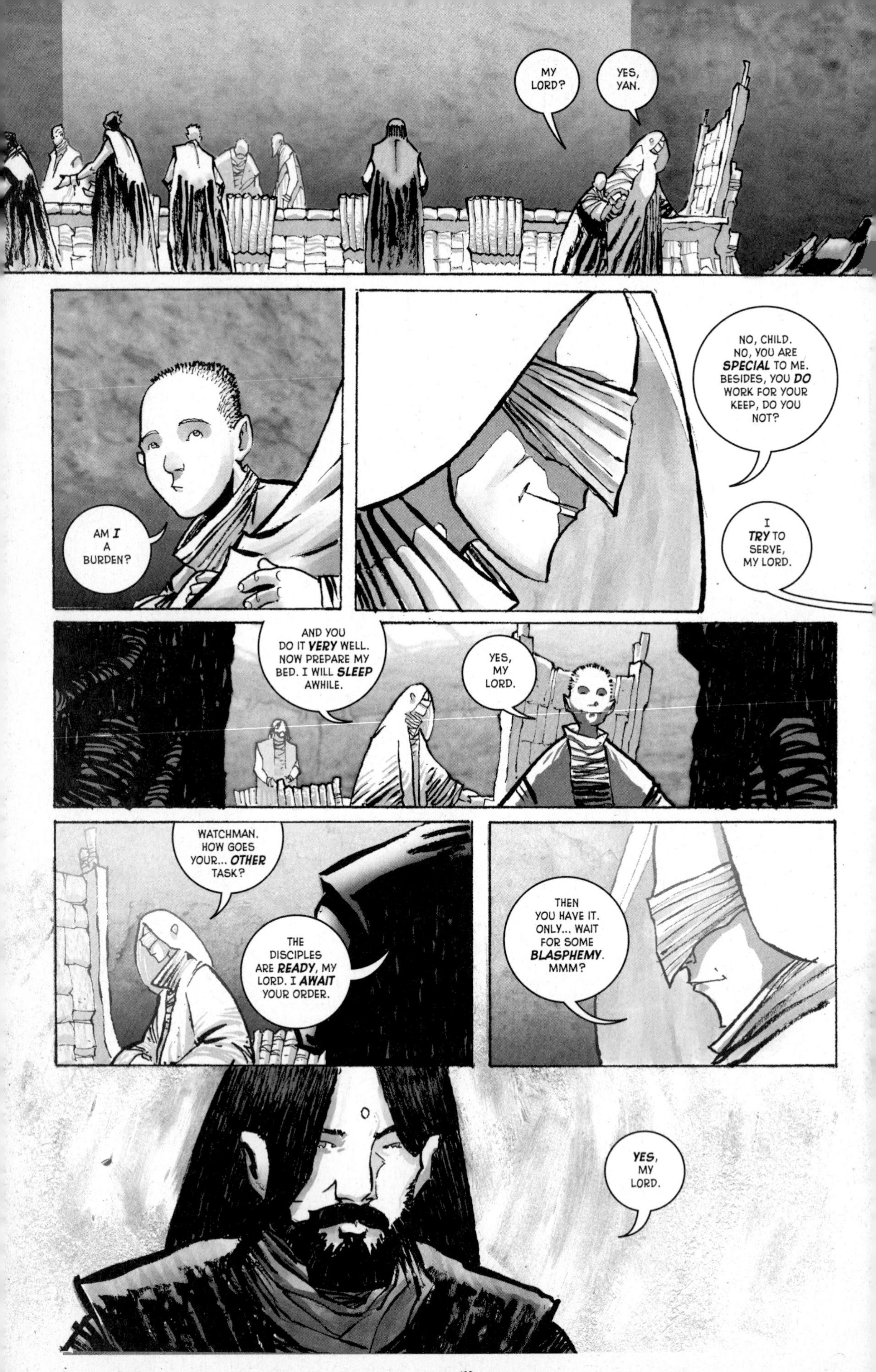
MY LORD?
YES, YAN.
AM I A BURDEN?
NO, CHILD. NO, YOU ARE SPECIAL TO ME. BESIDES, YOU DO WORK FOR YOUR KEEP, DO YOU NOT?
I TRY TO SERVE, MY LORD.
AND YOU DO IT VERY WELL. NOW PREPARE MY BED. I WILL SLEEP AWHILE.
YES, MY LORD.
WATCHMAN. HOW GOES YOUR... OTHER TASK?
THE DISCIPLES ARE READY, MY LORD. I AWAIT YOUR ORDER.
THEN YOU HAVE IT. ONLY... WAIT FOR SOME BLASPHEMY. MMM?
YES, MY LORD.

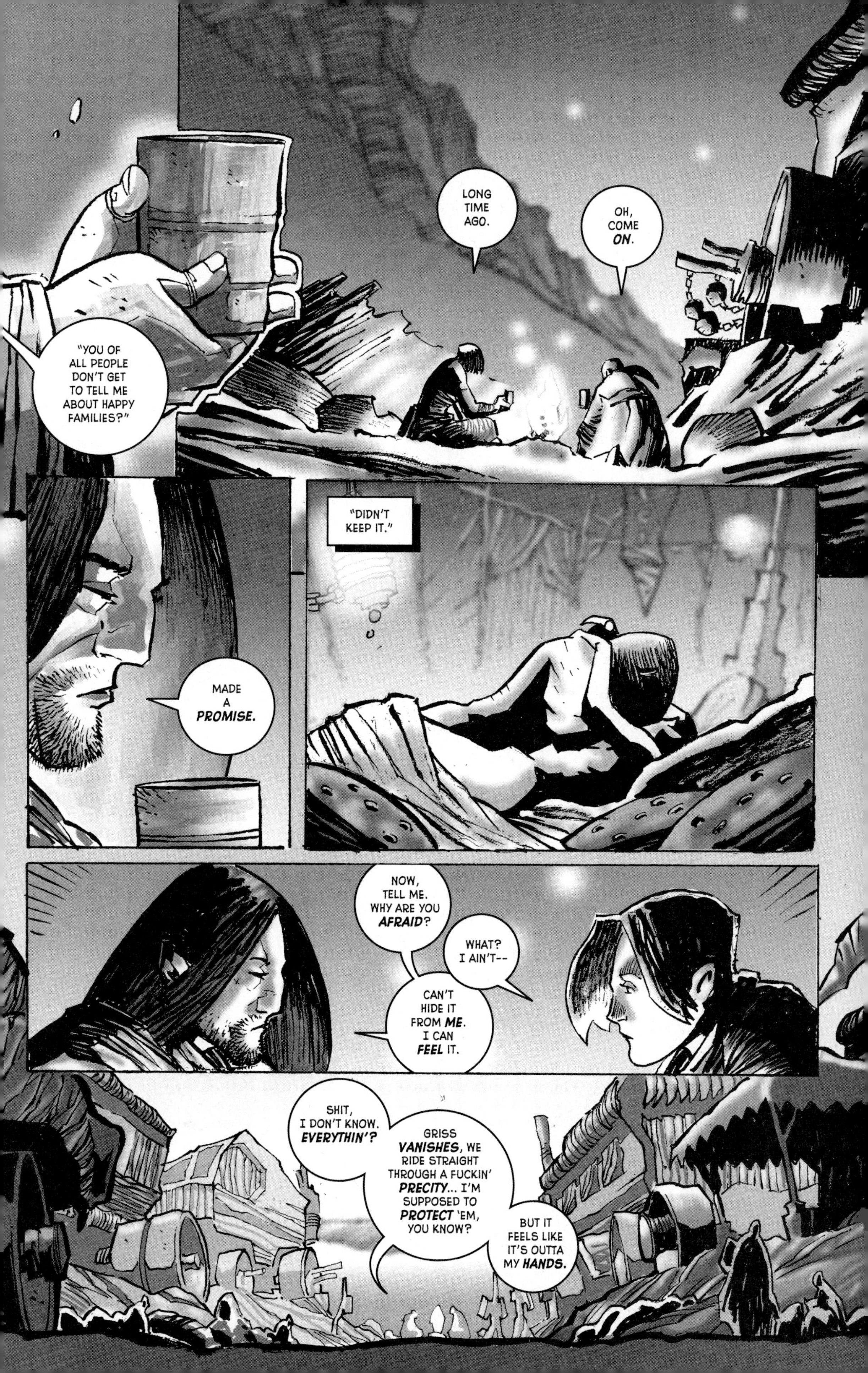

LONG TIME AGO.
OH, COME ON.
"YOU OF ALL PEOPLE DON'T GET TO TELL ME ABOUT HAPPY FAMILIES?"
MADE A PROMISE.
"DIDN'T KEEP IT."
NOW, TELL ME. WHY ARE YOU AFRAID?
WHAT? I AIN'T--
CAN'T HIDE IT FROM ME. I CAN FEEL IT.
SHIT, I DON'T KNOW. EVERYTHIN'?
GRISS VANISHES, WE RIDE STRAIGHT THROUGH A FUCKIN' PRECITY... I'M SUPPOSED TO PROTECT 'EM, YOU KNOW?
BUT IT FEELS LIKE IT'S OUTTA MY HANDS.

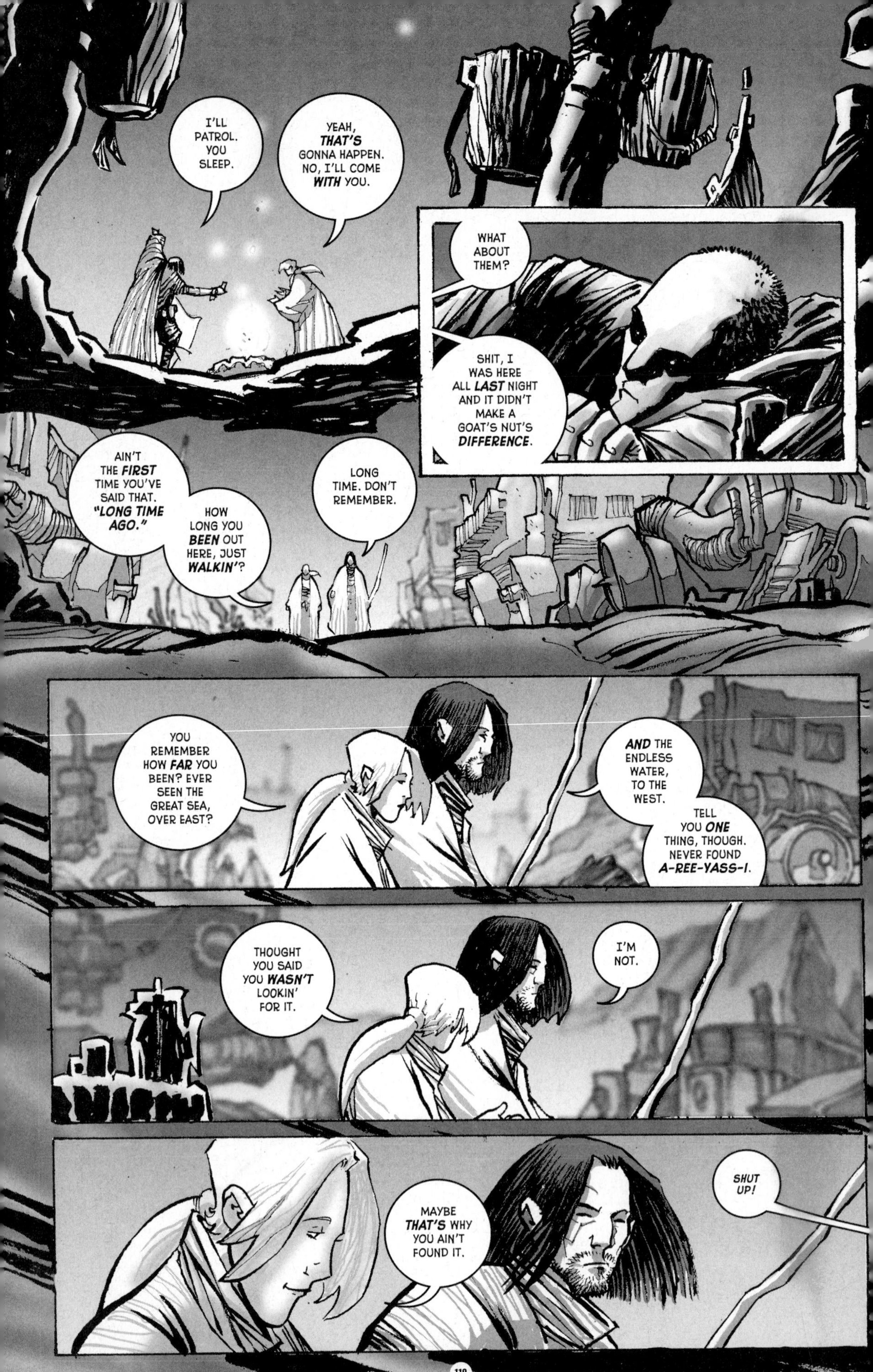
I'LL PATROL. YOU SLEEP.
YEAH, THAT'S GONNA HAPPEN. NO, I'LL COME WITH YOU.
WHAT ABOUT THEM?
SHIT, I WAS HERE ALL LAST NIGHT AND IT DIDN'T MAKE A GOAT'S NUT'S DIFFERENCE.
HOW LONG YOU BEEN OUT HERE, JUST WALKIN'?
LONG TIME. DON'T REMEMBER.
AIN'T THE FIRST TIME YOU'VE SAID THAT. "LONG TIME AGO."
YOU REMEMBER HOW FAR YOU BEEN? EVER SEEN THE GREAT SEA, OVER EAST?
AND THE ENDLESS WATER, TO THE WEST.
TELL YOU ONE THING, THOUGH. NEVER FOUND A-REE-YASS-I.
THOUGHT YOU SAID YOU WASN'T LOOKIN' FOR IT.
I'M NOT.
MAYBE THAT'S WHY YOU AIN'T FOUND IT.
SHUT UP!

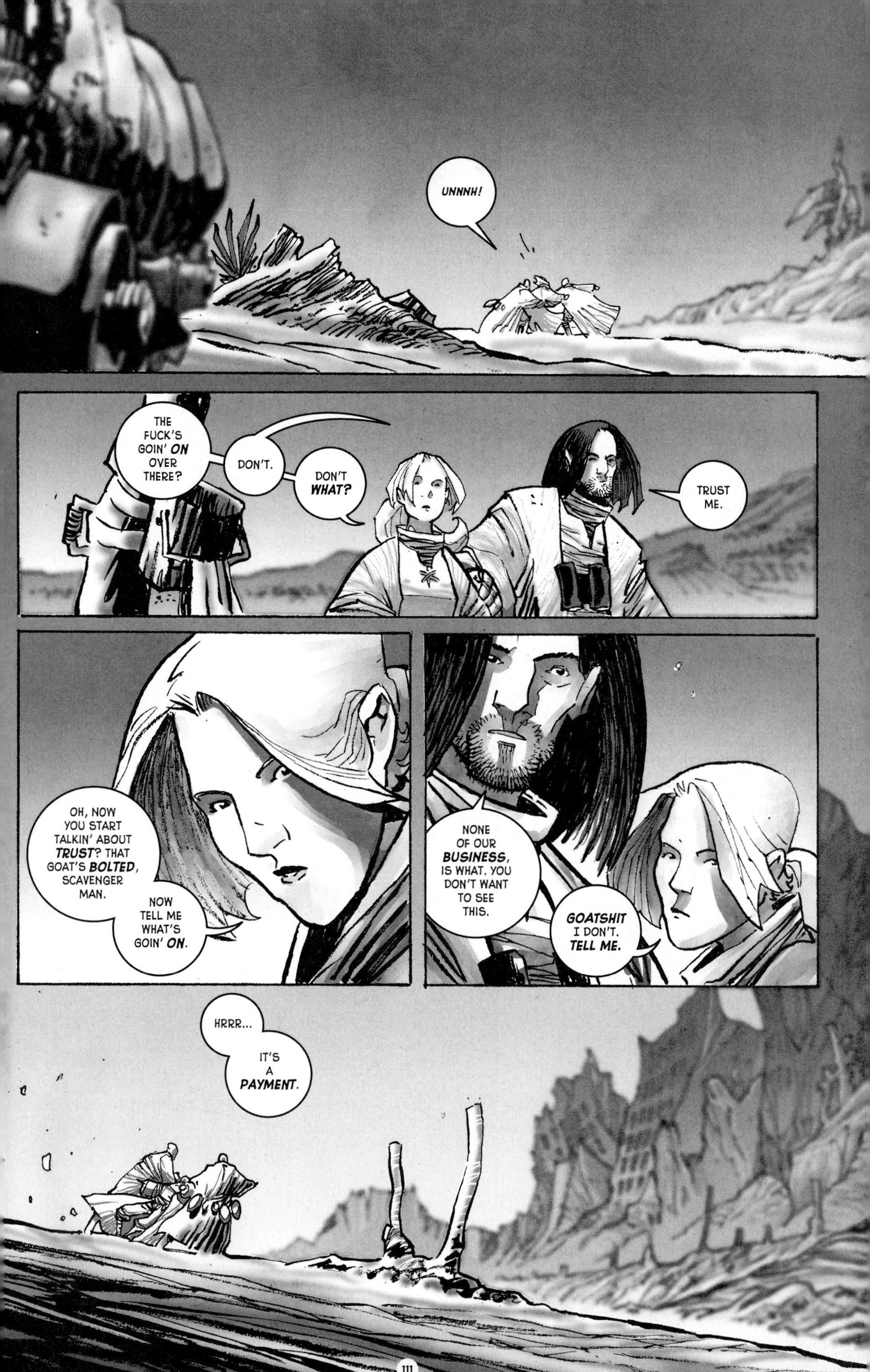
UNNNH!
THE FUCK'S GOIN' ON OVER THERE?
DON'T.
DON'T WHAT?
TRUST ME.
OH, NOW YOU START TALKIN' ABOUT TRUST? THAT GOAT'S BOLTED, SCAVENGER MAN.
NOW TELL ME WHAT'S GOIN' ON.
NONE OF OUR BUSINESS, IS WHAT. YOU DON'T WANT TO SEE THIS.
GOATSHIT I DON'T. TELL ME.
HRRR...
IT'S A PAYMENT.

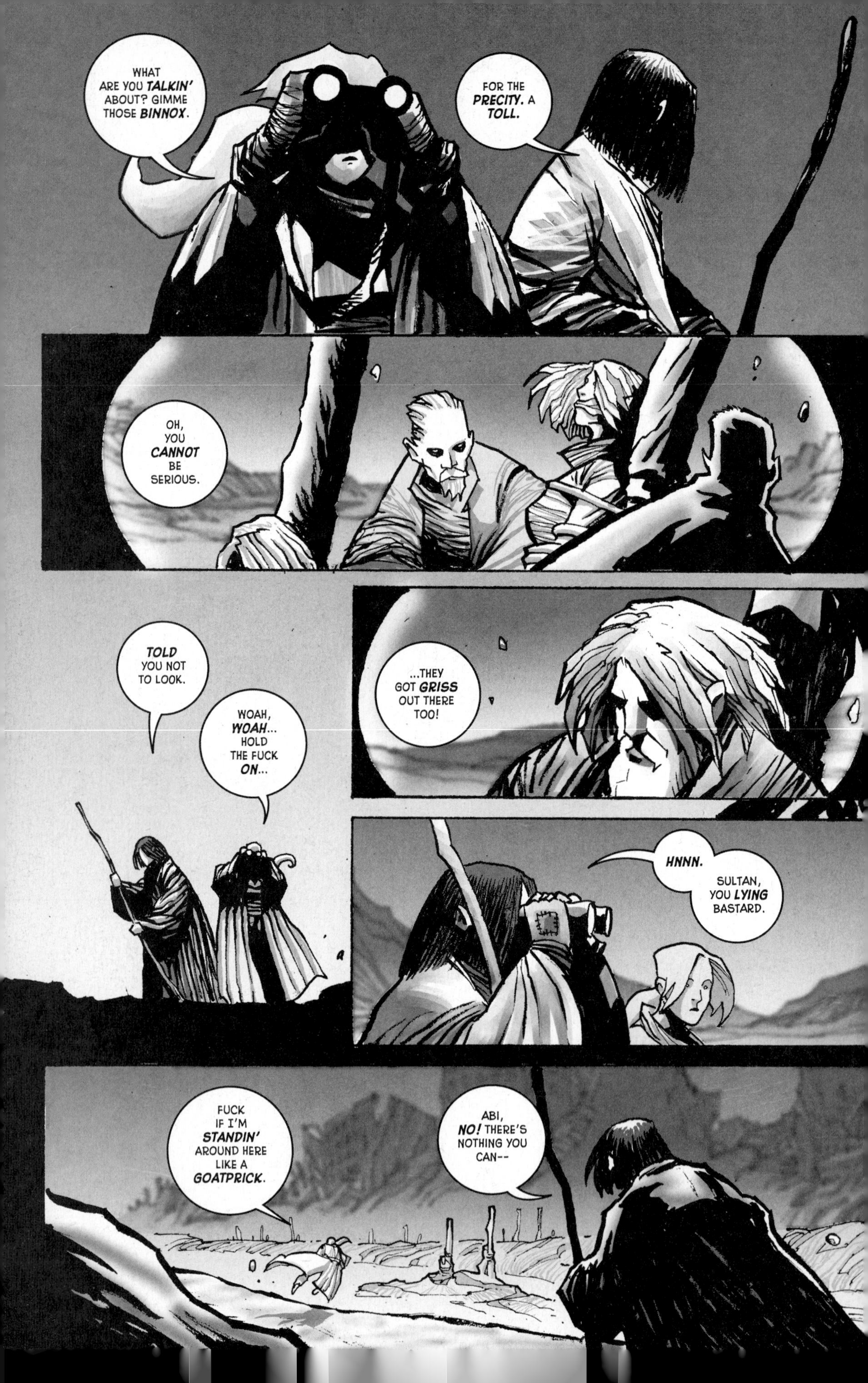
WHAT ARE YOU TALKIN' ABOUT? GIMME THOSE BINNOX.
FOR THE PRECITY. A TOLL.
OH, YOU CANNOT BE SERIOUS.
TOLD YOU NOT TO LOOK.
WOAH, WOAH... HOLD THE FUCK ON...
...THEY GOT GRISS OUT THERE TOO!
HNNN.
SULTAN, YOU LYING BASTARD.
FUCK IF I'M STANDIN' AROUND HERE LIKE A GOATPRICK.
ABI, NO! THERE'S NOTHING YOU CAN--

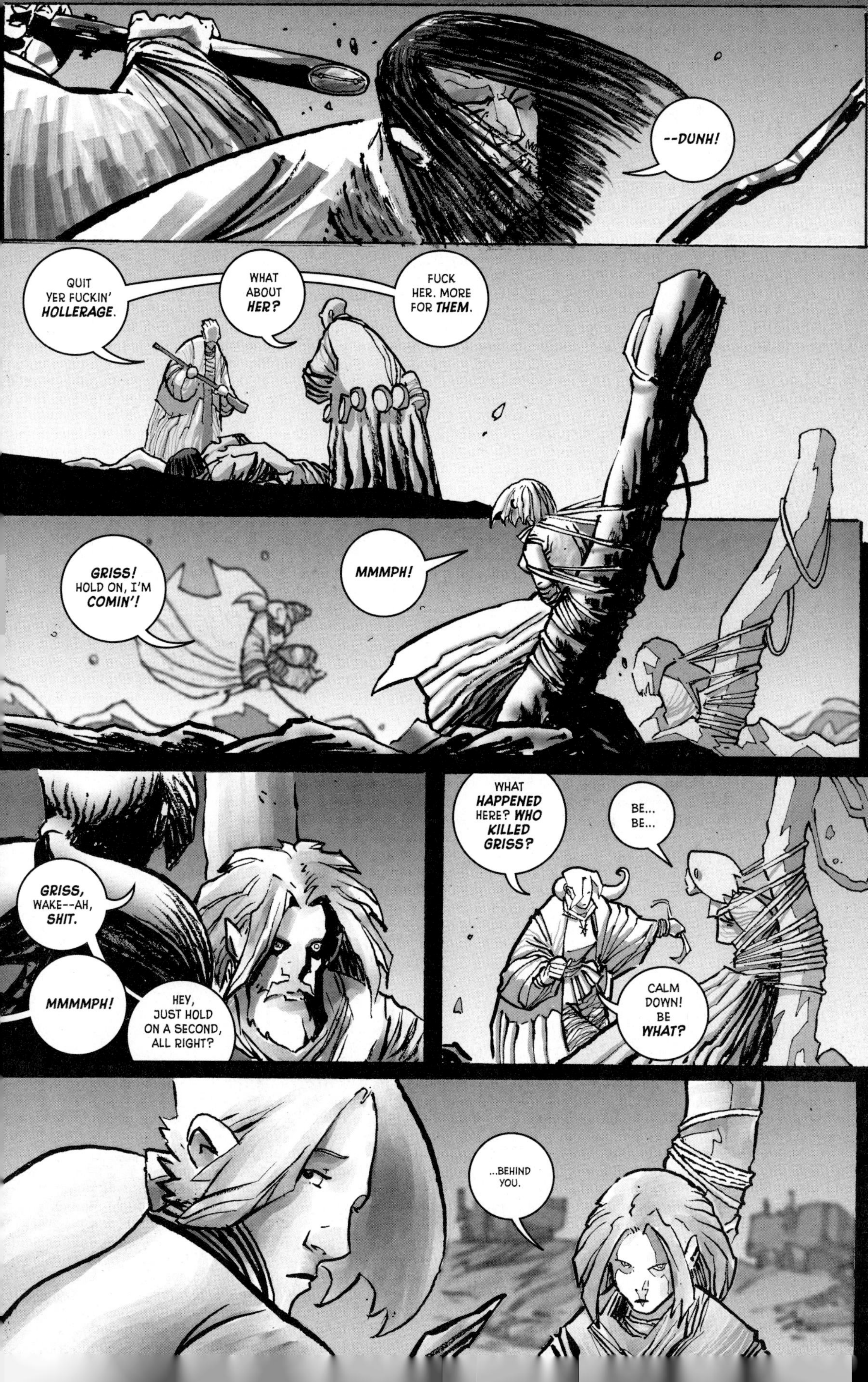
--DUNH!
QUIT YER FUCKIN' HOLLERAGE.
WHAT ABOUT HER?
FUCK HER. MORE FOR THEM.
GRISS! HOLD ON, I'M COMIN'!
MMMPH!
GRISS, WAKE--AH, SHIT.
MMMMPH!
HEY, JUST HOLD ON A SECOND, ALL RIGHT?
WHAT HAPPENED HERE? WHO KILLED GRISS?
BE... BE...
CALM DOWN! BE WHAT?
...BEHIND YOU.

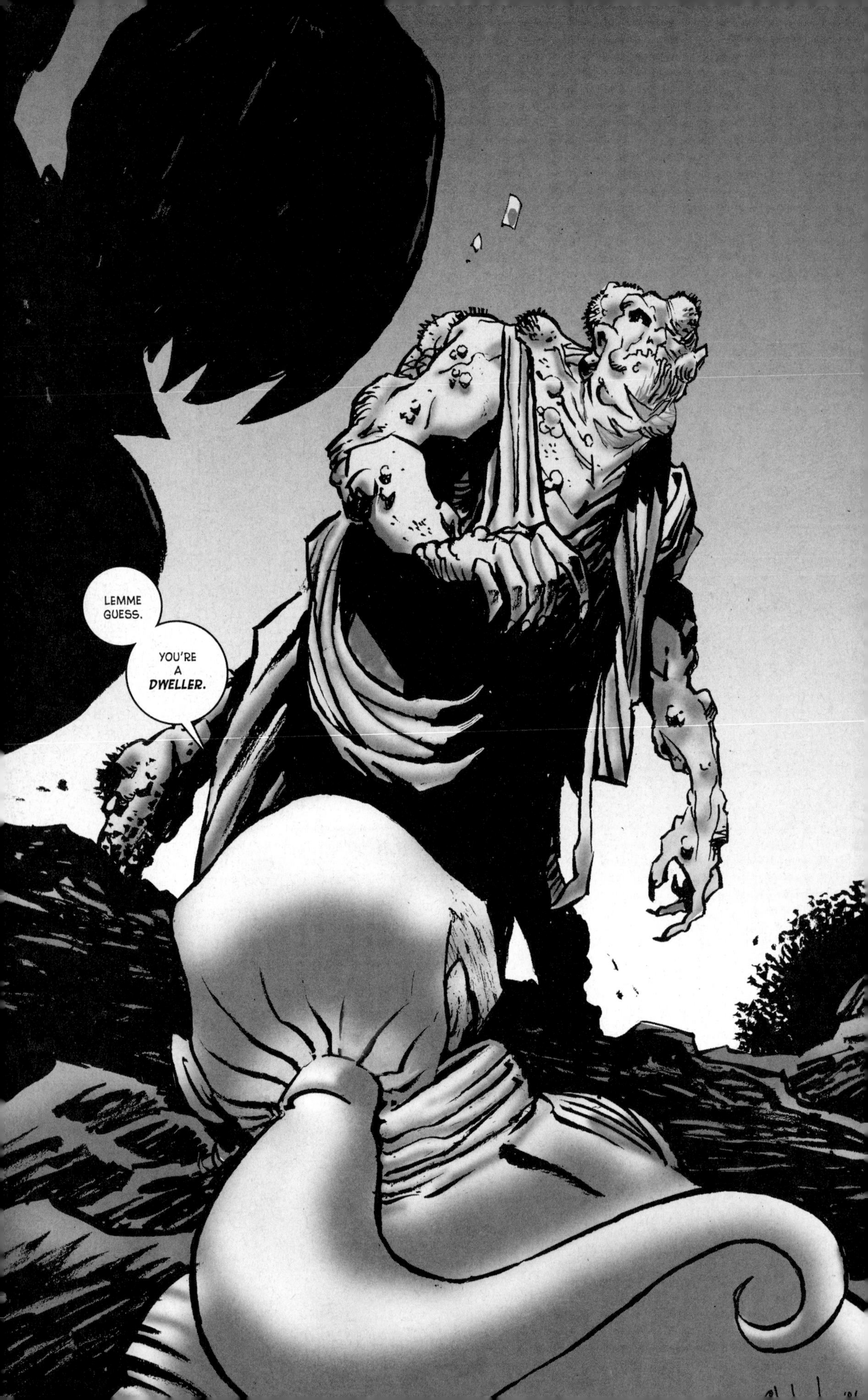
LEMME GUESS.
YOU'RE A DWELLER.

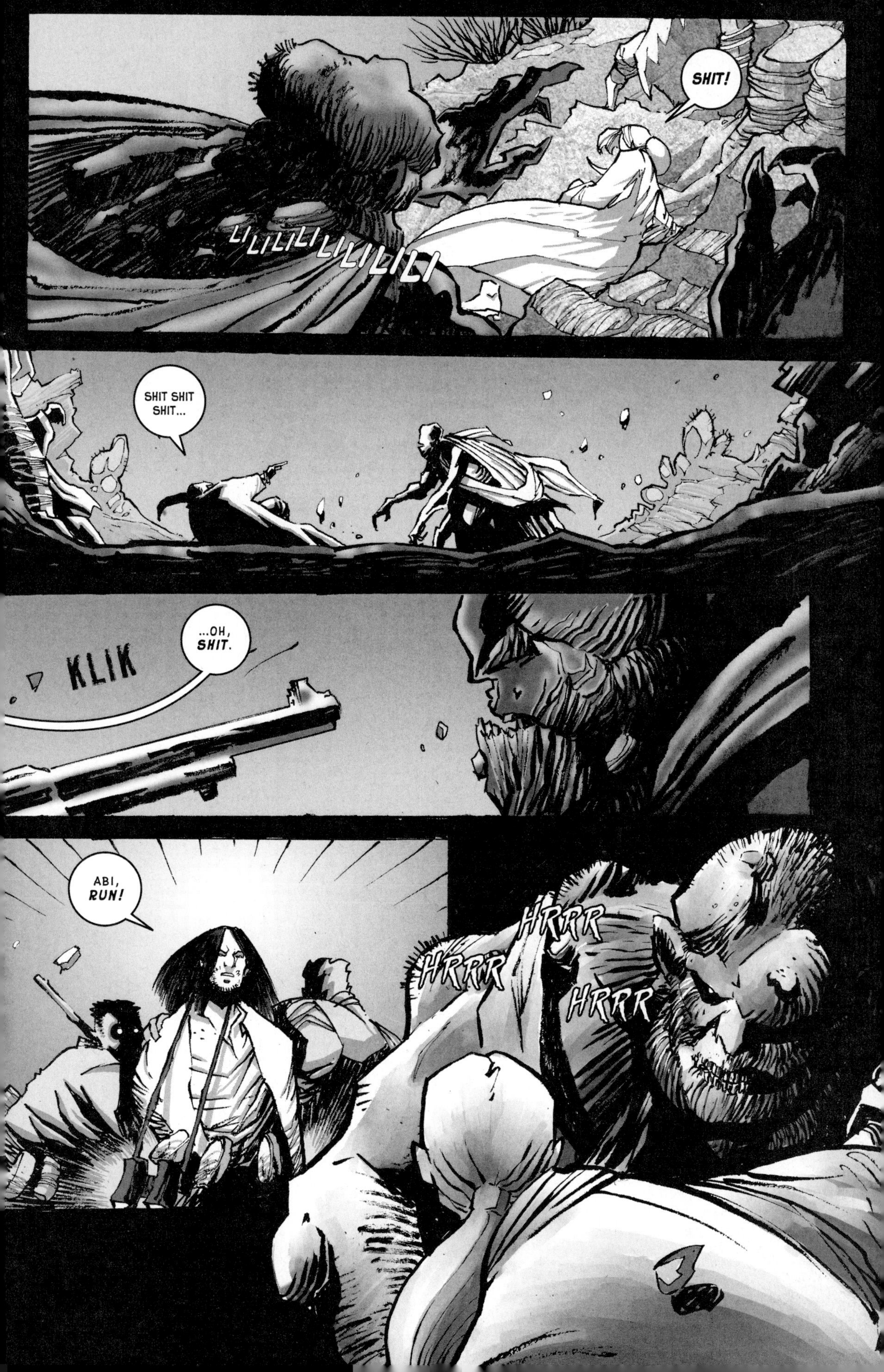
SHIT!
LILILILILILILILI
SHIT SHIT SHIT...
KLIK
...OH, SHIT.
ABI, RUN!
HRRR
HRRR
HRRR

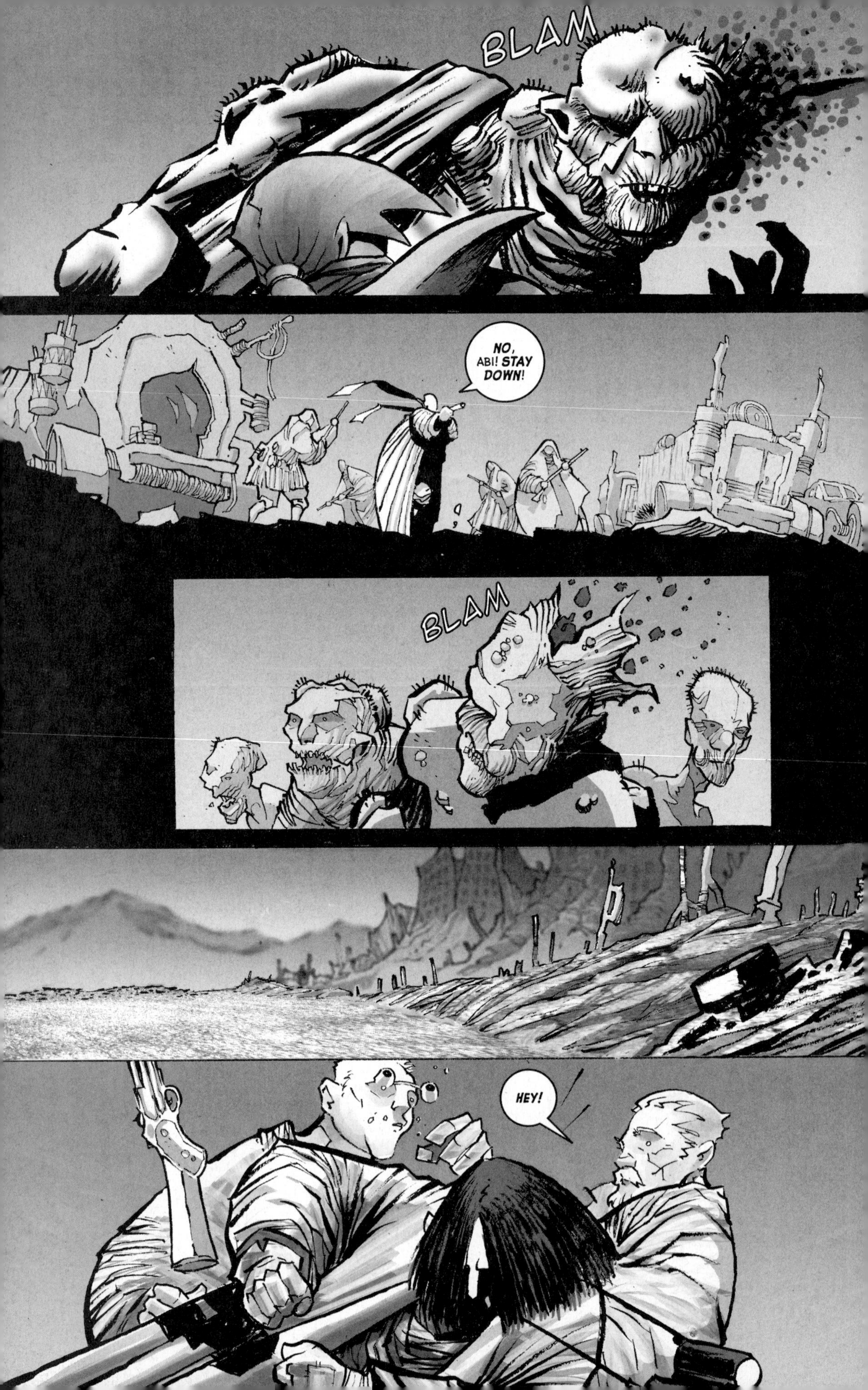
BLAM
NO, ABI! STAY DOWN!
BLAM
HEY!

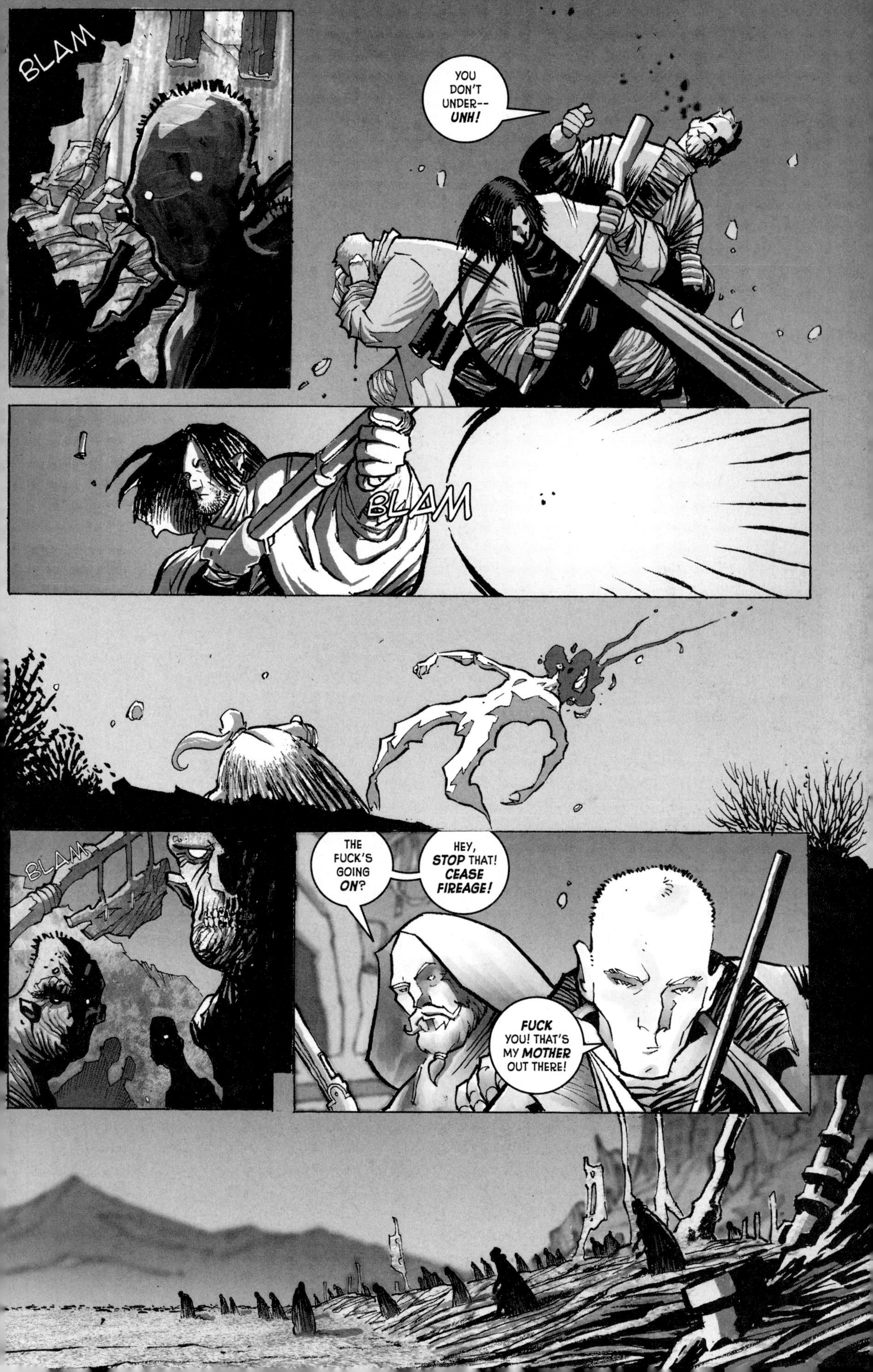
BLAM
YOU DON'T UNDER-- UNH!
BLAM
BLAM
THE FUCK'S GOING ON?
HEY, STOP THAT! CEASE FIREAGE!
FUCK YOU! THAT'S MY MOTHER OUT THERE!

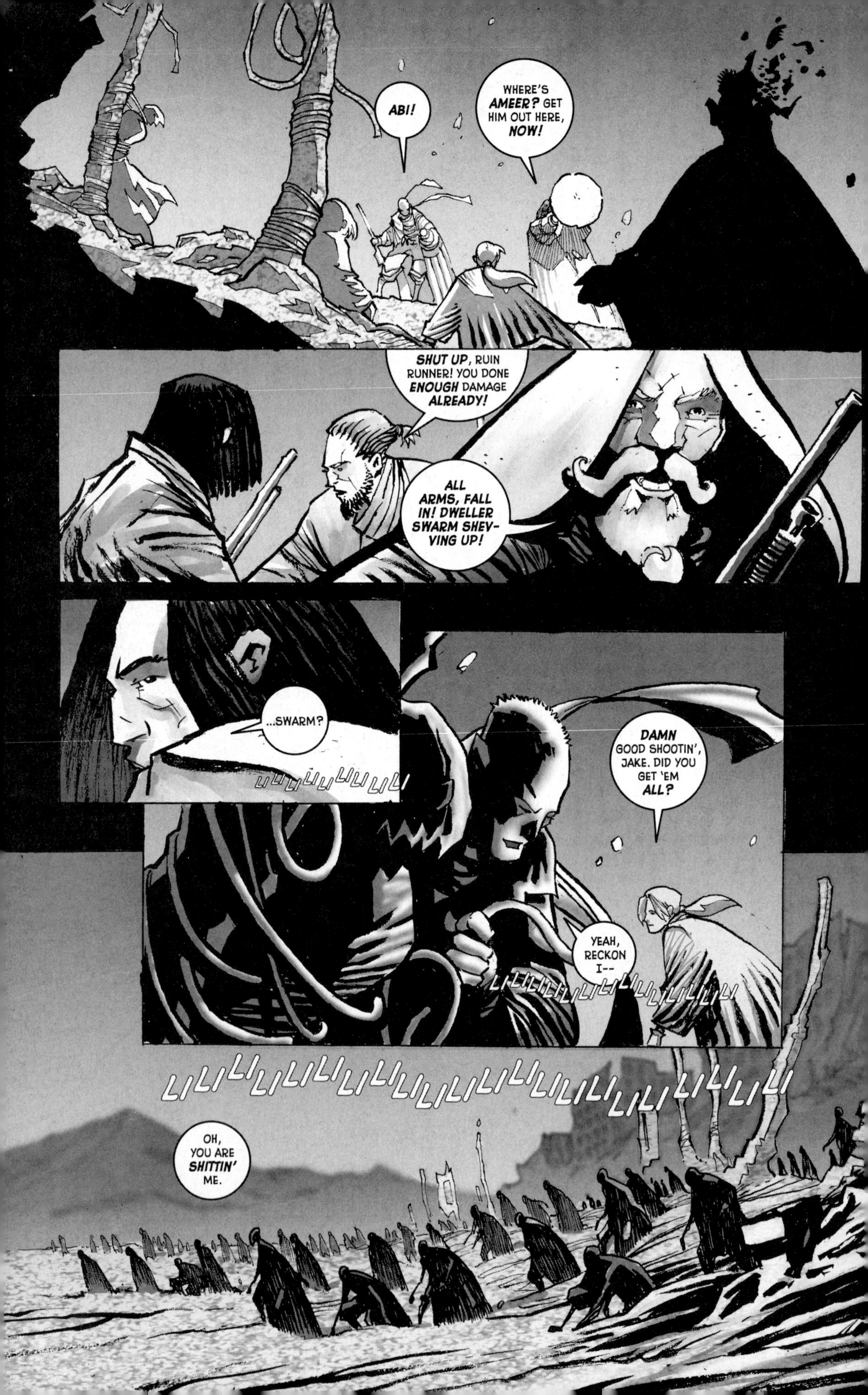
ABI!
WHERE'S AMEER? GET HIM OUT HERE, NOW!
SHUT UP, RUIN RUNNER! YOU DONE ENOUGH DAMAGE ALREADY!
ALL ARMS, FALL IN! DWELLER SWARM SHEV-VING UP!
...SWARM?
LILILILILILILILI
DAMN GOOD SHOOTIN', JAKE. DID YOU GET 'EM ALL?
YEAH, RECKON I--
LILILILILILILILILILILILILILI
LILILILILILILILILILILILILILILILILILILILI
OH, YOU ARE SHITTIN' ME.

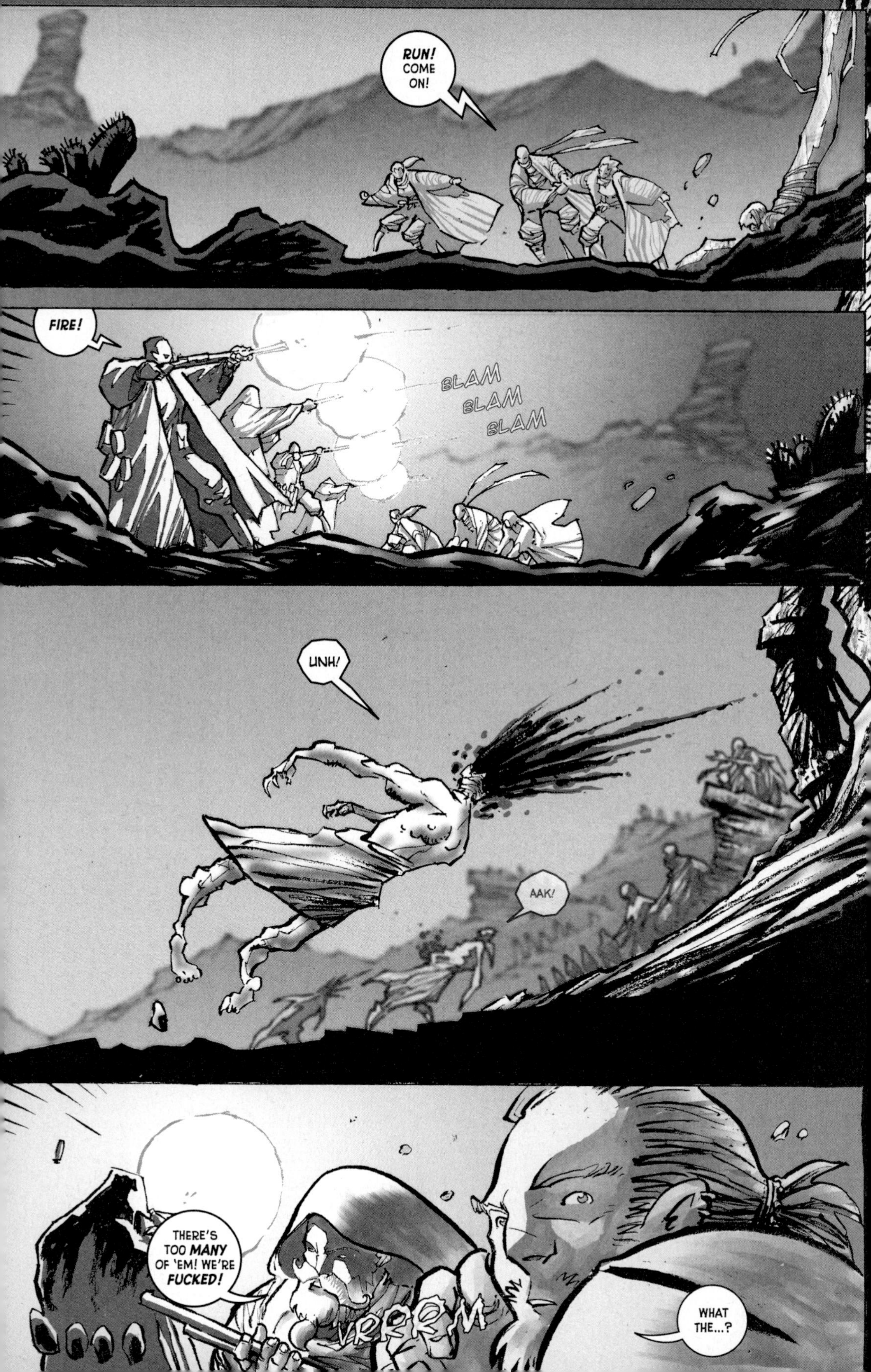
RUN! COME ON!
FIRE!
BLAM
BLAM
BLAM
UNH!
AAK!
THERE'S TOO MANY OF 'EM! WE'RE FUCKED!
VRRRRM
WHAT THE...?

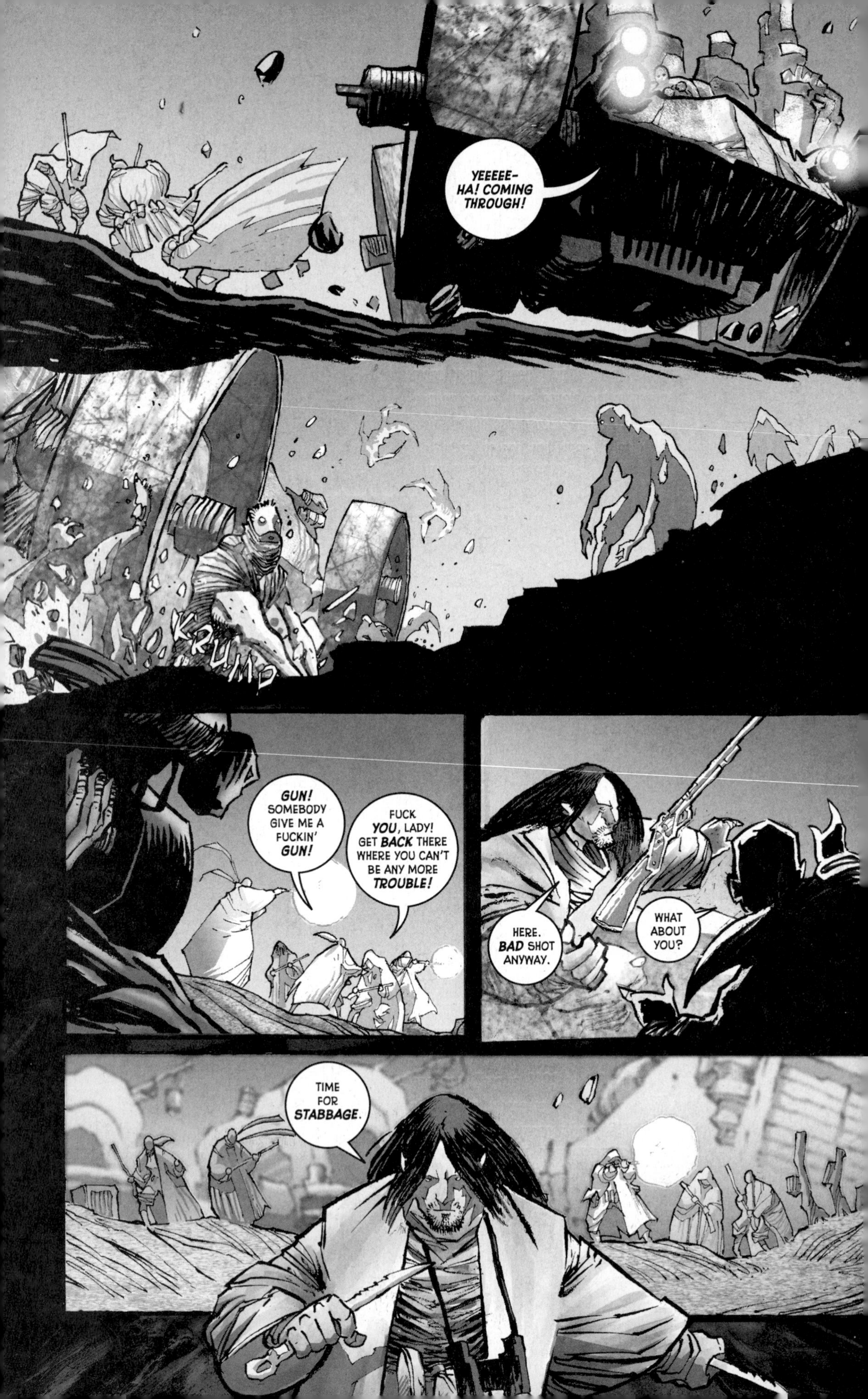
YEEEEE-HA! COMING THROUGH!
KRUMD
GUN! SOMEBODY GIVE ME A FUCKIN' GUN!
FUCK YOU, LADY! GET BACK THERE WHERE YOU CAN'T BE ANY MORE TROUBLE!
HERE. BAD SHOT ANYWAY.
WHAT ABOUT YOU?
TIME FOR STABBAGE.

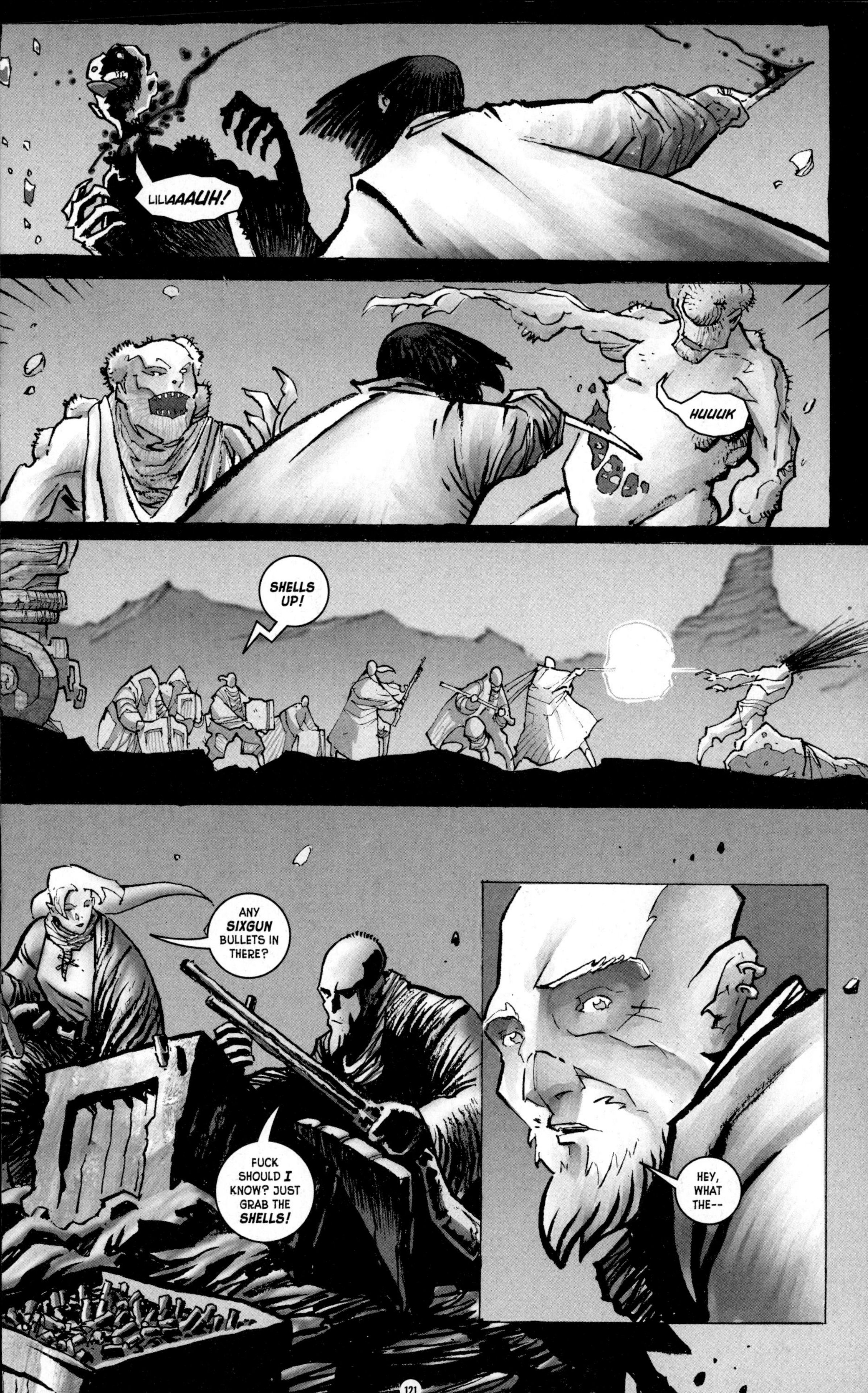

LILIAAAUH!
HUUUK
SHELLS UP!
ANY SIXGUN BULLETS IN THERE?
FUCK SHOULD I KNOW? JUST GRAB THE SHELLS!
HEY, WHAT THE--

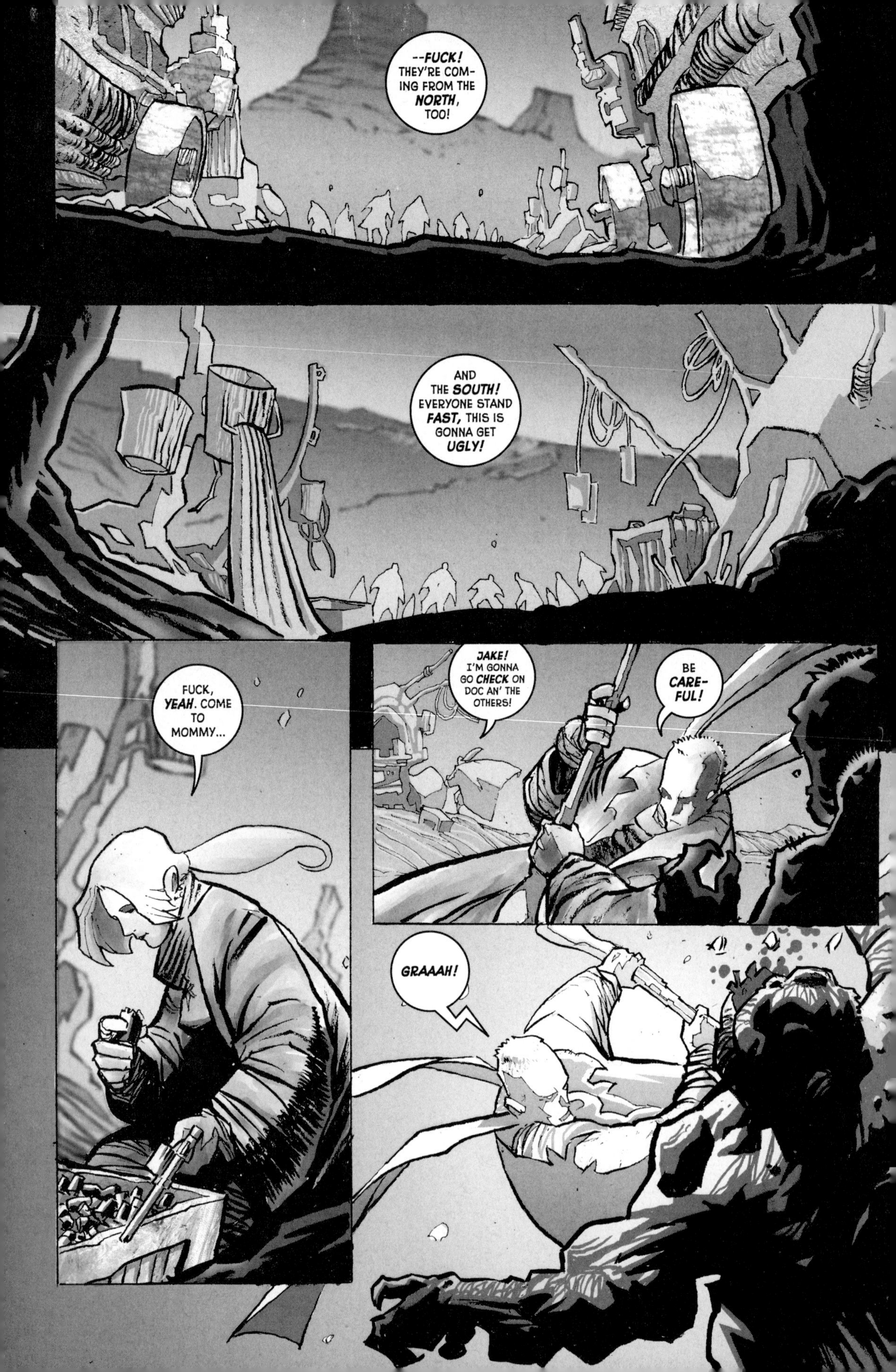
--FUCK! THEY'RE COMING FROM THE NORTH, TOO!
AND THE SOUTH! EVERYONE STAND FAST, THIS IS GONNA GET UGLY!
FUCK, YEAH. COME TO MOMMY...
JAKE! I'M GONNA GO CHECK ON DOC AN' THE OTHERS!
BE CAREFUL!
GRAAAH!

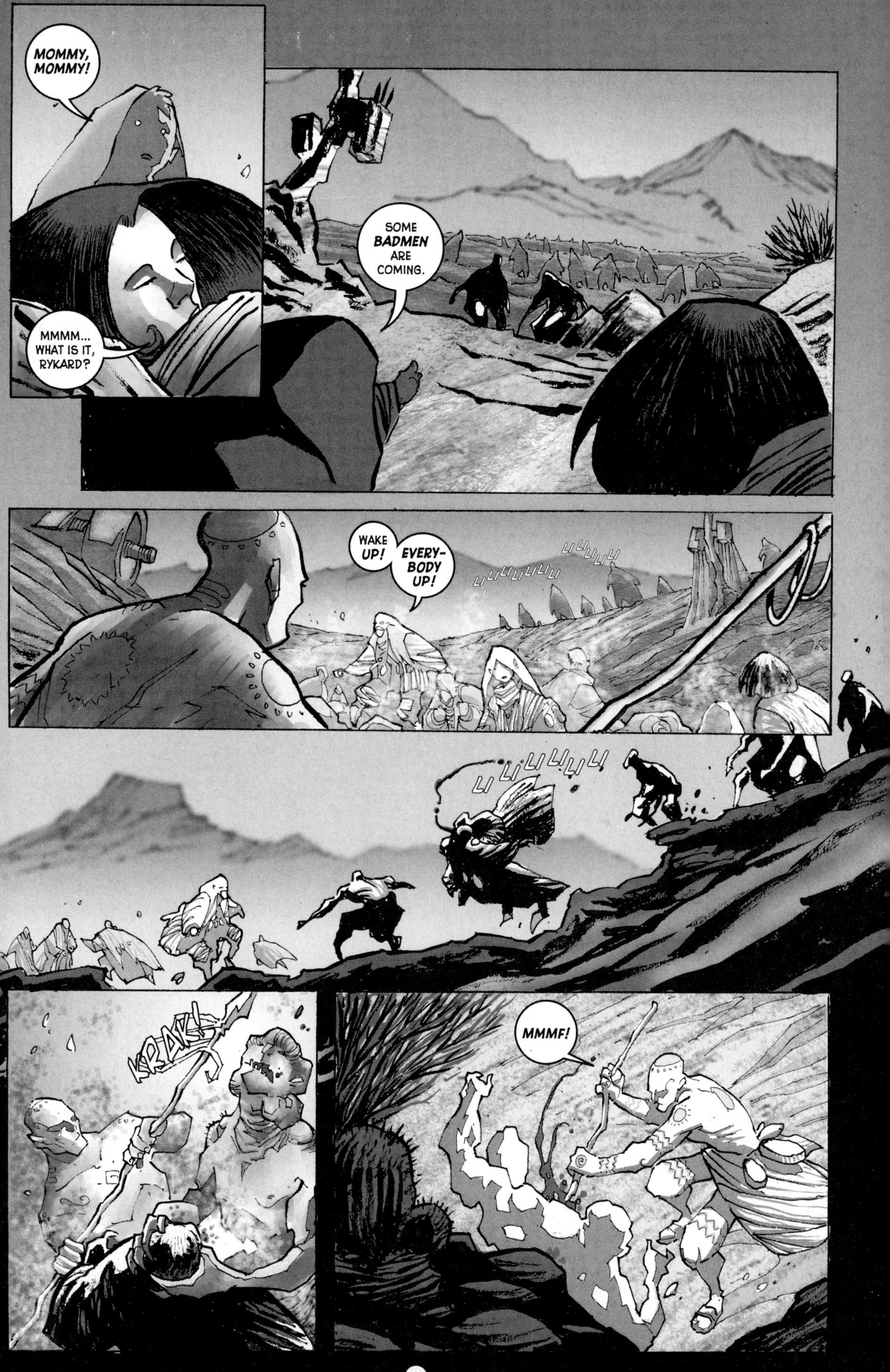
MOMMY, MOMMY!
MMMM... WHAT IS IT, RYKARD?
SOME BADMEN ARE COMING.
WAKE UP!
EVERY-BODY UP!
KRAK!
MMMF!

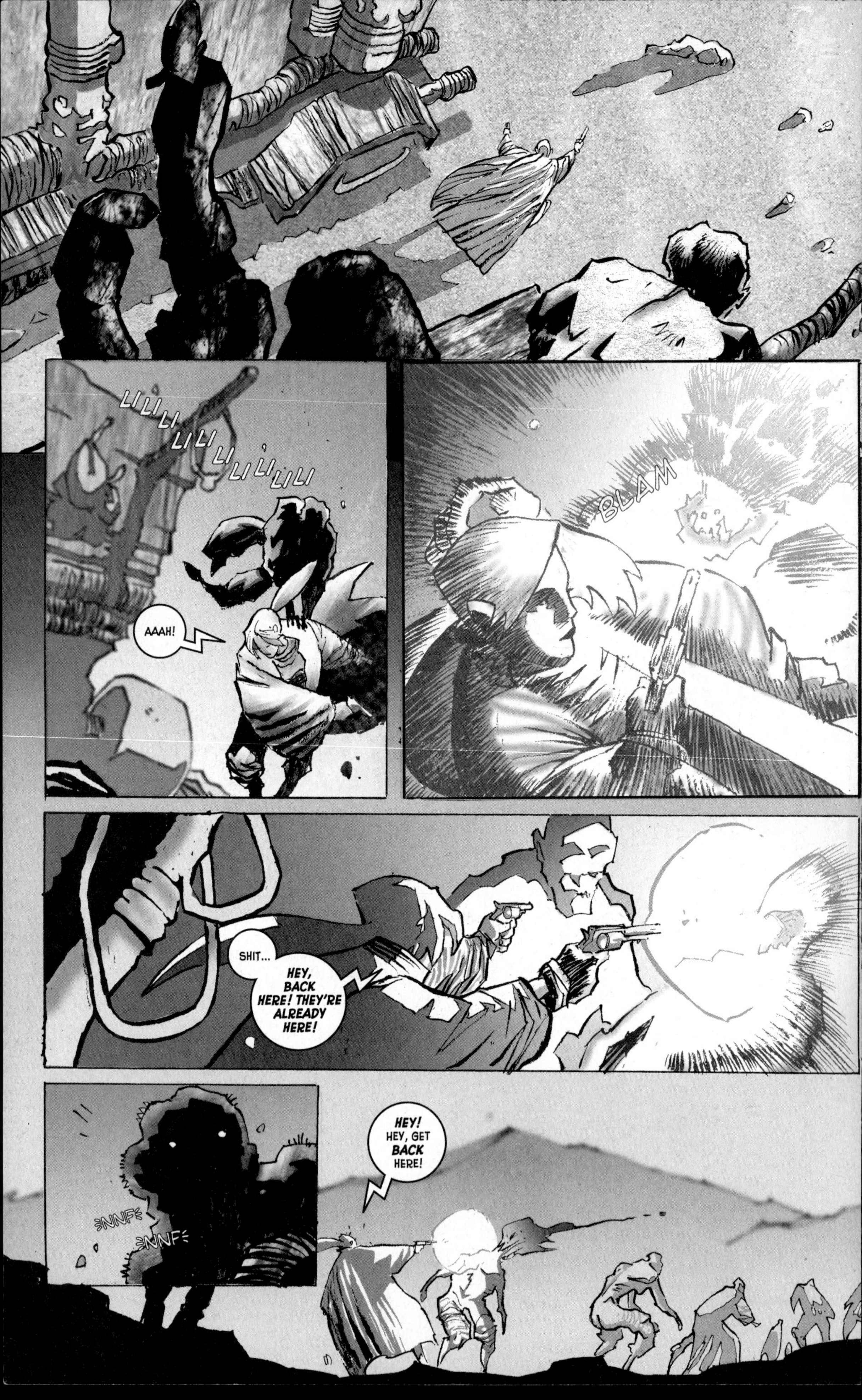
LI LI LI LI LI LI LI LI LI LI
AAAH!
BLAM
SHIT...
HEY, BACK HERE! THEY'RE ALREADY HERE!
NNF
NNF
HEY! HEY, GET BACK HERE!

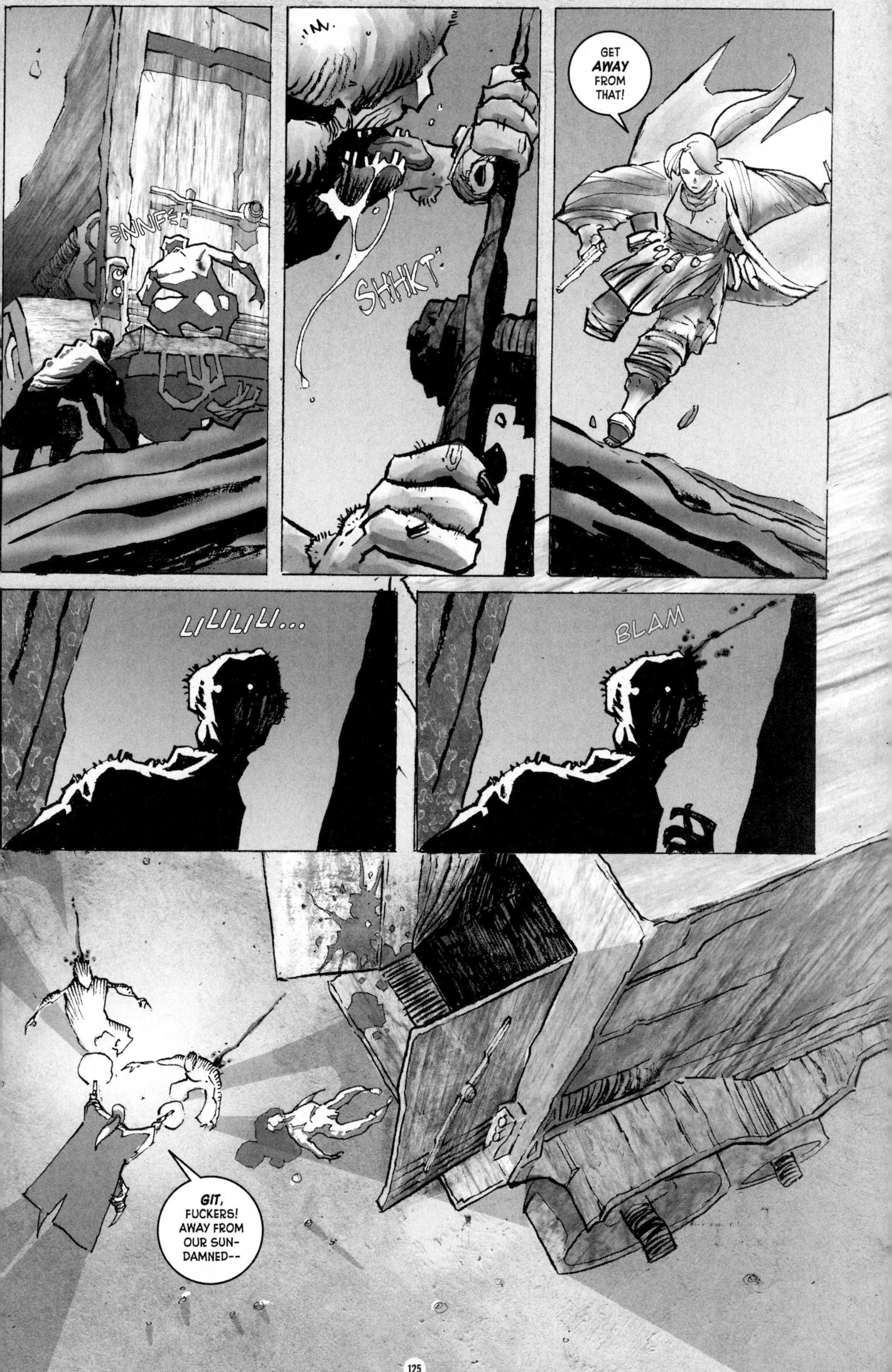
NNF
MM
SHHKT
GET AWAY FROM THAT!
LILILILI...
BLAM
GIT, FUCKERS! AWAY FROM OUR SUN-DAMNED--

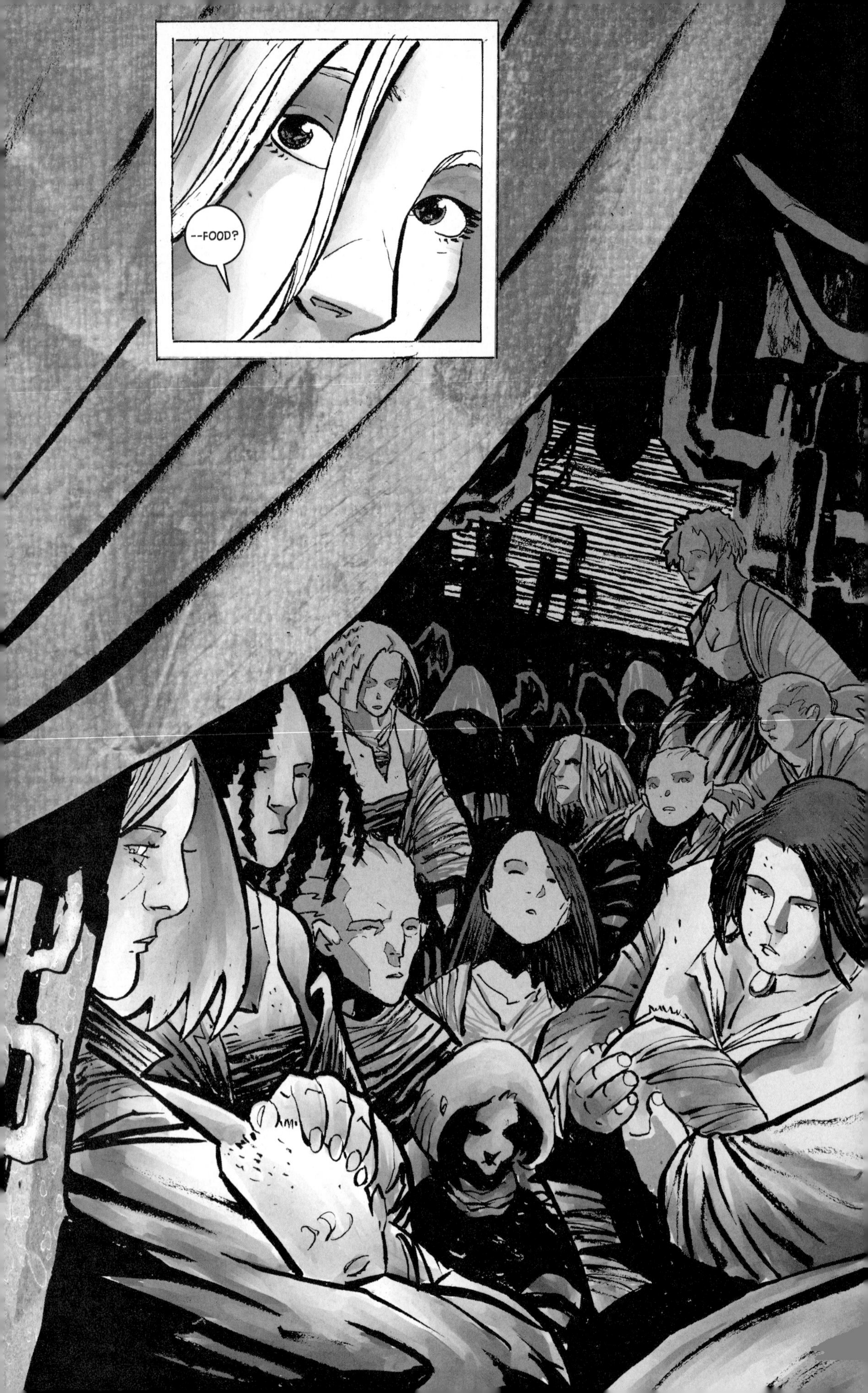
--FOOD?

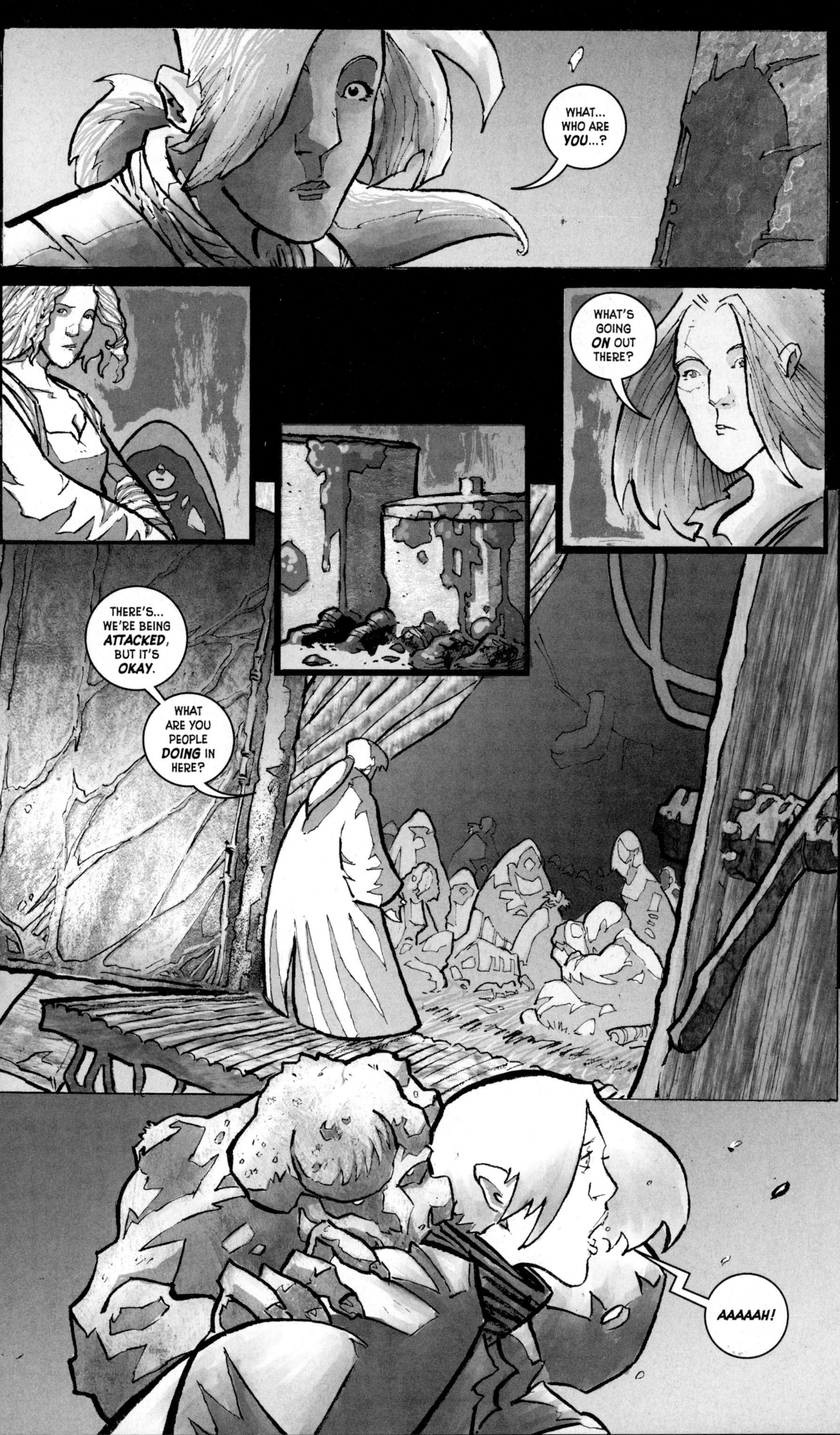
WHAT... WHO ARE *YOU*...?
WHAT'S GOING *ON* OUT THERE?
THERE'S... WE'RE BEING *ATTACKED*, BUT IT'S *OKAY*.
WHAT ARE YOU PEOPLE *DOING* IN HERE?
AAAAAH!

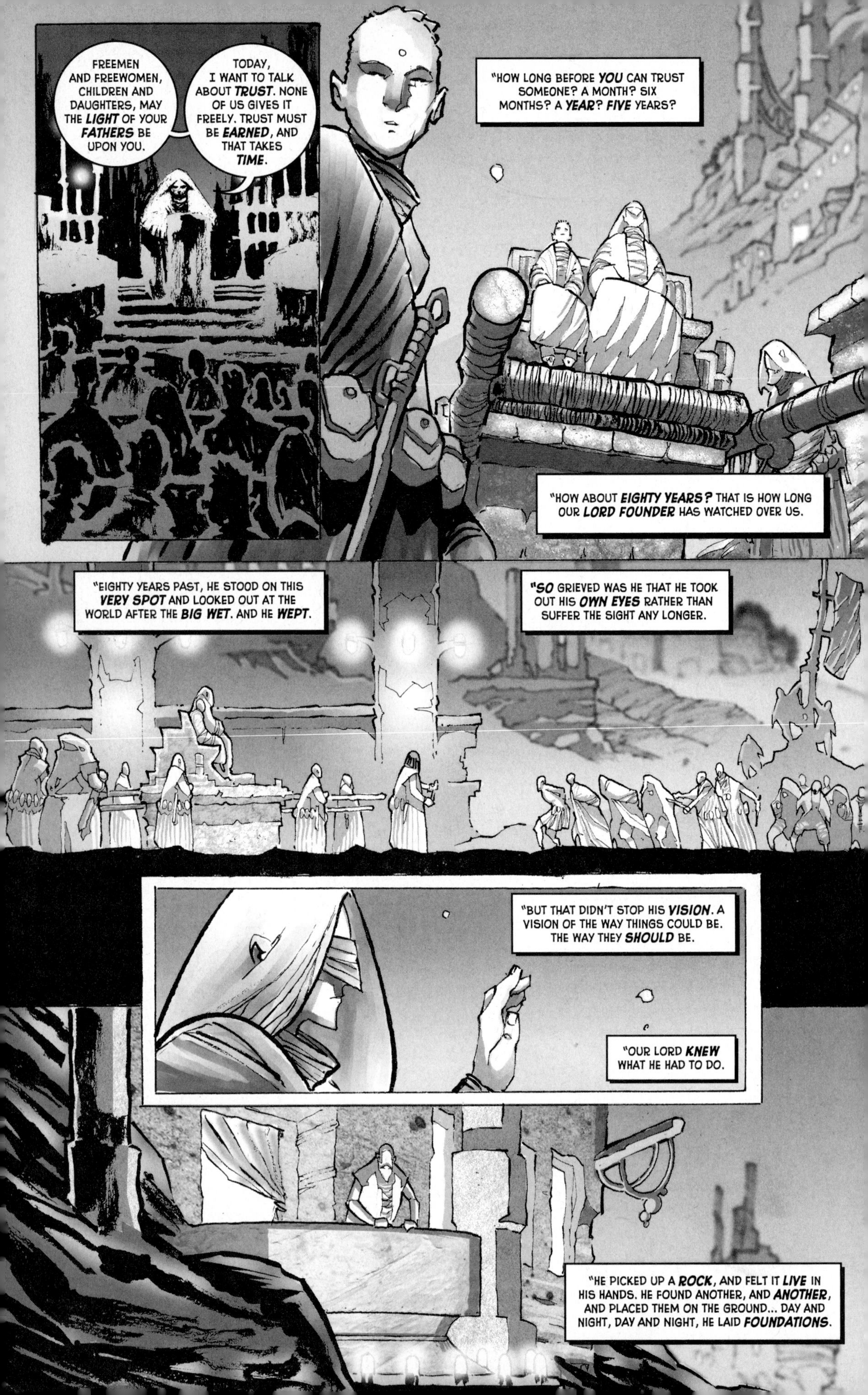
FREEMEN AND FREEWOMEN, CHILDREN AND DAUGHTERS, MAY THE LIGHT OF YOUR FATHERS BE UPON YOU.
TODAY, I WANT TO TALK ABOUT TRUST. NONE OF US GIVES IT FREELY. TRUST MUST BE EARNED, AND THAT TAKES TIME.
"HOW LONG BEFORE YOU CAN TRUST SOMEONE? A MONTH? SIX MONTHS? A YEAR? FIVE YEARS?
"HOW ABOUT EIGHTY YEARS? THAT IS HOW LONG OUR LORD FOUNDER HAS WATCHED OVER US.
"EIGHTY YEARS PAST, HE STOOD ON THIS VERY SPOT AND LOOKED OUT AT THE WORLD AFTER THE BIG WET. AND HE WEPT.
"SO GRIEVED WAS HE THAT HE TOOK OUT HIS OWN EYES RATHER THAN SUFFER THE SIGHT ANY LONGER.
"BUT THAT DIDN'T STOP HIS VISION. A VISION OF THE WAY THINGS COULD BE. THE WAY THEY SHOULD BE.
"OUR LORD KNEW WHAT HE HAD TO DO.
"HE PICKED UP A ROCK, AND FELT IT LIVE IN HIS HANDS. HE FOUND ANOTHER, AND ANOTHER, AND PLACED THEM ON THE GROUND... DAY AND NIGHT, DAY AND NIGHT, HE LAID FOUNDATIONS.

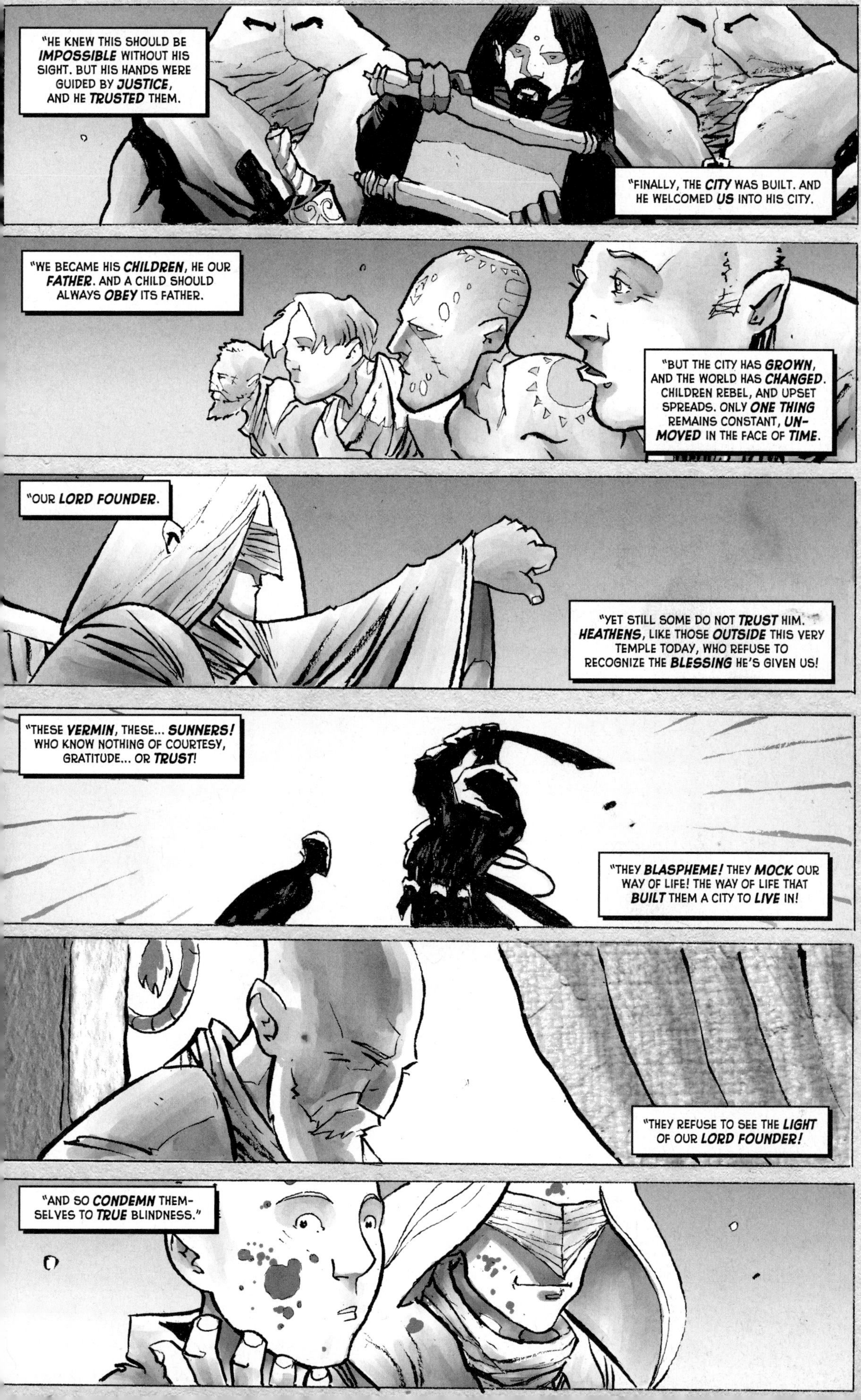
"HE KNEW THIS SHOULD BE IMPOSSIBLE WITHOUT HIS SIGHT. BUT HIS HANDS WERE GUIDED BY JUSTICE, AND HE TRUSTED THEM.
"FINALLY, THE CITY WAS BUILT. AND HE WELCOMED US INTO HIS CITY.
"WE BECAME HIS CHILDREN, HE OUR FATHER. AND A CHILD SHOULD ALWAYS OBEY ITS FATHER.
"BUT THE CITY HAS GROWN, AND THE WORLD HAS CHANGED. CHILDREN REBEL, AND UPSET SPREADS. ONLY ONE THING REMAINS CONSTANT, UN-MOVED IN THE FACE OF TIME.
"OUR LORD FOUNDER.
"YET STILL SOME DO NOT TRUST HIM. HEATHENS, LIKE THOSE OUTSIDE THIS VERY TEMPLE TODAY, WHO REFUSE TO RECOGNIZE THE BLESSING HE'S GIVEN US!
"THESE VERMIN, THESE... SUNNERS! WHO KNOW NOTHING OF COURTESY, GRATITUDE... OR TRUST!
"THEY BLASPHEME! THEY MOCK OUR WAY OF LIFE! THE WAY OF LIFE THAT BUILT THEM A CITY TO LIVE IN!
"THEY REFUSE TO SEE THE LIGHT OF OUR LORD FOUNDER!
"AND SO CONDEMN THEM-SELVES TO TRUE BLINDNESS."

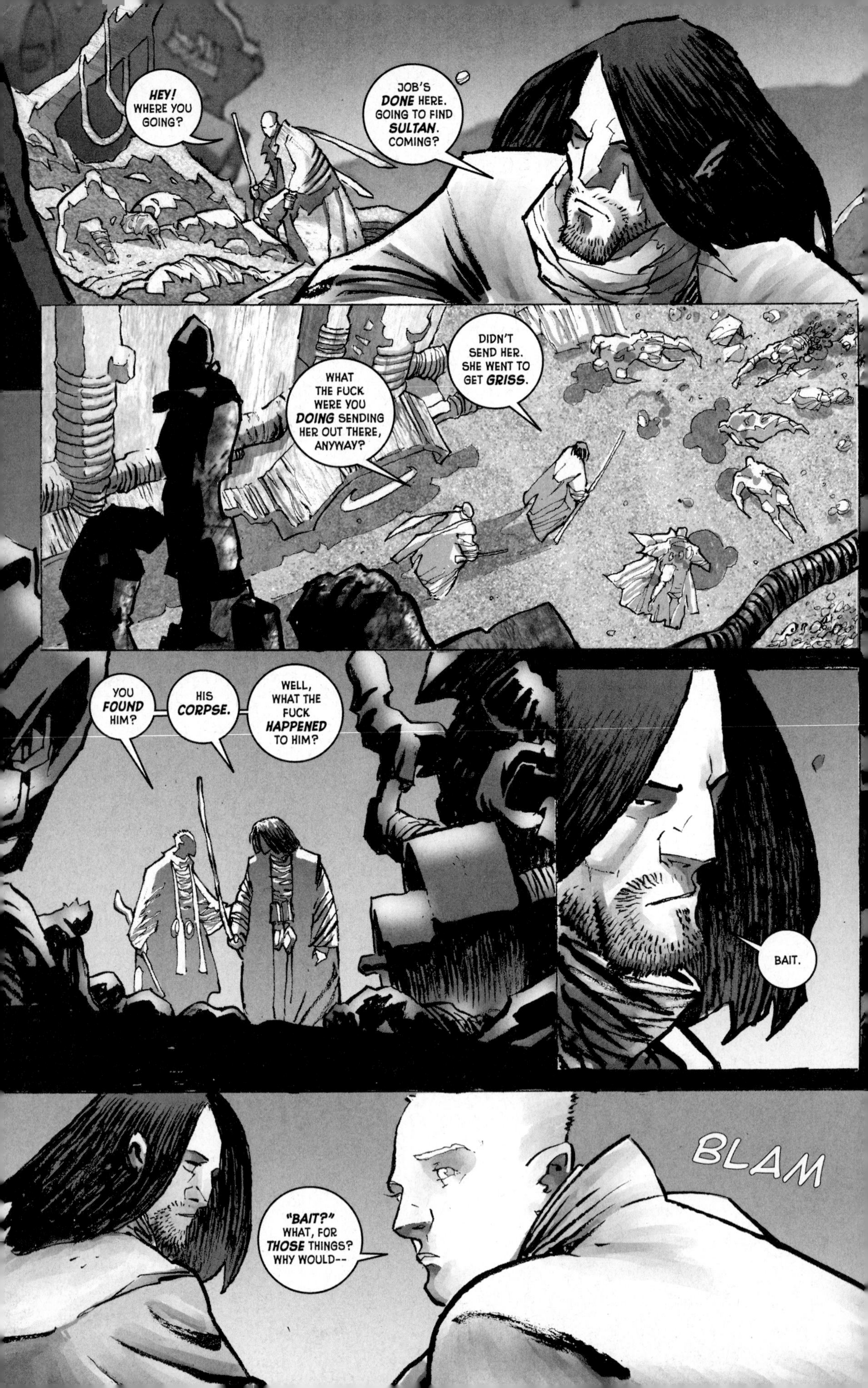
HEY! WHERE YOU GOING?
JOB'S DONE HERE. GOING TO FIND SULTAN. COMING?
WHAT THE FUCK WERE YOU DOING SENDING HER OUT THERE, ANYWAY?
DIDN'T SEND HER. SHE WENT TO GET GRISS.
YOU FOUND HIM?
HIS CORPSE.
WELL, WHAT THE FUCK HAPPENED TO HIM?
BAIT.
"BAIT?" WHAT, FOR THOSE THINGS? WHY WOULD--
BLAM

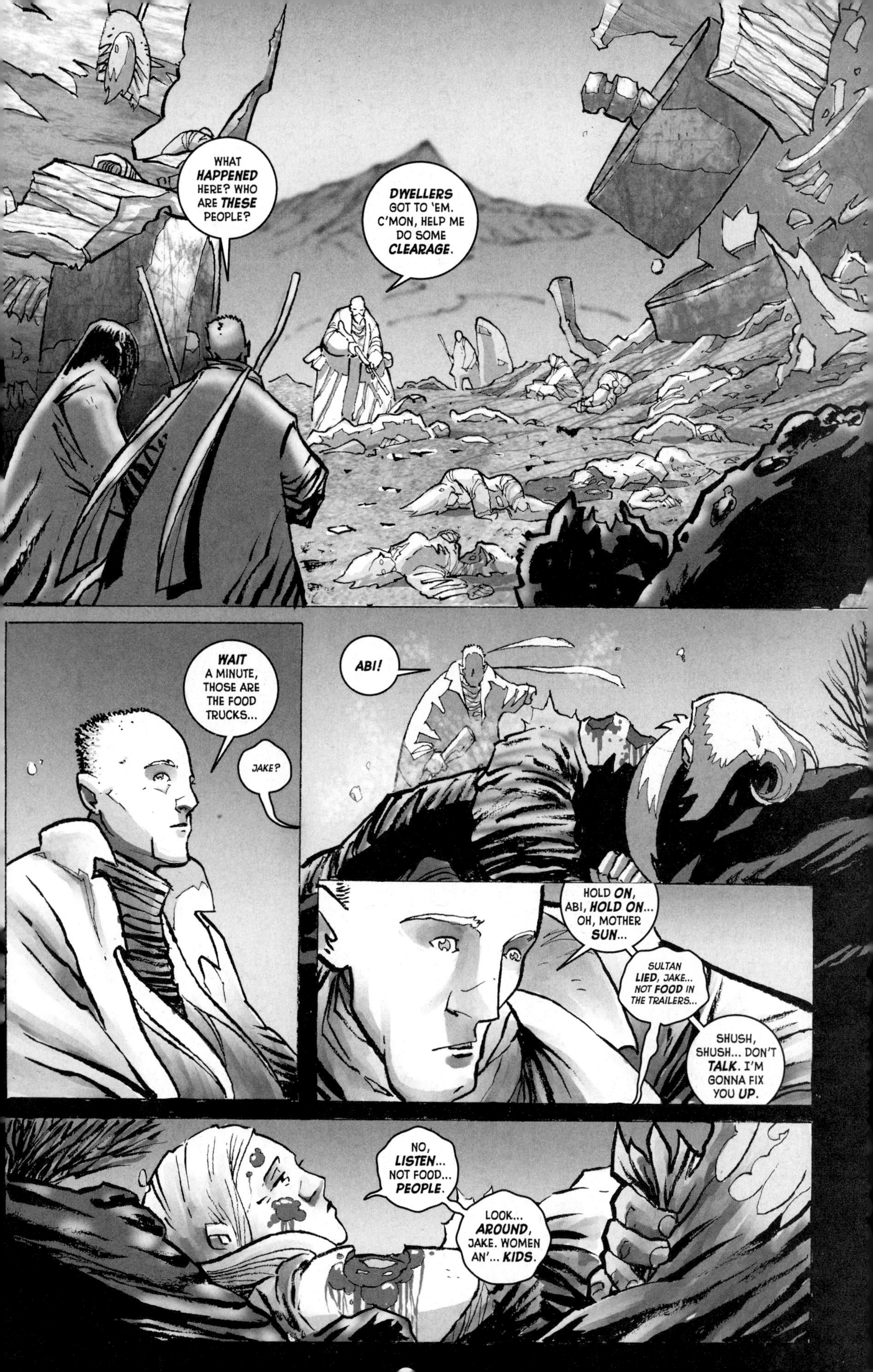
WHAT HAPPENED HERE? WHO ARE THESE PEOPLE?
DWELLERS GOT TO 'EM. C'MON, HELP ME DO SOME CLEARAGE.
WAIT A MINUTE, THOSE ARE THE FOOD TRUCKS...
JAKE?
ABI!
HOLD ON, ABI, HOLD ON... OH, MOTHER SUN...
SULTAN LIED, JAKE... NOT FOOD IN THE TRAILERS...
SHUSH, SHUSH... DON'T TALK. I'M GONNA FIX YOU UP.
NO, LISTEN... NOT FOOD... PEOPLE.
LOOK... AROUND, JAKE. WOMEN AN'... KIDS.

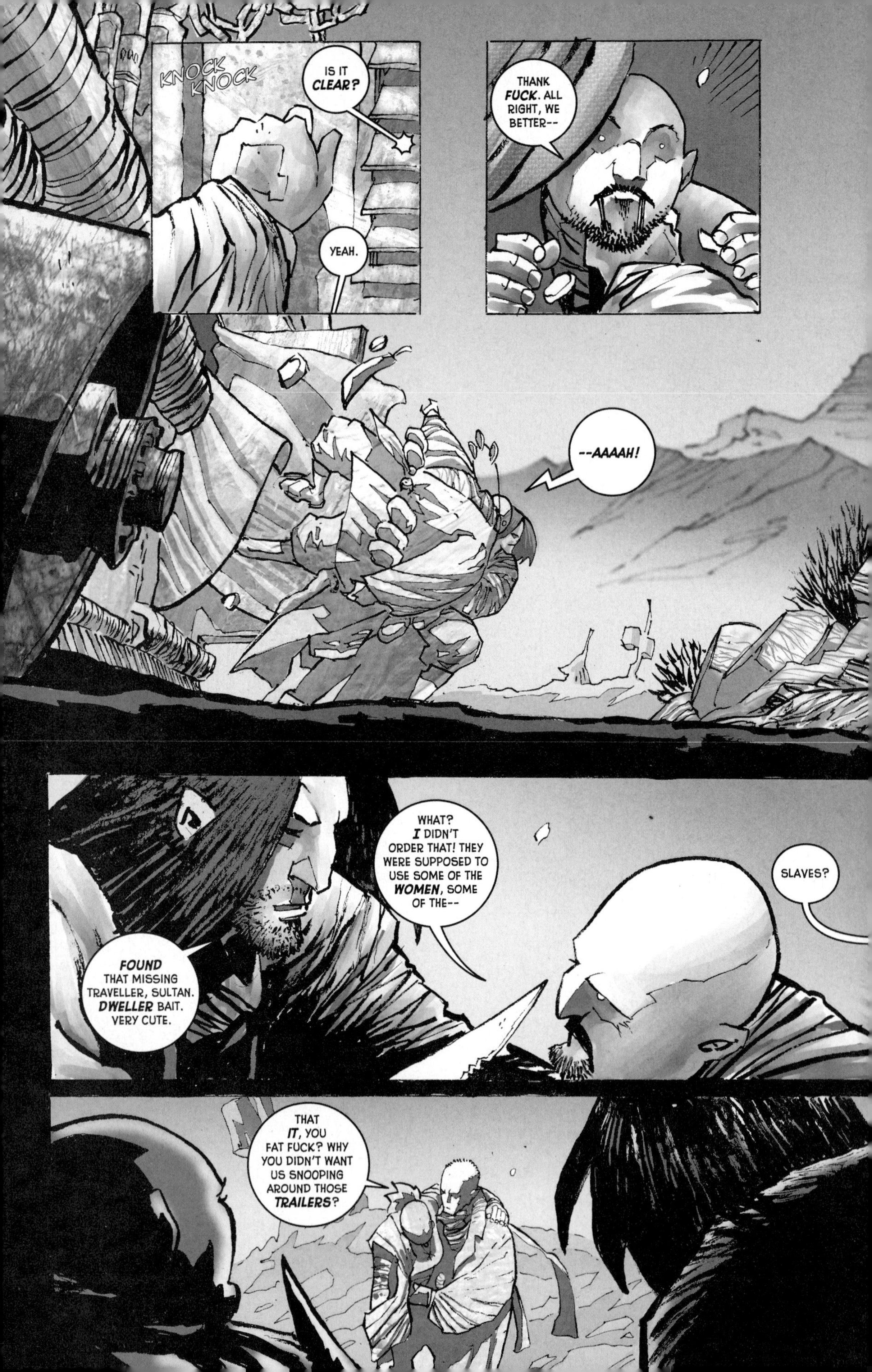
KNOCK KNOCK
IS IT CLEAR?
YEAH.
THANK FUCK. ALL RIGHT, WE BETTER--
--AAAAH!
FOUND THAT MISSING TRAVELLER, SULTAN. DWELLER BAIT. VERY CUTE.
WHAT? I DIDN'T ORDER THAT! THEY WERE SUPPOSED TO USE SOME OF THE WOMEN, SOME OF THE--
SLAVES?
THAT IT, YOU FAT FUCK? WHY YOU DIDN'T WANT US SNOOPING AROUND THOSE TRAILERS?

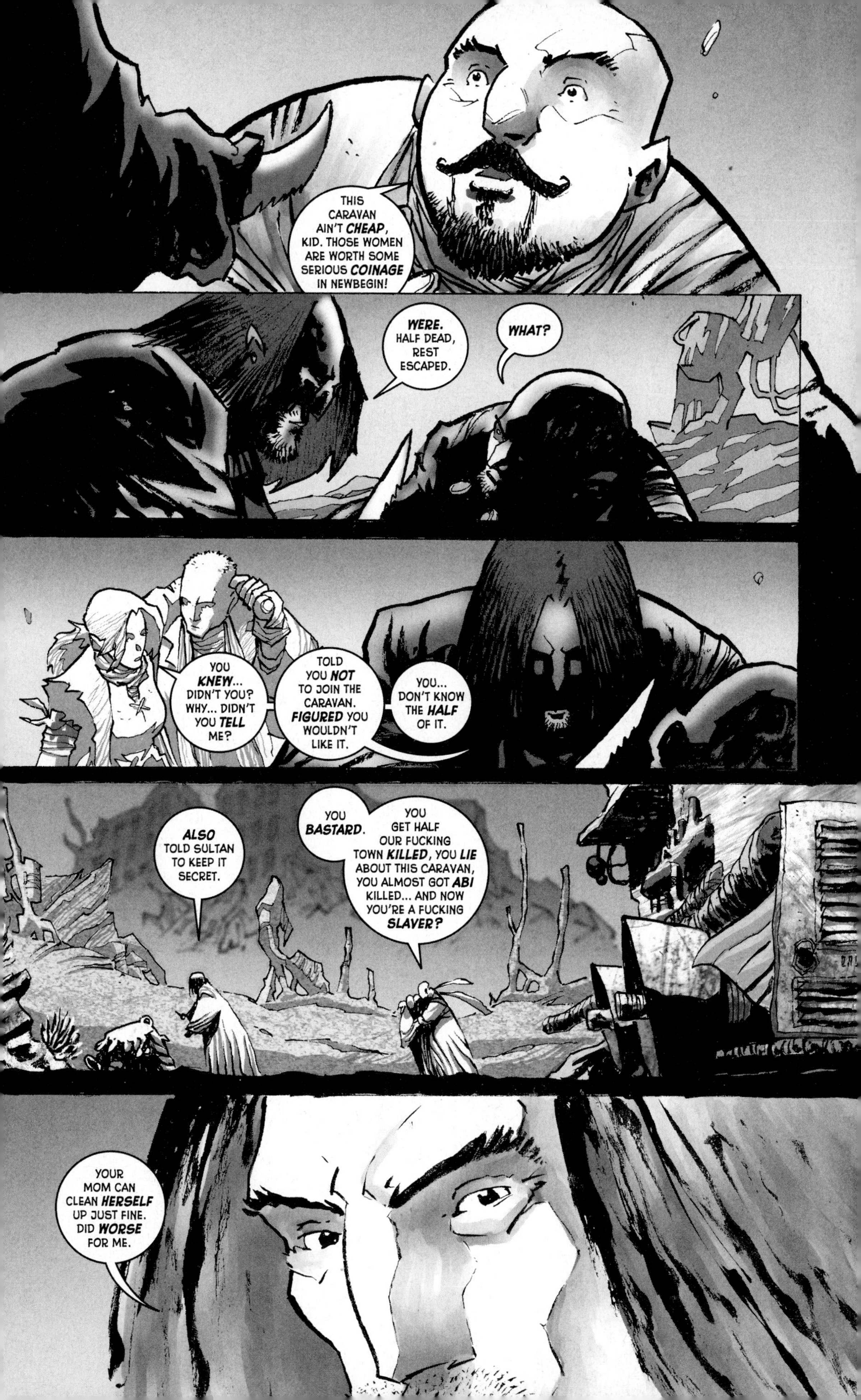
THIS CARAVAN AIN'T CHEAP, KID. THOSE WOMEN ARE WORTH SOME SERIOUS COINAGE IN NEWBEGIN!
WERE. HALF DEAD, REST ESCAPED.
WHAT?
YOU KNEW... DIDN'T YOU? WHY... DIDN'T YOU TELL ME?
TOLD YOU NOT TO JOIN THE CARAVAN. FIGURED YOU WOULDN'T LIKE IT.
YOU... DON'T KNOW THE HALF OF IT.
ALSO TOLD SULTAN TO KEEP IT SECRET.
YOU BASTARD.
YOU GET HALF OUR FUCKING TOWN KILLED, YOU LIE ABOUT THIS CARAVAN, YOU ALMOST GOT ABI KILLED... AND NOW YOU'RE A FUCKING SLAVER?
YOUR MOM CAN CLEAN HERSELF UP JUST FINE. DID WORSE FOR ME.

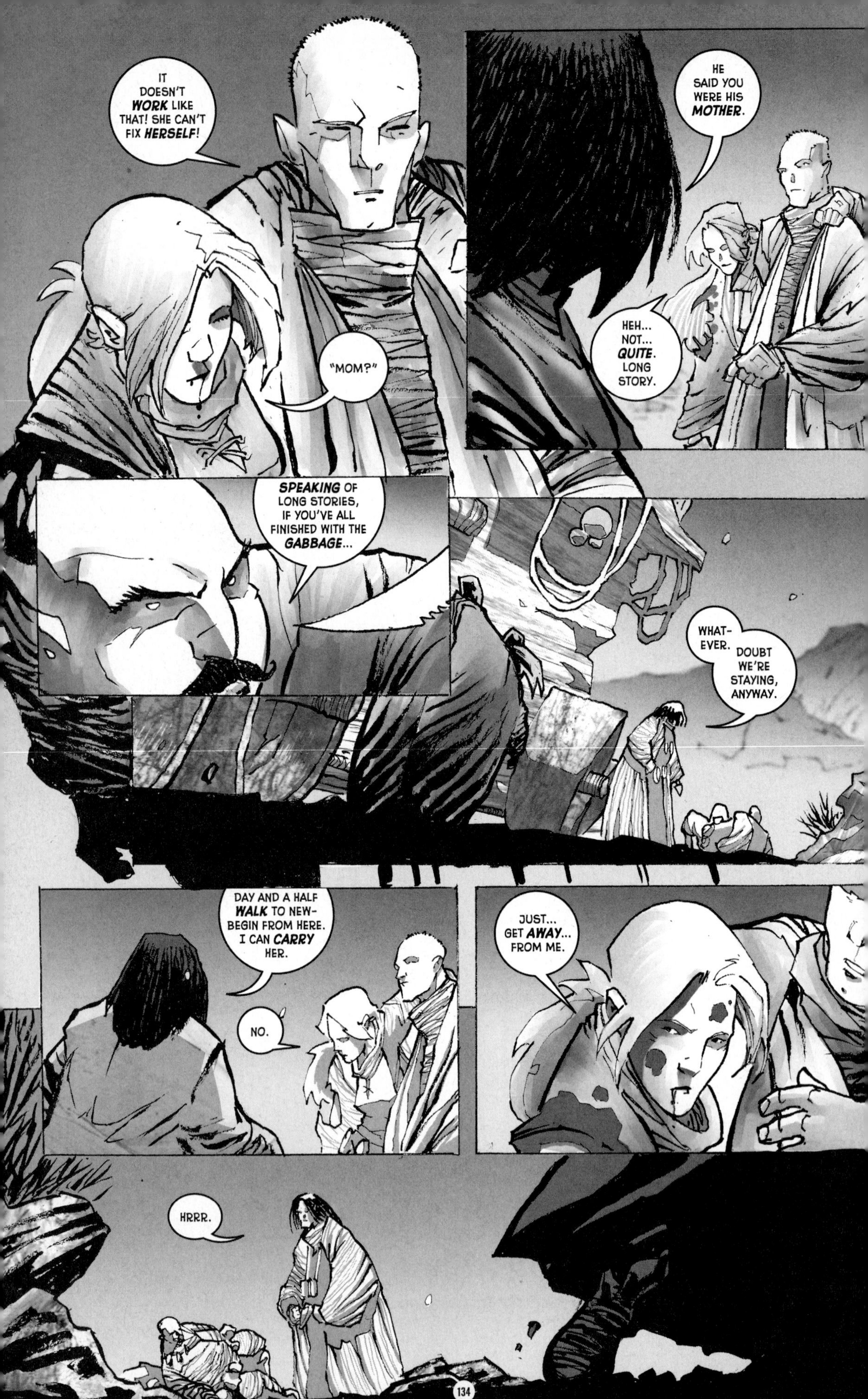

IT DOESN'T **WORK** LIKE THAT! SHE CAN'T FIX **HERSELF**!
"MOM?"
HE SAID YOU WERE HIS **MOTHER**.
HEH... NOT... **QUITE**. LONG STORY.
SPEAKING OF LONG STORIES, IF YOU'VE ALL FINISHED WITH THE **GABBAGE**...
WHAT-EVER.
DOUBT WE'RE STAYING, ANYWAY.
DAY AND A HALF **WALK** TO NEW-BEGIN FROM HERE. I CAN **CARRY** HER.
NO.
JUST... GET **AWAY**... FROM ME.
HRRR.

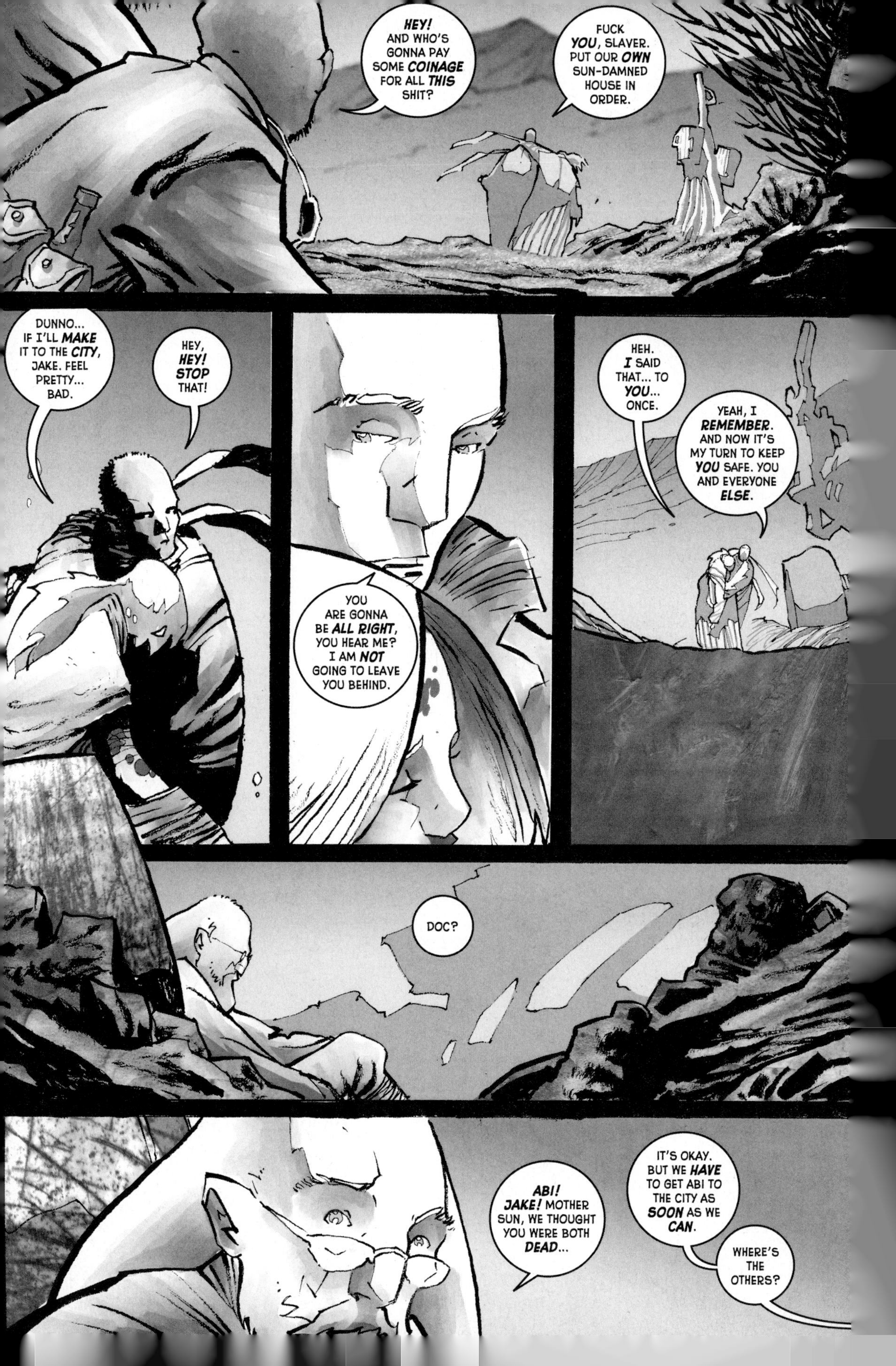
HEY! AND WHO'S GONNA PAY SOME COINAGE FOR ALL THIS SHIT?
FUCK YOU, SLAVER. PUT OUR OWN SUN-DAMNED HOUSE IN ORDER.
DUNNO... IF I'LL MAKE IT TO THE CITY, JAKE. FEEL PRETTY... BAD.
HEY, HEY! STOP THAT!
YOU ARE GONNA BE ALL RIGHT, YOU HEAR ME? I AM NOT GOING TO LEAVE YOU BEHIND.
HEH. I SAID THAT... TO YOU... ONCE.
YEAH, I REMEMBER. AND NOW IT'S MY TURN TO KEEP YOU SAFE. YOU AND EVERYONE ELSE.
DOC?
ABI! JAKE! MOTHER SUN, WE THOUGHT YOU WERE BOTH DEAD...
IT'S OKAY. BUT WE HAVE TO GET ABI TO THE CITY AS SOON AS WE CAN.
WHERE'S THE OTHERS?

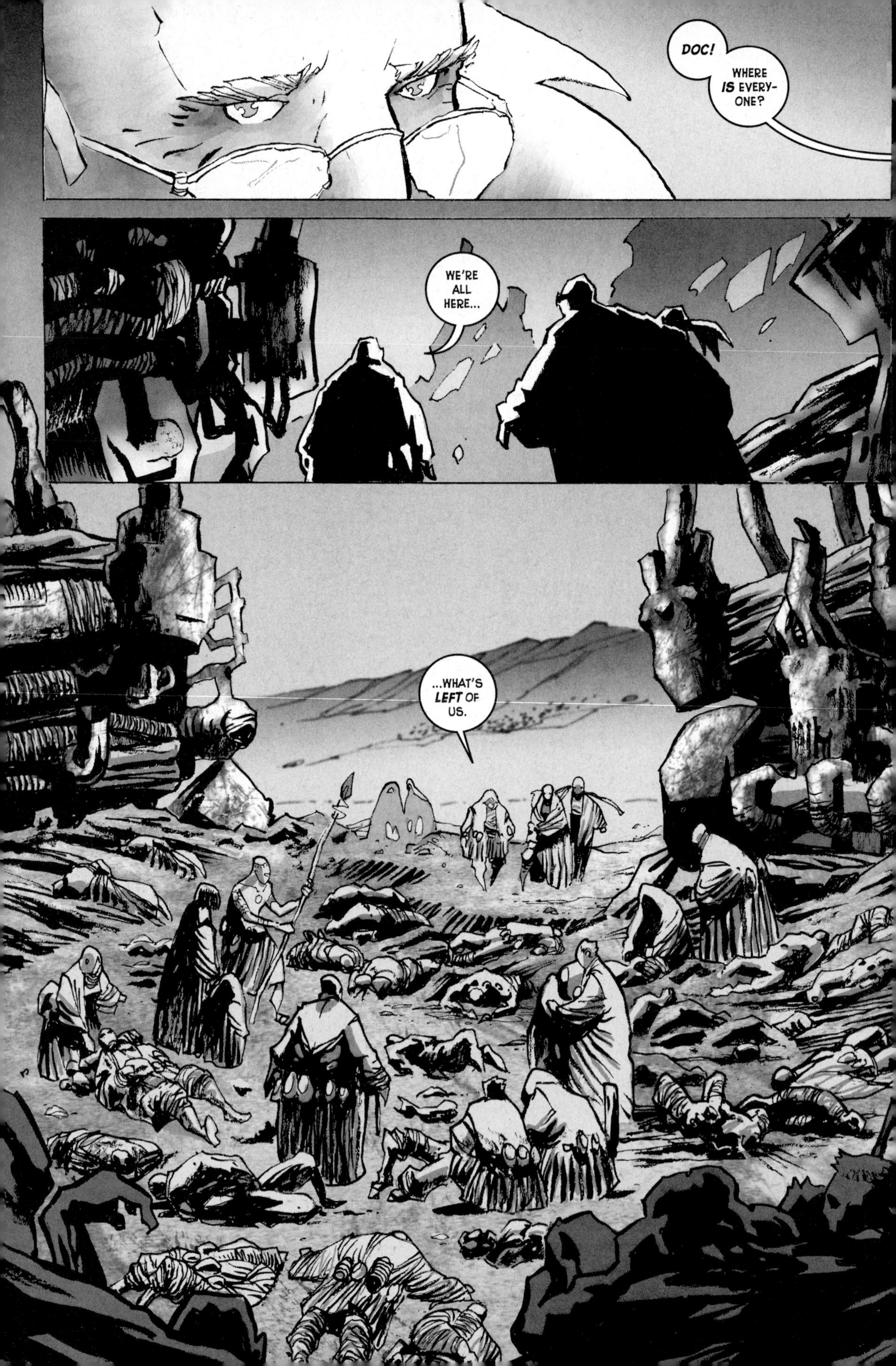
DOC!
WHERE IS EVERY-ONE?
WE'RE ALL HERE...
...WHAT'S LEFT OF US.

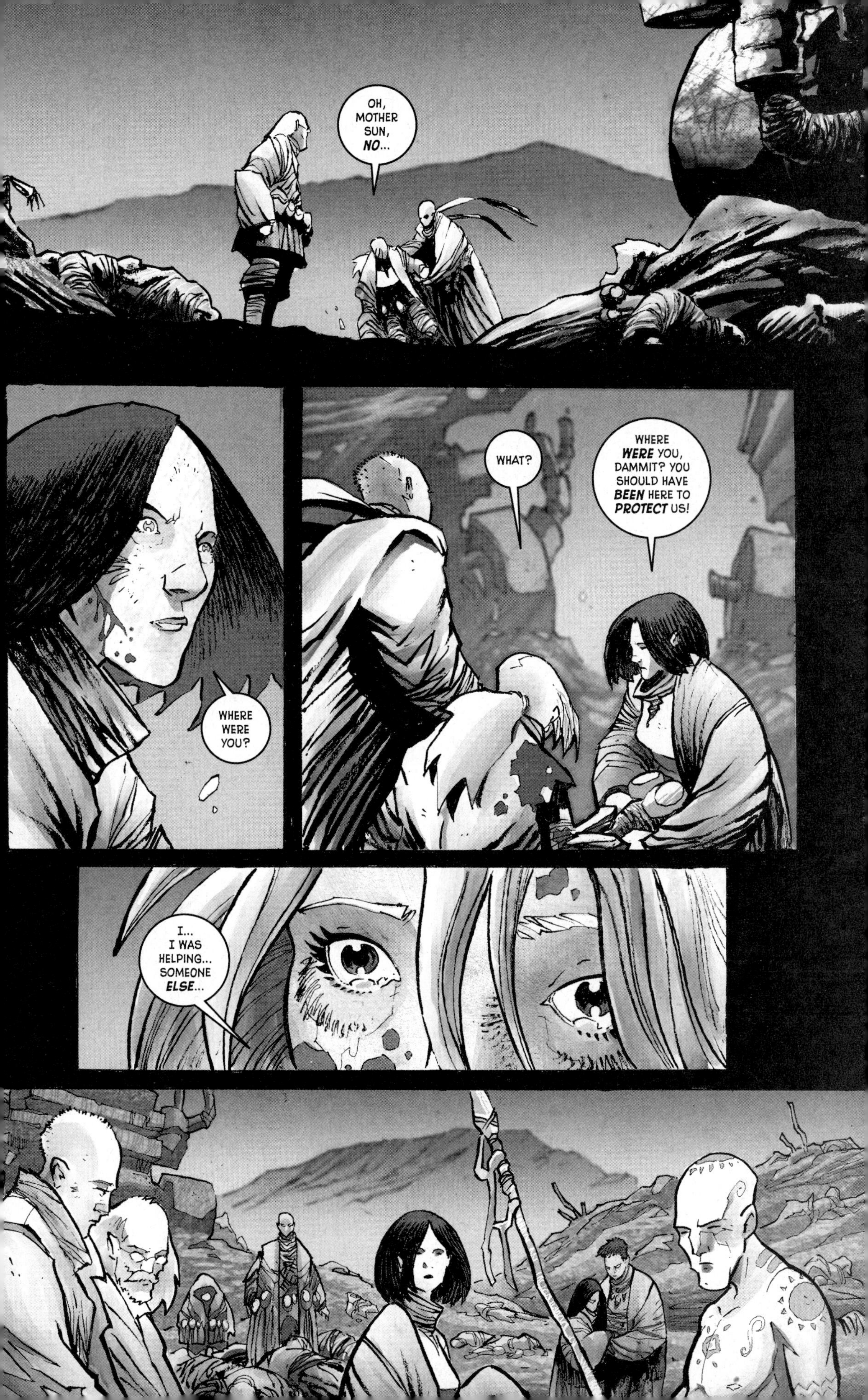
OH, MOTHER SUN, NO...
WHERE WERE YOU?
WHAT?
WHERE WERE YOU, DAMMIT? YOU SHOULD HAVE BEEN HERE TO PROTECT US!
I... I WAS HELPING... SOMEONE ELSE...

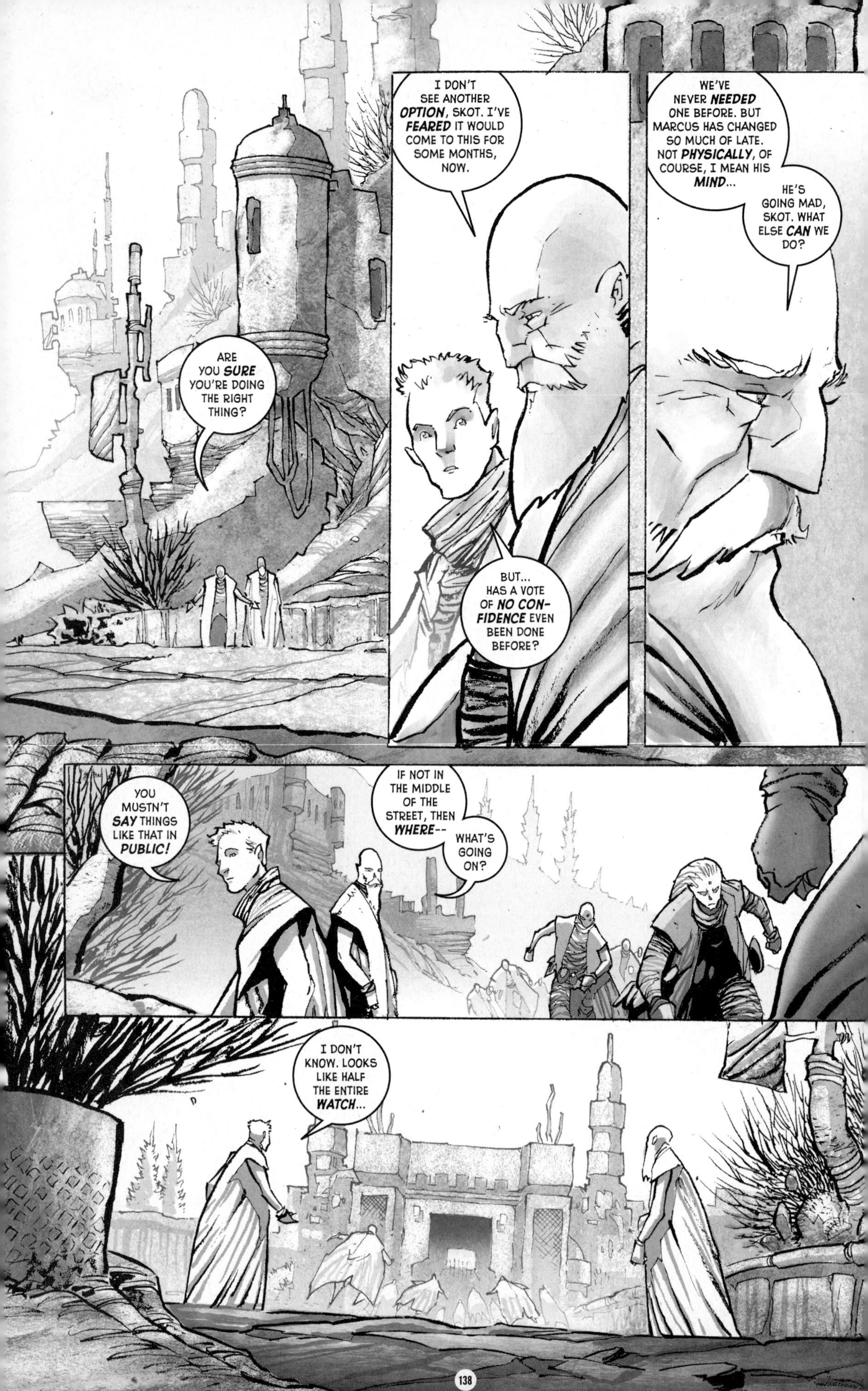
ARE YOU SURE YOU'RE DOING THE RIGHT THING?
I DON'T SEE ANOTHER OPTION, SKOT. I'VE FEARED IT WOULD COME TO THIS FOR SOME MONTHS, NOW.
BUT... HAS A VOTE OF NO CONFIDENCE EVEN BEEN DONE BEFORE?
WE'VE NEVER NEEDED ONE BEFORE. BUT MARCUS HAS CHANGED SO MUCH OF LATE. NOT PHYSICALLY, OF COURSE, I MEAN HIS MIND...
HE'S GOING MAD, SKOT. WHAT ELSE CAN WE DO?
YOU MUSTN'T SAY THINGS LIKE THAT IN PUBLIC!
IF NOT IN THE MIDDLE OF THE STREET, THEN WHERE--
WHAT'S GOING ON?
I DON'T KNOW. LOOKS LIKE HALF THE ENTIRE WATCH...

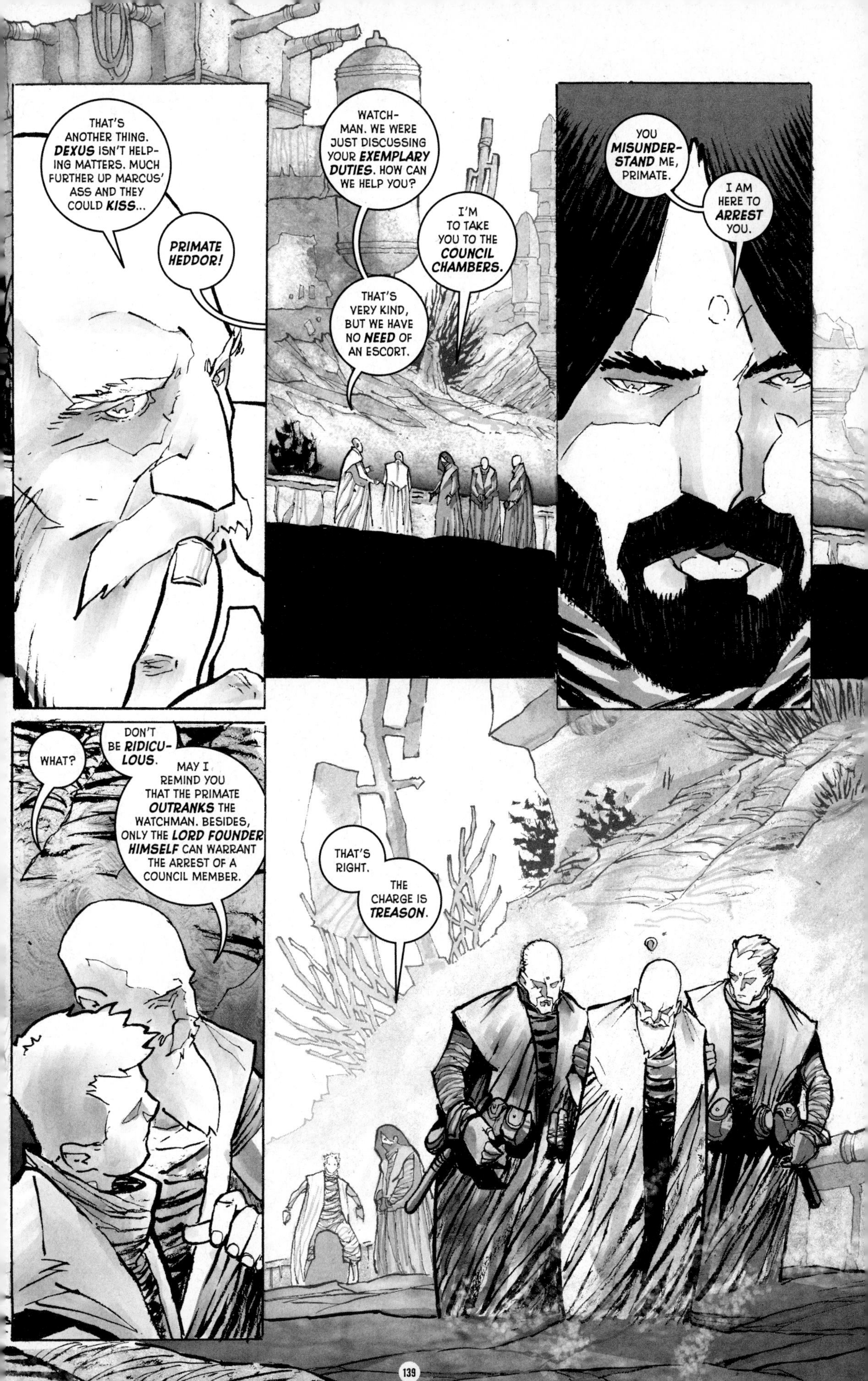
THAT'S ANOTHER THING. DEXUS ISN'T HELPING MATTERS. MUCH FURTHER UP MARCUS' ASS AND THEY COULD KISS...
PRIMATE HEDDOR!
WATCHMAN. WE WERE JUST DISCUSSING YOUR EXEMPLARY DUTIES. HOW CAN WE HELP YOU?
I'M TO TAKE YOU TO THE COUNCIL CHAMBERS.
THAT'S VERY KIND, BUT WE HAVE NO NEED OF AN ESCORT.
YOU MISUNDERSTAND ME, PRIMATE.
I AM HERE TO ARREST YOU.
WHAT?
DON'T BE RIDICULOUS.
MAY I REMIND YOU THAT THE PRIMATE OUTRANKS THE WATCHMAN. BESIDES, ONLY THE LORD FOUNDER HIMSELF CAN WARRANT THE ARREST OF A COUNCIL MEMBER.
THAT'S RIGHT.
THE CHARGE IS TREASON.

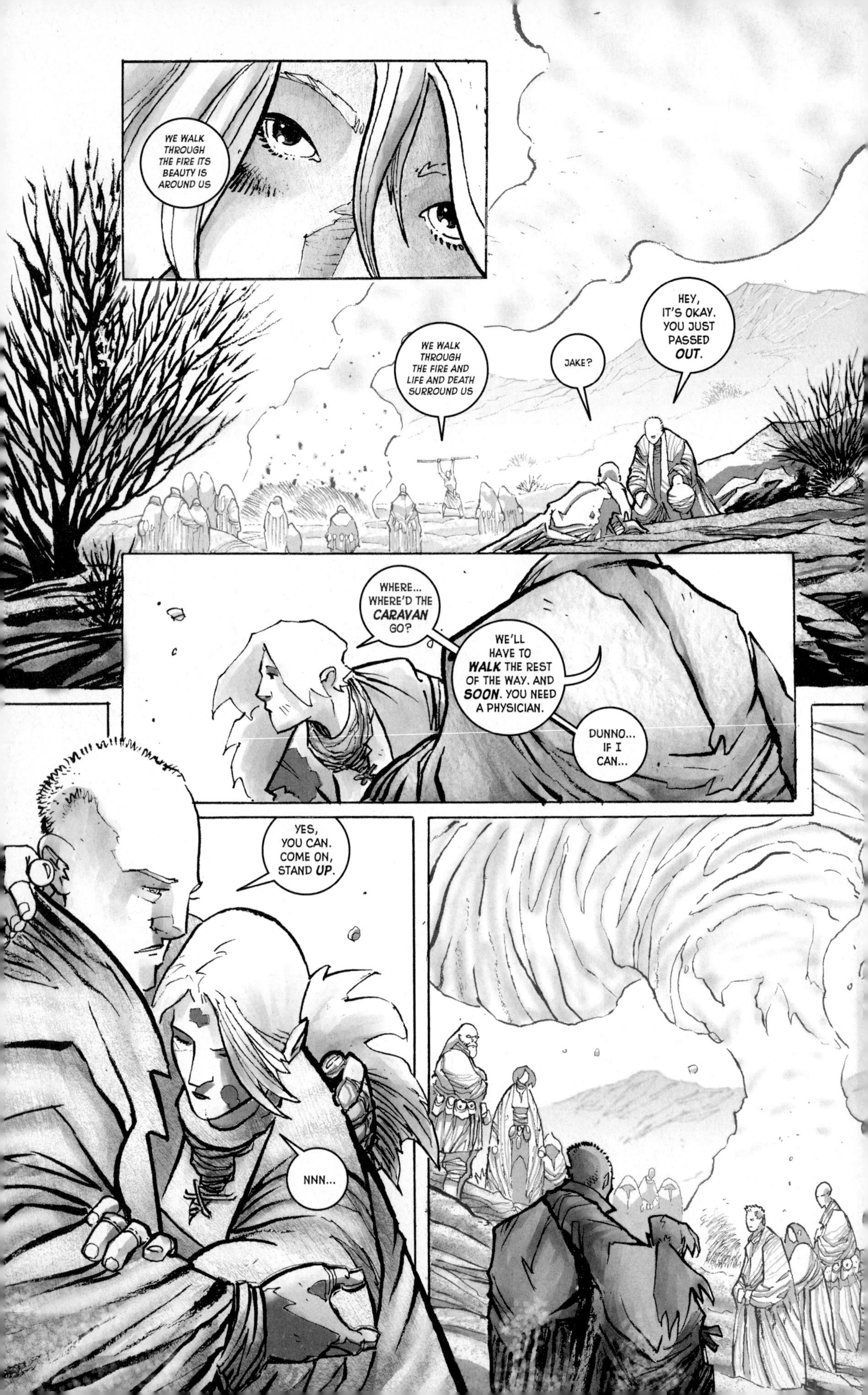

WE WALK THROUGH THE FIRE ITS BEAUTY IS AROUND US
WE WALK THROUGH THE FIRE AND LIFE AND DEATH SURROUND US
JAKE?
HEY, IT'S OKAY. YOU JUST PASSED OUT.
WHERE... WHERE'D THE CARAVAN GO?
WE'LL HAVE TO WALK THE REST OF THE WAY. AND SOON. YOU NEED A PHYSICIAN.
DUNNO... IF I CAN...
YES, YOU CAN. COME ON, STAND UP.
NNN...

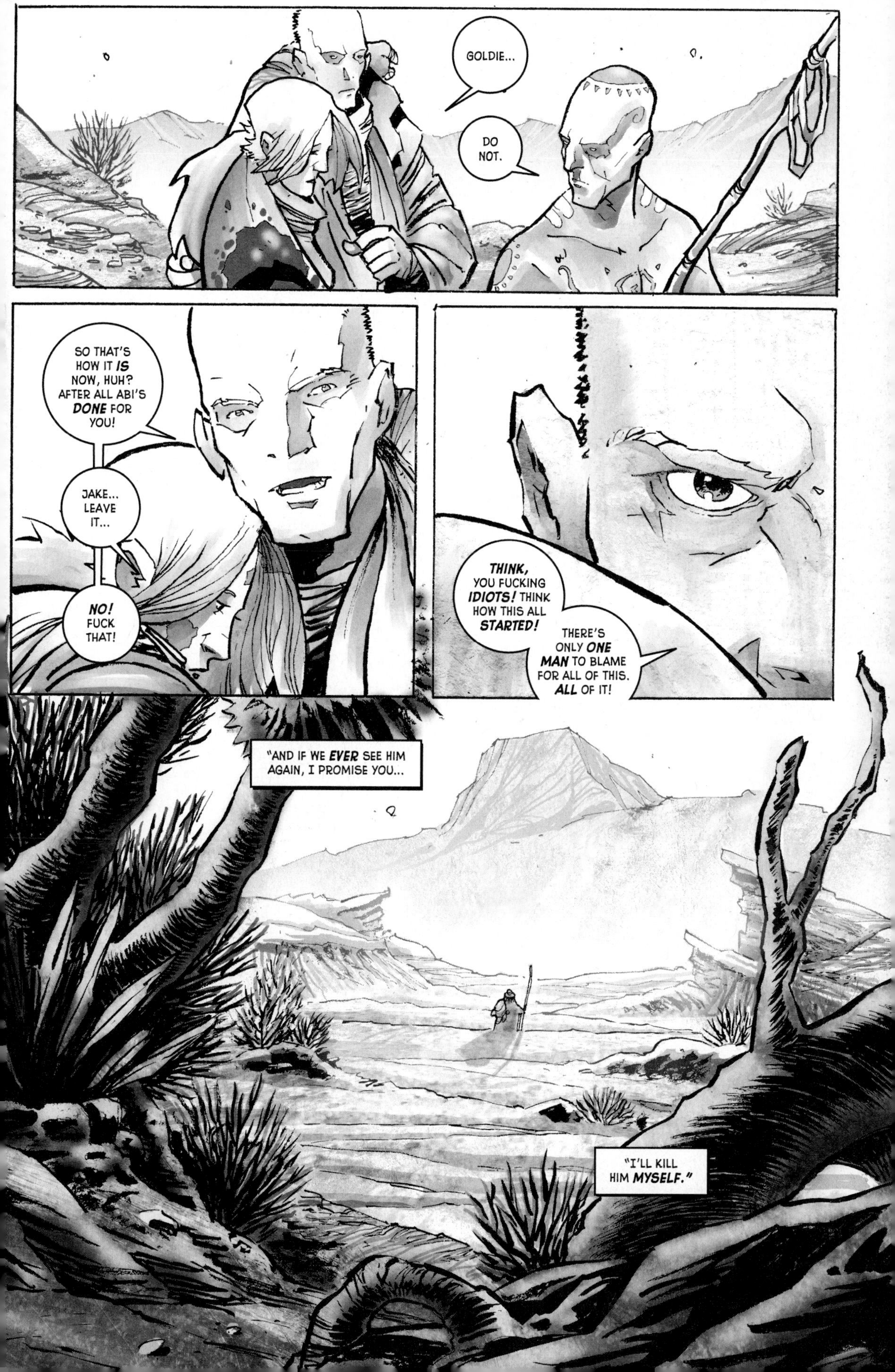
GOLDIE...
DO NOT.
SO THAT'S HOW IT **IS** NOW, HUH? AFTER ALL ABI'S **DONE** FOR YOU!
JAKE... LEAVE IT...
NO! FUCK THAT!
THINK, YOU FUCKING **IDIOTS!** THINK HOW THIS ALL **STARTED!**
THERE'S ONLY **ONE MAN** TO BLAME FOR ALL OF THIS. **ALL** OF IT!
"AND IF WE **EVER** SEE HIM AGAIN, I PROMISE YOU...
"I'LL KILL HIM **MYSELF.**"

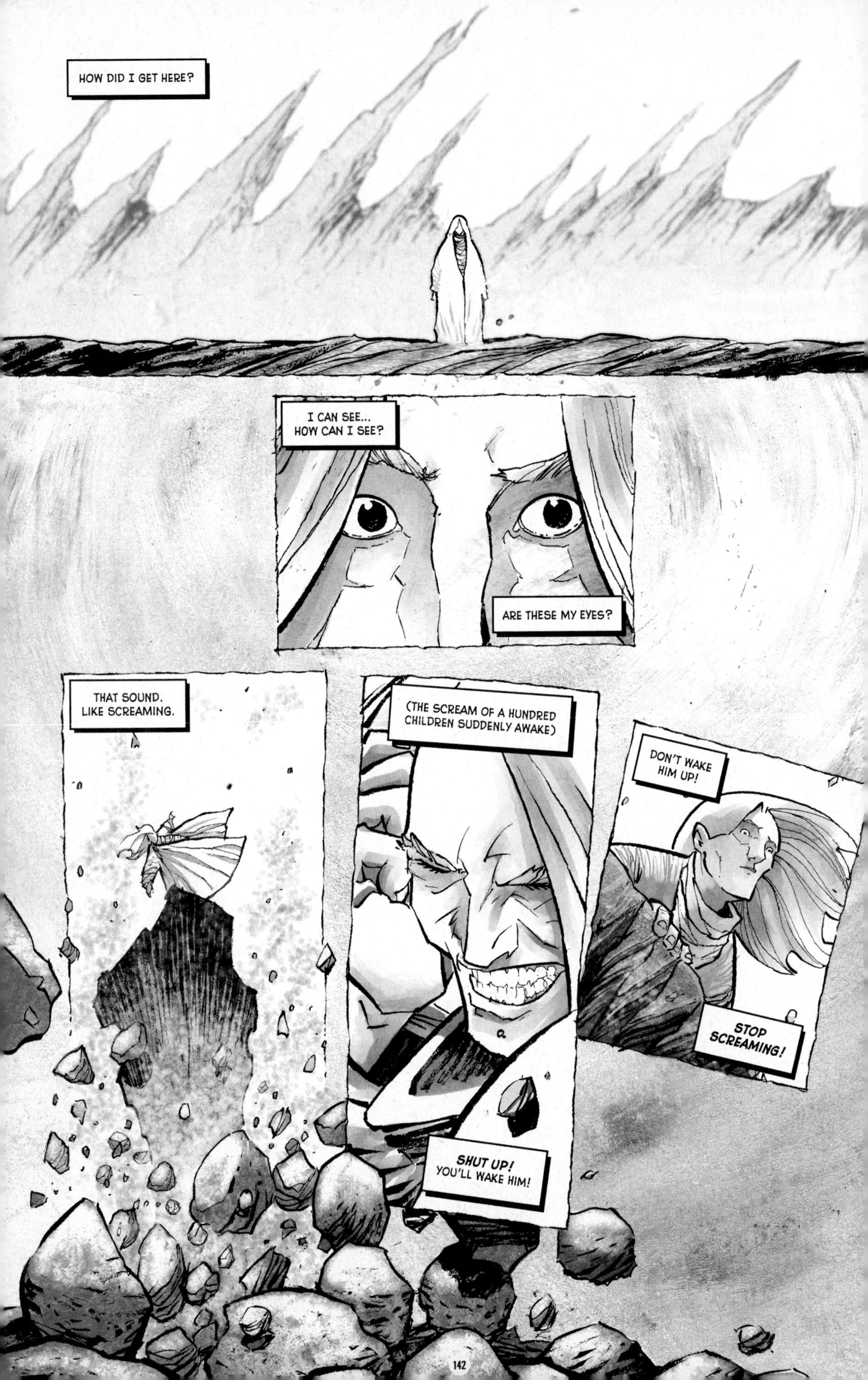
HOW DID I GET HERE?
I CAN SEE... HOW CAN I SEE?
ARE THESE MY EYES?
THAT SOUND. LIKE SCREAMING.
(THE SCREAM OF A HUNDRED CHILDREN SUDDENLY AWAKE)
DON'T WAKE HIM UP!
STOP SCREAMING!
SHUT UP! YOU'LL WAKE HIM!

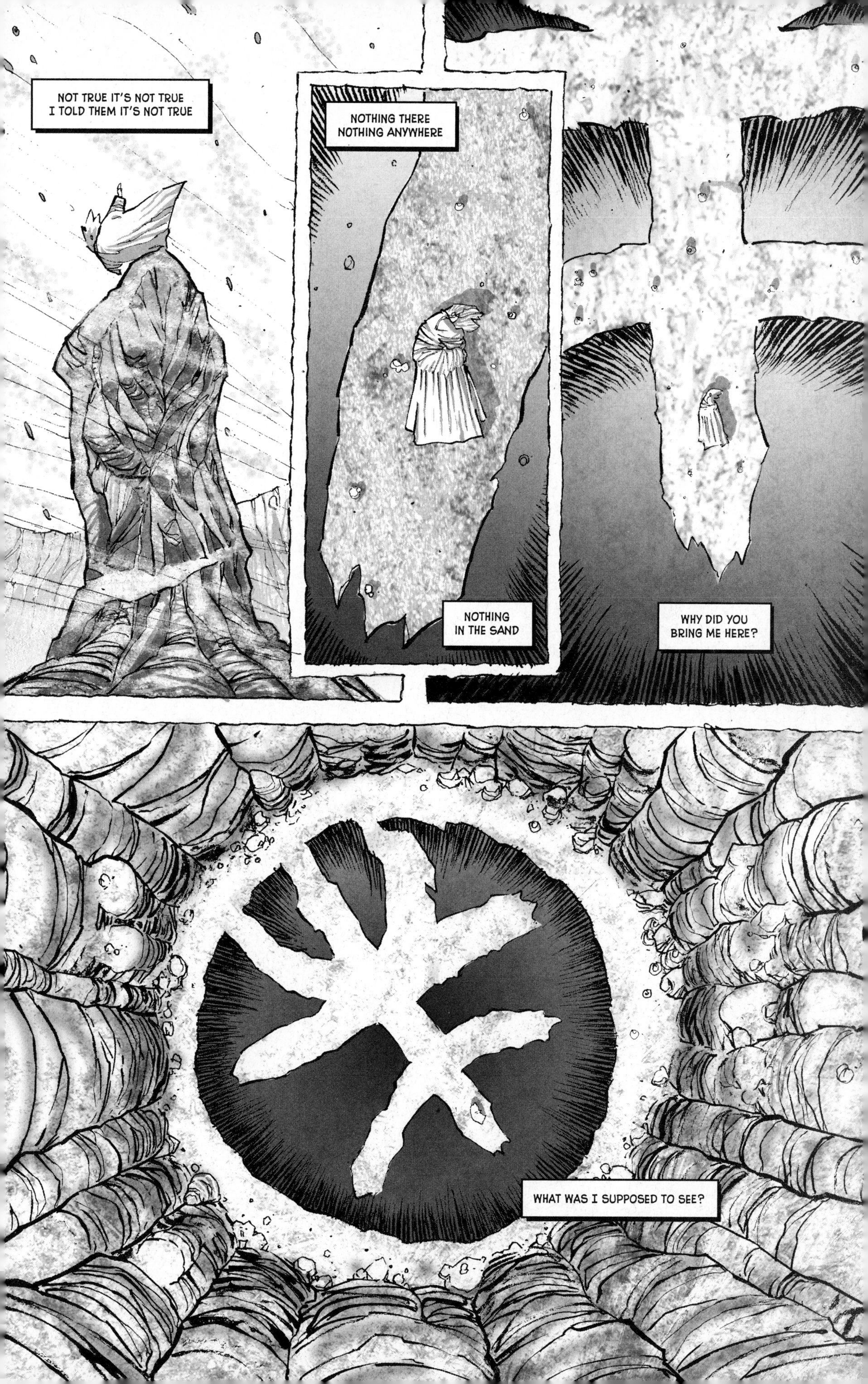
NOT TRUE IT'S NOT TRUE I TOLD THEM IT'S NOT TRUE
NOTHING THERE NOTHING ANYWHERE
NOTHING IN THE SAND
WHY DID YOU BRING ME HERE?
WHAT WAS I SUPPOSED TO SEE?

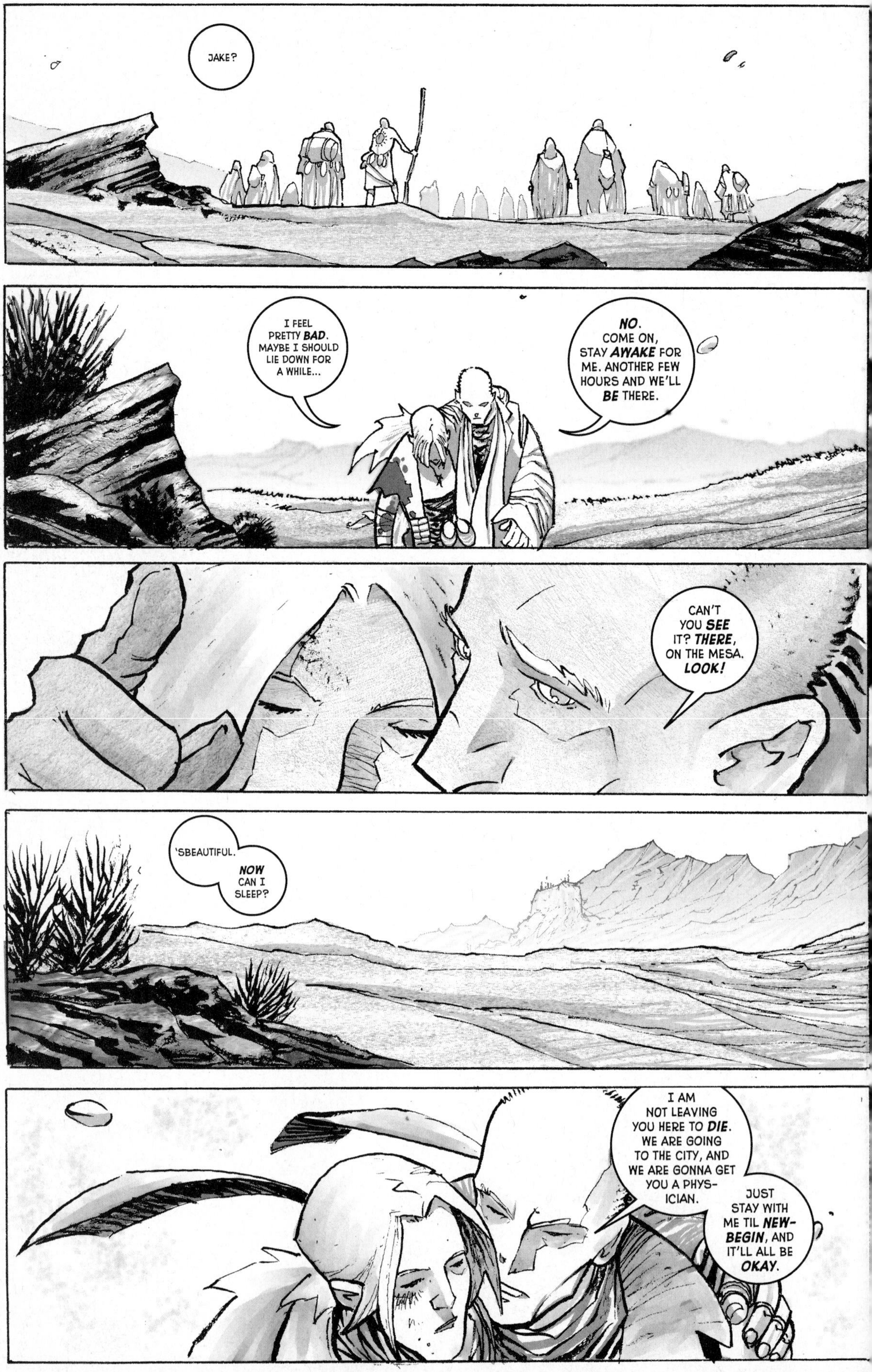
JAKE?
I FEEL PRETTY BAD. MAYBE I SHOULD LIE DOWN FOR A WHILE...
NO. COME ON, STAY AWAKE FOR ME. ANOTHER FEW HOURS AND WE'LL BE THERE.
CAN'T YOU SEE IT? THERE, ON THE MESA. LOOK!
'SBEAUTIFUL. NOW CAN I SLEEP?
I AM NOT LEAVING YOU HERE TO DIE. WE ARE GOING TO THE CITY, AND WE ARE GONNA GET YOU A PHYSICIAN.
JUST STAY WITH ME TIL NEW-BEGIN, AND IT'LL ALL BE OKAY.

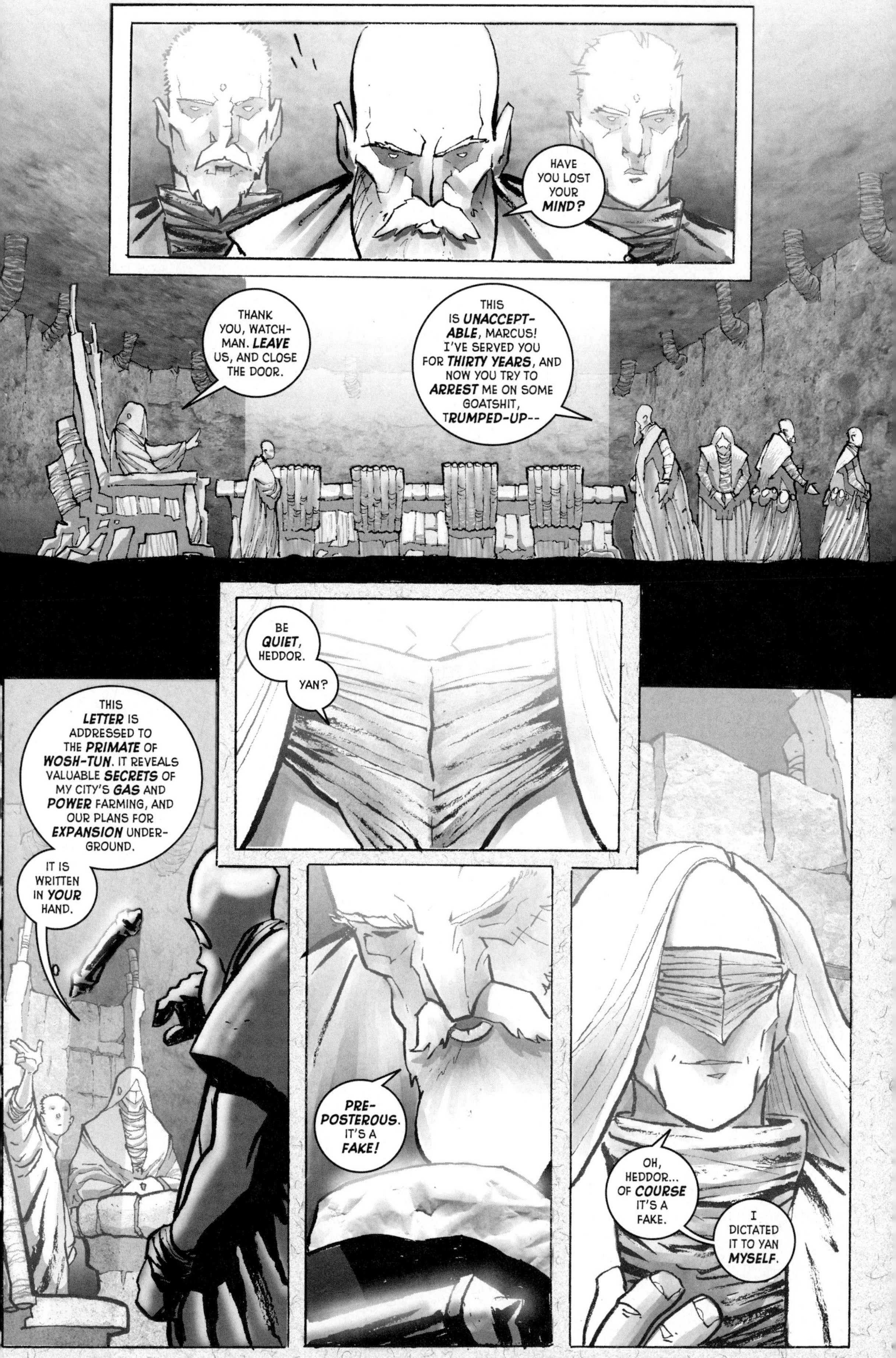
HAVE YOU LOST YOUR MIND?
THANK YOU, WATCH-MAN. LEAVE US, AND CLOSE THE DOOR.
THIS IS UNACCEPT-ABLE, MARCUS! I'VE SERVED YOU FOR THIRTY YEARS, AND NOW YOU TRY TO ARREST ME ON SOME GOATSHIT, TRUMPED-UP--
BE QUIET, HEDDOR.
YAN?
THIS LETTER IS ADDRESSED TO THE PRIMATE OF WOSH-TUN. IT REVEALS VALUABLE SECRETS OF MY CITY'S GAS AND POWER FARMING, AND OUR PLANS FOR EXPANSION UNDER-GROUND.
IT IS WRITTEN IN YOUR HAND.
PRE-POSTEROUS. IT'S A FAKE!
OH, HEDDOR... OF COURSE IT'S A FAKE.
I DICTATED IT TO YAN MYSELF.

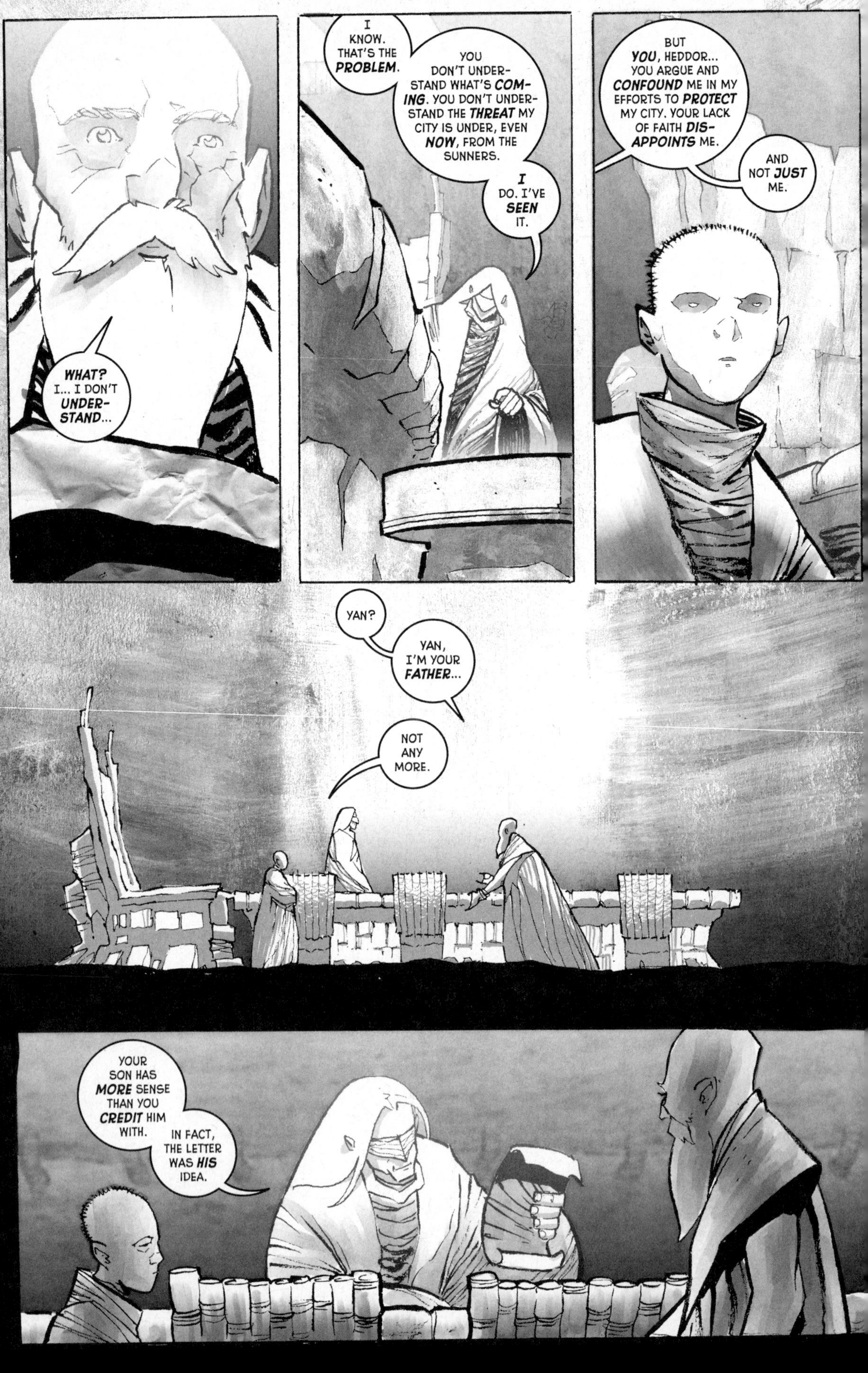
WHAT? I... I DON'T UNDER-STAND...
I KNOW. THAT'S THE PROBLEM.
YOU DON'T UNDER-STAND WHAT'S COM-ING. YOU DON'T UNDER-STAND THE THREAT MY CITY IS UNDER, EVEN NOW, FROM THE SUNNERS.
I DO. I'VE SEEN IT.
BUT YOU, HEDDOR... YOU ARGUE AND CONFOUND ME IN MY EFFORTS TO PROTECT MY CITY. YOUR LACK OF FAITH DIS-APPOINTS ME.
AND NOT JUST ME.
YAN?
YAN, I'M YOUR FATHER...
NOT ANY MORE.
YOUR SON HAS MORE SENSE THAN YOU CREDIT HIM WITH.
IN FACT, THE LETTER WAS HIS IDEA.

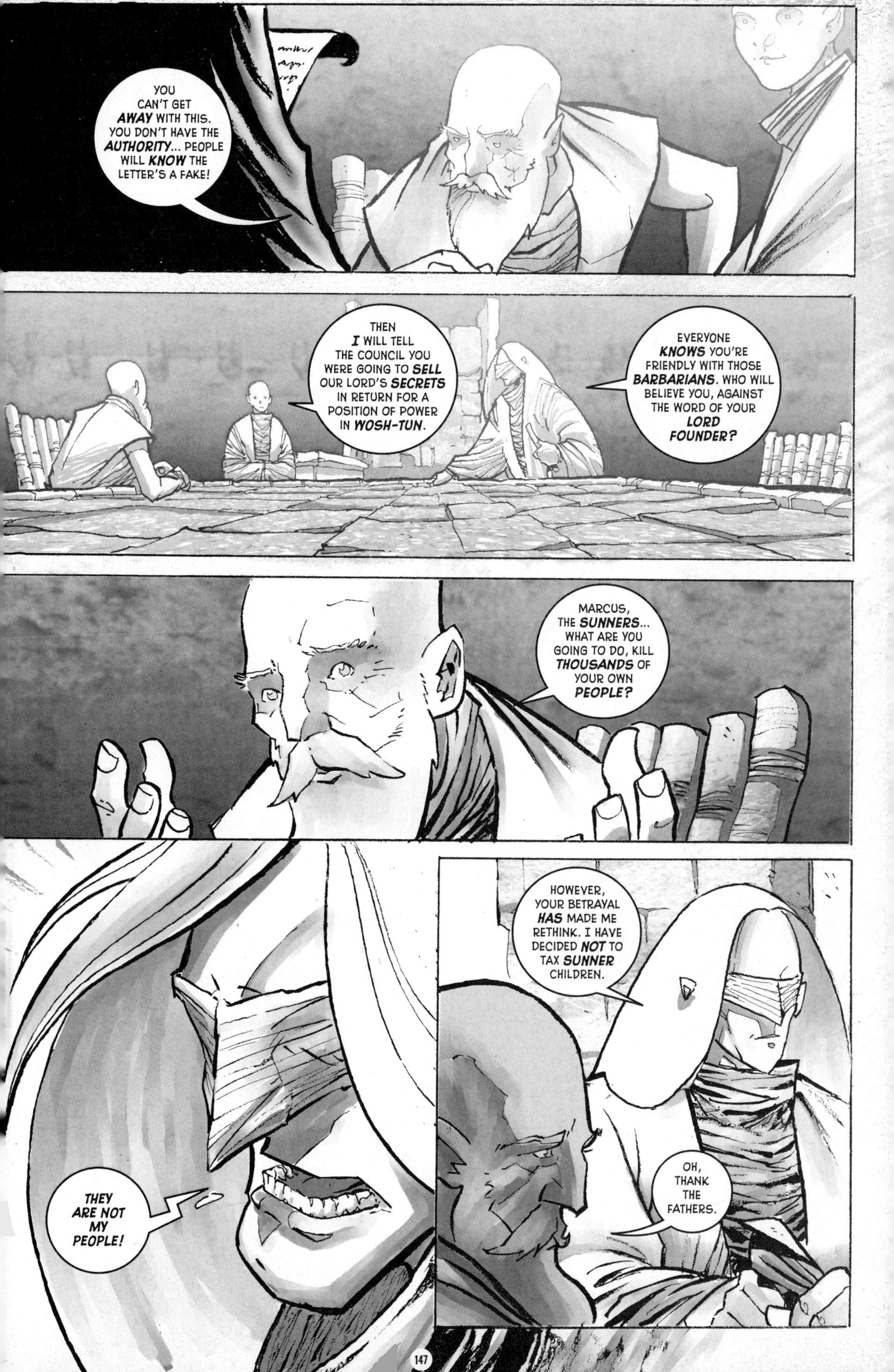
YOU CAN'T GET AWAY WITH THIS. YOU DON'T HAVE THE AUTHORITY... PEOPLE WILL KNOW THE LETTER'S A FAKE!
THEN I WILL TELL THE COUNCIL YOU WERE GOING TO SELL OUR LORD'S SECRETS IN RETURN FOR A POSITION OF POWER IN WOSH-TUN.
EVERYONE KNOWS YOU'RE FRIENDLY WITH THOSE BARBARIANS. WHO WILL BELIEVE YOU, AGAINST THE WORD OF YOUR LORD FOUNDER?
MARCUS, THE SUNNERS... WHAT ARE YOU GOING TO DO, KILL THOUSANDS OF YOUR OWN PEOPLE?
THEY ARE NOT MY PEOPLE!
HOWEVER, YOUR BETRAYAL HAS MADE ME RETHINK. I HAVE DECIDED NOT TO TAX SUNNER CHILDREN.
OH, THANK THE FATHERS.

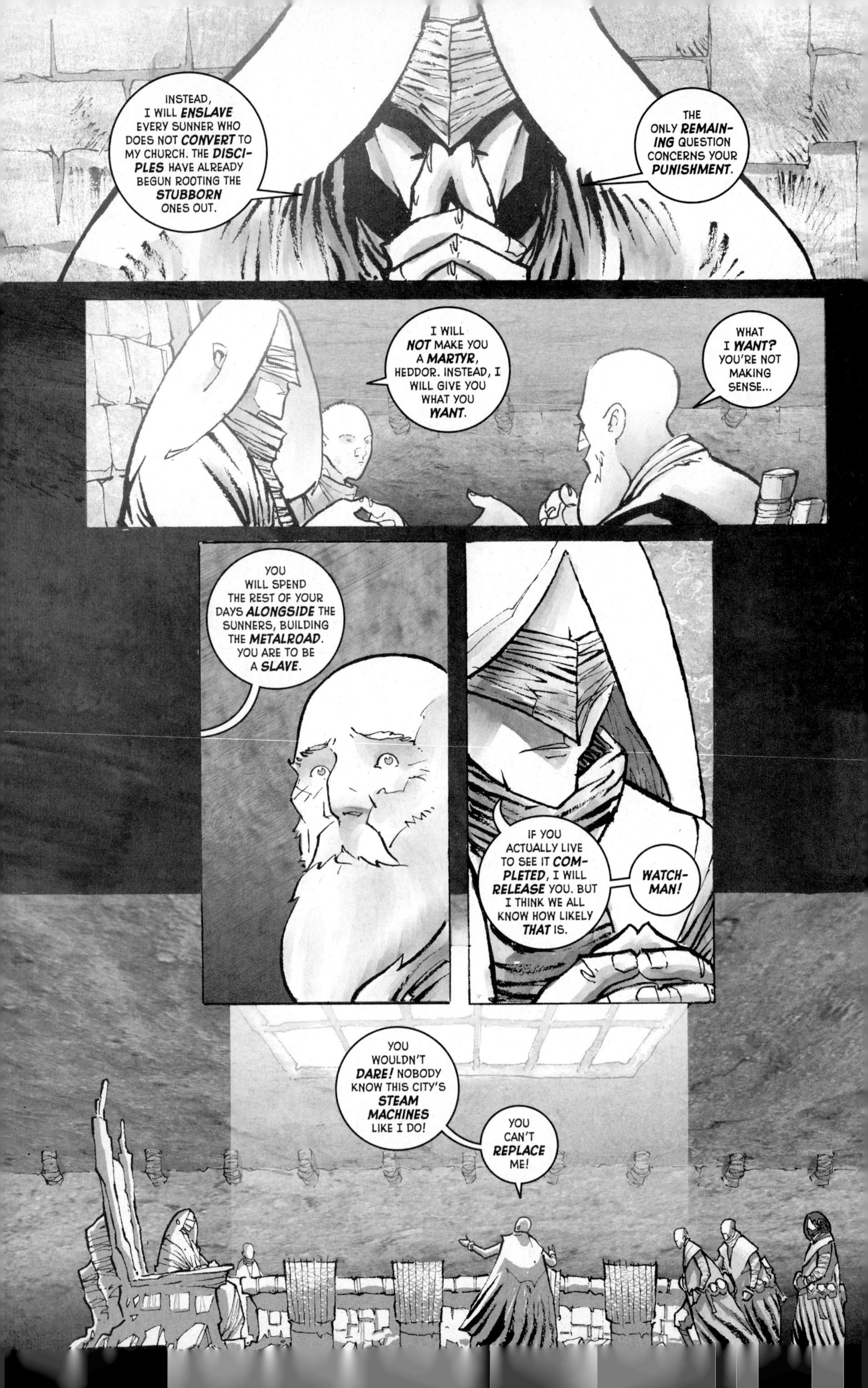
INSTEAD, I WILL ENSLAVE EVERY SUNNER WHO DOES NOT CONVERT TO MY CHURCH. THE DISCI-PLES HAVE ALREADY BEGUN ROOTING THE STUBBORN ONES OUT.
THE ONLY REMAIN-ING QUESTION CONCERNS YOUR PUNISHMENT.
I WILL NOT MAKE YOU A MARTYR, HEDDOR. INSTEAD, I WILL GIVE YOU WHAT YOU WANT.
WHAT I WANT? YOU'RE NOT MAKING SENSE...
YOU WILL SPEND THE REST OF YOUR DAYS ALONGSIDE THE SUNNERS, BUILDING THE METALROAD. YOU ARE TO BE A SLAVE.
IF YOU ACTUALLY LIVE TO SEE IT COM-PLETED, I WILL RELEASE YOU. BUT I THINK WE ALL KNOW HOW LIKELY THAT IS.
WATCH-MAN!
YOU WOULDN'T DARE! NOBODY KNOW THIS CITY'S STEAM MACHINES LIKE I DO!
YOU CAN'T REPLACE ME!

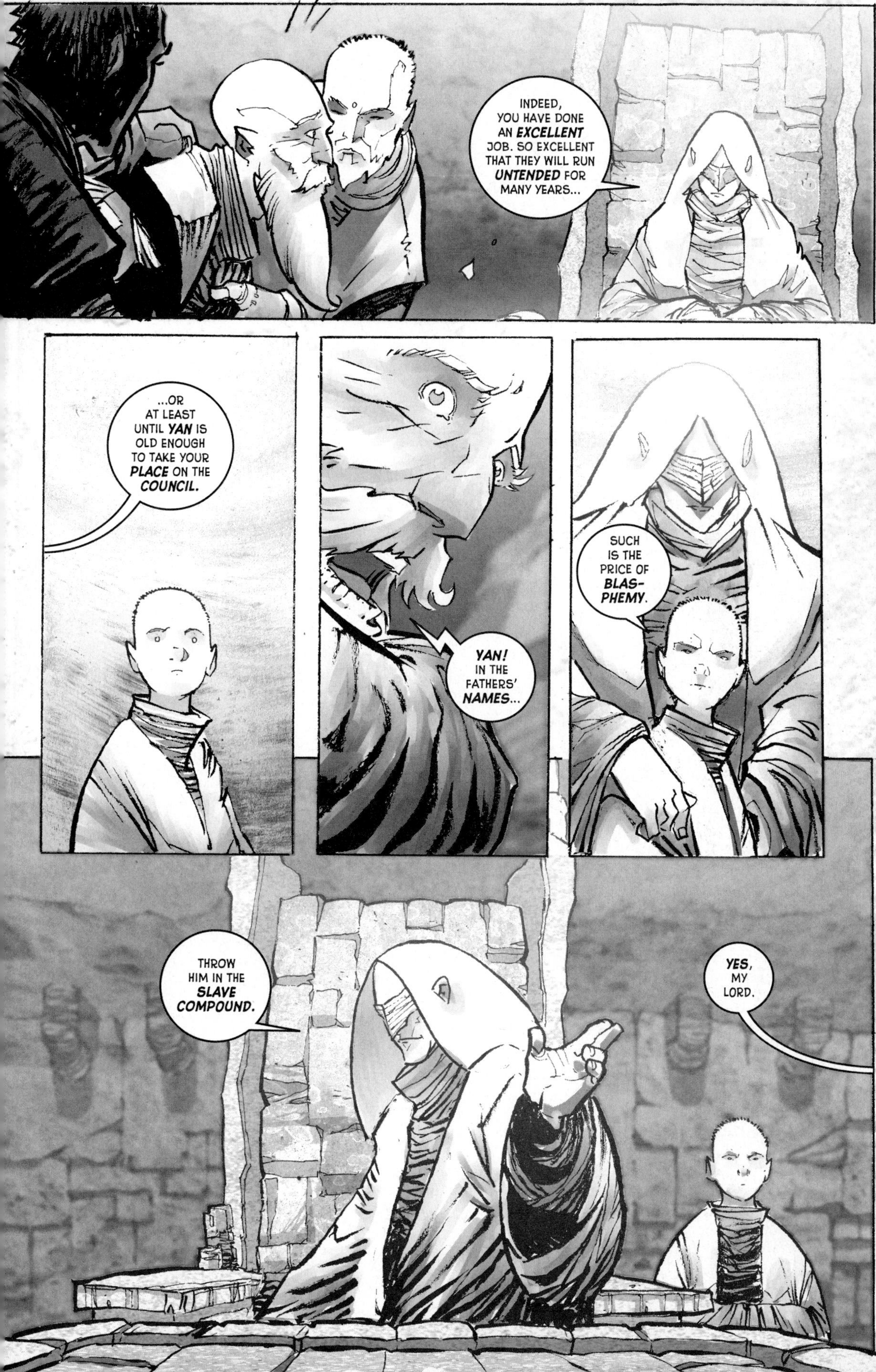
INDEED, YOU HAVE DONE AN EXCELLENT JOB. SO EXCELLENT THAT THEY WILL RUN UNTENDED FOR MANY YEARS...
...OR AT LEAST UNTIL YAN IS OLD ENOUGH TO TAKE YOUR PLACE ON THE COUNCIL.
YAN! IN THE FATHERS' NAMES...
SUCH IS THE PRICE OF BLAS-PHEMY.
THROW HIM IN THE SLAVE COMPOUND.
YES, MY LORD.

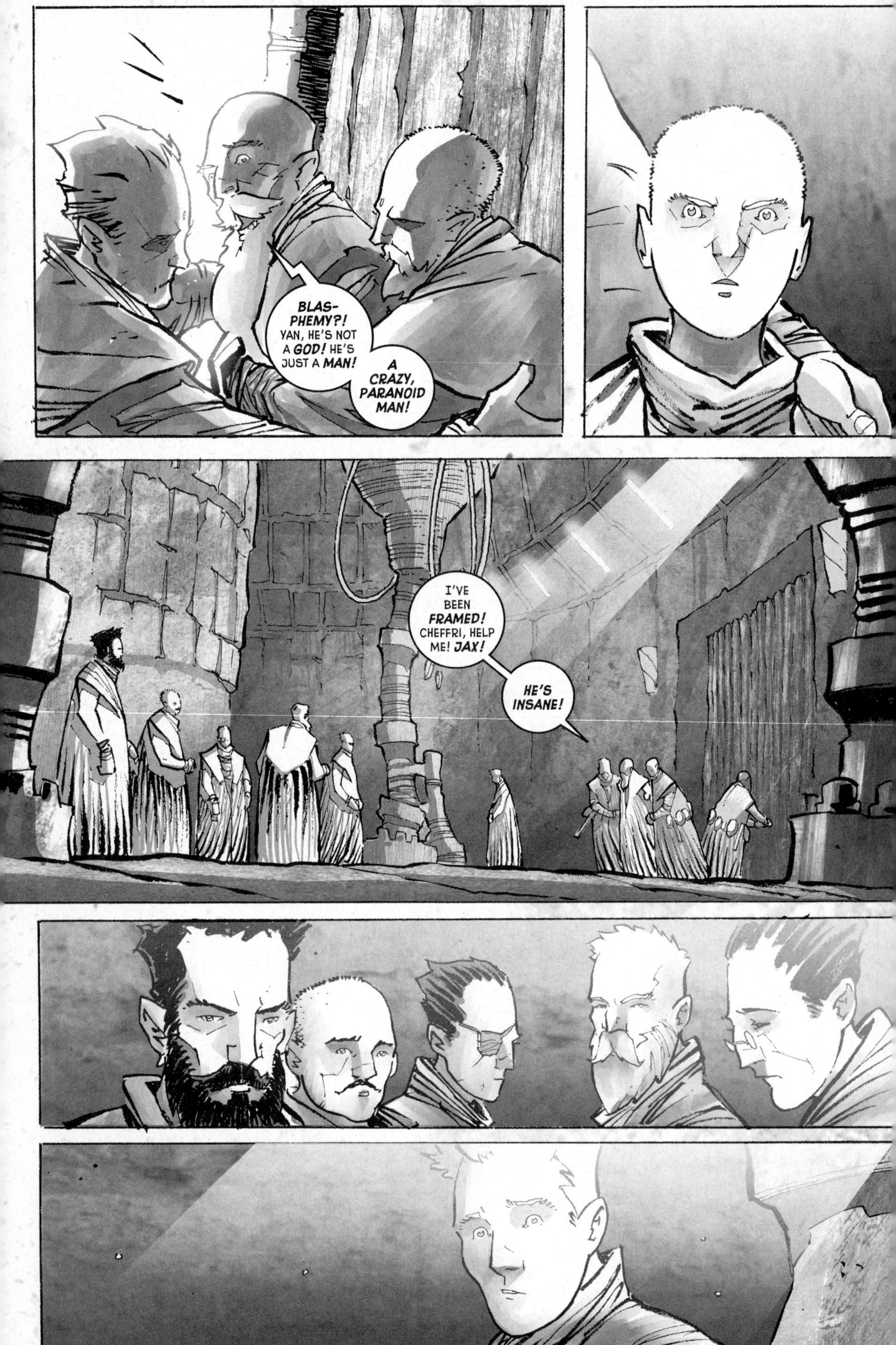
BLAS-PHEMY?! YAN, HE'S NOT A GOD! HE'S JUST A MAN!
A CRAZY, PARANOID MAN!
I'VE BEEN FRAMED! CHEFFRI, HELP ME! JAX!
HE'S INSANE!

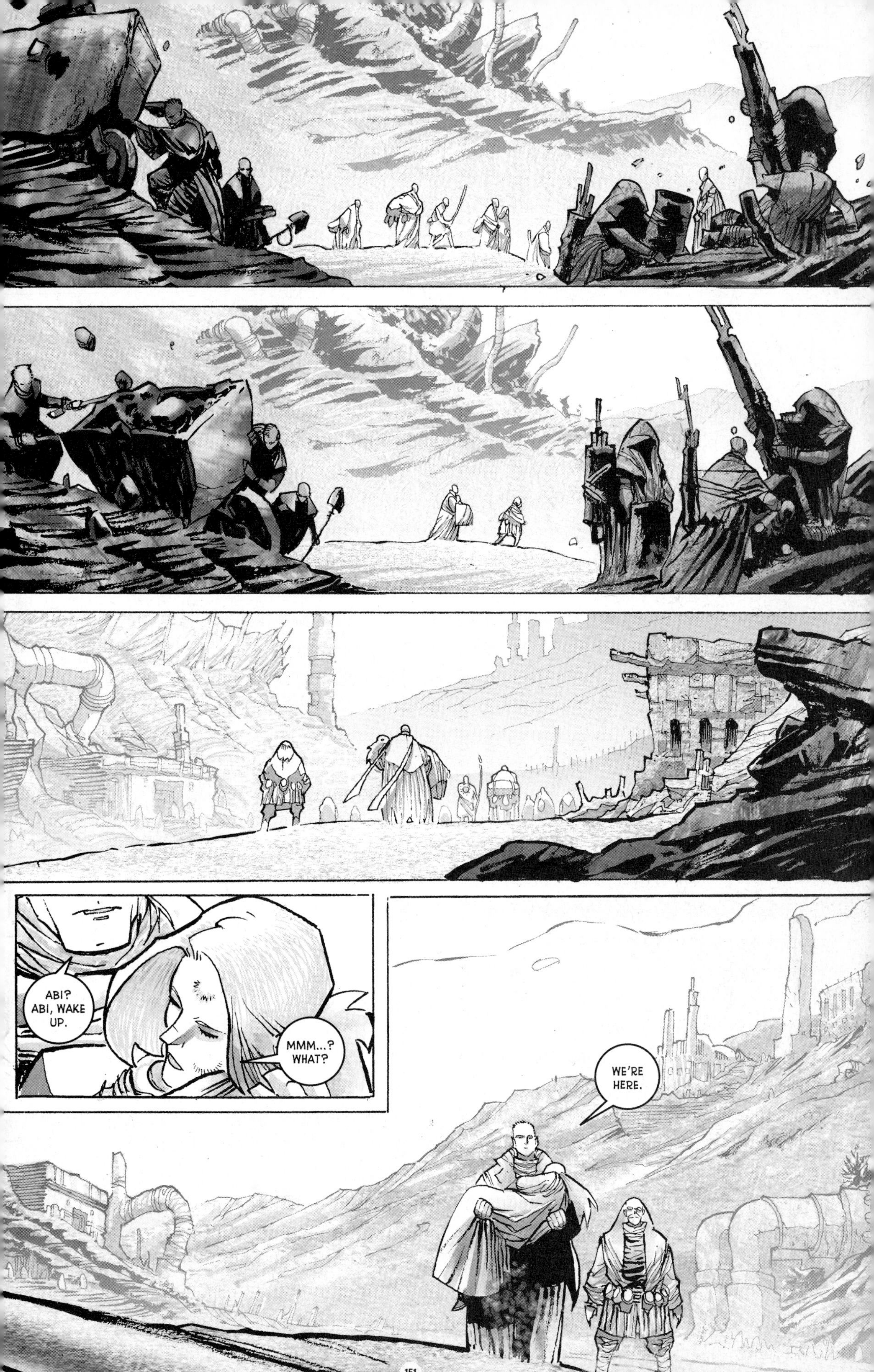
ABI? ABI, WAKE UP.
MMM...? WHAT?
WE'RE HERE.

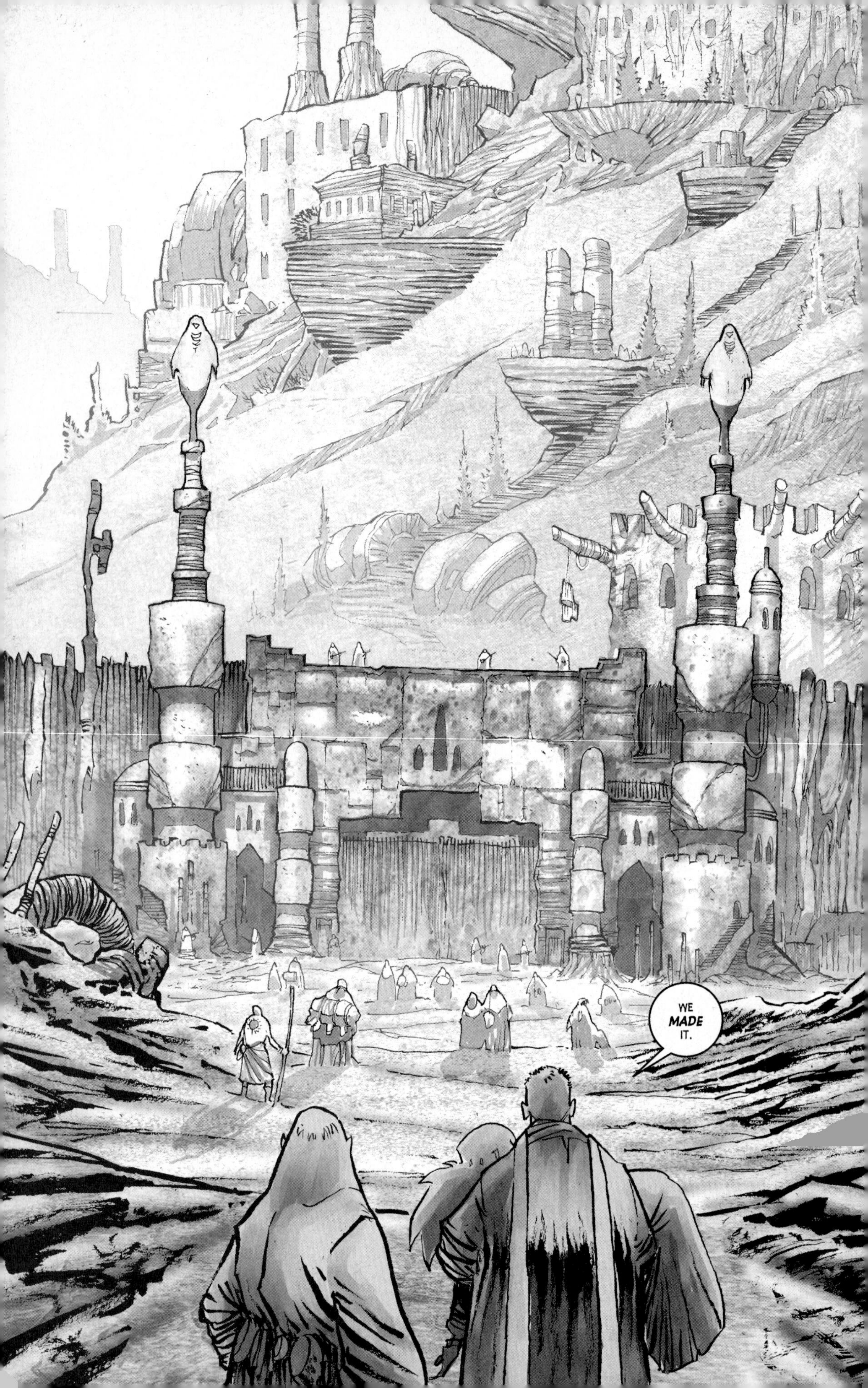
WE *MADE* IT.

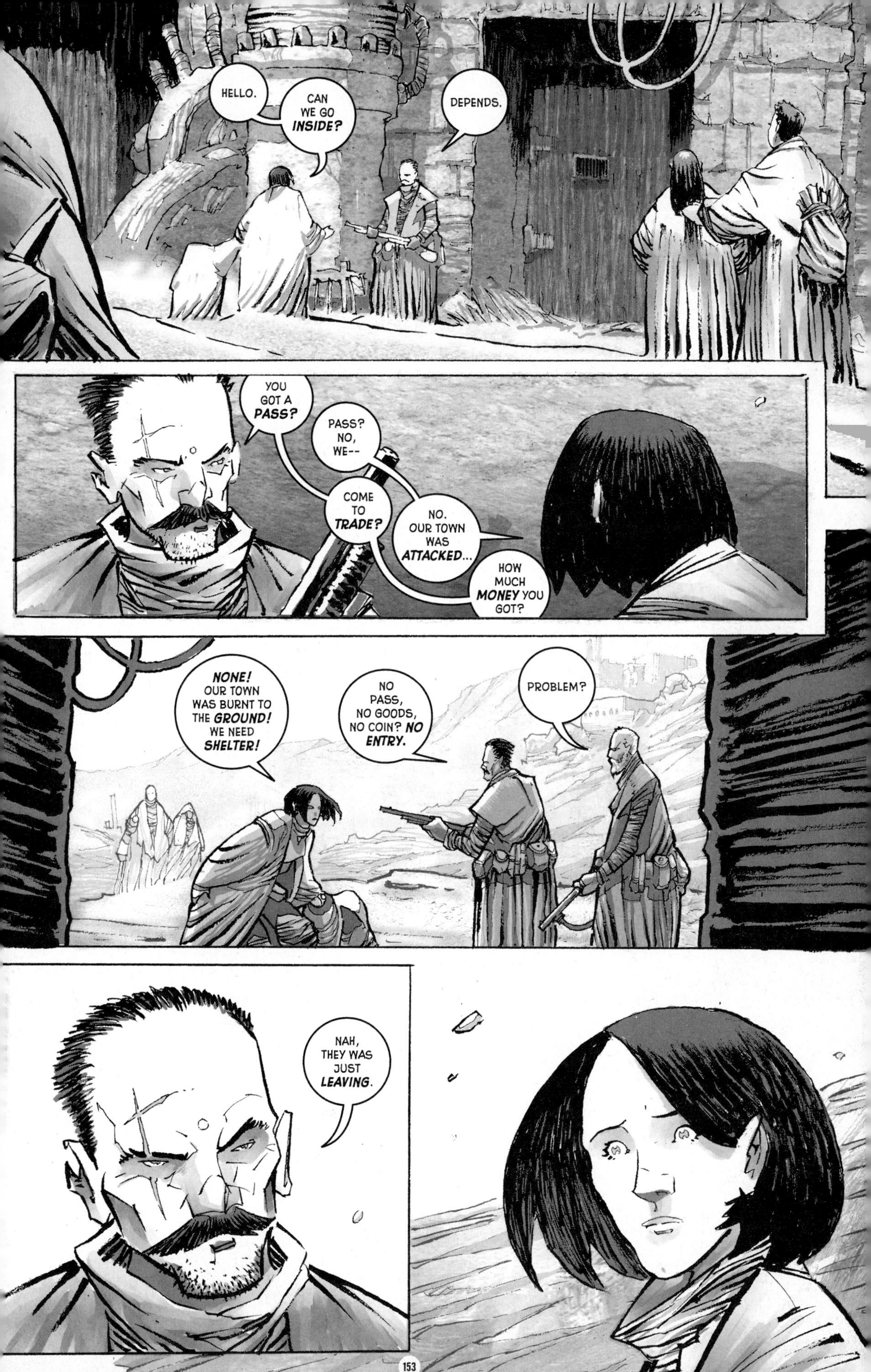
HELLO.
CAN WE GO INSIDE?
DEPENDS.
YOU GOT A PASS?
PASS? NO, WE--
COME TO TRADE?
NO. OUR TOWN WAS ATTACKED...
HOW MUCH MONEY YOU GOT?
NONE! OUR TOWN WAS BURNT TO THE GROUND! WE NEED SHELTER!
NO PASS, NO GOODS, NO COIN? NO ENTRY.
PROBLEM?
NAH, THEY WAS JUST LEAVING.

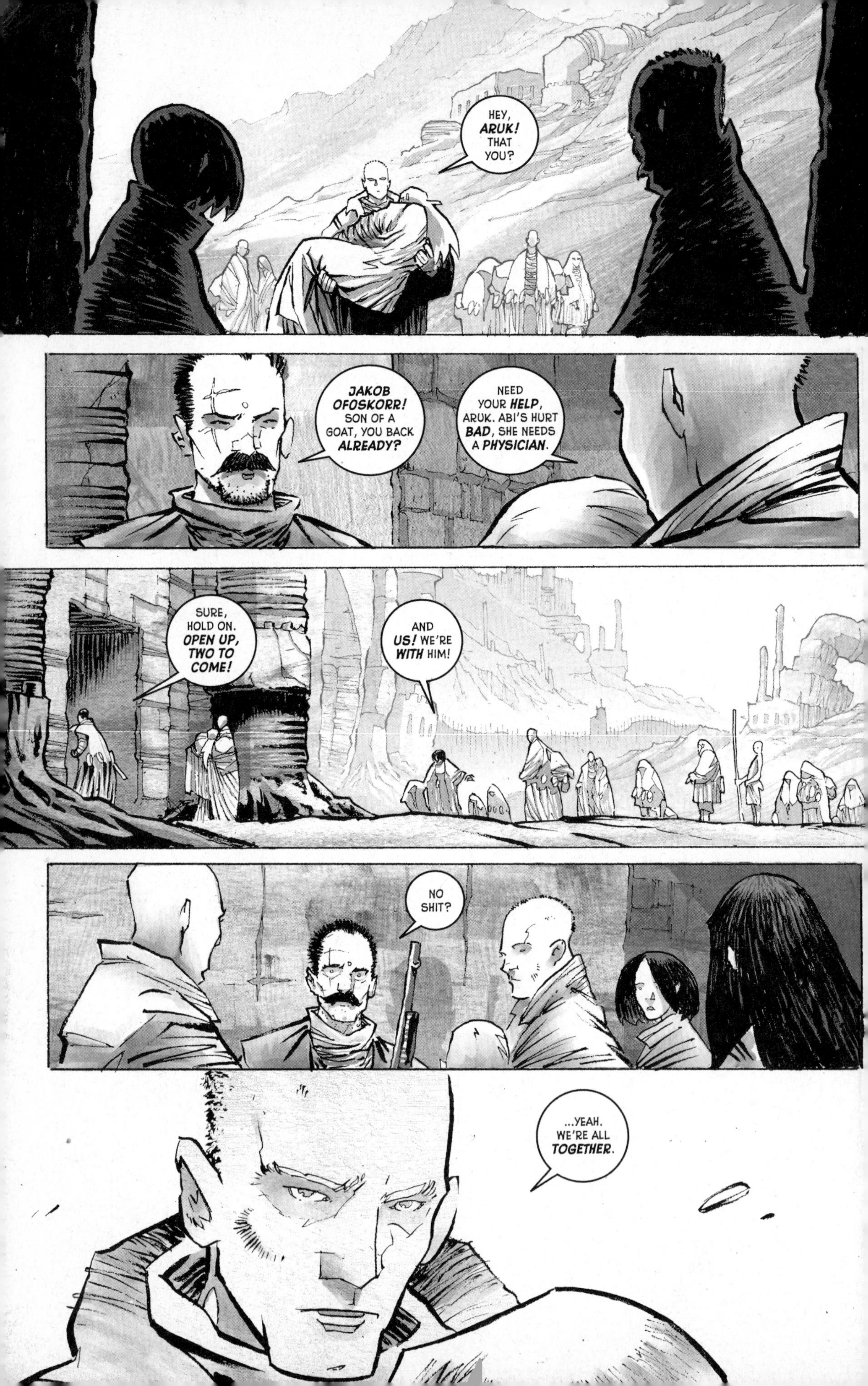
HEY, ARUK! THAT YOU?
JAKOB OFOSKORR! SON OF A GOAT, YOU BACK ALREADY?
NEED YOUR HELP, ARUK. ABI'S HURT BAD, SHE NEEDS A PHYSICIAN.
SURE, HOLD ON. OPEN UP, TWO TO COME!
AND US! WE'RE WITH HIM!
NO SHIT?
...YEAH. WE'RE ALL TOGETHER.

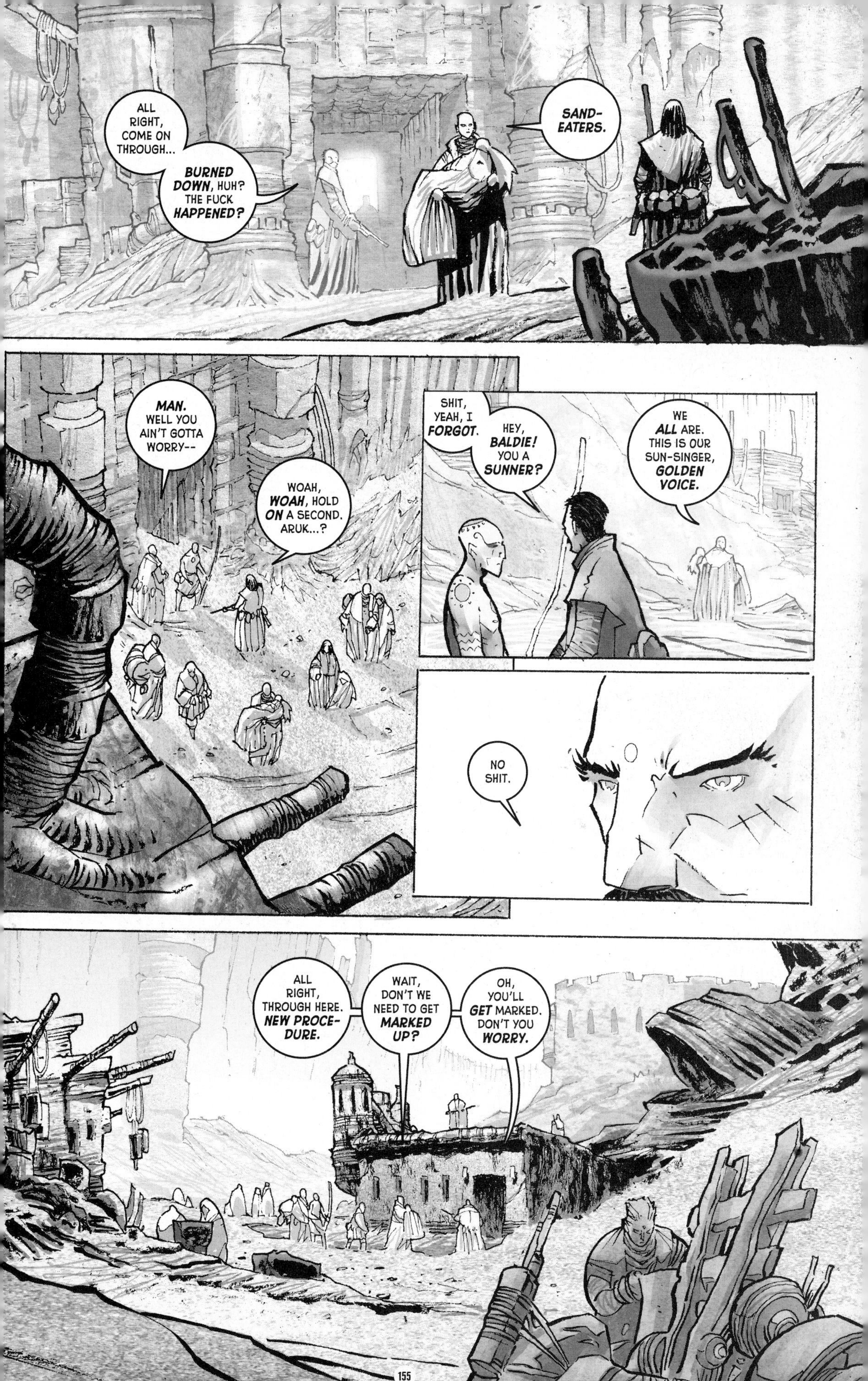
ALL RIGHT, COME ON THROUGH...
BURNED DOWN, HUH? THE FUCK HAPPENED?
SAND-EATERS.
MAN. WELL YOU AIN'T GOTTA WORRY--
WOAH, WOAH, HOLD ON A SECOND. ARUK...?
SHIT, YEAH, I FORGOT.
HEY, BALDIE! YOU A SUNNER?
WE ALL ARE. THIS IS OUR SUN-SINGER, GOLDEN VOICE.
NO SHIT.
ALL RIGHT, THROUGH HERE. NEW PROCE-DURE.
WAIT, DON'T WE NEED TO GET MARKED UP?
OH, YOU'LL GET MARKED. DON'T YOU WORRY.

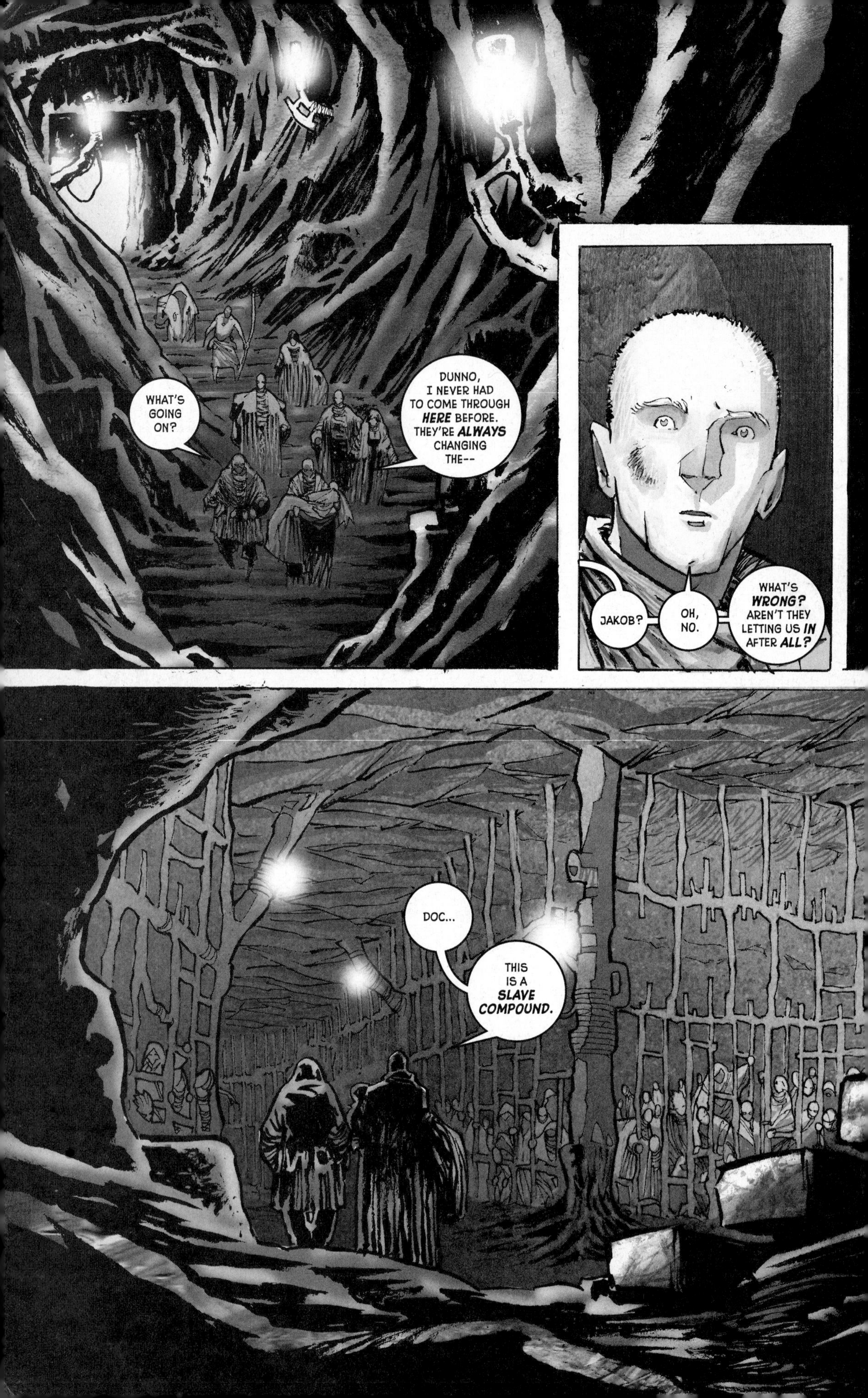
WHAT'S GOING ON?
DUNNO, I NEVER HAD TO COME THROUGH **HERE** BEFORE. THEY'RE **ALWAYS** CHANGING THE--
JAKOB?
OH, NO.
WHAT'S **WRONG?** AREN'T THEY LETTING US **IN** AFTER **ALL?**
DOC...
THIS IS A **SLAVE COMPOUND.**

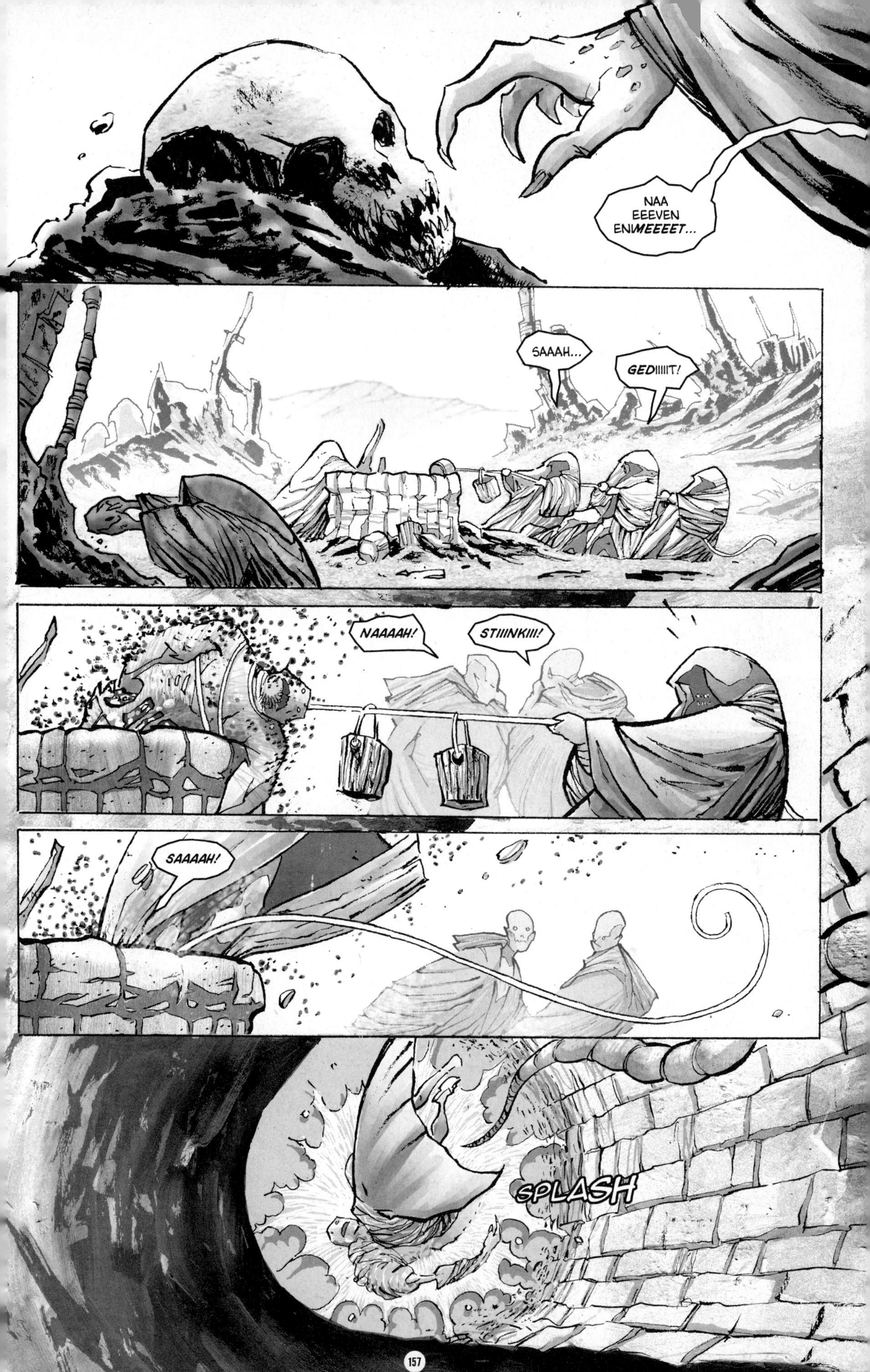
NAA EEEVEN ENIMEEEET...
SAAAH...
GEDIIIIIT!
NAAAAH!
STIIINKIII!
SAAAAH!
SPLASH

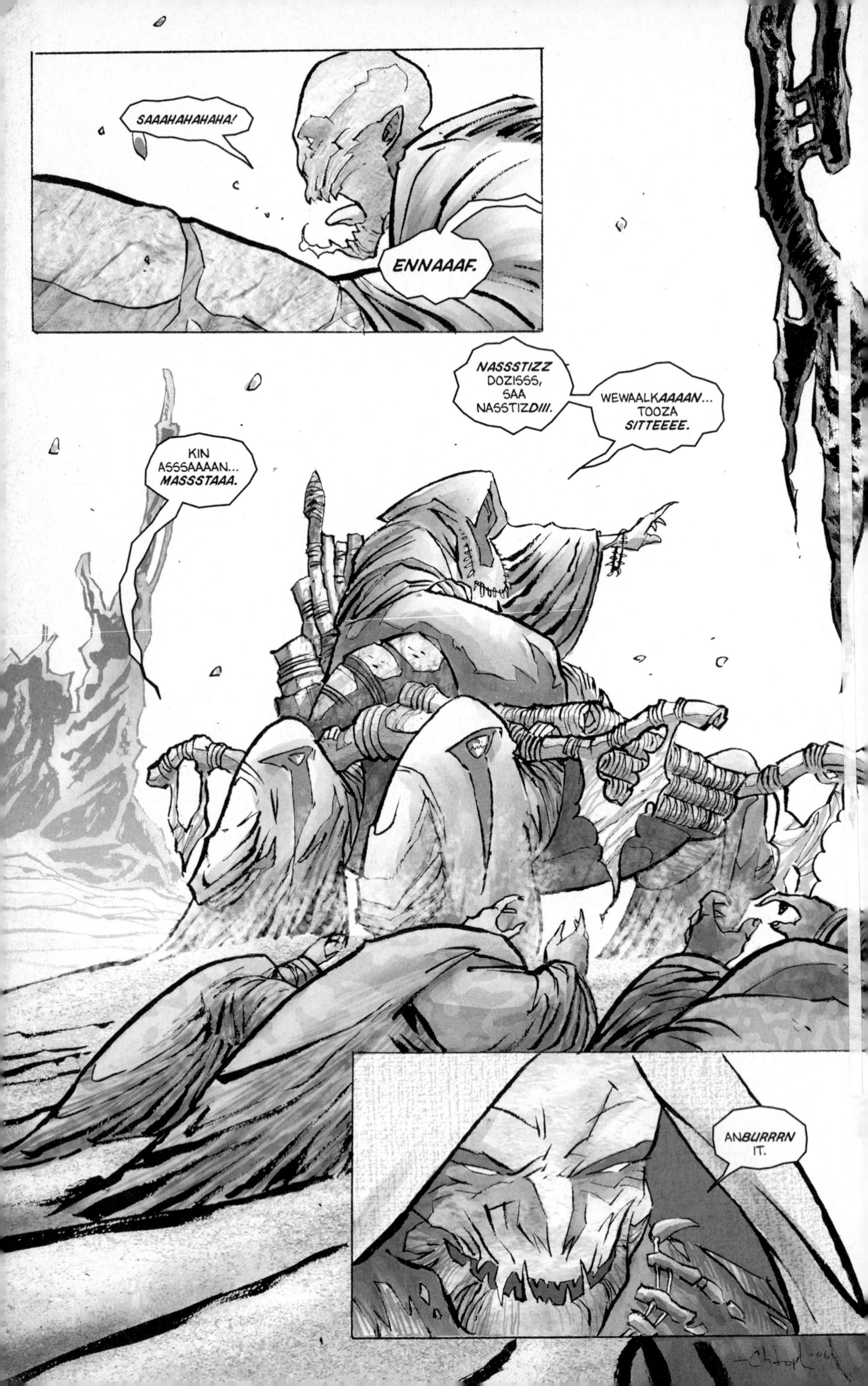
SAAAHAHAHAHA!
ENNAAAF.
NASSSTIZZ DOZISSS, SAA NASSTIZDIII.
WEWAALKAAAAN... TOOZA SITTEEEE.
KIN ASSSAAAAN... MASSSTAAA.
ANBURRRN IT.

TO BE **CONTINUED**

ANTONY JOHNSTON

Born and raised in central England, Antony is an award-winning writer in a wide range of genres and media. He has written more than a dozen graphic novels, several comics series, two novels and numerous short comic and prose stories. He lives in Northern England and wears a lot of black.
ANTONYJOHNSTON.COM

CHRISTOPHER MITTEN

Whisked from Wisconsin at the age of eight, Chris soon found himself having to navigate the misty wilderness of suburban Chicago where, for nearly twenty years, not much happened. Then in 2003 he fell face-first into comics, where he has provided the illustrations for, among others, PAST LIES and QUEEN & COUNTRY: DECLASSIFIED VOL. 3, his first collaboration with Antony Johnston.
CHRISTOPHERMITTEN.COM